PATTON'S WAY

PATTON'S WAY | A RADICAL THEORY OF WAR

James Kelly Morningstar

NAVAL INSTITUTE PRESS
ANNAPOLIS, MARYLAND

Naval Institute Press
291 Wood Road
Annapolis, MD 21402

© 2017 by James Kelly Morningstar
All rights reserved. No part of this book may be reproduced or utilized in any form or by any means, electronic or mechanical, including photocopying and recording, or by any information storage and retrieval system, without permission in writing from the publisher.

Library of Congress Cataloging-in-Publication Data
Names: Morningstar, James Kelly, author.
Title: Patton's way : a radical theory of war / James Kelly Morningstar.
Description: Annapolis, Maryland : Naval Institute Press, [2017] | Includes bibliographical references and index.
Identifiers: LCCN 2017007728 (print) | LCCN 2017012997 (ebook) | ISBN 9781612519784 (ePDF) | ISBN 9781612519784 (ePub) | ISBN 9781612519784 (mobi) | ISBN 9781612519791 (hardcover : alk. paper) | ISBN 9781612519784 (ebook)
Subjects: LCSH: Patton, George S. (George Smith), 1885–1945—Military leadership. | Generals—United States—Biography. | World War, 1939–1945—Campaigns. | United States. Army—Biography. | Military doctrine—United States—History—20th century.
Classification: LCC E745.P3 (ebook) | LCC E745.P3 M67 2017 (print) | DDC 355.3/31092 [B]—dc23
LC record available at https://lccn.loc.gov/2017007728

Maps created by Chris Robinson.

♾ Print editions meet the requirements of ANSI/NISO z39.48-1992 (Permanence of Paper).
Printed in the United States of America.

25 24 23 22 21 20 19 18 17   9 8 7 6 5 4 3 2 1
First printing

For Shannon, who makes my dreams come true

CONTENTS

List of Figures and Maps — viii
Preface — ix
Significant Events in George S. Patton's Life — xi

1. Legends and Lies — 1
2. A Series of Shocks — 20
3. Combined Arms — 55
4. Command and Control — 89
5. Intelligence — 122
6. Breakout: Conceptualization — 153
7. Breakout: Execution — 186
8. Death and Resurrection — 227
9. The Limits of Legacy — 277

Notes — 285
Selected Bibliography — 349
Index — 361

FIGURES AND MAPS

Figures

1. American Casualties by Month in the European Theater of Operations	10
2. Casualties of Divisions Associated with First or Third Army	12
3. Data Comparisons of Representative U.S. Tanks, 1917–41	70
4. Comparison of Combat Forces in Armored Unit Designs	85
5. Patton's Integrated Intelligence Systems	141

Maps

1. Sicily: Patton's End Run, 18 July–2 August 1943	45
2. Battle of the Bulge Third Army Movement, 19–22 December 1943	117
3. Patton/Bradley Plan Comparisons	178
4. Third Army Breakout, 28 July–2 September 1944	218

PREFACE

Much has been said about George S. Patton Jr. regarding his leadership, life, and accomplishments. Still, as a practitioner of war, Patton has been misunderstood. His success was a result not of bravado but of a well-thought-out and highly developed way of war, one at variance with accepted doctrine and often practiced in the face of interference by more conventional commanders. This book is an attempt to correct the record—to illuminate the principles at work in his methods and to demonstrate their real contribution to both the effort in World War II and the development of postwar U.S. Army doctrine.

I would like to thank the librarians and archivists at the Library of Congress, the National Archives at College Park, Maryland, the Pentagon Library, the United States Army War College Library, and the United States Military Academy Library. I would also like to thank Adam Nettina, Taylor Skord, Jonathan W. Jordan, Jon Sumida, John Nelson Rickard, Harold Winton, and Ed Yuen for their comments on this project. Special thanks to my parents Bernard and Sue Morningstar for their years of support. Finally, I would thank my wife Shannon and children Michael and Emily for their patience and encouragement; nothing in my life is possible without them.

SIGNIFICANT EVENTS IN GEORGE S. PATTON'S LIFE

- **1885** 11 NOVEMBER: Born in San Gabriel, California
- **1904** Enters United States Military Academy
- **1909** Graduates from West Point
- **1916** Assigned to Mexican Punitive Expedition Headquarters; promoted to first lieutenant
- **1917** MAY: Promoted to captain; assigned commander, Headquarters Company, Allied Expeditionary Force

    JUNE: Arrives in Paris

    NOVEMBER: Assigned to Tank Service
- **1918** SEPTEMBER: Leads 304th Tank Brigade in Saint-Mihiel offensive

    11 NOVEMBER: World War I ends
- **1919** Assigned commander, 304th Tank Brigade, Camp Meade, Maryland
- **1920** Tank Corps abolished

    Promoted to major

    Assigned commander, 3rd Squadron, 3rd Cavalry, Fort Myer, Virginia
- **1925** Assigned G-1 (Personnel) and G-2 (Intelligence), Hawaii Division
- **1926** G-1, G-2, and G-3, Hawaii Division
- **1928** Assigned to Office of the Chief of Cavalry, Washington, D.C.
- **1932** Distinguished Graduate from Army War College

    Assigned as executive officer, 3rd Cavalry, Fort Myer, Virginia
- **1934** Promoted to lieutenant colonel
- **1935** Assigned as G-2 (Intelligence), Hawaii Division
- **1938** Promoted to colonel
- **1940** Promoted to brigadier general
- **1941** Promoted to major general; commander, 2nd Armored Division, Fort Benning, Georgia

1942 JANUARY: commander, I Armored Corps

JULY: Assigned to Washington, D.C., to organize and plan invasion of Morocco; commands Western Task Force during invasion of North Africa

1943 MARCH: commander, II Corps, Tunisia, French North Africa

Wins first American victories over Germans at Gafsa and El Guettar

Promoted to lieutenant general

APRIL: Relieved from II Corps to plan invasion of Sicily

10 JULY: Leads Seventh Army in invasion of Sicily; defeats German attacks

22 JULY: Captures Palermo

AUGUST: Slapping incidents in Sicily

17 AUGUST: Beats Montgomery to capture Messina, ends Sicily campaign

2 SEPTEMBER: Eisenhower reprimands Patton, orders Seventh Army broken up

1944 26 JANUARY: commander, Third Army, in United Kingdom

6 JUNE: Allied forces invade Normandy

6 JULY: Arrives in France

25 JULY: Operation Cobra begins

28 JULY: Bradley assigns Patton as shadow commander over VIII Corps

1 AUGUST: Bradley makes Third Army operational; XV Corps ordered north to close Falaise Gap

15 AUGUST: Bradley halts Third Army efforts to close Falaise Gap

27 SEPTEMBER–13 DECEMBER: Battle for Metz

16 DECEMBER: Germans begin Battle of the Bulge

26 DECEMBER: Relieves Bastogne

1945 MARCH: Crosses Rhine River, failed raid on Hammelburg

14 APRIL: Promoted to general

4 MAY: Bradley authorizes Third Army to advance to Pilsen; Germany surrenders four days later

6 OCTOBER: Relieved of command of Third Army

21 DECEMBER: Dies in Heidelberg, Germany, after being paralyzed in automobile accident on 9 December

PATTON'S WAY

LEGENDS AND LIES | 1

> Patton deserves his legend, but
> posterity deserves history and not myth.
> —*Harry Yeide*

On a cold, wet, and gray Wednesday, 6 September 1944, Lieutenant General George S. Patton Jr., commander of the Third United States Army, conducted one of his habitual tours of the front. With aides Lieutenant Colonel Charles Codman and Major Al Stiller, he rode in an open-top jeep through Verdun, Etain, and Conflans in western France to see his 2nd, 5th, and 90th Infantry Divisions and the 7th Armored Division on the front line. Since the last days of July, Patton and his Third Army had conducted a historic drive across the country and turned stalemate into breakout. Now they were poised to pierce the border and stab into the heart of Germany—but it was not to be. At this emblematic moment, Supreme Allied Commander General Dwight D. "Ike" Eisenhower and his staff diverted logistical support from Patton's rampaging forces to other parts of the Allied armies. At the front, Patton found his commanders frustrated, his spearheads blunted, and his losses mounting. "All this comes from the fatal decision of the Supreme Commander to halt Third Army until the Pas-de-Calais was cleared up," he wrote in his diary that night, "a fateful blunder."[1] For the last three years, Ike had often left Patton on the sidelines of war or limited him to supporting roles, but this episode was worse. Cutting Patton's logistical support not only denied him a glorious victory, it also effectively obscured the historical import of Patton's way of war.

Patton's well-publicized personality had long been a source of amusement and resentment among his competitive peers. His seeming unwillingness or inability to comply with doctrine added equal parts of frustration and dismissiveness to the mix. Few could understand or appreciate his divergent theories regarding the roles of battle, infantry, mechanization, fire, and maneuver. His reliance on subordinate initiative appeared to others as poor command and control. Patton's carefully orchestrated web of intelligence operations remained invisible to those who supposed he just had a remarkable sense of intuition. Yet his obvious triumphs and the praise he received from many quarters seemingly contradicted the doctrinaire dismissal of his methods and spurred critics to construct incomplete theories attributing his success to his reckless daring, his emphasis on tanks, and his hallmark determination.

Patton's frustrations sprang partly from inevitable conflicts of personality—both natural and crafted. He consciously constructed his flashy costume of polished helmet, riding breeches, and ivory-handled pistols as a means of motivating a generation of young men reared on dime-store novels and comic books. In July 1941, a *Life* cover story reported, "Because of his snappy helmet and costumes," Patton was "sometimes called 'General Flash Gordon' or the 'Green Hornet.'"[2] General Omar Bradley knew the effect was by design, years later recalling Patton as "an actor—almost everything he did was designed to create a dramatic effect."[3] In 1931 Patton explained his intent: "A cold reserve cannot beget enthusiasm. . . . It then appears that the leader must be an actor."[4] His act included staged outbursts of anger, scripted in the language of the troops.[5] Patton wrote: "The greatest gift a general can have is a bad temper (under control). A bad temper gives you a sort of divine wrath, and it is only by the use of a divine wrath that you can drive men beyond their physical ability in order to save their lives."[6] In time, however, the image eclipsed the man. Close associate General Albert Wedemeyer explained, "The American people were given a picture of him only as a swashbuckling, intrepid combat leader; but he had a scholarly bent and a profound knowledge of strategy, tactics, and military and political techniques."[7] Unfortunately, the image crafted to motivate some simply irritated others.

Many Army professionals found Patton and his methods objectionable—and not without reason. Eisenhower wrote, "He talks too much and too quickly and sometimes creates a very bad impression. Moreover, I fear he is not always a good example to subordinates, who may be guided by only his surface actions without understanding the deep sense of duty, courage, and service that make up his real personality."[8] Even George C. Marshall once said, "Patton [was] not only indiscreet, [he] descended almost to buffoonery at times."[9] A number of war correspondents frankly despised him. Andy Rooney, for example, wrote: "Many of the soldiers in Patton's army hated him. . . . He was a loudmouthed boor who got too many American soldiers killed for the sake of enhancing his own reputation as a swashbuckling leader in the Napoleonic style."[10] Patton recognized this backlash against his over-the-top motivational style and admitted, "I have somewhat of an impish nature and frequently like to shock people. In fact I have shocked people so efficiently that it has militated against my success."[11]

Patton's deliberate practice of shocking people was just one point of conflict with the more traditional aloofness of Eisenhower, Bradley, and British general Bernard "Monty" Montgomery.[12] Patton was abrasive, while Montgomery was condescending, Bradley was irritable, and Eisenhower was, at turns, distant, imperious, friendly, political, frayed, and put upon. Each trod upon history's stage worried about his pending reviews. Patton lusted for glory, while Montgomery expected it as his due. Bradley coyly hid his desire for fame, while Eisenhower tempted it. Moreover, to use Samuel P. Huntington's categorizations, Patton was a true military professional working among craftsmen.[13] Eisenhower, Montgomery, and Bradley operated within the practiced customs of their trade; Patton mastered his vocation but remained unrestrained by its norms. Like his artistic contemporaries Louis Armstrong or Pablo Picasso, he was a modernist whose rapid, bold strokes contradicted the craftsman's traditional philosophies and practices and confounded conventional critics.

This conflict of personalities compounded a very real lack of understanding of Patton's unorthodox techniques. U.S. Army doctrine embraced increasingly industrial models of established methods of attritional warfare built on well-planned and controlled operations. Capstone interwar regulations directed that all military operations should aim to create battles designed to destroy the enemy's forces.[14] Before World War II, Eisenhower, Bradley, and even Marshall had only commanded tactical infantry units in peacetime with which they practiced official doctrine, using maneuver to bring destructive firepower on the enemy. Patton, having commanded a tank brigade in combat in World War I, held different ideas. He decided it was best to avoid battle—to go around and behind the enemy. He rejected doctrine targeting enemy forces and instead took aim at the enemy's will.[15] Patton developed a new calculus of war: fire to enable maneuver; maneuver to create shock; shock to frustrate enemy decisionmaking; frustrate decisionmaking to destroy enemy morale; and destroy morale to collapse the enemy's will. To his more conventional peers, it was not a calculus that added up to victory.

In breaking with doctrine, Patton also broke its focus on the infantry. As Kenneth Finlayson observed, the U.S. Army experience in World War I "reinforced the prevailing belief system that positioned the individual rifleman as the centerpiece of the tactical doctrine."[16] It was true that during the war, "infantry" expanded to include machine guns, mortars, and sometimes tanks, but all were slaves to the pace and range of the riflemen. The U.S. Army *Field Service Regulations 1923* commanded that "the coordinating principle which underlies the employment of the combined arms is that the mission of the infantry is the general mission of the entire force."[17] Doctrine also stressed, "The special missions of the other arms are derived from their powers to contribute to the execution of the infantry mission."[18] At the U.S. Infantry School, instructors such as Marshall and Bradley cautioned students: "When used habitually, tanks may tend to reduce the self-reliance and aggressive spirit of the infantry."[19] Patton exasperated such minds by preaching the contrary, urging the placement of mechanized forces at the heart of combined arms teams and refusing to restrict his operations to capabilities of the foot soldier.

The change in emphasis from infantry to mechanized force reflected an important difference in philosophy. When Bradley talked "open warfare or 'a war of movement'," he meant something far different from Patton's "Mobile Strategy."[20] The Infantry School endorsed General John Pershing's concept of "open warfare" as employed by the American Expeditionary Force as shorthand for a desire to avoid trench warfare.[21] Pershing defined the term as "driving the enemy out into the open and engaging him in a war of movement."[22] In practice, "open warfare" could resemble Ulysses S. Grant's frontal assaults in the Battle of the Wilderness in 1864—or those of Mark Clark in Italy or Bradley at Aachen in 1944. Patton was more inclined to follow Napoleon Bonaparte's advice: "Never attack a position in front which you can gain by turning."[23] And like Napoleon, he sought strategic maneuver: "the art of bringing forces to the battlefield in a favorable position."[24] The difference can be seen, for example, in the Operation Overlord plan where Eisenhower simply set the objective as "to secure a lodgment on the Continent from which further offensive operations can be developed," but Patton instead called for a "reverse Schlieffen plan" to envelop the Germans in Normandy.[25]

"Open warfare" embraced factors such as speed, initiative, and flexibility, but only at the tactical levels of regiment and below. In its endorsement of attrition, Army doctrine and its practitioners discounted higher-level maneuver. After World War I, General Tasker Bliss voiced the official U.S. Army opinion that classical strategy had died on the fields of France.[26] The vast size of modern armies, the advent of aerial reconnaissance, and the speed of communications meant it was no longer possible to gain an advantageous position on an enemy. The outcome of battles therefore depended on frontal assaults, determination, and superior firepower. The Army school system ingrained this lesson into several generations of officers who went on to the highest tiers of command in World War II.

Patton countered that army and corps commanders should focus on *where* to beat an enemy more than *how* to beat them.[27] Like Napoleon, he embraced the concept of *coup d'oeil*—the "strike of the eye"—to determine the *where*.[28] Clausewitz defined the term, applicable in both tactics and strategy, as "the quick recognition of a truth that the mind would ordinarily miss or would perceive only after long study and reflection."[29] In essence, the term refers to the ability to see how events under way will unfold and quickly decide how to direct efforts toward decisive ends. William Duggan explored this concept and concluded: "Patton fought by *coup d'oeil*. Eisenhower and Bradley were classic Jomini planners. While his two superiors plodded along . . . Patton broke out."[30] This difference between them added to the friction in their relationships. Bradley was mystified by Patton's suggestion that the Overlord plans did not "go far enough."[31] Supreme Headquarters Allied Expeditionary Force (SHAEF) failed to grasp the urgency in Patton's calls for attacking the Siegfried Line in late August 1944.[32] Likewise, his arguments for strategic maneuver—to cut to the sea in Tunisia, to take Palermo and Messina, to encircle the Germans at Falaise or along the Seine, to swing east of the Bulge, to dash across the Rhine, or to take Berlin—not only failed to move his superiors but also irritated them. The exclusivity of his vision has even today led such critics as Stanley P. Hirshson to incorrectly argue, "Clearly, Patton was a better tactician than strategist."[33]

During the great pre–World War II maneuvers, Patton's "victories" brought greater criticism from traditionalist umpires and observers.

As Bradley put it, "Patton broke all the old-fashioned rules, smashing his mechanized forces ever onward with dazzling speed and surprise. [Yet] he was criticized by the umpire-generals for his unorthodoxy, for leaving his command post and prowling the 'front line,' for running his division 'roughshod' over the 'enemy.'"[34] The chief of staff of the Army General Headquarters, General Lesley J. McNair, pronounced, "This is no way to fight a war."[35] During the war, Patton's relentless advances transformed conventional cavalry *pursuit* (the last phase of victorious battle) into a prime mission for fast-moving combined arms columns in *exploitation* (the decisive phase of a campaign). Few understood his logic. When Ike offered the compliment, "Patton had an instinct for pursuit, and that was his great capacity," 4th Armored Division commander Major General John S. Wood corrected, "'Pursuit,' indeed! A fair measure of Eisenhower's military genius—this evaluation of George Patton. A pity neither he nor Bradley nor even Montgomery knew so little about *exploitation.*"[36]

To traditionalists, the speed and flexibility of Patton's operations were signs of a lack of command and control. U.S. Army doctrine instructed, as James Corum described, that "battles must be fought by plan, there is little consideration for the 'fog of war,' and individual initiative is not encouraged."[37] Infantry School texts emphasized, *"A unit must be engaged in accordance with a definite plan. It must not be permitted to drift aimlessly into battle."*[38] Commanders were to make circumstance bend to plans—to bring order to chaos. Patton, on the contrary, accepted German field marshal Helmuth von Moltke's view, "No plan of operations reaches with any certainty beyond the first encounter with the enemy's main force."[39] In 1926 he shared his belief with Eisenhower that execution was more important than plans.[40] In the margin of *Infantry in Battle*, he scribbled: "Execution is to plan as 5 is to 1."[41] He did not dismiss plans, he transformed them. Rather than highly detailed, complicated products, Patton issued simple, flexible plans that relied on adjustments during execution. He preached, "It may be of interest to future generals to realize that one makes plans to fit the circumstances, and does not try to create circumstances to fit plans."[42]

Simple plans required an emphasis on subordinate initiative during execution. Patton urged his men to "use their imagination . . . act on their own best judgment."[43] This style of command and control remained completely unfathomable to his peers. The Infantry School, the source of official doctrine, insisted: "Control is essential to success in battle. . . . This requirement is absolute; for no plan can be carried through, no previously conceived maneuver executed, no fleeting opportunity grasped, unless a leader has control of his unit."[44] Similar traditionalism in Britain convinced Bernard Montgomery: "The plan of operations must always be made by the commander and must not be forced on him by his staff, or by circumstances, or by the enemy. . . . A commander must be very thorough in making his tactical plans; once made, he must be utterly ruthless in carrying out and forcing it through to success."[45] There is little wonder, then, that Patton's contrasting methods looked inadequate at best and sloppy at worst. Bradley complained, "Patton did not give a damn about [planning] details, and his attitude was reflected by his staff."[46] He quietly harbored constant condemnation of Patton's "impetuous habits."[47] Eisenhower thought Patton's methods limited him to "certain types of action" and believed army commander was his promotion ceiling.[48] When results contradicted these impressions, critics could only express bewilderment.

Betraying their lack of comprehension of his methods, many Patton observers often suggested he had an inexplicable divine star guiding his operations. Bradley once marveled at his apparent clairvoyance and surmised, "Patton's intuition may have been based in part on the excellent work of his G-2, Oscar Koch."[49] Koch explained, "Many times the question has been asked whether Patton possessed an intuition—a sixth sense or whatever—which contributed to the exploits of his commands and to his ability to catch the enemy unaware. If one can call anticipation of enemy reactions based on a lifetime of professional training and on thinking and application 'intuition,' he had it."[50] That lifetime of study provided Patton with unique insights divergent from doctrine and therefore inscrutable to his peers and to many later historians.

After Patton's death, the leading generals refought the war in the pages of their memoirs. In 1947 his wife Beatrice drew mainly from his diaries to guide the completion of his only book, *War as I Knew It*. She left in his many criticisms of his contemporaries. Undersecretary of War Robert P. Patterson reported to President Harry Truman: "He steps on other people's toes pretty freely. He was that way—impulsive, explosive, far from impartial."[51] In 1948 Ike published *Crusade in Europe*, which in turn sparked Montgomery to write: "A pity you should have thought it necessary to criticize me and my ways. . . . I feel sad when an officer I have tried to serve loyally criticizes me publicly."[52] Ike described Patton as a limited field commander, emotional and impetuous.[53] Bradley followed three years later with his first memoir, *A Soldier's Story*, condemning Montgomery as an egoist and calling Patton indifferent to supply, lacking self-discipline, and essentially lucky.[54] Monty sought the last word in 1958 with his *Memoirs*. Eisenhower told a friend it would be "a waste of time to read if I was looking for anything constructive."[55] Finally, in 1983, the last man standing—Bradley—released a second memoir in which he rewrote events and further castigated the other players.

Out of this babble of the generals, a skewed picture of Patton and his methods emerged. A number of historians, such as British writer Charles Whiting, concluded that "in essence, Patton was neither a great man nor a great soldier. If he had not lived, it would not have mattered one little bit. . . . Nor was he a Great Captain. He initiated no new tactics, such as Guderian's and von Manstein's concept of the Blitzkrieg."[56] A popular ranking of the "100 Most Influential Military Leaders of All Time" placed Patton at number ninety-five behind Frederick Sleigh Roberts, Garnet Joseph Wolseley, and Kim Il Sung—a full seventy-nine slots behind George C. Marshall, seventy-seven behind Eisenhower, forty-nine behind Bradley, and thirty-two behind Montgomery.[57]

These historians' assessments contradict some notable impressions relayed by wartime leaders regarding Patton's much-needed singular abilities. When the Navy asked for a more malleable general for the North African invasion, Marshall declined and told Admiral Ernest King that Patton was "indispensable."[58] Following the "slapping incidents," Ike implored reporters to sit on the story, saying, "Patton is indispensable to the war effort—one of the guarantors of our victory."[59] Appreciation of Patton's skills crossed the battlefront. Erwin Rommel conceded: "Even [in Tunisia], the American generals showed themselves to be very advanced in the tactical handling of their forces, although we had to wait until the Patton Army in France to see the most astonishing achievements in mobile warfare."[60] General Hermann Balck, who faced him on the German border, acknowledged, "Patton was the outstanding tactical genius of World War II. I still consider it a privilege and unforgettable experience to have had the honor of opposing him."[61] Commander in chief Field Marshal Gerd von Rundstedt reportedly thought Patton "a far more dangerous opponent" than Montgomery.[62]

Rundstedt told an Allied interviewer after the war: "Patton was your best."[63] (Harry Yeide has suggested some laudatory German generals were currying favor with the postwar North Atlantic Treaty Organization [NATO], but by then Eisenhower, Montgomery, and Bradley were actively discrediting the Patton legend and had already largely removed "Patton's boys" from positions of influence in NATO.[64])

The rank and file also gave kudos to Patton. Soldiers tend to be skeptical of commanders in general, and flashy commanders in particular, but they are loyal to leaders who accomplish their missions without putting undue hardship on their men. Soldiers were loyal to Patton. Hearing that he was coming to II Corps after the Kasserine disaster, one officer wrote: "The old soldiers, who knew him as Gorgeous Georgie or Flash Gordon, rejoiced at his coming, even though they feared his rashness. They knew that he would demand much, but that there would be a pat on the back for every kick in the pants, and that their interests would be his interests."[65] A Navy lieutenant recalled that upon seeing Patton, "You get the same feeling, as when you saw Babe Ruth striding up to the plate. Here's a big guy who's going to kick the hell out of something."[66] A major on his staff said, "I knew I was with a winner. . . . He had the reputation of being a winner from Africa and Sicily."[67] While visiting wounded American soldiers in British hospitals, Undersecretary Patterson noted with surprise: "When asking a patient what unit he was in, men from other Armies invariably named their regiment or division, very few knowing what Army they were in, or the name of their Commanding General. But a Third Army man always replied: 'I was with the Third Army.' And he not only knew who commanded it, but usually had a personal anecdote about Patton."[68] Such connections planted a legend in popular memory.

Patton's reputation as someone who gained ground quickly with fewer casualties is only vaguely supported by aggregate numbers (see figure 1). Casualties, however, make for a troublesome metric in measuring the efficiency of combat methods. Units carried out different missions of different difficulties, they switched headquarters or subordinate units, and sometimes they failed to report accurate numbers. Men carried on rosters as "missing" one month migrated to "killed," "captured," or "returned to active duty" the next.

A close examination of 12th Army Group G-1 (Personnel) reports, however, provides an interesting perspective. 12th Army Group employed

Figure 1.
American Casualties by Month in the European Theater of Operations

Source: "Battle Casualties by Type of Casualty and Dispositions, And Duty Branch: 7 December 1941–31 December 1946," in Army Battle Casualties and Nonbattle Deaths in World War II, Final Report 7 December 1941–31 December 1946 at http://www.ibiblio.org/hyperwar/USA/ref/Casualties/Casualties-Intro.html

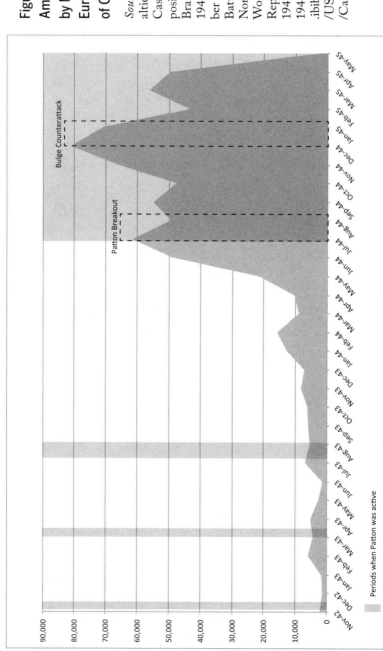

thirty-four infantry divisions, thirteen armored divisions, and three airborne divisions in Europe, but only nine spent the entire campaign exclusively with either the First or Third Army (once the Third was activated). The 1st, 2nd, 9th, and 83rd Infantry and 3rd Armored Divisions stayed with First Army; the 5th and 35th Infantry and 4th and 6th Armored Divisions remained with Third Army. Reported casualties (see figure 2) show those exclusive First Army infantry divisions suffered 7.9 killed and 35.8 wounded per day. Third Army's permanently associated infantry divisions suffered about 7.4 killed and 34.6 wounded per day, only about 6 percent fewer deaths and 4 percent fewer wounded. In armored divisions, however, First Army's permanently assigned divisions suffered 7.6 killed and 21.8 wounded per day compared to Third Army's armored division average of about 4.3 killed and 14.5 wounded per day. That difference of 43 percent fewer tanker deaths and 33 percent fewer wounded is significant. The differences are especially notable when one considers that the 4th Armored Division, the unit most closely associated with Patton's methods, repeatedly spearheaded his battles and suffered the fewest casualties per day—especially when one factors in the severity of the unit's fights caused by the cut to Patton's gas and Eisenhower's orders to drive into the center of the Bulge.

The contradiction between Patton's overt achievements and his critics' perceptions have made him a fixture in public fascination. As a field army commander, he was a peer of Alexander Patch, William Simpson, and Courtney Hodges—men now generally forgotten—yet numerous books and websites count Patton among a pantheon that includes Bradley, Montgomery, Eisenhower, and Marshall. Edgar Puryear, for example, included him alongside Marshall, Eisenhower, and Douglas MacArthur in his seminal study of command. Victor Davis Hanson wrote of Patton in a study with Epaminondas and William T. Sherman. A History Channel television series focused on the interwar lives of Adolf Hitler, Winston Churchill, Joseph Stalin, Benito Mussolini, Charles De Gaulle, MacArthur, and Patton.[69] A recent Google search returned over 28 million hits on George S. Patton Jr. compared to almost 18 million for Montgomery, 16 million for Eisenhower, and a little over 10 million for Bradley.[70] A similar search of the Amazon.com website showed 7,975 results for books on Patton as compared to 1,074 about Montgomery and 926 on Bradley.[71] This interest is all

DIVISION	ARMY	CORPS	KILLED TOTAL	KILLED DAILY	WOUNDED TOTAL	WOUNDED DAILY	MISSING TOTAL	MISSING DAILY	CAPTURED TOTAL	CAPTURED DAILY	TOTAL BATTLE TOTAL	TOTAL BATTLE DAILY	NON BATTLE CASUALTIES TOTAL	NON BATTLE CASUALTIES DAILY
1ST INFANTRY	FIRST	VII CORPS	1973	5.9	11448	34.1	951	2.8	631	1.9	15003	44.7	13832	41.1
2ND INFANTRY	FIRST	V CORPS	2999	8.9	10924	32.5	109	0.3	1034	3.1	15066	44.8	10605	31.6
9TH INFANTRY	FIRST	VII CORPS	2905	8.6	14066	41.9	792	2.4	868	2.6	18631	55.4	15191	45.2
83RD INFANTRY	FIRST	VII CORPS	2735	8.1	11678	34.8	547	1.6	288	0.9	15248	45.4	8584	25.4
3RD ARMORED	FIRST	VII CORPS	2540	7.6	7331	21.8	106	0.3	128	0.4	10105	30.1	5919	17.6
5TH INFANTRY	THIRD	XX, XII CORPS	2057	7.3	9110	32.5	1038	3.7	101	0.4	12312	43.9	10729	38.3
35TH INFANTRY	THIRD	XV, XII, III CORPS	2071	7.4	10,286	36.7	1032	3.7	460	1.6	13219	47.2	9293	33.1
4TH ARMORED	THIRD	VIII, XII, III CORPS	1210	4.3	3953	14.1	494	1.8	1	0	5661	20.2	4324	15.44
6TH ARMORED	THIRD	VIII, XII, III CORPS	1163	4.2	4164	14.9	147	0.5	7	0	5481	19.6	6966	24.9

FIRST ARMY UNITS CALCULATED FOR 336 DAYS (6 JUNE 1944 TO 8 MAY 1945)
THIRD ARMY UNITS CALCULATED FOR 280 DAYS (1 AUGUST 1944 TO 8 MAY 1945)

Source: "G-1 Section 12th Army Group: Report of Operations (Final After Action Report) Volume II" Box 1314, Records Group 407, National Archives and Records Administration, College Park, Maryland

Figure 2. Casualties of Divisions Associated with First or Third Army

Source: "G-1 Section 12th Army Group: Report of Operations (Final After Action Report) Volume II," box 1314, records group 407, National Archives and Records Administration II, College Park, Md.

the more remarkable considering Patton's lesser position, his extensive time spent idle, his early death, and the harsh postwar critiques.

Historians have struggled to reconcile the odd combination of Patton's persistent legend with his brusque persona and mystifying methods. One popular theory explaining Patton presents him as a lucky gambler who, as Terry Brighton rationalized, combined "the dash of the cavalry and the taking of risks, the outcome of which could not be calculated in advance."[72] Carlo D'Este agreed that "what separated him from his peers and cemented his reputation was his daring, freewheeling approach to modern warfare."[73] As proof of Patton's essential risk-taking nature, critics cite his constant calls for boldness and the "foolhardy" Hammelburg raid.[74] Some even interpreted Patton's apparent penchant for risk as an outgrowth of his brash persona. S. L. A. Marshall said, "I think he was half mad. Any man who thinks he is the reincarnation of Hannibal or some such isn't quite possessed of all his buttons."[75] This "bold gambler" theory, however, fails to see there was indeed method to Patton's madness. His *coup d'oeil* operated within an unconventional strategy targeting the enemy's will.

Another prominent theory attributes Patton's success to his expertise with tanks. As new chief of staff, Marshall proclaimed, "Patton is by far the best tank man in the Army."[76] According to Hubert Essame, "Patton was unquestionably the outstanding exponent of armored warfare produced by the Allies in the Second World War."[77] More recently, Trevor Royle attributed Patton's triumphs to his unique status as "an American soldier imbued with his country's military doctrine of speed, maneuver and surprise and then the deployment of overwhelming force to crush the opposition."[78] But America's doctrine was really more mundane, and as Alan Axelrod noted, "Although he loved the cavalry and was a passionate advocate of armor, Patton never limited himself to a single arm."[79] No tank fanatic or one who only applied cavalry doctrine to armor warfare could have created the operations Patton executed in World War II. He acted in opposition to "his country's military doctrine" and followed his own methods of warfare.

A related theory suggests that Patton's natural rambunctiousness produced positive results only when placed under proper command and control. In other words, he was like an attack dog, valuable when leashed by more capable commanders. According to this model, the one-dimensional Patton ran into problems when left to his own devices. Eisenhower felt the need to promise Marshall that Patton would never rise higher than Army command.[80] Bradley's aide, Chester Hansen, said of Patton: "With Bradley to control and guide him, with [Third Army Chief of Staff Hugh] Gaffey to hold down his administration, Patton provides the leadership and aggressiveness needed to make an army aggressive and going concern.... There is no doubt that he is capable. But he is more of a sledgehammer than a skillful commander. He has more punch than he has knowledge of tactics."[81] This was the rationale for putting Bradley over Patton in France.

While recognizing "a need for a commander who sees nothing but the necessity of getting ahead," Ike wanted the "emotionally stable" Bradley to govern Patton.[82] Marshall concurred and reportedly told a correspondent, "Bradley will lead the invasion, but he is just a limited objective general. When we get moving, Patton is the man with the drive and the imagination to do the dangerous things fast."[83] In 1946 Eisenhower corrected a writer who credited Patton for victories: "His army was part of a whole organization and his operations part of a great campaign. Consequently, in those instances where Patton obeyed orders, the story only hurts itself by assuming that Patton conceived, planned, and directed operations in which he was in fact—the brilliant executor."[84] The record suggests otherwise. Patton conceived, planned, and directed his operations using nondoctrinal *Auftragstaktik*, subordinate initiative, and simplicity to produce flexibility, agility, and speed.

Probably the most accepted theory on Patton ascribed his success to his relentless drive—in Essame's words, his "eagerness to seize opportunities and to exploit them to the full, the ruthless overriding of the opposition, the love of the unconventional, the ingenious and the unorthodox, the will to win whatever the cost and, above all, in the shortest possible time."[85] Ian Hogg expanded on this idea: "In World War II there was still room for the flamboyant leader, the man who could impress his own personality on the troops he led and, to some extent, on the enemy."[86] Victor Davis Hanson added, "Patton proved that the idea of a great democratic march, an ideological trek in which a fiery commander might put his spirit of vengeance into his citizen soldiers, was not lost.... Patton alone of the American generals accomplished that feat."[87] Even John Nelson Rickard acknowledged, "Though it is impossible to quantify, Patton probably transferred some of his energy and enormous self confidence to his subordinates."[88] Patton's aide,

Charles Codman, described the "key to General Patton's success" as his "uncanny gift for sweeping men into doing things they do not believe they are capable of doing."[89] But if determination in the attack alone brought victory, Burnside's Bridge, Little Big Horn, and the Fields of Flanders would all tell different tales. Patton inspired determination, but there was more to his way of war. He relied on a refined intelligence system and a knowledge of military history and theory to exploit opportunity and unbalance his opponent. In other words, he knew what he was doing.

Unfortunately, proponents of these theories derived from suppositions of Patton as recklessly aggressive have turned mining for his faults into a cottage industry. Restrictions and limitations imposed by higher commanders on Patton's troops, supplies, or freedom of maneuver in Tunisia, Sicily, and Metz and during the drive to Houffalize have created rich veins for exploration. Some, such as Rickard, offered insightful studies of these difficult battles.[90] Others, such as Charles Whiting, delivered broad critiques impelled by questionable motives. Testimony from those Patton pushed too hard or confounded with his methods fueled the critics. Hirshson's "officers who took part in or later studied his campaigns" were men aggrieved by Patton: Bradley and Lucian Truscott in Sicily, Wood in Brittany, and Robert Icks in Metz.[91] Needless to say, no commander is without critics or faults, but Patton's case often reminds one of Margaret Thatcher's belief that if her critics saw her walking across the Thames, they would say it was because she could not swim.

Patton died without leaving an adequate explanation of his success. He provided only clues in tailored speeches, letters, and orders. In July 1943, for instance, he confessed in a letter: "I knew perfectly well in my own case that I am not a brilliant soldier. So far I have been quite a successful one because I am always fully confident that I can do what I am told to do, and have had my sense of duty developed to the point where I let no personal interest or dangers interfere."[92] That confidence, however, grew out of a faith in his methods honed by many years of intense study and practice. Dennis Showalter might have come closest to explaining the true Patton:

> A lifetime of reading and reflection focused on war developed a mental sophistication that enabled him to think ahead, anticipating moves and developing counters, forcing

the pace of battle to points where neither his enemies, his superiors, nor his subordinates could readily keep pace. Patton's concepts of war led him away from conventional approaches, toward a nonlinear paradigm whose pace and impact compelled the enemy to fight at a disadvantage, to surrender, or to flee. Often presented as designed to avoid enemy contact, Patton's way of war accepted combat, but sought to make it brief and decisive: the final element in throwing the enemy fatally off-balance through sophisticated use of time, space, and mass.[93]

The same issue of *Life* that noted Patton's flashy costume also inadvertently outlined his embryonic, unorthodox methods. "The brief action of the tanks," it begins, "combined with the reports of scouting parties, engineers and parachutists has revealed to him how large the enemy forces are, how they are disposed and, most important, where their weakest positions are located. Now, General Patton can plan his all-out tank, infantry and artillery attack."[94] Synthesized intelligence systems, planned flexibility, and combined arms—these were his hallmarks. The article continues: "Because enemy forces are larger than he had expected, he must strengthen his main shock force . . . if he is to be successful in breaking through enemy positions and penetrating enemy lines."[95] The final element, shock, completes the recipe of his success.

British historian S. D. Badsey argued that Patton "was anything but a theorist."[96] Again, the record suggests otherwise. Patton was one of the Army's few deep thinkers and an astute theoretician. He possessed a superior intellect evidenced by his appointments to the Virginia Military Institute and the United States Military Academy and (although he never went) his admission to Princeton University.[97] Despite failing mathematics one year, he graduated forty-sixth in a class of 103 at West Point, well ahead of classmates Robert Eichelberger (who would become superintendent of the academy) and William Simpson (who would command the Ninth U.S. Army in World War II). Bradley was forty-fourth in his class and Eisenhower sixty-first in his. Patton was an honor graduate of the Command and General Staff College and a distinguished graduate of the Army War College. Roger Nye marveled that Patton "left behind the most complete record of exhaustive professional study of any World War II general—or any general in American history, for that matter."[98] Victor Davis Hanson added, "Critics forget that behind the foul mouth, sometimes offensive and near-lunatic pronouncements, and showy dress, Patton was without question the best-educated, most experienced, and most widely read general in the American army."[99] Patton spent his intellectual life concentrating on a singular purpose: the study and improvement of ways of war.

Contrary to the opinion of Charles Whiting, Patton mattered a great deal. After each of the two greatest reversals under his command, at Kasserine Pass and the Battle of the Bulge, Eisenhower turned to Patton as his one-man fire brigade. Without Patton, the Allied effort struggled. In Africa, Eisenhower failed to beat the Germans to Tunisia and suffered disaster at Kasserine. The Allies slogged into Tunis. Montgomery got stuck in Sicily. Mark Clark faltered in Italy. Bradley and Montgomery stalled in Normandy. Montgomery failed in Market Garden. Bradley could only wage bloody attrition warfare at Aachen and in the Hürtgen Forest and was caught catastrophically flat-footed by the German attack in the Bulge. As Wedemeyer said upon hearing Eisenhower criticizing Patton, "Hell, get on to yourself, Ike; you didn't make him, he made you."[100]

This is not to say that Patton was perfect. He was not. He admitted to two mistakes: the ill-conceived raid on Hammelburg and his persistence in direct assaults against Metz.[101] Patton tried his habitual multiple probes around Metz with the intention to follow "whichever assault makes a hole" but failed to get results.[102] A captured German colonel frankly told Patton, "There is no city in Germany which looks quite so well [for defense] as Metz."[103] Patton pressed his frontal attacks toward Metz too long, but his raid on Hammelburg was even more poorly decided and ineptly designed. He tried to combine a stealthy liberation raid with an essentially incompatible diversion effort. Even so, these examples are less indicative of faults within Patton's theory of war than illustrative of the costs of violating it. They are exceptions that prove the rule.

To discern Patton's theory of war, one must look at not only his writings, orders, and speeches but also the operations in which he had a free hand. Unfortunately, these are few. As noted, his operations were most often truncated by limitations and restrictions emplaced by higher headquarters. The hardest blow for Patton was the decision to cut his supplies, airpower, and troops in France, thereby giving the Germans time to regroup and reinforce significant defenses as the weather turned foul. Bradley once commented, "Without meaning to detract from his extraordinary achievements, Patton's great and dramatic gains, beginning in Sicily and continuing through Brittany and on across the Seine at Mantes, Melun and Troyes, had been made against little or no opposition. . . . I was not sure how good a tactician he would be in a tough fight."[104] This misses the point: Patton *intended* to seek out and exploit points of "little or no opposition," not create the conditions for doctrinal battles of attrition. In a tactical battle, Patton may have been less successful than in his preferred way of war, but he still compared favorably to his peers. Even with limited support from SHAEF, his set-piece victory at Metz contrasts well with the roughly concurrent operations by Bradley at Aachen and the Hürtgen Forest along the German frontier and by Montgomery in Market Garden in Holland—*especially* as a secondary effort. Even in Montgomery's paradigm set-piece victory at El Alamein against a worn-out foe that he outnumbered 6 to 1, Monty lost more than 13,000 men and nearly half of his 1,200 tanks (against 200 effective Axis tanks).[105]

Postwar developments muddled Patton's legacy. The shift to diplomatic generals such as Eisenhower, Bradley, and Joe Collins and the reliance on traditional infantry-artillery–based attrition doctrine in Korea and Vietnam shunted aside Patton's theory of war. Not until a series of unexpected events led to its resurrection on the road to the "AirLand Battle" did his ideas gain favor in U.S. Army doctrine. On that gray September day in 1944, however, these events were far off.

When SHAEF first cut his fuel Patton observed, "It is terrible to halt, even on the Meuse. We should cross the Rhine in the vicinity of Worms and the faster we do it the less lives and munitions it will take."[106] The man next to him was one of the very few who understood. John Wood would later write, "George Patton was the outstanding warrior of them all in Europe. He understood the nature of combat and the essentials of victory better than any of those placed ahead of him, including Montgomery."[107] Wood was schooled in Patton's way of war: a theory crafted from revolutionary ideas on strategy based on shock, combined arms operations, flexible command and control, and integrated intelligence systems.

Strategist William Duggan wrote, "One thing no one disputes: Patton was the best Allied general of the war."[108] Many critics do in fact dispute Duggan's observation. Even those who defend Patton rarely understand his methods. The following chapters expand on the elements of his way of war as a way of explaining his methods.

2 | A SERIES OF SHOCKS

> He out-blitzed those who made the blitzkrieg famous.
> —Robert Coram

Patton's exceptional success derived from his rejection of attrition strategy and his adoption of something completely new: a strategy of shock. His vision was unique. Not only did he see more than his peers, he also looked for different things. His peers looked for enemy strength to target. Patton differed, said Oscar Koch, by searching for "enemy capabilities."[1] Capabilities delineated opportunities. Patton looked for ways to exploit enemy weaknesses, to present sudden and unexpected threats, and to sustain such operations at a pace faster than the enemy's ability to react. Where his peers counted damage done to enemy forces, Patton sought to frustrate enemy decisionmaking and thereby undermine their morale. By turning battle into a campaign of unrelenting and frustrating continuous shocks, he sought to cause the enemy will to collapse. These aims produced the metrics of success in Patton's way of war.

Unlike his peers, Patton fought by *coup d'oeil*, which Baron Henri de Jomini termed "the most valuable characteristic of a good general."[2] In the days of Frederick the Great, the term described the ability to rapidly read the terrain and adjust operations accordingly. Patton's eye embraced much more. He operated within Edward Mead Earle's narrow definition of strategy, "the art of military command, of projecting and directing a campaign."[3] Patton set campaign objectives that would exploit enemy weakness and then attack their morale. Breaking with doctrine, he eschewed set-piece battles and tactical pauses, restrictive plans, and top-down control and instead pursued flexible, relentless advances calculated to overwhelm enemy planners. He reasoned that an enemy unable to react effectively would suffer a loss of morale and an eventual collapse of will.

Today, the U.S. Army has clear definitions of strategy, tactics, and operational art. Doctrine defines *strategy* as "a prudent idea or set of ideas for employing the instruments of national power in a synchronized and integrated fashion to achieve theater, national, and/or multinational objectives."[4] At the strategic level, state leaders determine war-winning objectives and allocate national resources to achieve those objectives. Doctrine also defines *tactics* as "the employment and ordered arrangement of forces in relation to each other. Through tactics, commanders use combat power to accomplish missions."[5] Battles delineate this exchange of combat power in time and space. The use of battles to achieve strategic objectives is conceptualized as the *operational art*. As doctrine states: "Commanders use operational art to envision how to create conditions that define the national strategic end state."[6] These terms, however, were not so well defined in Patton's day.

Today's doctrine assigns to theater commanders the responsibility of connecting tactics and strategy through operational art. Lower-level commanders focus on tactics, or the application of combat power on enemy forces. By this definition in August 1944, Supreme Allied Commander Eisenhower directed the "operational art" while land component commander Montgomery directed tactical operations. Army groups (as under Bradley) and armies (as under Patton) were purely tactical commands.[7] Bradley, Montgomery, and Patton were thus expected to only apply combat power against the enemy.

Operational art was not yet part of the U.S. Army doctrine in 1944; it was borrowed in the 1980s from the study of German and Russian army operations.[8] In the 1920s and 1930s Soviet general Vladimir Triandafillov imagined a two-staged "shock army" to create deep penetrations to disrupt enemy organization.[9] He envisioned fast-moving forces transcending the battlespace to undermine enemy theater plans, but his work would be virtually ignored until very late in World War II. The 1970s writings of General Alexei Radzievskii, commandant of the Frunze Academy, illustrated renewed Russian appreciation for this connection of tactics and strategy.[10] In World War II, the Soviet Union's enemy thought a little differently. "The tradition in the German army," Robert Citino noted, "was for the commander to 'shape' the campaign so that it resulted in a great battle of annihilation. . . . Operational commanders, then, must do more than simply assemble divisions, corps, and armies, and march them off in the general direction of the enemy. Rather, they must have the end result in mind at the start of the operation."[11] To the Germans, the operational art was to create decisive tactical battle.

Eisenhower practiced a form of operational art as a "concentration and mass against the main German armies."[12] In essence, he conducted theater operations in a tactical fashion, closing with the enemy and piling on combat power against their forces. In executing this strategy of attrition, Ike followed U.S. doctrine and tradition.[13] The manpower-strapped British, on the other hand, preferred an economical application of force tailored to decisive battles. To them, as chief of the Imperial Staff Field Marshal Alan Brooke lamented, "Ike knows nothing about strategy and is quite unsuited to the post of Supreme Commander as far as running the strategy of the war is concerned!"[14] Montgomery added, "It was always very clear to me that Ike and I were poles apart when it came to the conduct of the war."[15] Monty rejected what he saw as Eisenhower's desire to attack with all units all the time as too "expensive in life" and preferred instead a doctrine "based on unbalancing the enemy while keeping well-balanced myself."[16] Whether defending or attacking, Monty sought to get the enemy to commit his reserves on a wide front before committing his own reserves on a narrow, concentrated point and then quickly turning to reconstitute his reserves faster than the enemy. Montgomery's doctrine, therefore, sought decision through selective concentration in the tactical battle. Disciples of these two strategies—attrition versus decision—became frustrated with each other. Neither grasped the alternative practiced by Patton two links down the chain of command.

As John Nelson Rickard observed, "Patton had no ability to shape ground operations at the theater level, the way Montgomery and Bradley did, but Third Army was a grand tactical (operational) headquarters because it did more than simply fight the current battle. The function of his headquarters and his decision-making range equated to the operational level of war as it is understood today."[17] Technically, Patton was a tactical commander, but, as Rickard noted, he engaged in operational art, seeking to marry tactics to strategic ends. Many decades later some would call Patton a prototypical "operational leader" who translated "theater strategic objectives into a series of operational objectives accomplished through a series of major operations as part of a single campaign."[18] This view contradicts Patton's assigned duties and limited authority.

Patton often had to set his own strategic objectives at variance with Eisenhower's attrition operations. Moreover, he was not a conventional "operational art" commander. Instead of following the German, British, or Soviet model of shaping operations to achieve a decisive battle, he did something distinctive. He constructed operations to unbalance the enemy, to confront them with rapidly changing conditions, by advancing to positions most threatening to their intentions. In this way he reformed Napoleon's "strategic thinking" which, as Robert Leonhard noted, "ultimately was aimed at bringing the enemy to battle and seeking decision in one bloody contest."[19] Instead of using maneuver to bring firepower upon the enemy, Patton would use firepower to enable maneuver.

Maneuver was Patton's key to undermining the enemy's will. As his aide Charles Codman noted during the breakout from Normandy, "General Patton felt that this was the time to make an all-out effort by using highly mobile units, widely separated, moving in every direction. He was convinced that we could create such confusion in the German rear that they, having practically no communications, would eventually find themselves in a state of chaos."[20] That chaos—a fearful state of not knowing what threats might appear—set the conditions for creating shock.

Shock has seemingly faded from the military lexicon. It once described the physical "battering ram" impact of ancient massed Greek and Swiss phalanxes.[21] That impact could break a unit's will to stand its ground. Shock quickly took on this added psychological dimension, soon associated with the charge of heavy cavalry such as the Byzantine cataphracts or medieval knights. As one British infantryman said of Napoleon's cuirassiers, "The appearance was of such a formidable nature, that I thought we would not have the slightest chance with them."[22] By suddenly appearing with menacing force at the points most threatening to enemy forces and plans, cavalry could—in Jomini's words—"have a great influence in giving a turn to the events of a war."[23] Jomini added: "It may excite a feeling of apprehension at distant parts of the enemy's country, it can carry off his convoys, it can encircle his army, make his communications very perilous, and destroy the *ensemble* of his operations."[24] In fact, Jomini equated far-ranging cavalry operations to the overall effect of a mass popular uprising in troubling an army and "reducing a general to a state of entire uncertainty in his calculations."[25] Fear, doubt, apprehension, and uncertainty—these were the results of the appearance of unexpected force upon an enemy. Patton took to heart this linkage of maneuver to shock.

To arrive at the proper points at the right time to most likely affect the enemy morale, shock required rapid maneuver guided by strategic design. Maneuver had to catch the enemy unaware and unready to react. This implicitly meant acting more quickly than the enemy. Furthermore, Patton realized that while maneuver in space could unbalance the enemy, only continuation in time could overwhelm them. The attacker needed to maintain a series of shocks—to continue beating the enemy in an ever-accelerating series of decision cycles—in order to completely frustrate enemy morale and cause their will to collapse. Such warfare required a complete break from official doctrine, however.

Patton's ideas of warfare were rooted in his early appreciation for the role of morale in combat. Like many of his generation and social status, young George was homeschooled. Among his informal teachers was his surrogate grandfather, Colonel George Hugh Smith. This former commander of the 25th and 62nd Virginia Infantry Regiments in the Civil War shared with the boy valorous tales of forefathers battling in the Shenandoah Valley, at Gettysburg, and at Cold Harbor. Patton once wrote, "My grandfather, Colonel George S. Patton was my earliest hero, and I learned to ride on the saddle from which he was killed [at the Battle of Opequon in 1864]. In fact, there is a nick on the pommel by the shell which finished him."[26] He internalized concepts of glory and demoralization, the decisiveness of maneuver, and the horrors of attritional battle. Lessons in mobility, surprise, and shock were learned first-hand at the knee of his neighbor, famed Confederate guerrilla leader John Singleton Mosby.[27] Patton absorbed Thomas Stonewall Jackson's mantra to "never take counsel of your fears" and came to rationalize, "The enemy is more worried than you are. Numerical superiority, while useful, is not vital to successful offensive action. The fact that you are attacking induces the enemy to believe that you are stronger than he is."[28] As part of his education he memorized accounts of history's "great captains" and learned Napoleon's dictum regarding the three-fold greater importance of the moral to the physical in war.[29] Upon such stories the youth would build his theories of war.

When Second Lieutenant George S. Patton Jr. graduated from West Point in 1909, he entered an Army with a doctrine still modeled on Ulysses S. Grant's dogged methods of closing with the enemy and destroying them through massed firepower. As Russell Weigley noted, Grant and his disciples "returned decision to the war by prolonging battle through the whole campaign, inflicting casualties until he won not a dramatic Napoleonic victory but the peace of exhaustion."[30] They instilled in the Army a creed of determination, massed combat power, and attrition. The infantry supported by artillery carried the battle, with cavalry in a peripheral role. Taught this formula at West Point, Patton no doubt weighed its attrition focus against the moral perspective he absorbed in his youth.

As a young cavalryman, Patton first expressed conceptual rejection of traditionalist doctrine targeting the destruction of the enemy force. While serving as an aide to Brigadier General John J. "Black Jack" Pershing in the futile Punitive Expedition chasing Pancho Villa in Mexico in 1916, he began to break from infantry-artillery canon with its carefully planned and controlled battles. With motorized vehicles and aircraft at hand, Patton saw that pauses in the advance enabled the enemy to get away. During the campaign he wrote notes theorizing means "for the march to be continuous," arguing, "The Advance Guard must not stop and assume the defensive on seeing a hostile patrol."[31] He also saw how failure to catch the enemy hurt morale. On the other hand, when he shot down Villa's bodyguard Captain Julio Cardenas in a gunfight near Lake Itascate, he saw how action could boost morale. He strapped Cardenas and two other dead bandits over the hood of his staff car and drove to headquarters, where a delighted Pershing said: "We have a real bandit in our ranks, this Patton boy! He's a real fighter!"[32] Hungry for news, reporters put Patton in their reports, giving him a first taste of being in national headlines.

Patton again served on Pershing's staff as the American Expeditionary Force (AEF) entered World War I. Here was a much different conflict. Pershing pulled together a million-man army in France and fell in with the Allied strategy that Weigley described as "frontal collision in the hope destroying the enemy armies" even while criticizing the Allies for being too defensively minded in their acceptance of static lines and attrition.[33] The AEF head of training, Colonel Harold B. Fiske, complained, "The French do not like the rifle, do not know how to use it, and their infantry is consequently too entirely dependent upon a powerful artillery support."[34] Pershing would show his Allies how the United States massed foot soldiers to achieve fire superiority and grind forward to victory.[35]

To assist the infantry, Pershing investigated new weapons, including tanks. He sent a delegation from the Army War College to inspect British and French tank operations but cautioned, "Close adherence is urged to the central idea that the essential principles of war have not changed, that the rifle and bayonet remain the supreme weapons of the infantry soldier and that the ultimate success of the army depends upon their proper use in open warfare."[36] French marshal Philippe Pétain boasted of the psychological lift tanks provided his demoralized soldiers; the presence of tanks was strongly linked to morale. His minister of munitions explained, "There are two kinds of infantry; men who have gone into action with tanks, and men who have not; and the former never want to go into action without tanks again."[37] When Pershing decided to create an American Tank Corps to assist his infantry, Patton was first to volunteer.

Captain Patton went to the front to interview soldiers. American infantrymen of the 1st Division who had fought alongside French tankers were "most enthusiastic" about the vehicles.[38] Officers in French tank units near Saint Martin-aux-Bois talked "of 1914 with longing and never speak of the present *'salle affaire'*."[39] A major told Patton, "Ah, how I loved that war of movement, it was exciting. But this one is very annoying."[40] Though the tanks moved barely faster than a foot solider, the link between movement—possible with tanks—and morale registered with Patton: advance raised friendly morale and simultaneously undermined enemy morale. This echoed Napoleon: "A rapid march augments the *moral* of an army, and increases all the chances of victory."[41]

The Great War increased Patton's abhorrence of attrition warfare. He saw his men killed and suffered his own grievous wounds. Crawling over a French battlefield one night he studied the many corpses about him and found himself trying to repress thoughts of their mothers. His daughter Ruth Ellen remembered, "Suddenly the whole concept seemed unbearable, and he decided that the only way to survive under such stress was to try to think of soldiers as numbers, not as individuals, and that the sooner the allies won, the sooner the slaughter of innocents would cease. However, no matter what he said, he could never quite do that. To him men were individuals, people and responsibilities, always."[42] The erudite Codman once observed, "The simple truth of the matter is that all his life General Patton has been obsessed with an almost neurotic aversion to suffering and cruelty in any and every form."⁴³ During World War II, Patton revealed his disgust with a general who boasted of his losses as a sign of toughness and said, "I see no use in paying unnecessary casualties for victory."⁴⁴ His aversion to losses compelled Patton to find a more altruistic way of war.

In his copy of the 1910 edition of Sun Tzu's *The Art of War*, Patton underlined and marked "good" the line: "Thus it is that in war the victorious strategist seeks battle after the victory has been won, whereas he who is destined to defeat first fights and afterwards looks for victory."⁴⁵ To Patton, maneuver could make Sun Tzu's idea a reality and reduce casualties. During the breakout from Normandy, for example, he noted, "The 6th [Armored Division] is too careful, and so gets shot up. I told them to use more dash and keep going."⁴⁶ Maneuver reduced exposure to fire, it made the enemy reposition, and it enabled attacks on softer targets. Maneuver in the face of fire, however, required boldness.

On 10 June 1918 Patton issued a subtly brilliant pamphlet entitled "Brief Notes on the Tactical Employment of Tanks" in which he wrote, "It must never be forgotten that boldness is the key to victory. The tank must be used boldly. It is new and always has the element of surprise. It is also very terrifying to look at as the infantry soldier is helpless before it."⁴⁷ Tanks produced shock—which runs contrary to boldness—in the helpless infantry facing the crash of the new armored cavalry. Patton continued, "Tanks like cavalry must depend on rapidity and shock for success, or as a rear guard in an active retreat but never as adjuncts to a passive defense. . . . Like all new weapons they justify extreme boldness, even rashness, in their employment."⁴⁸ As Jomini had noted, "With cavalry more than with infantry the *morale* is very important."⁴⁹ Patton sensed that the same held for tanks.

The 1916 *Cavalry Drill Regulations* dictated, "Cohesion in the line and vigor in the shock are essential to the success of the saber charge. High speed is necessary for the desired shock."⁵⁰ Cohesion required discipline. When Patton established the American light tank school in France, he wrote, "There should be at least one regular officer per company to enforce discipline, as it is a well-known fact that working with machines has a very disastrous effect on discipline. It seems to run out of men as the oil soaks into them."⁵¹ He wrote his wife, "I am getting a hell of [a] reputation for a skunk," and added, "I bet the Tank Corps will have discipline if nothing else."⁵² First Lieutenant Will Robinson remembered, "If there was anything he wanted, it was to make the Tank Corps tougher than the Marines and more spectacular than the Matterhorn."[53] Patton intended to translate garrison discipline into battlefield cohesion.

Patton began submitting ideas for the employment of tanks in battle. Tank Corps chief of staff Lieutenant Colonel Daniel Pullen sent a mild rebuke to Patton: "I do not think this is the time to propose any tactics for the Tank Corps. . . . A great deal of what we say will be looked upon as hot air."[54] Ceding cavalry roles to tanks was not popular just when Pershing—himself an old cavalryman—pushed the War Department for eight horse regiments for the AEF.[55] Undeterred, Patton continued with his radical contemplations for the temporal use of tanks in "the assault, the counterattack, the exploitation of a success, advance and rear guards in a war of movement, raids with cavalry or special infantry units, and small, independent operations."[56]

Sequential echelons could produce sequential shocks, employing tanks for "riding the enemy to death," but the timing had to be right.[57] Patton complained to the AEF deputy chief of staff about an exercise with an eleven-minute delay between the commitment of the first and second waves of troops. "Subsequent reflection on my part has convinced me that this halt is an error," he wrote. "The second wave of infantry supported by a line of tanks preceding them should 'leapfrog' on at once. For the reason that if they do not the enemy will have nothing on his mind except the shelling of the tanks and the infantry at the intermediate objective, while if the line goes right on he will have something else to think about."[58] Patton believed that sustaining shock required rapid action by the follow-on echelons; otherwise, pauses in the attack would enable the defenders to regroup. Only continuous advance could keep the enemy off balance.

Patton learned firsthand the difficulty of maintaining a continuous advance when he led American tanks into their first combat in the Saint-Mihiel offensive on 12 September 1918. Across the front his men moved in fits and starts. Forced off a tank in Pannes by German machine guns, he could not get a nearby infantry commander to advance.[59] Asked to send a soldier to retrieve a tank under fire, the commander replied, "Hell no. It ain't my tank."[60] Still, Patton noted, "the appearance of five tanks had so disheartened the Germans that they could be seen retreating."[61] Meanwhile, the AEF battered ahead with massed forces to clear the Saint-Mihiel salient, capturing more than 15,000 Germans at a cost of 7,000 U.S. casualties.⁶² Yet, as Robert B. Bruce noted, "The battle of St. Mihiel had provided a dangerous reinforcement to Pershing's illusion that American ardor and bayonets could swiftly and easily overcome an entrenched opponent."⁶³ For all his efforts to propose maneuver, Patton's tanks had simply been part of a great attrition machine.

In the second American attack two weeks later, Patton found the advance again descended into chaos across the front. Against increasing machine gun fire, he rounded up small groups of disoriented infantry and retrieved tanks from several trenches. Answering the men's fears about the enemy, he said, "To Hell with them—they can't hit me."⁶⁴ He recalled, "I was trembling with fear when suddenly I thought of my progenitors and seemed to see them in a cloud over the German lines looking at me. I became calm at once, saying aloud, 'It is time for another Patton to die,' called for volunteers and went forward to what I honestly believed to be certain death."⁶⁵ Five of his accompanying 6 men fell dead. Patton was struck through the leg and was dragged off the field by Private First Class Joseph T. Angelo. He was just one of more than 100,000 U.S. casualties in the Meuse-Argonne offensive. Army leaders came away convinced of the validity of U.S. doctrine; Patton thought there had to be a better way to wage war.

While still convalescing from his battle wounds, Patton began a 249-page essay, "A Study of the Combat of Cavalry up to and Including the World War." As David Jablonsky noted, a consensus then existed that the mechanization "demonstrated the inadequacy of classical strategy to deal with modern warfare."⁶⁶ Armies were just too large and too dependent on massed artillery to gain any advantageous position on an unsuspecting enemy. Aircraft spotted movement, long-range artillery broke up maneuver, machine guns and barbed wire blunted attacks. Strategy thus migrated to the highest levels of command.⁶⁷ Corps became tactical units, their commanders trained to close with and destroy the enemy by massed firepower.

Oblivious to these views, Patton began his own examination of the war and concluded: "Strategy merely leads up to battle. The end of all effort and maneuver in war is successful combat *or to cause the enemy to give up because of his fear of that combat* [emphasis added]."⁶⁸ He therefore saw strategy in the traditional German view as leading to a decisive battle, but he added a key insight: there was advantage gained in creating in the enemy a perception of threat caused by the *direction* of the advance. Here was a classical understanding of strategy, in accordance with Jomini's description of Napoleon's grasp of the concept: "Strategy decides where to act."[69] Patton would develop this concept.

In a second paper entitled "German and Allied Theory of War," Patton noted newly revealed tactics in which specially trained German *Stosstrupp* (shock troop) patrols sought out and slipped through weak points in the Allied lines and then called forward follow-on troops to exploit their breakthroughs. Attacks therefore were freed from predetermined plans that might or might not conform to the facts on the ground. Patton had read in Sun Tzu: "Military tactics are like unto water; for water in its natural course runs away from high places and hastens downward. So in war, the way is to avoid what is strong and to strike what is weak."[70] Patton wrote in the margin, "A very good Field Service Regulations."[71] While recognizing a need for frontal attacks to hold the enemy's attention, he embraced the idea of maneuver to exploit weak spots. He wrote, "Strategical maneuvers will return with the diminution of the front attacks but it will always be fire backed by the threat of bayonet which now as in the time of Gustavus Adolphus decided the fate of war."[72] Patton sought maneuver to produce that threat of force.

American doctrine once endorsed Jominian interpretations of Napoleonic strategic maneuver. In 1835 Winfield Scott's *Infantry Regulations* began with a quote from Prussian field marshal Karl von Bülow: "I call STRATEGY, the hostile movement of two armies, made beyond the view of each other; or—if it be preferred—beyond the effect of cannon."[73] The Civil War saw attrition strategy rise to prominence, and World War I enshrined its dominance.[74] Military minds reframed Clausewitz's term: "Strategy is the use of the engagement for the purpose of war."[75] Industrial armies now employed strategies designed to erode the enemy through prolonged firepower, emphasizing Clausewitz's particular passages on mass and concentration geared toward the destruction of enemy forces.[76] Theorists selectively cited the Prussian: "Every combat is therefore the bloody and destructive measuring of the strength of forces, physical and moral; whoever at the close has the greatest amount of both left is the conqueror."[77] Such attrition obviously had little need of maneuver.

Patton countered that strategy was wholly connected with maneuver, which was needed to gain position against the enemy in time and space.

Properly executed, such maneuver could create sudden and threatening shock that, when repeated faster than the enemy could react, could undermine enemy morale and will without the losses intrinsic to attrition warfare. In this belief, Patton stood opposed to official doctrine expressed by the preeminent instructor in the U.S. Army school system, Colonel W. K. Naylor. In 1922 Naylor wrote: "I wish to stress this point; that warfare means fighting, and that war is never won by maneuvering. . . . History shows that the surest way to take the fighting spirit out of a country is to defeat his main army."[78]

With the Great War won, budgets slashed, and maneuver rejected, the U.S. Army abolished its Tank Corps in 1920, sending Patton back to the cavalry. He entered the Cavalry School's Field Officers' Course at Fort Riley, Kansas, in 1923 and found a curriculum, in Lucian Truscott's words, "dominated by the experience of trench warfare of the World War, so fresh in the minds of military men."[79] Guided by *Field Service Regulations 1923*, the school flatly taught: "The ultimate objective of all military operations is the destruction of the enemy's armed forces in battle."[80] Patton graduated to the General Service School at Fort Leavenworth (later renamed the Command and General Staff College), where instructors taught that the right amount of firepower combined with frontal assault by infantry could break any defensive position.[81] Leavenworth, David E. Johnson observed, "remained riveted on conservative doctrines, largely ignoring emerging, competitive perspectives such as mechanization and air power."[82] As late as 1938 the school provided nearly two hundred hours of instruction on the ponderous square infantry division and fewer than thirty hours on mechanization.[83]

Immense pressure compelled students to conform to doctrine. Truscott recalled, "Officers were made to feel that their entire future careers depended on their class standings. . . . Some officers broke under the strain."[84] A surge of student suicides caused such a scandal that the school was temporarily closed, only to reopen still dedicated to conformity. Maxwell Taylor explained that the mission at Leavenworth was to produce officers "all speaking the same professional language, following the same staff procedures, schooled in the same military doctrine, and thus ready to work together smoothly in any theater of war."[85] Historian D. K. R. Crosswell noted that the Leavenworth students learned that "military science rested upon the single-minded determination to feed irresistible power into frontal assaults all along the line until the opportunity arose for exploiting the enemy's weakness and destroying him."[86] Strategy meant massing firepower to physically destroy the enemy, and only by adhering to this doctrine could an officer make general. It comes as no surprise that Eisenhower later admitted, "I know of no single year in my whole service that I go back to in my memories more than my student year at Leavenworth."[87]

Carlo D'Este wrote, "Patton and Eisenhower emerged from Leavenworth with a discernable difference in philosophy, which would one day contribute to the rupture of their friendship. Although there was an obvious overlap, Eisenhower perhaps believed more firmly in the need for efficacious plans, while Patton placed more faith in their execution."[88] Even though Patton chafed under Leavenworth's dogmatism, he still finished as an honor graduate, twenty-fifth out of 248 students.[89] That achievement came with suspicion: he was once reported by a classmate for studying late at night under a "strange blue light." Brought before an academic board, Patton admitted it was true; the light was a device he purchased in hopes of curing his ever-increasing baldness.[90] The complaint was dismissed.

At Leavenworth, Patton made a careful study of doctrine and spent subsequent years working and reworking the class problems, adding new ideas to a notebook of best solutions. He loaned more than one hundred pages of his carefully reworked notes to Eisenhower, who used them to graduate first in his Leavenworth class in 1926.[91] This remarkable triumph catapulted the career of the previously undistinguished Ike. When a grateful Ike returned his notes, Patton replied: "I don't try for approved solutions any more but rather to do what I will do in war. . . . First read *Battle Studies* by [French colonel Ardant] Du Picq (you can get it at Leavenworth) then put your mind to a solution."[92] Among his catalogue of typed notes on numerous military works were 138 on du Picq's 1868 book that included an intellectual contemplation on shock in war.[93] Du Picq wrote, "In studying ancient combats, it can be seen that it was almost always an attack from the flank or rear, a surprise action, that won battles. . . . Maneuver being a threat, of great morale effect, the cavalry general who knows how to use it, can contribute largely to success."[94] Patton copied out this dictum in capital letters.[95]

Du Picq went on: "If cavalry unexpectedly appears, he [the infantryman] is lost. Cavalry conquers merely by its appearance."[96] He explained: "In the terror of the shock. Yes. In the shock, No! It lies only in the determination. It is a mental ends not a mechanical condition. . . . Courage, dash, and speed have a value beyond that of mere mass."[97] These ideas resonated with Patton's growing faith in boldness, tempo, maneuver, and the avoidance of pauses in the attack. Patton considered tanks an improved means for implementing du Picq's ideas, writing, "The tank is primarily and only a shock weapon. Its efficiency resting on its ability to produce mental shock by the never realized threat of physical shock."[98] Patton's philosophical break with official doctrine's focus on the physical destruction of the enemy was complete. He now looked for ways of inflicting decisive shock on the enemy. He wrote to the Cavalry Board his belief that "it is the enemy's soul rather than his body which is defeated. For the same reason the formation which a charge is executed is immaterial; determination and speed are the only requisite."[99] Patton was now on a doctrinal island.

Patton reported to Hawaii on the last day of March 1925, where he would serve stints as division G-1 (chief of staff for Personnel), G-2 (Intelligence), and G-3 (Operations and Plans). The assignments provided him unique opportunities to investigate staff operations, large unit functions, and field exercises. In November 1926, for example, his examination of advance guard operations brought him to some interesting conclusions. "In the general case," Patton complained, "the normal purpose of an attack is the infliction of death, wounds and destruction on the enemy troops with a view of establishing both physical and moral ascendency over them. The gaining of ground in such a combat is simply an incident; not an object."[100] He protested this general case. During exercises Patton cited confusion upon contact with the enemy, inadequate advance guards, habitual failure to envelop, and lack of coordinated fire and maneuver routinely as causing pauses in the attack that ceded initiative and prolonged exposure to enemy fire. He contended, "In battle a man going forward enters a lottery, with death the stake, and the odds the laws of probability. The only saving clause in his venture are time and the effect on the enemy's nerves of his rapid approach: why waste these benefits in futile sacrifices to lost Gods of Indian Wars [i.e., searching for cover to fire from]."[101] Patton pressed for boldness, speed, and movement forward.

By 1928 talk of tanks so threatened the horse cavalry that the chief of cavalry sent for America's foremost tanker to defend the branch against mechanization. Patton began this assignment by emphasizing moral factors in "Tactical Employment of Armored Cars, Experimental": "Oil and

Iron do not win battles—Victory is to men not machines."[102] He readily advocated the primacy of human factors in war, but for any more he was in a tough spot. As D'Este explained, "He accepted that the cavalry of the future must be mechanized to replace the horse, but as a representative in high standing of the chief of cavalry, he could hardly recommend the demise of his own service, and, in the end, supported the cavalry."[103] While Patton spent several years working for the horsemen, his writings always hinted at his faith in tanks as the primary weapon in future wars.

In 1930 Major General Frank Parker, now War Department G-3, produced a supplement to *Field Service Regulations 1923* titled *A Manual for Commanders of Large Units* (MCLU). Based largely on a 1921 French manual, Parker described the MCLU as adequately covering "the functions and needs of larger units and the specific responsibility of their commanders."[104] The MCLU included much-needed guidance on strategy—in a total of four paragraphs. Unlike modern doctrine, it described strategy as the province of the theater commander, who allocated resources and established missions, planning the next campaign while subordinates executed current plans.[105] The goal of strategy was the concentration of forces "so that the forces may be launched without delay against their objectives"—in other words, battle.[106] Critics such as chief of infantry Major General George A. Lynch thought MCLU espoused an inappropriate "doctrine of the successive effort"—echeloned attacks rather than one massed effort—contradicting the "doctrine of the concentrated blow" in *Field Service Regulations 1923*.[107] The successive effort described, however, was actually successive concentrated blows to produce sequential battles of attrition.

By this time, Patton had written: "Victory results from the infliction of a series of moral shocks to which the infliction of death, wounds and destruction are but contributory influences."[108] He thus codified his rejection of doctrine. Despite his conscripted support for the horse cavalry, he argued mechanized maneuver was the desired means to the proper ends of warfare. In the article "Mechanized Forces," published in *Cavalry Journal* in 1933, he advocated for a force of "armored cars, tanks and foot fighters" to be used in "wars of maneuver."[109] Abhorring "the appalling losses of a war of attrition," he noted that tanks restored maneuver to tactics and that the British had expanded "the idea of mechanization to the field of strategy, in the hope that by its use they could restore movement and so pave the way for shorter and more decisive wars."[110] His article was a radical rebuff to Army doctrine. Even more, he called for infantry and artillery to execute holding attacks so that a tank-led "maneuvering force can launch an attack against the enemy's rear or flank."[111] Patton's subject was horse cavalry, but his writing again confirmed his faith in mechanized mobile warfare.

Patton's belief in the primacy of moral factors in war found support in a lecture, "Battlefield Psychology," presented in March 1933 by Major General Hanson E. Ely (Ret.), who had commanded troops in the Philippines, Mexico, and France.[112] Ely stressed the importance of leadership to morale. He noted the centrality of chaos in battle and warned his audience, "You find yourself without communications and have to strike in the dark."[113] The solution he drew from du Picq: "For me as a soldier, the *smallest* detail caught on the *spot* and in the heat of action is more instructive than all the Thiers and the Jominis in the world."[114] It was therefore vital that leaders adapt to conditions found during battle and not attempt to adhere to preconceived plans. Finally, Ely noted, men in combat were dominated by a fear of death and, he wrote, "Fear of death is fear of the unknown."[115] Only unit coherence ingrained through discipline could compensate for the fear of the unknown ever present in battle. Patton would hence keep a transcript of Ely's speech in his personal files.

Patton began devouring Military Intelligence Division translations of contemporary foreign military writings as war clouds gathered.[116] He read G-2 translations of Heinz Guderian and Erwin Rommel that called for massed armored formations to spearhead attacks and defeat the static defenses.[117] Guderian's 1937 *Achtung-Panzer!* proposed concentrations of tank formations to conduct breakthroughs and exploitations.[118] Patton agreed, but with a caveat. Guderian proposed maneuver to close on and destroy the enemy.[119] Patton sought maneuver to inflict a series of moral shocks.[120] Guderian advocated maneuver to enable fire; Patton proposed fire to enable maneuver.

Despite all his study and writings, Patton's career seemed to go nowhere. July 1938 brought him to the command of the 5th Cavalry Regiment of the 1st Cavalry Division at Fort Clark, Texas. A biographer described it as "the country's most somnambulant Cavalry post, where superannuated officers, given their colonelcy as a parting gesture, were usually allowed a pleasant last fling before retirement."[121] Indeed, the outgoing commander, Colonel

Robert C. Richardson, retired. If it was to be the end, Patton decided to make the most of it. As D'Este described: "Colonel George S. Patton blew in like a Texas dust storm to disturb what had been years of tranquility. . . . He conducted sand table exercises, made them *walk* through mock battles, instructing them that this was the way they would have to fight in the next war, and preached that horses were obsolete."[122] He trained his surprised men in his vision of war—to shock the enemy with fire from the rear. It would not be the last time that, faced with career termination, he felt freed to do as he wished.

Patton's regiment took part in Third Army field exercises testing mechanization in central Texas. On the second day he wrote his wife, "Yesterday we marched 35 miles in the worst heat I have ever seen and secured our objective without a fight. . . . Tomorrow night we may march around his flank but it will be a very long trip over slippery roads."[123] He wrote to Brigadier General Daniel Van Voorhis, "We had a great war in the Third Army Maneuvers and on the last day got right back of the enemy. . . . They had so absorbed the bull butting tactics of the World War that they forgot they had to keep their pants buttoned or get buggared [*sic*]."[124] Hirshson noted, "Even with horses, Patton demonstrated on the last day of the maneuvers what a daring and imaginative officer could do against unimaginative opponents. . . . Moving 'about ten miles mostly at a gallop,' the cavalrymen got into the enemy's rear, capturing artillery, kitchens, a command post, and the colonel of the 69th Artillery."[125] Patton did not turn to attack the main force from the rear; he instead made them react to the shock of his threatening presence.

The 5th Cavalry attracted attention. The soon-to-be Army chief of staff, General George C. Marshall, began collecting officers he believed would be valuable in any future war and noticed the "madman" of Fort Clark he had first met during World War I on Pershing's staff.[126] In December Patton was abruptly transferred to command Fort Myer and the 3rd Cavalry Regiment outside Washington, D.C. There on 22 July 1939 he wrote to the new commander of the 5th Cavalry Regiment: "We are about to have a maneuver in the vicinity of Manassas, which, as far as I can see, is cleverly designed to prevent the Cavalry and the Field Artillery from doing anything. However, we may have an opportunity to break loose, and if we do we shall do our level best to demonstrate the value of horse cavalry."[127] He would also demonstrate the value of his ideas.

Patton avidly followed news of the German blitzkrieg across Europe. Military Intelligence Division bulletins cited French commanders complaining that the Germans attacked so quickly they were unable to reconcile their preconceived plans with the unfolding events. General Édouard Réquin of the French Fourth Army said, "*The development of this strategical exploitation is so rapid*, that the reorganization of a constituted front in order to limit the effects thereof, becomes impossible [emphasis in original]."[128] Patton instantly understood what the Germans had accomplished: a continuous series of shocks that overwhelmed the French command's ability to respond. The demoralized French soon lost the will to resist. Patton explained the German victory to the 2nd Armored Division: "How did they do it? By attacking the soul of the leaders, by attacking the means of signal communication and the means of supply—that is what we are for. In terms of football, an armored division is that element of the team which carries out the running plays. We straight-arm and go around and dodge and go around."[129] The Germans proofed his theories.

As James Corum observed, the French entered World War II with a doctrine "essentially frozen in the year 1918," emphasizing time-consuming, detailed planning and extensive command and control.[130] As they entered the planning cycle for one situation, the Germans, spearheaded by Guderian, confronted them with another. He was at Sedan, then the Meuse, then farther west, then turning north—all without pause. No sooner had the French begun to react than a different reaction was needed. French officer Marc Bloch wrote, "The whole rhythm of modern warfare had changed its tempo."[131] In his exposition on decision cycles, John Boyd argued that the German tempo "paralyzed" the French ability to react.[132] Ad hoc, Guderian demonstrated how an aggressive, mechanized tempo could destroy the enemy coherence and, as a result, cause their will to resist to collapse.

In May 1940 Patton served as an umpire in maneuvers in Louisiana. He objected to the artificialities employed in proving doctrinal theories. Afterward, he submitted his observations to the chief control officer: "This exercise demonstrated headlong tactics to overwhelm the enemy by quick thrusts all along the front. These tactics appeared to be successful. It is believed, however, that in actual combat the losses suffered would have caused greater delay than were assessed."[133] Returning to Fort Myer, he set his theory of war into a simple maxim: "The secret of success in mounted operations is to GRAB THE ENEMY BY THE NOSE AND KICK HIM IN THE PANTS."[134] Given command of the new 2nd Armored Division at Fort Benning, he instructed his officers: "We must find out where the enemy is, we must hold him, and we must get around him."[135] He would lead with tanks, bring up infantry and artillery to hold the enemy's attention, and bounce his tanks around their flanks. Secretary of War Henry L. Stimson recalled observing a Patton exercise that featured, in quick sequence, reconnaissance patrols to find enemy weak spots, air and artillery bombardments to fix the enemy front line, and tanks with infantry slipping around their flanks and breaking through.[136] In this Patton contradicted doctrine that 2nd Armored soldiers had learned: "Once you gain contact with the enemy, never lose that contact; *advance against resistance*, pursue and destroy [emphasis added]."[137]

With the 2nd Armored Division at Fort Benning, Patton constructed a huge amphitheater, the "Patton Bowl," to personally address his 15,000 men. In May 1941 he gathered them with the umpires for upcoming maneuvers and reminded them that, contrary to doctrine, in his vision it is "the mission of this division to attack weakness rather than strength" and that "we prefer to go around the end."[138] He added, "The only defensive flank which you can produce is by attacking, because the fact that you attack induces the enemy to think that you are stronger than he is."[139] He lamented, "The effect of surprise as to time or direction of attack should be given tremendous weight. In reading over the rules I find no emphasis placed upon this."[140] He instructed his men: "Remember that the great advantage possessed by an Armored Division is its ability to produce in the minds of its opponents a fear of the unknown. To do so you must keep moving."[141] Finally, he repeated his "favorite remark about the whole essence of war being to grab the enemy by the nose and kick him in the pants."[142] Patton was to practice what he preached.

In September 1941 Patton assembled his men to build their morale.[143] With references ranging from the Romans to the Great War, he stressed: "War is a killing business. You've got to spill their blood or they'll spill yours. Rip them up the belly, or shoot them in the guts."[144] Private Vincent Hooper vividly recalled some fifty years later, "I am positive the Patton image was born on the first day he spoke in that bowl. . . . At the end of the speech he said, 'I am taking this division into Berlin and when I do, I want every one of your tracks to be carrying the stench of German blood and guts.'"[145]

The apparent contradiction between his long-developed ideas of strategy set on avoiding battle and these bloody exhortations to his men would confuse many. To Patton, fighting and killing was an unavoidable part of war for soldiers, but not an inescapable aim for commanders. Soldiers had to attack to give credence to shock.

It was easy to mistake Patton's violent exhortations for a philosophy of war. Stenographer Corporal Joe Rosevich watched Patton, clad in slippers and wearing pince-nez glasses, thoughtfully draft a speech before rehearsing it with purple fury. Patton paused. "He said," Rosevich remembered, "that the performance we had just watched was exactly that—a performance, a put-up show, a calculated and rehearsed act of bravado. He was convinced, he said, that the young men of America needed such a toughening because they had grown soft. . . . You have to shock them out of their ordinary habits and thinking with the kind of language you've just heard in the speech."[146] Rosevich added, "I had occasion to see that I was serving two men rather than one. General Patton was the fusion of two men who lived in different worlds. One was his own world of calm efficiency, discipline and order. The other was the world of his immediate environment—our world of extreme tension and nervous strain."[147] Likewise, Patton's incitements to his men were separate from his view on strategy.

Patton's men understood him. A 2nd Armored Division history states, "We learned by doing and were soon initiated into the facts of strategic mobility and surprise; great fire power; maneuverability, as in the old cavalry; shock action (physical and morale effect); armor protection and obstacle ability."[148] *Strategic mobility* and *shock action*: Patton's concepts were made real in exercises. When they deployed for the great Louisiana Maneuvers, a soldier recalled, "The Blitzkrieg tactics developed in Tennessee were to be polished in Louisiana. We were now the HELL ON WHEELS division. We saw Patton as the great star among the 400,000 soldiers in Louisiana and all of us, down to the lowliest private, *prayed with Patton at the altar of violent force and audacity* [emphasis in original]."[149] In one famous instance, Patton's division conducted a 186-mile "end run through western Louisiana and east Texas" to circumvent the enemy—"the longest and most completely self sustaining maneuver ever made by a large force in a short time."[150] Even veteran British observers were amazed by the speed with which Patton overwhelmed his enemy's methodical and meticulous command style.[151]

Umpires monitored the great prewar maneuvers for unity of effort against decisive points and only allowed for independent action that doctrinally contributed "directly to success in the main battle."[152] Again and again, Patton confounded them by avoiding strength and outmaneuvering the enemy. He argued:

> There is a wide-spread belief that the function of an Armored Division is to attack and destroy an enemy. This is erroneous. The only time an Armored Division should attack is when it is necessary to do so in order to attain a position astride the enemy's line of communication. Having attained that position, all that the Armored Division has to do is to disrupt his means of communication and his supply system and wait for nature in the form of lack of supplies and information to take its inevitable cause. The attack that destroys the enemy after he is immobilized by the Armored Divisions is put on by the motorized divisions or the regular foot infantry divisions.[153]

Here was Patton's doctrine: avoid attacking strength, do not prioritize the destruction of the enemy force, use maneuver to threaten the enemy, cut off his support, make the enemy unaware by cutting off his "information." Lieutenant Oscar Koch observed, "The empirical formula worked. Hold the enemy by the nose while you kick him in the pants."[154] Others, such as U.S. Army ground forces commander General Lesley McNair, who wished to demonstrate that the Army could defeat panzers, were not happy. McNair complained, "The Army has not yet learned how to handle armored divisions."[155] Amusingly, observers who criticized Patton's widest sweeping maneuver in Louisiana praised the officer they credited with his plan—Colonel Dwight Eisenhower—who coincidentally put the plan to paper *after* a visit from his old friend Patton.[156]

His first campaign of World War II, Operation Torch, provided Patton little opportunity to test his ideas on warfare. Eisenhower intended to race to Tunisia to cut off the Afrika Korps, but he approved Mark Clark's selection of two cautious infantrymen, II Corps' Lloyd Fredendall and the 34th Infantry Division's Charles Ryder, to lead the dash. This accorded with Marshall's instructions forbidding Ike from "under any circumstances" making "a reckless advance toward the border of Libya."[157] Patton was left behind in Morocco while the Allies bogged down in Tunisia against German reinforcements that came to hold open Rommel's lines of communications. Biographer Stephen Ambrose observed that Eisenhower "lacked that ruthless, driving force that would lead him to step into a tactical situation and, through the power of his personality, extract the extra measure of energy to get across the final barrier. He never forced his subordinates in the field to the supreme effort, and as a result until almost the very end of the war there would be, at critical moments, an element of drift in the operations he directed."[158] Ike lacked Patton's ability to drive subordinates forward, but more important, he also lacked Patton's vision. Ike sought to grapple with and destroy the enemy, but without overwhelming numbers, it proved a damned hard thing to do.

Without Patton, the Americans suffered disaster at Kasserine Pass. Circumstances just did not support an attrition strategy, and the Americans knew no other way. British general Harold Alexander complained, "There has been no policy and no plan. The battle area is all mixed up with British, French, and American units."[159] After the battle—and after Mark Clark and Ernest Harmon declined it—Eisenhower offered the command to Patton. Ike's aide, Captain Harry Butcher, USN, commented, "If you ask me it should have been Patton in the first place. . . . Ike told me a week ago he wished he had sent Patton."[160] Noting that while Eisenhower and Bradley excelled at team sports and Patton was a fencer and Olympian pentathlete, some have implied the high command feared Patton was not a "team player." Actually, Patton played team sports and was a world-class polo player. There simply comes a time when every team needs a star performer.

A War Department report noted, "The prevailing attitude is that the North African operation is just another maneuver with live ammunition. The enemy is regarded as the visiting team, and this is *not* a major game. Even units suffering heavy casualties did not evince hatred of the enemy. . . . Both officers and men are psychologically unprepared for war."[161] Alexander found the Americans "soft, green and quite untrained. . . . They lack the will to fight. . . . There is no doubt that they have little hatred for the Germans and Italians and show no eagerness to get in and kill them."[162] Ike sent Patton to remedy this situation, explaining, "The troops had to be picked up quickly. For such a job Patton had no superior in the Army."[163] Patton saw the moral dimension of war.

Without the time or resources to get better equipment or retrain his men, Patton attacked their attitude. After a week of harshly enforcing all matters of discipline and increasing supply efficiency, he took II Corps forward in several successful small engagements. He wrote, "When we first started fighting, we were a little bit too platonic in our relations with the enemy, but I believe that in the future he had better look out unless he wants to get very badly hurt."[164] As Charles Whiting noted, "For the rest of the campaign, even when Patton had gone again, the II Corps proved its fighting ability in spite of the fact that it absorbed 5,000 green replacements."[165] Yet Patton regretted the harsh reputation he gained in the effort to rally the troops. He admitted to an old friend, "This 'Blood and Guts' stuff is quite distasteful to me. I am a very severe disciplinarian, because I know, and you as an old soldier know, that without discipline it is impossible to win battles, and that without discipline to send men into battle is to commit murder."[166] The mask of command was a tool, not a goal.

In Tunisia, Patton was denied decisive maneuver and was ordered "to go slow, and warned not to go too far."[167] His mission was to "draw off" enemy reserves from Montgomery, occupy airfields to support Montgomery, and establish a forward maintenance area for Montgomery.[168] Patton wanted to drive to the east coast of Tunisia and cut off Rommel's retreat but wrote, "It is noteworthy that these instructions definitely prohibit an American advance to the sea."[169] In short, he was ordered to attack strength and wage battles of attrition as a supporting, limited effort. After successfully completing this mission, Ike ordered him to turn over his command to Bradley and begin planning the American portion of Husky, the invasion of Sicily (a strange decision if Patton was thought to be a poor planner). Bradley would command the Americans in the victorious slow march to Tunis.

Patton's idea of strategic maneuver was never part of the Sicily plan, either. After failing to cut off Rommel in North Africa, Ike would never again set a clear end state for a campaign. The original Husky plan had Patton landing near Palermo and Montgomery near Syracuse, both with supply ports and situated to drive on Messina and cut off all Axis forces on the island.[170] Monty complained, "The planners, and everyone else, had been concentrating on *where* to land; nobody had considered how the campaign in Sicily should be *developed*."[171] He concluded, "The Husky planning is an awful mess."[172] Husky was changed to place Patton at Gela, without a port and relegated to protecting the British flank. A U.S. Army history noted: "The problem was that Alexander never drew up any detailed plans for the land campaign beyond the initial landings, preferring instead to make those decisions once the troops were firmly ashore and the operation was under way."[173] Alexander lacked Patton's vision.

With Patton's Seventh Army dependent on the British Eighth Army for supply through Syracuse, Montgomery controlled the main effort. As Andrew J. Birtle noted, the American position "clearly reflected British skepticism about American capabilities, a skepticism borne of the debacle at Kasserine Pass a few months before."[174] Even Alexander conceded, "The risk was unevenly divided and almost the whole of it would fall on Seventh Army."[175] Patton entertained his own ideas.

For the landings at Gela, Patton deliberately placed his only corps headquarters (under Bradley) closest to Monty where it could handle the detailed coordination required of adjacent large units, thus freeing his Seventh Army headquarters to exploit other opportunities. He hinted at his intentions before departing North Africa. Captain William Sullivan, USN, who was supervising port operations in Bizerte, refused an Army lieutenant colonel who asked him to send jeeps and trucks to Patton. The next day Patton arrived. Sullivan recalled, "He said a certain son of a bitch was trying to slow him up in Sicily, but when he hit Sicily he was going to go through that place like a dose of salts. He needed every truck he could get, steal or hijack. He knew I had no need for trucks until we took Palermo. He would have to take Palermo before we could start working there. How about it? I had his word that I could have all the trucks I needed once we hit Palermo. I said OK."[176] Where Ike and Alexander lacked vision, Patton provided his own.

On 5 June Patton issued guidance reminding his commanders that they should "never attack strength," that "rapidity of attack" reduces exposure to enemy fire, and that "battles are won by frightening the enemy." He explained again: "Fear is induced by inflicting death and wounds on him. Death and wounds are produced by fire. Fire from the rear is more deadly and three times more effective than fire from the front, but to get fire behind the enemy, you must hold him by frontal fire and move rapidly around his flank. . . . Never take counsel of your fears. The enemy is more worried than you are."[177] He added, "WHEN IN DOUBT, ATTACK! . . . We can only conquer by attacking."[178]

For a week after landing on Sicily, Seventh Army busily repelled German counterattacks and moved forward against heavy resistance. Then the Germans turned on Montgomery. By 17 July, Monty's attack stalled north of Syracuse, so he cut west, effectively cutting the U.S. II Corps out of the fight. Blocked by Monty from advancing north, Patton went unannounced to Alexander's headquarters and proposed a movement to sweep around western Sicily.[179] Patton recalled his surprise when Alexander said he had "planned to do just what I asked but that his chief of staff had failed to tell me when issuing the order."[180] Seventy-two hours later, Patton's tanks completed a more than one-hundred-mile end run on converging routes into Palermo, seizing ten thousand enemy soldiers, including two Italian generals. Patton wrote, "It reminded me very much of the way the 5th Cavalry got behind the enemy gun line in the Texas Maneuvers. In fact, the idea was probably implemented by memories of that."[181] Clausewitz famously observed "that war is not merely an act of policy but a true political instrument, a continuation of political intercourse, carried on with other means."[182] Patton's rapid movement had such political value: the loss of the Sicilian capital, in combination with the initial Allied bombing of Rome, incited the Italian people to overthrow Benito Mussolini.

Harry Yeide has argued, "Patton was well aware that the Axis forces were withdrawing to the northeast, so when he made his decision to race for Palermo, there was nothing bold about it."[183] But that was not so. Sweeping maneuver through rugged terrain invited enemy counteraction. Moreover, Patton's maneuver changed the balance in Sicily. As Yeide conceded, by 24 July the Germans understood Patton was now the major threat, and they fell back from their positions in front of Monty. Eisenhower wrote of Patton's sweep: "His rapidity of movement quickly reduced the enemy ports to the single one of Messina; it broke the morale of the huge Italian garrison and placed Patton's forces in position to begin the attack from the westward to break the deadlock on the eastern flank."[184] Critics of Patton's sweep are silent on the alternative: what value could be associated with him remaining stationary behind Eighth Army?

From Palermo, Patton spurred his commanders on to Messina. Yeide wrote that this did not faze the Germans and added, "Their assessment of the

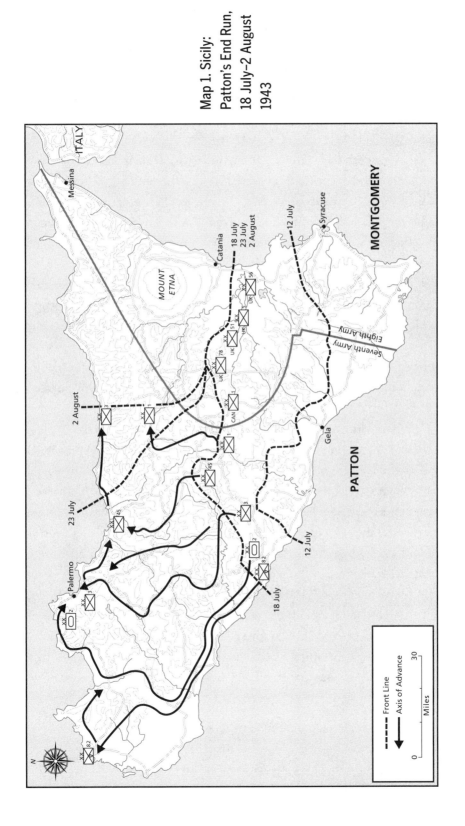

Map 1. Sicily: Patton's End Run, 18 July–2 August 1943

American performance once the smash-mouthed fighting erupted along the northeastern perimeter suggests that [Patton] did not much impress them then either. . . . Patton was hesitant in the clinch."[185] Indeed, the rugged and bare mountainous terrain greatly favored the defense and constricted avenues of advance. The 1st Infantry Division commander Terry Allen once explained to reporters, "Had we kept up just a frontal attack, it would have meant just a bloody nose for us at every hill. . . . This was as stubborn as any resistance we've encountered so far."[186] Even so, Patton irritated his subordinates by refusing to pause and ordered: "This is a horse race in which the prestige of the U.S. Army is at stake. We must take Messina before the British. Please use your best efforts to facilitate the success of our race."[187] Bradley, revealing his conventional view of strategy, wrote, "I confess that while no strategic purpose would be served by it, I was equally anxious to beat Monty to Messina, if it were possible without recklessness or undue casualties. For a long time now, our men had been ridiculed and abused by the British media in Sicily. It seemed fitting revenge to rob Monty of the triumphant march into Messina."[188] There was, however, true strategic purpose in getting behind the Germans.

Patton explained the methods that brought success in Sicily: "When you get the enemy on the run, keep him there. Had I ever stopped to let myself or the soldiers rest, the Germans would have dug in, and it would have cost many thousands more lives to have moved them out."[189] By continuing to press and shock the enemy in the race to Messina, Patton reduced the time of exposure to enemy fire and also established the Americans as equal to the British in the field. The front line German troops certainly were impressed. Bradley's G-2 brought him a letter found on a dead German soldier that complained, "These astonishing Americans. They fight all day, attack all night, and shoot all the time."[190] Alexander congratulated Patton for "the speed, dash and skill you have shown in the Sicilian operation."[191] The "Commander-in-Chief's personal representative" also praised the unhesitating Patton and congratulated Seventh Army for "a continuous, unrelenting campaign."[192] Ike reported of Patton:

> He has conducted a campaign where the brilliant successes scored must be attributed directly to his energy, determination, and unflagging aggressiveness. The operations of the

Seventh Army in Sicily are going to be classed as a model of swift conquest by future classes in the War College in Leavenworth. The prodigious marches, the incessant attacks, the refusal to be halted by appalling difficulties in communication and terrain, are really something to enthuse about. This had stemmed mainly from Patton. He has fine division and corps commanders, but it is obvious that had he been willing to seize on an excuse for refitting, these commanders would have done nothing.[193]

Unfortunately, Patton's brash command style, compounded by the reprehensible "slapping incidents" in Sicily, eclipsed his performance. Eisenhower saw them as further proof that Patton was unsuited for anything above an army command.[194] He promoted Bradley, Patton's subordinate, to command the U.S. forces in the invasion of France, yet the evidence suggests that Ike made this decision long before the slapping incidents. He had relieved Patton early from command of II Corps to give Bradley a chance to gain command experience and notoriety.[195] Ike even asked famed war correspondent Ernie Pyle to "discover" Bradley so as to raise the general's profile.[196] After Messina, Ike promoted Bradley over Patton before the slapping incidents became public and seemed contained. Ike was just more comfortable with Bradley; they were of the same Leavenworth mind.

Ike's subsequent plans for Normandy merely got men ashore to confront the enemy. Patton instinctively sought strategic maneuver to gain an advantageous position to threaten the Germans.[197] In his planning notes he explained his thoughts: "First—surprise, find out what the enemy intends to do and do it first. Second—rock the enemy back on his heels—keep him rocking—never give him a chance to get his balance or build up. Third—relentless pursuit—*à l'outrance* as the French say—beyond the limit. Fourth—mop him up."[198] Overlord established a lodgment and sought to expand it. Patton offered options for cutting off the Germans in Normandy, and when they were declined, he executed his own ideas to accomplish it. A comparison of SHAEF's and Patton's plans indicates a significant difference in philosophy. Where SHAEF planned a deliberately paced, linear advance toward delineated phase lines, Patton designated a series of nonlinear decision points, places where he could adapt to emerging opportunity.

The former supported executing preconceived plans; the latter enabled rapid adjustment to developments.

The success of Patton's breakout (see chapter 7) not only shocked the Germans, it also stunned the Allies. By constantly outflanking the Germans, refusing to pause in the advance, and driving to positions that threatened the enemy with envelopment, Patton had unbalanced, disrupted, and demoralized the enemy. After nearly 2 months of stagnation in Normandy without Patton, Third Army raced 328 miles to the east in 12 days.[199] By then Patton's lines stretched nearly 700 miles from west to east, and he stood 180 miles from the Rhine. In early September, Eisenhower confided in his journal, "The defeat of the German Army is complete and the only thing now needed to realize the whole conception is speed."[200] Ironically, Ike then opted to divert Patton's supplies to Montgomery. Patton and his men could not believe SHAEF wanted them to pause and disrupt the series of shocks they were inflicting on the Germans. In 4th Armored Division, Major Albin Irzyk thought, "No, this just could not be! The shock was so great, so difficult to comprehend and accept, that it momentarily stiffened us."[201] The next day, Hitler gave to Gerd von Rundstedt Army Group G under Generaloberst Johannes Blaskowitz with orders to stop Third Army.

With proper support, Patton could have exploited his position and likely disrupted the German buildup for the Ardennes counteroffensive. Recognizing this, Hitler rushed reinforcements to Blaskowitz.[202] Stephen Zaloga wrote, "Hitler believed that a violent panzer attack against Patton's Third Army was both the most necessary and the most promising option."[203] Within 3 days of Patton's enforced halt, Blaskowitz assembled 106,700 infantry and 78,000 Panzer troops—with more than 200,000 additional less-effective troops—into formidable fortifications around Metz.[204] Eisenhower's pause let Germany close the gate, just as Patton feared.

When Eisenhower cut Patton's supplies, forces, and momentum, he cut his ability to continue and accelerate the delivery of shocks upon the enemy. Third Army was left with only two understrength corps, the XX and the XII.[205] Half of the XIX Tactical Air Command was sent to support VIII Corps in Brittany.[206] Patton's front was too wide for his corps fire direction centers to mass fires, reducing mass and response times.[207] An Army history explained, "Thus, at the outset of the Lorraine campaign, Third Army was logistically starved, depleted in strength, and denied the full use of its air assets."²⁰⁸ Patton had knocked the enemy off balance, but headquarters enabled them to regain their equilibrium. Even Bradley recalled on 26 September, "Patton would go on the defensive. This was yet another poor decision. . . . Stopping Patton, a proven ground gainer, to favor Monty, who wasn't, simply made no sense at all."²⁰⁹

Eisenhower's orders were part of his attrition strategy. On 18 October he announced, "The plan of battle is as follows: The enemy is stretched to the breaking point, straining every nerve to stave off defeat. We propose to keep on hitting him at every sensitive point until he cracks. He is bound to crack if we keep on hammering him without let-up."²¹⁰ Patton calculated that there was not enough ammunition in SHAEF to attack with three armies but there was "enough to attack with only one of the three and to do it now."²¹¹ His arguments for priority support were declined. No army broke through.

Patton was forced to fight a deliberate, set-piece battle. In October at Metz, Third Army suffered more than 9,000 casualties while reporting that the Germans facing them had 43,200 casualties.²¹² In comparison, Monty, with priority SHAEF support, suffered 17,000 casualties in Market Garden and another 18,000 just in clearing the Scheldt. When General Jacob Devers' 6th U.S. Army Group and General Courtney Hodges' First Army began their major attacks, Bradley wrote, "The spearheads jumped off as planned but soon bogged down. . . . What followed over the next several weeks was some of the most brutal and difficult fighting of the war. The battle—known as Hürtgen Forest—was sheer butchery on both sides."²¹³ First Army suffered more than 38,000 casualties in the Hürtgen Forest and Aachen, but Ike and Bradley believed they were realizing "tremendous relative gains," noting that "the daily enemy losses were double our own."²¹⁴ Frustrated, Montgomery complained, "The war of attrition in the winter months, forced on us by our faulty strategy after the great victory in Normandy, was becoming very expensive in human life."²¹⁵ It was a price Britain could no longer afford.

At a commanders' conference in Maastricht on 7 December, Ike reiterated his broad-front attrition campaign. Like Ulysses S. Grant in the Wilderness Campaign, he was convinced that the enemy could not continue to take heavy losses much longer without breaking, especially after the Russians launched their expected winter offensive.²¹⁶ Bradley noted, "SHAEF analysts reported, our continuing pressure all along the front was costing the Germans some 9,000 permanent or long-term casualties a day, the equivalent in manpower of five divisions per week."[217]

The German counteroffensive out of the Ardennes on 16 December against First Army changed things dramatically. The next morning Patton reviewed the enemy situation and observed, "Had the V and VIII Corps of the First Army been more aggressive, the Germans could not have prepared this attack; one must never sit still."[218] Operations chief Colonel Halley Maddox spotted opportunity and noted, "If they will roll with the punch up north, we can pinwheel the enemy before he gets very far. In a week we could expose the whole German rear and trap their main forces west of the Rhine."[219] Patton responded, "You're right that would be the way to do it. But that isn't the way those gentlemen up north fight. They aren't made that way. That's too daring for them. My guess is that our offensive will be called off and we will have to go up there and save their hides."[220] The Allies needed Patton to counterattack—but where?

Bradley summoned Patton, expecting him to be angry at having to stop his advance east. "My fears turned out to be groundless," he later recalled. "Patton grasped the necessity for the change in the strategy at once and immediately became its most unrestrained champion."[221] Patton rationalized, "What the hell, we'll still be killing Krauts."[222] Given command of the southern half of the Bulge, he wanted VIII Corps to evacuate Bastogne and wrote, "I told [General Troy] Middleton to give ground and blow up bridges so that we can get the enemy further extended before we hit him in the flank."[223] It would have been the smart move, changing the correlation of forces at the point of attack. "However," Patton added, "on Bradley's suggestion, in which Middleton strongly concurred, we decided to hang on to Bastogne, because it is a very important road net, and I do not believe the enemy would dare pass it without reducing it."[224] Patton then argued for exploiting the situation by enveloping the Germans on the east and gaining position on the Rhine before the Germans could defend it, but Eisenhower and Bradley balked.[225] Patton explained to the press, "If you got a monkey in a jungle hanging by his tail, it is easier to get him by cutting his tail than kicking him in the face —and the same is true here."[226] Danny Parker noted, "Consequently, Eisenhower opted to attack further to the west—a cautious strategy Generalfeldmarshal von Rundstedt would note with irony in his war diary as the Allied version of the 'Small Solution.'"²²⁷ The blinders of traditional doctrine trumped Patton's vision.

Eisenhower opted for a counterattack "only with a methodical advance to the Bastogne area."²²⁸ With this direction set by higher command, Patton's speed of attack was his only means for achieving shock. He succeeded. In the end, as one correspondent reported, "The Germans . . . were defeated morally and damaged materially . . . but it was the moral shock which brought home to them the hopelessness of their cause."²²⁹ The predictable direction of attack still had its cost: by the end of January, the Third Army's total casualties exceeded 100,000 men, one-sixth from battle and half of those in the Bulge.²³⁰ Paul Harkins recalled thinking, "The Third was compelled to a course which would have horrified any tactics professor."²³¹ Patton believed the choice of direction of an attack was the key to producing shock against enemy morale; Ike only saw it as the means for getting firepower onto the enemy force.

After the Bulge, Eisenhower drafted plans to close up on the Rhine without Third Army. Patton thought the plans lacked boldness and restricted the American armies to secondary, limited actions.²³² In support of SHAEF's plan, Bradley ordered Patton to clear the rugged Eifel north of the Moselle and link up with Hodges. Patton saw opportunity. As Codman described: "For months he had eyed the concentration of two German armies in the Palatinate (between the Rhine, the Moselle, and the Sauer)."²³³ He sent XII Corps along the north bank of the Moselle through Bitburg and on to Coblenz with an eye on being positioned to cross the Rhine while also gaining position on the northwest edge of the Saar-Moselle triangle ready to open the Trier-Coblenz corridor through the Palatinate to flank the Siegfried Line in the Saar.²³⁴ From such a position he could threaten the enemy in multiple directions. The shock created by his subsequent advance into the Palatinate led to the collapse of two German armies.

Speed of attack on unexpected lines of advance enhanced shock. Patton reached Trier on 1 March, sent a corps across the Saar at Saarburg (making the Germans think he was going south), then quickly turned north to take the city and "took them completely by surprise."²³⁵ He then sprinted northeast along the north bank of the Moselle to reach the Rhine at Coblenz, leading the Germans to expect him to cross the Rhine there. Patton noted, "Bradley was anxious for me to coordinate my plan with [Seventh Army

Commander Alexander] Patch, but since he cannot jump until the 15th, I am going to attack as soon as possible, because at this stage of the war, time is more important then [*sic*] coordination."²³⁶ With XX Corps and Seventh Army fixing the enemy from the west and southwest, Patton suddenly sent his army south, unexpectedly crossed the Moselle and Hunsrück Mountains, and sliced down the west bank of the Rhine, cutting off the Germans in the Palatinate. Looking at the extended arrows on a map depicting the operation, air marshal Arthur Tedder commented, "There goes Patton with another of his phallic symbols."²³⁷

These maneuvers presented the enemy with an unfolding series of shocks that overwhelmed and paralyzed their ability to react. An observer noted, "Patton's forces seemed to be everywhere at once—attacking the *Westwall*'s concrete casements from the rear, racing through the center of the Palatinate, sweeping southward along the Rhine itself."²³⁸ Third Army reported, "Now the enemy faced a tactical situation similar to that of the historic FALAISE pocket, the 4th Armored Division having swept across his rear in the Palatinate triangle, bounded by the RHINE, MOSELLE and SAAR Rivers. Third U.S. Army was threatening the envelopment of all the enemy's forces and defensive positions in the triangle."²³⁹ After 72 hours, the German resistance collapsed. Rampaging columns took Saarlautern, Kaiserslautern, and Bad Kreuznach on the run. In 6 days, Third Army captured 80,000 German soldiers and drew the Germans away from First Army.²⁴⁰ As Robert S. Allen wrote, "The enemy's vitals had been pierced. An Armored poniard was stabbed squarely in the middle of his rear and athwart his main line of communications. That night, Patton set the final kill in motion."²⁴¹ With the German Army Group G torn asunder, Patton redirected columns to secure Rhine crossing points at Oppenheim, Mainz, and Worms. He received a message from V Corps commander Leonard Gerow: "Congratulations on enveloping three armies, one of them American."²⁴² Patton had cut off the German First and Seventh Armies—and Patch's Seventh U.S. Army. German major general Richard Schimpf of the German 3rd Paratroop Division called Patton's Palatinate campaign simply "phenomenal."²⁴³

Now fighting his way of war, Patton wanted to sustain the shocks. He urged his commanders and staff, "There is only one thing to remember from now on. Roads don't matter; terrain doesn't matter; exposed flanks don't matter. The only thing that matters is to keep on top of the Hun and to keep him on the run. That's the only thing that will win the war. We've got to kill him or run him to death."[244] Speaking from experience, he instructed his men: "The enemy is in chaos on our front. But if we delay 72 hours, he will reorganize and we will have to fight to push him out of our way. We must not give him that chance, no matter what political machinations are going on up above. I don't give a goddamn what they're planning. I don't propose to give the Hun the opportunity to recover from the killing we've just given him."[245]

The next night, 22 March, Patton gave XII Corps approval to conduct a hasty assault over the Rhine—a full day before Montgomery's long-awaited priority crossing. "I think that there is a strong chance that the operation will be successful," he wrote, "because the Germans are so used to build-ups prior to attempts to cross rivers that they will not think it feasible."[246] Here again, Patton exploited shock. At 2300 hours that night, the 5th Infantry Division crossed the Rhine near Nierstein. Attacking at the unexpected place without any artillery preparation, Major General Stafford Irwin's men caught the enemy completely off guard and encountered almost no resistance. At SHAEF, British general Frederick Morgan marveled that "while the British assault on the river was prepared with ponderous formality, General Patton's armor roared through the Palatinate and hopped lightly across the East Bank as and where it suited them."[247] The low eastern shore offered poor defensive terrain and invited a rapid exploitation and, unlike Eisenhower at Remagen, Patton was not about to pause. He wrote, "This surprise crossing, I believe, sets the climax to a very magnificent operation."[248] In 10 days of attack since 14 March, the Third U.S. Army liberated more than 3,000 towns and 6,482 square miles of territory, captured more than 90,000 Germans soldiers, destroyed 2 armies, and breached the Westwall.

The operations in the Palatinate and across the Rhine served as a nearly perfect example of Patton's vision. He shunned traditional attrition doctrine and instead sought out and targeted the enemy's will, avoided strength and attacked weak spots, created uncertainty, unbalanced the enemy, and pushed relentlessly forward. By rapid, unexpected advance he delivered a continuous series of shocks that frustrated enemy reaction, overwhelmed their decisionmaking ability to react, and defeated their morale and collapsed their will to resist.

Patton's success derived from his vision. He could see the places where his forces could best threaten the enemy's forces and plans. He saw that rapid movement to advantageous positions undermined the enemy's ability to coherently react, disorganized their responses, eroded their morale, and ultimately destroyed their will. Appreciating that the enemy was a moving target, he envisioned secondary and tertiary opportunities before they emerged and was prepared to seize fleeting chance when it presented itself in the relative movement of the two sides. In execution—when free from interference from higher command—he proved the efficacy of his preferred methods while at the same time confounding traditionalists bent on waging battles of attrition. To successfully wage his style of warfare, however, Patton needed more than just a strategic vision: he needed the tools to carry it out.

COMBINED ARMS | 3

> His grasp of the capabilities of the weapons and
> equipment at his disposal was unexcelled.
> —Carlo D'Este

When Marshall became Army chief of staff in 1939, he identified Patton as the Army's premier tanker, saying, "I know this from the First World War. I watched him closely when he commanded the first tanks we ever had."[1] Even by that time, however, Patton was more than just a "tank man"—he was a skilled *combined arms* commander. An early advocate of tank and infantry cooperation, he quickly embraced rapid and accurate artillery support and innovated methods for marching fire. He also tested and incorporated motorized logistical support and developed unique air-ground liaison to provide effective tactical air support. In the end, his decades of study and practice produced lethal combined arms columns tailored to carry out his vision of rapid, sustained shock.

When Patton entered the ranks of the U.S. Army, each of the major combat branches—infantry, cavalry, and artillery—stood as a world unto itself. The Army's barely 84,000 men were so scattered in small, isolated posts that in 1911 it took more than 90 days to form a single division of 13,000 men.[2] When regiments of various arms with motorized and aircraft support were finally brought together in Mexico, Patton was quick to grasp the "almost UNIMAGINED benefits."[3] Yet even the new lieutenant understood the inter-arms politics in play. Former Army chief of staff Leonard Wood—a member of Patton's social circle—wrote him, "Don't let the mounted infantry get control of the cavalry. Cavalry has never been in more demand in history than it is on the Eastern front at the present time and the French and English are carefully building up their cavalry forces on the Western Front and expect to have a tremendous demand for it soon as the final break up begins."[4] In fact, the cavalry's days were numbered.

At the start of World War I, Patton was with Pershing as he set out to knit the branches together in the rapidly expanding AEF while trying to figure ways to best incorporate modern arms. In June 1917 Pershing formed the American Expeditionary Tank Board (AETB) "to make a careful and confidential study" of tanks."[5] Drafting the board's report, Lieutenant Colonel Frank Parker told the operations officer of the Royal Tank Corps, British colonel J. F. C. Fuller, that he believed any hopes for breakthrough at the front would rest on a mechanized force of infantry and tanks supported by tactical aircraft practiced in methods to create, widen, and penetrate a breach deep into the enemy's lines.[6] Fuller, then planning the first large tank attack at Cambrai, wrote, "Lieutenant Colonel Parker's report makes good reading; not only is it virile but sound."[7] The AETB report foreshadowed most future theories of armor warfare.

Parker crafted a revolutionary conceptualization of combined arms. He called for tanks to punch a thirty-kilometer-wide hole through the "*whole German formation* deep enough to uncover a line of communication to a flank attack."[8] Machine gun companies with a second line of tanks would then secure the flanks and widen the breach. Parker termed it "the old 'flying wedge' of football" with tanks as linemen, motorized machine gun carriers as blockers, and the horse cavalry carrying the ball.[9] Patton read the AETB report thoroughly and discussed it with Parker, who had been an instructor at West Point when Patton was a cadet.

On 3 October Pershing's headquarters commandant, Robert Bacon, endorsed the first application for the Tank Corps: "I consider Capt Patton unusually well equipped and fitted in every way for the command."[10] A month later, Patton went with Parker to meet with Fuller during the battle of Cambrai. Despite his characteristic truculence toward intellectual underlings, Fuller took the time to tutor Patton on the need for good weather, firm ground, and thorough coordination and communications with other arms for successful tank operations.[11] Fuller also passed along his beliefs that stodgy conservatives failed to grasp the potential of the modern machines. As Fuller's boss, General Hugh Elles, confided, "Fighting the Germans is a joke compared with fighting the British."[12] Mechanization escalated interarms politics to a new level.

Patton spent several weeks at the French tank school at Chamlieu where he quizzed instructors on maintenance and tactics and drove, fired, and crawled all over the Renault, Schneider, and Saint-Chamond tanks. He then drafted a curriculum for the new U.S. tank school he was building at

Langres. He met several times with the pioneering French brigadier general Jean-Baptiste Estienne, who explained his ideas of using swarms of light tanks as a means of assisting infantry across no-man's land. In contrast, at the British tank school near Arras, Fuller told Patton he considered it a mistake to try to "harmonize" tanks with infantry and artillery. Fuller argued, "In fact, the tank idea, which carries with it a revolution in methods of waging war, has been grafted onto a system it is destined to destroy, in place of being given free scope to develop on its own lines."[13] That said, Fuller still suggested a means for harmonizing artillery and tanks in the current fight. The three hundred British tanks at Cambrai would advance without the customary lengthy preparatory artillery barrage. Instead, Brigadier General H. H. Tudor, an artillery officer in the 9th Scottish Division, individually registered guns so as to avoid alerting the enemy of the impending attack and to preserve firm ground for the tanks.[14]

Fuller tried to synchronize tanks and infantry using aerial photographs. He drew up six-by-four-mile "tank section attack areas" for teams of tanks and infantry. Tanks dropped bundles of logs—fascines—in trenches to cross over, infantry leapfrogged forward to knock out antitank guns, and together they penetrated 5 miles into the German lines. For the first time in the war, church bells rang across England in victory—but they were premature. In the center, General G. M. Harper of the 51st Highland Division feared that his tanks would attract artillery onto his infantry, and so he ordered the vehicles to stay 150 to 200 yards *behind* his soldiers.[15] The infantry, however, failed to advance without the tanks. The German commander, artilleryman General von Walter, had his men pick off the stalled landships with direct fire from protected positions.[16] The attack stopped. The British paused 10 days to reorganize, and the Germans rallied 20 divisions to eventually take back more ground than they had lost. The lesson for Fuller was clear: forget working with the infantry, he told Patton.

Drawing on his talks with Parker, Estienne, and Fuller and on his own lessons learned, Patton wrote a fifty-eight-page report, "Light Tanks," which he sent to the not-yet-filled office of chief of the Tank Service on 12 December. As Dale Wilson observed, "The document served as the foundation for subsequent tank developments in the AEF."[17] Patton covered in detail the mechanics, organization, supply, maintenance, tactics, training, and history of tanks and tankers.[18] He highlighted lessons from every battle involving tanks. Synthesizing the divergent French and British concepts, he drafted a distinctive U.S. doctrine describing two phases of operations for tanks in the attack: first, cooperating with the infantry to break the enemy lines, and second, assuming a role traditionally held by the cavalry. He explained, "When the final objective has been consolidated they must push on at their own initiative and seek every opportunity to become pursuit cavalry."[19] He added, "If resistance is broken and the line pierced the tank must and will assume the role of pursuit cavalry and 'ride the enemy to death.' The ever present chance of this last role is the chief reason for the deployment in depth and the maintenance of a reserve."[20] Combined arms could spring loose the tanks and make shock possible. Patton later noted, "I think it is the best technical paper I ever wrote."[21]

In January 1918 Patton began a series of lectures to sell his doctrine to the AEF. Reflecting both a salesman's deference to the doctrinal sensibilities of his audience and his belief in combined arms, he said, "For tanks in common with all other auxiliary arms are but a means of aiding infantry—on whom the fate of battle ever rests—to drive their bayonets into the bellies of the enemy."[22] Critically, he added, "Two of the determining factors in war are weapons and movement. Movement naturally separates its self into two parts: approach and attack. In the approach movement is paramount to weapons. In the attack weapons assert themselves to allow movement by killing."[23] Movement brought firepower onto the enemy, but fire then enabled decisive movement. Infantry and tanks would work together in the approach, but tanks would "ride the enemy to death" and thereby decide the battle.

Meanwhile, Patton threw himself wholeheartedly into his new command, despite old mentors advising him to "get out of vaudeville, and get into the legitimate."[24] By mid-April, the newly promoted lieutenant colonel was running his fleet of ten tanks ragged at his tank school in many exercises with the 16th Infantry Regiment.[25] He quickly learned: "It is a very complicated affair to get all the guns and infantry and tanks to the same place at the same time."[26] Effective synchronization of arms would bedevil all doctrinal innovators until the arrival of radio communications. In April 1918 Patton spent more than a month experimenting with and studying radios on his tanks but found it only possible to set up the needed antennas when the tanks were stationary and in protected positions.[27]

The War Department envisioned a limited role for tanks. On 18 May it issued Document No. 804, *Infantry and Tank Co-operation and Training*, an exact copy of a British manual of the same title, which emphasized the prominence of the assault and the priority of the infantry: "Tanks, like all other auxiliary arms, assisted the assaulting infantry."[28] On 10 June Patton issued his own "Brief Notes on the Tactical Employment of Tanks" calling for tanks to both lead infantry *and* conduct the pursuit. In his suggested doctrine, two companies of tanks from a light tank battalion would go forward with the assault echelon of infantry while the remaining company stayed with the reserve echelon.[29] Traditionalists in the War Department seemed to think of tanks as mobile pill boxes supporting the infantry, but Patton envisioned larger roles.

Patton continued to tinker with means for tailoring artillery to his tank-infantry doctrine. On 22 July he wrote to his wife, "I was walking around inspecting things just now when all at once a completely new tank tactics popped into my head. It is really a great idea and I believe it is pregnant with far reaching possibilities."[30] He put his epiphany to paper in "Further Notes on the Use of Tanks in Various Operations including Open Warfare," calling for tanks to attack with simultaneous bursts of artillery as the infantry followed in echelons. This was neither the normal preparatory artillery deluge nor Tudor's individual register method. By calling for artillery to pace their barrage not by the routine one-hundred-meter increments for infantry but by two hundred to four hundred meters to allow rapid advance by tanks, he broke with accepted infantry-centric doctrine.[31] After refining his ideas in several more papers over the next thirty days, Patton demonstrated them before three hundred officers and nine generals, using nine hundred tankers to replicate infantry.

Orthodox plans for inter-arms cooperation troubled Patton. The orders for the Saint-Mihiel offensive called for tanks to follow three hundred meters *behind* the infantry. Patton instead told his men: "Remember that you are to make paths in the wire and put out machine gun nests for the infantry; hence do not leave them, never get more than a hundred and fifty yards ahead of them and never let them get ahead of you or if they do hurry to regain your place."[32] He could not let go of his tank-centric vision.

On 12 September Patton's fifty-one tanks attacked with the 1st Infantry Division. They reached Jonville on the Hindenburg line before realizing that they were eight miles beyond friendly lines. There, Lieutenant Ted McClure's tank section bagged a battery of 77-millimeter (mm) field guns and twelve machine guns before enemy artillery forced his withdrawal. It was a rare demonstration of deep penetration in the Great War and, as D'Este noted, hinted at Patton's later "trademark employment of armor."[33] On the German side, Crown Prince Wilhelm reported "no danger" from the poorly planned American infantry attacks "but their tanks pierced our lines—one man every twenty meters—and fired on us from behind."[34] Patton thought that with reinforcement, he could have driven into Germany.

Prior to his next attack Patton sent a paper, "Memorandum on Plan for the Use of Tanks," to I Corps chief of staff Brigadier General Malin Craig in an effort to improve coordination between the infantry, artillery, and his tanks.[35] He asked to concentrate his tanks toward a specific point in *three* waves: the first to assist the infantry in breaking the enemy lines, the second to pass through and achieve a deep penetration, and a third *to seize any possibilities for exploitation*.[36] The change in suggested organization was an attempt to exploit emerging opportunities, such as the breakthrough to the Hindenburg line, found in the inescapable chaos of battle. Although Craig forwarded Patton's memorandum to each division commander, none agreed to his plan.

Two weeks after being wounded in his second battle, Patton was released from the hospital. He quickly sent a paper, "A Suggested Method of Attack," to the AEF training and plans staff. Worried that without his intervention his men would suffer under orthodox orders, he again advocated for tanks to lead the infantry in coordinated rushes.

Recuperating in the weeks following the armistice, Patton wrote "German and Allied Theory of War," a consideration of German *Stosstrupp* (shock troop) tactics in which special infantry patrols found weak points in the Allied lines and called forward follow-on echelons. These tactics received a boost from an old artillery officer, Colonel Georg Bruchmüller, who, like Tudor, tailored sporadic preparatory fires to specific targets but then added rolling barrages to support the advance. Patton imagined infantry and tank teams working together in *Stosstrupp* fashion to overcome the kind of static defenses seen on the Western Front.

Fresh out of the hospital in January 1919, Patton sent his thoughts on tanks to the G-3 of the Second Division. He described their value in delivering fire without risking troops and noted, "The tank, in other words, is the answer to the machine gun. Tanks are then a separate weapon as truly new and original as the aeroplane. They are not mechanical cavalry, neither are they artillery or armored infantry."[37] He concluded, however, that "like all other phases of war, success in the operation of tanks with infantry depends upon teamwork."[38]

The U.S. Tank Corps' after action report listed nine "Tactical Conclusions" that emphasized the need for better understanding of tanks by infantry officers, improved liaison between tanks and infantry, and changes in tactical employment for a better utilization of tanks in mass and depth.[39] The tankers asked the infantry to adapt to them; the infantry did not agree. Patton then initiated a new series of lectures on "Tank Tactics" to convince the infantry that they needed tanks to cut wire, suppress machine guns, mop up enemy pockets, repel counterattacks, and disrupt enemy artillery and reserves—and to remind them that tanks needed good terrain and cooperation with infantry.[40] He argued: "The tank is new and for the fulfillment of its destiny it must remain independent."[41] It was a tough sell. After a briefing to Army Staff College generals, Patton reported, "It was a rotten affair as they all went to sleep. They were the culls and they looked it."[42]

In a following paper, "Light Tanks in Exploitation," Patton expanded on his ideas for tanks in breakthrough operations. "In other words," he explained, "the crust has been broken and we are about to eat the pie."[43] After infantry and tanks together solved "the organized zone" of trenches and strongpoints, following echelons of tanks would spring forward.[44] "The defeated and demoralized enemy has been run to earth," he wrote, "we are upon him; it only remains to finish him."[45] To traditionalist ears this sounded like a call for tanks to replace cavalry, if not to assume infantry's primary role in battle outright. In France, Estienne had already given Pétain a remarkable paper, "Study of the Missions of Tanks in the Field," that proposed a 100,000-man French army with 4,000 tanks and 8,000 support vehicles in formations combining tanks, motorized infantry, self-propelled artillery with mechanized reconnaissance, supply, and maintenance, and supported by aircraft. Politicians rejected Estienne's ideas as "too offensively minded, too aggressive" for postwar France.[46] They reassigned Estienne as inspector of tanks, a position in which he remained until his retirement in 1927.

In Britain, a new paper by Fuller, forwarded to Patton by Colonel Henry E. Mitchell, called for "tank fleets" to attack "not against the body of the enemy's army but against his brains . . . the billets of the German headquarters. . . . What then is the body going to do, for its brain is paralyzed?"[47] Fuller had become so enamored with tanks that he openly dismissed all other arms.[48] He argued that "specialists" such as tanks and infantry could not cooperate efficiently and that because tanks were more capable and better protected, they "therefore, can replace infantry."[49] When Fuller argued that "weapons form 99% of victory" and that "the main factor in future warfare will be the replacing of man-power by machine-power," Patton strongly disagreed.[50] Unfortunately, Estienne and Fuller placed American traditionalists fully on guard against similar tank advocates.

In the war's wake Patton assumed command of the Army's sole tank brigade at Camp Meade, Maryland, with a new deputy, Major Dwight Eisenhower. Together they directed numerous field exercises, despite having only about one-sixtieth of their wartime fuel supply.[51] Once, they completely disassembled and reassembled a Mark VIII tank. Ike boasted, "So carefully had we done the work, that no pieces were left over and the machine operated when we were finished."[52] Camp Meade served as Patton's private laboratory, and he was bubbling with theories to test.

In "Desirable Features in Proposed Tank," Patton described his ideal suspension, motor, hull, armament, and speed for tanks. He thought the hull "should afford as few straight surfaces susceptible of normal impact to hostile projectiles as possible."[53] Sloped armor would become a standard for tanks about thirty years later. Patton also called for rotating turrets, "periscopic" sights, and tanks that could move on wheels or tracks. He continued experimenting with radios on tanks and even invented a coaxial mount that linked a machine gun to the main cannon for gunnery practice. He shared such ideas with a new acquaintance, innovative engineer J. Walter Christie, at his workshop in Hoboken, New Jersey. Throughout his life Patton continued to explore, dream up, and experiment with ideas for improving tanks: two days after the German surrender in World War II, he inspected the Skoda Munitions Plant in Pilsen and proudly photographed a "new form of bogie suspension" for U.S. Army consideration.[54] Unlike his peers, Patton desired to know not only what his weapons could do but also what they could become.

Selected as a member of the Tank Board, Patton inspected Christie's Front Drive Motor Company and saw his prototype M1919 tank, the first motorized vehicle purposely built to Army specifications. It had wheels, removable tracks, a turret designed to carry a 57-mm main gun, and angled hull armor. The vehicle could top sixty miles per hour on the road and cross a seven-foot trench.[55] Patton thought it "the greatest machine in the world. It is far ahead of the old tanks as day is from night."[56] The potential of the M1919 struck him hard and he wrote, "In the Christie we are buying a principle not a vehicle."[57] Unfortunately, the Army was not interested in Christie or his tank.

In a notable essay, "Tanks in Future Wars," published in *Cavalry Journal* in May 1920, Patton argued that, contrary to popular opinion, tanks would become the dominant instrument in future wars. He warned observers, such as those on the various Army boards reviewing doctrine and organizations, not to mistake present tank inadequacies for future limitations. He maintained that "the discovery of other means for combating tanks" was vital for the infantry, artillery, and cavalry.[58] Patton reasoned that future wars would *not* repeat the World War I experience, writing: "The tank officer must know by theory and practice the tactics of the other arms. Further, he must know his own diversified potentialities so thoroughly that in the prompt movements and uncertainty of battles in a war of movement he may follow instantly and correctly the lead given him by the arm with which he is operating. Above all he must know tanks."[59] Know theory and practice potentialities so thoroughly that proper movement comes naturally in the chaos of battle: this was Patton's maxim for leaders in combined arms warfare.

With the "war to end all wars" over, Congress slashed budgets and manpower. Pershing commissioned a Superior Board to recommend postwar changes for the Army and—unlike Patton—board members operated under the assumption that "future wars will follow the tactics of the offensive and defensive battles of 1918."[60] Not surprisingly, the board endorsed the primacy of infantry and warned, "Too much reliance was placed by the infantry on the auxiliary arms and not enough on the means within the infantry itself."[61] The endangered Tank Corps leadership pledged, "The tank is primarily an aid to the advance of the infantry engaged in a vigorous offensive either in the assault of works or in open warfare situations."[62] Congress nevertheless eliminated the Tank Corps in 1920 and handed the tanks to the infantry.

At war's end the Army stood at 2,395,742 men. Within 2 years that number was cut 91 percent, to 204,292; some 70,000 more would go in the next 3 years.[63] Correspondingly drastic budget cuts left the tenured infantry and cavalry branches fighting for fiscal survival against arrogant newcomers in tanks and airplanes. The infantry contended that it *had* adapted to the requirements of modern war by greatly increasing its "fire superiority."[64] As William Odom explained, "The infantry of 1914 was a formation of riflemen. In contrast, the infantry of 1918 included riflemen, machinegunners, grenadiers, mortarmen, and 37-mm gunners."[65] To traditionalists, combined arms meant infantry arms.

Back in the cavalry, Patton resumed his studies: Field Marshal Colmar Von Der Goltz's *The Conduct of War* (1896), Major General Douglas Haig's *Cavalry Studies, Strategical and Tactical* (1907), General Friedrich von Bernhardi's *The War of the Future* (1913), General von Verdy du Vernois' *A Tactical Ride* (1906), Sun Tzu's *The Art of War* (1910 British translation), General Erich von Ludendorf's *Ludendorf's Own Story August 1914–November 1918*, Lieutenant General Hugo von Freytag-Loringhoven's *Deductions from the World War*, General Erich von Falkenhayn's *The German General Staff*, Lieutenant Colonel R. M. P. Preston's *The Desert Mounted Corps*, and W. T. Massey's *The Desert Campaigns*.[66] All had a common theme: mobile operations.

In a 1921 *Cavalry Journal* article, "Cavalry Tanks," Patton rebutted arguments that certain locations were limited to horse cavalry and claimed the war proved how horsemen had to "await the breakthrough made by tanks."[67] The next year his essay "What the War Did for Cavalry" rejected "tactics based on a crushing artillery," reliance on "Air, Gas, or Tank" specialists, and the "futility of trench warfare" and proposed instead that dismounted firepower should be used "as pivots of maneuver, that is, to use their fire to pin the enemy to the ground while the mounted elements use their mobility to attack the flanks or rear of the enemy so held."[68] Here was the first incarnation of his combined arms doctrine: "hold them by the nose and kick them in the ass."[69]

Patton's 1924 article "Armored Cars with Cavalry" (by law, *tanks* now belonged to the infantry, so the cavalry called their tracked vehicles *armored cars*) presciently envisioned a future battlefield in which commanders in chemical gas–proofed armored vehicles watched little motion picture screens depicting live images of the forward battlefield as transmitted by radio signals from cameras on helicopters circling overhead.[70] It would be seventy years before this scene neared reality. Patton closed by calling for a lightweight, mechanically simple, open-topped gun vehicle (similar to later tank destroyers) for the cavalry. He believed tanks would fight tanks but regretted there were no tanks "AVAILABLE FOR ISSUE in this country" up to the job.[71] The existing U.S. tanks were too slow, too thin-skinned, and too lightly armed to effectively engage other tanks. Without a robust budget this situation was not going to improve. Patton never allowed his enthusiasm to surpass his recognition of budgetary and political reality.

After completing postwar reviews, the Army issued new doctrine in *Field Service Regulations 1923* that would stand unchanged for sixteen years, the longest such period in the Army's history. The doctrine underscored that "the mission of the infantry is the general mission of the entire force. The special missions of the other arms are derived from their powers to contribute to the execution of the infantry mission."[72] Commanders were to carefully calibrate all supporting arms to the parameters of the infantry. The subaltern status of tanks and tankers was clear. Patton received a message from his commander in the war, Brigadier General Samuel D. Rockenbach, in February 1924: "I have gotten my promotion, as some of my stupid friends inform me, in spite of the Tanks, but I believe in Tanks, I believe that the machines that we have in manufacture at the present time are going to win many of our opponents and are going to force you, cavalryman, to adopt them."[73] Patton understood.

Elsewhere, change happened fast. Patton studied intelligence digests describing how the chief of the German general staff Hans von Seeckt rewrote his army's doctrine to emphasize tanks.[74] As Robert Citino noted, von Seeckt "was no tank fiend like Fuller," believing instead that "only in harmony and close cooperation with the traditional arms did tanks have a future."[75] In September 1922 American attaché Colonel Arthur Conger sent a ninety-two-page report on a German two-day field exercise praising the Germans' execution and mobility and noted their simulated use of tanks that were then denied to them by the Versailles Treaty.[76] His reports during the winter of 1923–24 even described rudimentary field tests of air-ground coordination, which was also banned.[77] By 1925 the *Reichswehr* was conducting divisional exercises, and the next year it began multidivisional exercises.

Back in the United States, multidivision exercises remained a pipe dream. Combined arms operations were limited. The Infantry School warned its instructors that "habitual" use of tanks was detrimental to the "self-reliance and aggressive spirit of the infantry."[78] A student later recalled, "There was a tank battalion at Benning, but its equipment was utterly obsolete and our contact with the unit was limited to watching rolling demonstrations—mere parades—in the boondocks. We did not actually integrate tank developments or movements into our infantry problems, a regrettable lapse."[79] The Army preached "practice as you will fight," when regrettably it would fight as it practiced.

Try as it might, the U.S. Army could not avoid modernization. First Cavalry Division commander Brigadier General George Van Horn Moseley complained to the chief of cavalry, "When the cowboy down here is herding cattle in a Ford we must realize that the world has undergone a change."[80] His division tested motorized vehicles and airplanes in 1923.[81] The next year, the 4th Infantry Division's 34th Infantry Regiment experimented with trucks. Press coverage of the Billy Mitchell trial compelled the Calvin Coolidge administration to look anew at modernization.[82] Secretary of War Dwight D. Davis visited the British Experimental Mechanization Force (EMF) exercises featuring the new turreted British Vickers Company Mark "C" tank carrying a 57-mm main gun and traveling at twenty miles per hour.[83] There was nothing like it in the U.S. inventory. Davis directed Army chief of staff General Charles Summerall to establish an American EMF. Summerall passed the task to his G-3, Brigadier General Frank Parker, the same officer who first introduced Patton to tanks. Leading Parker's staff was another of Patton's friends, Major Adna Chaffee Jr.

Patton found ways to investigate combined arms operations. In March 1927 as G-3 in the Hawaiian Division, he read a report from a board chaired by Major Henry "Hap" Arnold on aircraft attacks on mobile ground columns.[84] He then devised and tested in the field tactics for transitioning from a column on the march into a formation that would enable every gun to engage attacking aircraft within thirty seconds.[85] A test by the 3rd Battalion of the 35th Infantry Regiment convinced him that speed and volume of fire were the keys to defending against aircraft. Conversely, these tests also proved to him how dangerous tactical airpower could be against mechanized columns.

In March 1928 Parker submitted to Summerall another groundbreaking report, *A Mechanized Force,* calling for the creation of a combined arms mechanized force supported by aircraft with tanks, artillery, engineers and—unlike the British EMF—mechanized infantry.[86] Parker foresaw this force spearheading corps or army attacks, conducting counterattacks, guarding flanks, and seizing "distant key positions."[87] These were all traditional cavalry missions in support of large units. In July Summerall pulled together an Experimental Mechanized Force of two light tank battalions, a medium tank platoon, an infantry battalion, an armored car troop, a field artillery battalion, an ammunition train, chemical and ordnance maintenance platoons, and a provisional motor repair section. The unit differed from the British EMF in its large number of infantry and its lack of serviceable tanks. As Timothy Nenninger commented, "Obsolete wartime equipment, which often broke down, proved the greatest handicap."[88] Without large exercises or better equipment, the EMF tests proved inconclusive at best.

There was a solution to the EMF equipment problem. On 19 February 1929 the chief of cavalry requested the Ordnance Department purchase the new Christie chassis, recently put through vigorous tests at Fort Leonard Wood, Missouri, and Fort Myer, Virginia. Patton kept a copy of the request and wrote on the bottom, "Probably a very momentous paper."[89] He foresaw the vehicle supporting cavalry in battle "both in fire and shock action."[90] Unfortunately, the Ordnance Department was not interested. Patton had to advise the Cavalry School to tone down instruction on tanks and armored cars: "It is evident that the tactics of armored cars and the technique of their handling and maintenance depend to a great deal on the material in use. So far as the American Army is concerned this material is in a wholly nebulous state, so that it is impossible to base tactics or technique on it."[91] Between 1920 and 1935, the United States would produce only thirty-five tanks.[92]

Patton followed the developments in mechanization from a distance but tried to get closer. He applied for duty in London. General Fox Conner wrote to him in February 1931: "I hear a rumor that you are likely to go to England as military Attaché. If this turns out to be correct, you will certainly see enough of the mechanized side. As I understand it, the British are going to the mechanical idea more than anyone else."[93] That effort came to nothing. Looking elsewhere, Patton asked for a copy of a book on French artillery doctrine recently written by his friend Colonel John S. Wood, who sent the edition with the note, "George—if you ever read this, you will, I guess, be the second person in the world who has done so."[94]

Meanwhile, the chief of cavalry summoned Patton for the assignment to write in defense of the horse branch. In Dennis Showalter's words, "During his time in the cavalry office, Major Patton was the cavalry's house intellectual, the go-to man for a few well-chosen words on any subject relating to the cavalry's welfare—a public relations officer without the title."[95] Patton, with Major C. C. Benson, opened his campaign with an article, "Mechanization and Cavalry," which examined the impact of "fast cross country fighting machines" on "not only the Cavalry, but also the Infantry, the Artillery, Engineers, Signal Corps, supply services and Air Forces."[96] He wrote that supply, terrain, and control factors meant horse cavalry could not be completely replaced by tanks. "Instead of rivalry," Patton maintained, "there should be union to insure strength."[97] Far from arguing against tanks, Patton wanted to employ them to augment the cavalry.

Over the next two years Patton's defense of the horse cavalry continued to cover his endorsement of tanks, especially better tanks. In "The Effect of Weapons on War," he presented the tank and the airplane as a continuation of the evolution that began with the chariot that would undoubtedly lead to adequate responses. While arguing that "few, if any, victories are traceable to weapons," he added that when it comes to weapons, "we must use them all."[98] A follow-up article, "Success in War," emphasized the human and moral factors in war and the transient impact of innovations.[99]

Privately, Patton pushed for better tanks. He wrote to influential friends in search of tanks with engines powerful enough to carry "plate sufficient to stop .50-caliber bullets" or lighter armor able to "stop or delay .30-caliber A.P. [armor piercing] bullets."[100] He sent to engineers and manufacturers his own designs on suspensions, coaxial guns, radio configurations, and a myriad of other ideal features for tanks.

With Patton assigned to defend the horse cavalry, tank advocacy passed to Chaffee who, as the son of an Army chief of staff, could afford to be more radical. Some thought Chaffee had the opportunity to develop a mechanized combined arms force to conduct operational level rapid and deep independent missions.[101] As the EMF evolved into the 7th Cavalry Brigade (Mechanized) at Fort Knox, Kentucky, however, Chaffee gradually limited the unit to cavalry missions. It did not become a counterpart to the new units in Britain and Germany. When Lieutenant Colonel Adolf von Schnell visited with a delegation of German officers, he said he thought the American .50 caliber machine gun too small for a tank. Colonel Daniel Van Voorhis explained that American tanks were not designed to engage other tanks. Von Schnell replied that the Germans would "hurl thousands of tanks against the enemy. . . . Infantry will then follow through, protected at close quarters by a small number of additional tanks which will mop up."[102] Chaffee's unit had no such number of tanks nor any such mission (see figure 3).

Patton confided to a fellow tank enthusiast: "The future of mechanization . . . lies in the creation with it of a small powerful striking force capable of operating for a specific purpose for a fixed time. In other words, an offensive reserve used to give the knock out punch after normal troops have fought the enemy sufficiently—several days probably—to determine his weak spot."[103] He now saw a mechanized force doing more than just cavalry missions: it would combine the ideas of Sun Tzu, *Stosstrupp* tactics, and his own infantry-tank echeloned breakthrough into a means for creating and maintaining a series of shocks upon the enemy. In his Army War College dissertation, he called for strategic mobility but cautioned, "Neither cavalry nor mechanized troops have sufficient combat mobility to secure a major victory unaided. Infantry is needed and to be effective it too must have a faster rate than its opponent."[104] Ideas for a true combined arms force were coalescing in Patton's mind.

In the 1930s Germany formed a mechanized, combined arms panzer corps, much along the lines suggested by Parker in 1918.[105] The new U.S. military attaché in Berlin, Major Truman Smith, reported that the Germans saw the "tank as a strategical weapon for achieving decisive battle success" and that "the infantry tank is an exploitation weapon—not a front line breaking weapon."[106] In 1931 the German *Wehrmacht* was known to have only fifty-five 5.4-ton Panzerkampfwagen Mark I training tanks. Two years later Germany fielded three full combined arms panzer divisions, nine to fifteen mechanized brigades, in its panzer corps.[107] In November 1935 Major Smith sent a fifteen-page report that held, "The German Panzer Division is the most important development (from an organizational standpoint) of the entire German rearmament program . . . a unique organization, without exact or even close parallel in other European countries."[108] He did not have to mention that there was also no equivalent at home.

Vehicle	Year	Maximum Armor	Weight	Main Weapon	Machine Guns	Maximum Speed	Operational Range
 Renault FT17	1917	22mm	6.5 tons	37 mm		4.3 mph	37 miles
 Mark VIII	1917	16mm	37 tons	Two 6-pounders	Five .30 cal	5.25 mph	50 miles
 T7 Armored Car	1937	16mm	11 tons	12.7mm machine gun	One .30 cal	35 mph on tracks 53 mph on wheels	110 miles
 M2A1 Light Tank	1939	32mm	18.7 tons	37mm	Seven .30 cal	26 mph	130 miles
 M3 Lee/Grant Tank	1941	51mm	30 tons	37mm & 75mm	Two to four .30 cal	26 mph	195 miles
 M4 Sherman Tank	1941	76mm	30.3 tons	76mm	Two .30 cal	30 mph	120 miles

Figure 3. Data Comparisons of Representative U.S. Tanks, 1917–41

Source: Peter Chamberlain and Christopher Ellis, *Pictorial History of Tanks of the World 1915–45* (London: Arms and Armour Press, 1972), and Ian V. Hogg and John Weeks, *The Illustrated Encyclopedia of Military Vehicles* (London: New Burlington Books, 1980).

The U.S. Army, divided by branch politics and budgetary competition, still assigned tanks to the infantry with only one authorized mission: "the neutralization of machine guns."[109] Sparse budgets, limited missions, and powerless sponsorship resulted in American tanks, as described by the German army weekly *Militär-Wochenblatt*, being the "perfect example of bad construction."[110] A "Modernization Board," looking for cost savings, moved tank, aviation, and antitank units to only corps or higher level commands. American observers in the Spanish civil war, led by former chief of infantry Major General Steven O. Fuqua, reported that tanks were only useful for infantry support.[111] All this contributed to the War Department's order in April 1938 that "combatant arms will fight in their traditional roles."[112] There would be no mobile combined arms operations; infantry still ruled.

When Germany invaded Poland in 1939, Military Intelligence Division reports indicated that after piercing the enemy front lines, German columns "*avoided combat* and were *pushed forward as far and as rapidly as possible*, breaking up enemy formations, disrupting his communication, and destroying his establishments and reserve depots of materiel and personnel [emphasis in original]."[113] A U.S. Army history noted, "German armor units disregarded their exposed flanks and raced ahead of the infantry divisions to cut the retreating Polish armies into smaller groups."[114] Patton avidly absorbed the lessons learned in the field by the panzer divisions: they were the tactics he had imagined for the past twenty years.[115]

Traditionalists countered that the German blitzkrieg was actually conventional, as John Mosier described, "revealing an advance on a broad front with the aim of defeating the enemy in detail as its troops appear or attempt to counterattack."[116] Indeed, the German general staff *had not* planned independent deep armor penetrations because they felt they had too few tanks for such operations.[117] There was no "blitzkrieg doctrine." Except for two corps, the Germans committed their panzers piecemeal.[118] Their infantry advanced across Poland at roughly the same rate that the German foot soldiers achieved during the Great War.[119] Cavalry advocates even noted that several Polish and German horse cavalry attacks met with success.[120] Analysts also reported the German reliance on "horse drawn supply columns."[121] Weeks after the Germans captured Warsaw, the U.S. chief of cavalry told students at the Army War College that Poland demonstrated that obviously "the machine cannot eliminate the horse."[122]

With combat engulfing Europe, on 1 October 1939 the War Department released Field Manual 100–5, *Tentative Field Service Regulations: Operations*, which ignored the German military developments that had profoundly transformed the pace, range, and nature of warfare.[123] The Army failed to learn what Patton understood. The new doctrine reemphasized that the infantry was the primary arm and all others supported it.[124] It added, "Normally tanks do not operate beyond the effective fire support of the infantry and other supporting arms."[125] Tanks were thus limited to about twenty miles of the front.

The fall of France the following June threw U.S. doctrine into question. By all accounts the French had been well positioned to stop the Germans. The 136 German divisions faced 94 French and 10 British divisions.[126] Each side had about 2.5 million men, and the Allies had the advantage of the strategic and tactical defense reinforced by the Maginot Line. While the Germans had 5,500 aircraft against 3,100 for the British and French, the Allies had quality antiaircraft systems on their side. The French also had 10,000 artillery pieces against only 2,500 for the Germans and 4,000 tanks compared to 2,600 for the Germans, and many of the French tanks were of superior quality.[127] Numbers, however, were only part of the equation in war.

The way the Germans applied force tipped the balance. Peter McCarthy and Mike Syron explained: "The French had completely failed to grasp the possibilities offered by tanks deployed independently and in concentration, instead sticking to the tired old formula of 'penny packing' their armor."[128] In the French army, Eugenia Kiesling added, "Concern for the tank's vulnerability in the face of increasingly effective anti-tank measures reinforced the widespread conviction that the tank could not be employed in any context other than that of methodical battle."[129] The French spread their tanks out to support their infantry in deliberately controlled operations. In contrast, the Germans concentrated their panzer divisions into a "heavy point," the *Schwerpunkt*, to punch through defenses and enable free-flowing attacks. Hitler personally selected an aggressive leader, Heinz Guderian, to lead that effort. Several times Guderian refused orders to halt to let the infantry catch up and instead sped across France.

Looking past media reports trumpeting the blitzkriegs, Patton saw in the Military Intelligence Division bulletins the effectiveness of the combined arms formations. He understood that the German combined tank, mechanized infantry, and close air support formations seeking to create decisive battles had produced ad hoc shocks that outpaced French reaction. In one analysis, General Édouard-Jean Réquin of the French Fourth Army reported, "*The decisive breakthrough*, tactically possible, but strategically utopia during the last war of 1914–1918, has become a reality thanks to the use of Large Armored Units and Aviation for the *exploitation* [emphasis in original]."[130] A later study identified commonalities between Patton and Guderian in the operational art: "centralized control of artillery; close cooperation of ground and air efforts; attacks to envelop or encircle the enemy at operational depths; execution of operations at high speed; acceptance of flank and logistical risk; and personal leadership at frontline units."[131] Yet Patton disagreed with the German reliance on tank-heavy spearheads, the armored corps built around the panzer divisions tailored for exploitation. He favored more balanced combinations of arms with armored divisions distributed across corps to enable more operational flexibility. In part his view was likely a concession to fiscal realities, but it also reflected his preference for flexible, agile formations.

As France fell, Patton joined a select group of officers brought together by Parker and Chaffee in the basement of a high school in Alexandria, Louisiana, to draft recommendations for creating an American panzer force. One officer present recalled, "The thought was not along the lines of the old Infantry and Cavalry tanks but of a Force separate from all current Arms and one that combined not only the combat elements but the essential support units to make a tactical entity."[132] The resulting "Alexandria Recommendations" sent to Chief of Staff Marshall called for the creation of combined arms tank divisions. A panzer corps—the spearhead of the blitzkrieg—was out of the question. General Headquarters chief of staff Lesley McNair wanted to beat a panzer corps, not make one. He explained: "It is believed that our general concept of an armored force—that it is an instrument of exploitation, not greatly different in principle from horse cavalry of old—is sound. However, some, particularly armored enthusiasts, have been led away from this concept by current events which have been misinterpreted."[133] Marshall tasked his staff to act on the recommendations and design an armored force.

On 16 July Patton joined the new 2nd Armored Division at Fort Benning, and a month later he was appointed to the division board to "review and make recommendations on such matters pertaining to equipment, training, and tables of organizations."[134] For the first time since Camp Meade, he was positioned to explore, test, and rework a mechanized force centered on tanks. Marshall gave Chaffee overall command of the new armored force, and Chaffee in turn designed the divisions along the lines of the EMF—for traditional cavalry operations and not deep, independent operations.[135] He put the division's striking power into a single tank brigade.[136] The brigade had no infantry; they were kept in a separate two-battalion infantry regiment.[137] In battle the Germans had already learned to increase the infantry in their panzer divisions to four battalions.[138] Moreover, as Christopher Gabel observed, "The 1940 [U.S.] armored division differed markedly from the panzer division, however, in that it could not subdivide into battle groups."[139] Contrary to Patton's advice, the tank divisions went to war unable to fight in combined arms teams. The U.S. armored division was only suited to rampaging unprotected rear areas *after* an infantry breakthrough.

Patton received command of the tank brigade in the new 2nd Armored Division before assuming command of the entire division in 1941. He quickly grasped, "These Armored Divisions are pure cavalry in their functions and tactics and all the foreign writers so state."[140] Still, considering the available light armored vehicles were not "real tanks," Patton experimented to determine the unit's full potential.[141] In December 1940 he led 1,100 vehicles and 16,000 men on a road march from Fort Benning to Panama City, Florida, and back—a trip of over 400 miles, the longest to date by an armored division—after which he remarked, "These new armored divisions are terribly powerful instruments of destruction and on account of size difficult to handle."[142] He earned his pilot's license and bought a Piper Cub to better observe his columns. In February 1941 he paraded the division's 15,000 men and 1,300 vehicles and noted, "The amazing thing, from my standpoint was that thirteen hundred vehicles passed the reviewing stand without any checks or stalls. We certainly could not have done that in 1918!"[143] In the Tennessee Maneuvers, Patton was pleased to report to Secretary of War Henry Stimson, "In spite of the long march, in some cases over 110 miles, every fighting vehicle in the division, except two tanks and a scout car, got to the place it was supposed to be in time to deliver the attack."[144] The ability to move his force long distances was essential to his ideas for strategic maneuver.

Early on Patton began intensive exercises with the 16th Observation Squadron to try to establish adequate air-ground coordination and called for "Cooperation Command" to coordinate ground operations, aerial reconnaissance, and tactical air support. The air service, however, feared exposing its aircraft to ground fire. Patton argued, "While it is technically correct, I presume, that high bombardment is certainly safer than dive bombing, nevertheless, it is apparent from what the Germans have done that the morale effect of the dive bombing cannot be over estimated. Furthermore it has the unmistakable advantage of hitting targets closer to the armored force."[145] After several months he became convinced that the ground troops had to "coordinate their attack with the air rather than the other way around."[146] He asked for local air support for the hour of attack and then made certain to conduct his attack when air support was available. "This is not an ideal solution," he wrote, "but I think at present it is the only one that will work."[147]

In May 1941 the Army released a new edition of Field Manual 100–5, *Operations*.[148] It now stated: "The armored division is organized primarily to perform missions that require great mobility and firepower. It is given decisive missions."[149] It explained that "other large units of the combined arms" would break through the enemy lines, and then the armored divisions would conduct "offensive operations against hostile rear areas."[150] Yet the field manual also explicitly reaffirmed the primacy of infantry, and its section on tanks consisted of just the final 3 of the book's 280 pages.[151] Tanks in successive echelons with the first wave, accompanied by artillery and combat aviation, *attacked enemy antitank guns*. A second wave would *overrun the enemy position*, destroying "the hostile automatic weapons which have survived the preparatory fires."[152] Clearly tanks still supported infantry by attacking enemy strength.

Patton believed in the primacy of tanks in modern battle. "But," he told his troops, "the tanks do not attack alone."[153] He conducted field exercises with an airplane squadron and reconnaissance battalion to locate the enemy, two regiments of artillery to "jellify" them, and engineers and infantry to "do with their flesh and blood what the armor is unable to accomplish."[154] Patton emphasized that "each weapon must support the others. Team play wins."[155] In an apt metaphor he said, "An Armored Division is not a unit composed of artillery, infantry, tanks, engineers, and so forth, each in its own little shell like eggs in a crate. An Armored Division is an omelet in which all the eggs have been broken out of their shells and combine to form a palatable and nutritious whole."[156] Armor units were not separate aids to the infantry as in doctrine, but interlocked parts of a whole.

In the Great Maneuvers in Louisiana, Tennessee, and Carolina, higher command's insistence on charging tank-pure formations into prepared anti-tank gun defenses in accordance with doctrine frustrated Patton. Umpire rules overestimated the effectiveness of antitank guns while tanks, as Gabel noted, "could not knock out anti-tank guns with gunfire at all, but only by charging and overrunning them."[157] Patton fumed to a friend, "You would be surprised at the profound ignorance in higher places as to the use of tanks. People are still obsessed with the belief that tanks are invulnerable and try to send them head-on into prepared positions."[158] He attributed this to "undigested memories" from World War I and noted "that the teachings of that period and the action at Cambrai were based on the invulnerability of tanks. That invulnerability no longer exists, and hence the use of tanks in mass is futile and suicidal."[159] He was perhaps the only man in the world to personally experience the change. Patton told his assembled division, "I can think of nothing more futile to send expensive tanks against a prepared position. The doctrine for so doing was originally written by me and was based on the fact that in 1918 tanks were invulnerable, but a careful analysis of what the Germans have done leads me to a totally different solution for present day armored forces."[160] He taught that infantry and tanks needed to work together in the tactical battle to solve the enemy's defensive zone, and that tanks could not charge defenses on their own. After the maneuvers, however, Patton privately complained to General Jacob Devers, the new armored forces chief, that his forces had been slaved to infantry and that needed to change.[161]

The debate over methods of direct attack hid a more important point. Whereas the Army saw such attacks as the heart of tactical battle—the focus of attrition strategy—Patton saw them as secondary to decisive maneuver. They were but a means for holding the enemy by the nose or exploiting a weak spot while his combined arms columns sprung into the enemy rear to create the series of shocks that would overwhelm enemy reactive capabilities, erode their morale, and collapse their will. The great exercises were only designed to exercise doctrine, however, not to test Patton's ideas.

Contrary to the direct methods prescribed by the umpires, Patton developed a combined arms battle drill he thought more effective against antitank guns. After detecting the guns, he opened a heavy artillery barrage augmented by dive bombers; he then "stalked" the guns with armored reconnaissance detachments and dismounted troopers. Finally, his reconnaissance and dismounts held the guns' attention with frontal fire while "other vehicles" outflanked them. "The result," Patton wrote, "is that the anti-tank guns have the choice of withdrawing, in order to avoid being enveloped, or of sticking it out and being enveloped. When they attempt to withdraw for the purpose of avoiding envelopment, they are immediately followed and destroyed by the tanks moving in direct pursuit."[162] The drill became a model for all his wartime operations.

In March 1942 Marshall sent Patton to the Mojave Desert to establish a Desert Training Center and prepare U.S. Army units for possible fighting in North Africa. Patton explained to the training units that although they would follow "the fundamental principles of tactics as laid down by Field Service Regulations," they would learn "certain new techniques with which our officers are in the main totally unfamiliar."[163] The desert became another laboratory. He trained units as task forces "comprising all of the elements of an armor division."[164] As such, much of their training focused on detailed operations of all arms formations.[165] Training ran at a tempo of one major tactical exercise every two days, including overnight maneuvers, providing a reasonable simulation of Patton's expected wartime pace.

In the desert Patton was everywhere, prodding and poking, to both train the men and learn their limits. He was quickly impressed with the two-and-a-half-ton truck and the 4x4 Jeep, but not so much with the scout cars. He found value in commanding movement from the air by radio but believed commanders should be on the ground during battle. He once spotted a truck moving on a surfaced motorway, contrary to a standing order to only travel off road, and made a note of the driver's problems with a certain type of transmission.[166] Through these and thousands of other observations, Patton came to understand the promise and deficiencies in combined arms formations. He especially found fault in the organization of the armored division but promised Devers he "would certainly never suggest" changes to anyone other than the armored force commander.[167]

Indeed, the U.S. Army entered World War II lacking in combined arms. Patton carefully planned a 72-hour campaign for Morocco beginning 8 November, to end in a combined arms attack on Casablanca. With the only available airfield in the north and the only port capable of offloading tanks in the south, he put his Center Landing Group of 19,000 soldiers nearest the Moroccan capital, a Northern Landing Group to secure the Port Lyautey airfield for 77 P-40 fighters, and a Southern Landing Group to deliver tanks through the artificial harbor at Safi.[168] As he had at Fort Benning, he timed advances to sequence reconnaissance, air bombardment, naval artillery, and finally the ground assault on Casablanca.[169] It was to be the first fully synchronized U.S. combined arms attack in theater, but when the French surrendered at the last moment, Patton called off the attack.

Though brief, the fighting in Morocco revealed several lessons on combined arms warfare. In the north, Major General Lucian Truscott attempted several fruitless infantry assaults on the Kasbah, a French fortress, before finally calling for Navy dive bombers that convinced the defenders to surrender after only a few direct hits.[170] Patton noted, "The Navy-Air was very fine and really showed up the Army, at least based on my maneuver experience with the latter. In one case a Navy torpedo plane dropped a 500-pound bomb on a column of French tanks with the result that three of them were never again seen."[171] Communication was bad with the Navy and nonexistent with air support. A U.S. Army history noted, "Neither infantry nor armored divisions proved to be completely satisfactory during combat because they lacked all the resources habitually needed to operate efficiently."[172] A tanker from the 1st Armored Division—a division not trained by Patton—explained, "There was no infantry at Fort Knox, so we never trained with infantry. And although there was one battalion of artillery there, we never trained with them."[173] Left behind while the Allies moved to Tunisia, Patton studied the problems of combined operations from a distance.

When the Allies bogged down and the weather worsened, Eisenhower suspended his offensive and candidly wrote to the War Department: "I think the best way to describe our operations to date is that they have violated every recognized principle of war, are in conflict with all operational and logistical methods laid down in text-books, and will be condemned, in their entirety, by all Leavenworth and War College classes for the next twenty-five years."[174] Lloyd Fredendall, commander of II U.S. Corps, so frequently piecemealed units from the 1st Armored Division that Major General Orlando Ward complained, "Never have I seen anything like this before. Here I'm a Division Commander, my division has been taken away from me, all I have left is a medical battalion."[175]

At Kasserine Pass in February 1943, the lack of combined arms formations resulted in disaster. McNair's pet antitank systems operated alone and were picked off. Armor units counterattacking without infantry were slaughtered. On the first evening British First Army commander General Kenneth Anderson reported to Eisenhower, "The II Corps cannot continue to battle with its tanks because it no longer has any."[176] Patton took over II Corps and quickly issued his first order: divisions would no longer be committed piecemeal. Ward and 1st Infantry Division Commander Major General Terry Allen were more than willing to take the reins. Visiting the 1st Infantry Division, Benjamin "Monk" Dickson noted, "We found morale was sky high as the Big Red One was fighting as a division for the first time since its November landings."[177]

Ike instructed Patton in Tunisia: "Large forces are not to be passed beyond the line Gafsa-Maknassy-Faid-Fondouk"—Patton was to draw the enemy away from the British Eighth Army.[178] At Gafsa, he used the now-concentrated 1st Infantry Division against the Italians to produce the U.S. Army's first well-coordinated combined arms attack in the war. British correspondent John D'Arcy-Dawson reported, "I arrived back at Gafsa in time to see the finest battle yet waged by American troops."[179] Patton then combined the 1st Armored Division and 60th Regimental Combat Team to take the high ground near Senad Station. At El Guettar, tipped by intelligence, he delivered the first U.S. victory over German troops, highlighted by the effective use of artillery. Patton confessed to an old friend, "As an artilleryman, you will be interested to note that I have changed my mind about your old arm and am now a most enthusiastic supporter."[180] Terry Allen credited the victory "to having the division together as a unit."[181] In his May 1943 notes on combat, Patton listed lessons hard learned in the use of infantry, artillery, tanks and armored reconnaissance, tank destroyers and antitank guns, air, and miscellaneous troops.[182]

Officially, II Corps reported: "Our operation during the entire period was brilliantly supported by the XII Air Support Command."[183] Unit reports painted a different picture. The 1st Infantry Division reported, "We had no fighters to protect us. . . . We dug holes so deep you could call them graves."[184] Patton complained, "Total lack of air cover for our units has allowed German air force to operate at will."[185] The problem was coordination. Eisenhower issued guidance, "Combat Aviation in Direct Support of Ground Units," that put the onus on ground commanders: "As a general rule, only those targets which cannot be reached quickly and effectively by artillery should be assigned to combat aviation."[186] By this order, commanders had to submit target lists so early that strikes on targets of opportunity became impossible.

Air-ground coordination was no better when the Allies attacked Sicily in July. Admiral H. Kent Hewitt complained, "When we went to Sicily, we strove to get the air to join with us in making plans. They never did, and so we put to sea without knowing what the Air Force plan was."[187] Truscott noted, "We had no information as to what, if any, air support we could expect on D-Day. We had no knowledge of the extent of fighter protection we would have. . . . This lack of air participation in the joint planning at every level was inexcusable."[188] Marshall's plans officer, Brigadier General Albert C. Wedemeyer, argued against theater air commanders air chief marshal Sir Arthur Tedder and General Carl Spaatz, who decided "that air power should be used in direct support of troops only when enemy air forces had been neutralized."[189] Even then, procedures for requesting tactical air support took from twelve to twenty-four hours, too long to be effective.[190] As overall commander, Eisenhower could have forced coordination, but, as Patton noted, "Here it was that Ike missed being great. He could have faced the issue but sat mute."[191]

To ensure combined arms in the initial assaults into Sicily, Patton reinforced the 3rd Infantry Division with one ranger battalion and tanks from the 2nd Armored Division, and added to the 1st Infantry Division two ranger battalions with a reserve from the rest of the 2nd Armored Division.[192] Ashore at Gela, he personally intervened to get naval gunfire and tanks to defeat German counterattacks.[193] He revealed his unique understanding of the capabilities of his formations prior to sweeping around western Sicily when he observed that ground forces commander General Harold Alexander "has no idea of either the power or speed of American armies. We can go twice as fast as the British and hit harder."[194] He knew, as Martin

Blumenson explained, "American vehicles, particularly the 2½-ton truck, were so much better than British transport that Americans could move more rapidly on roads and cross-country."[195] Across Africa, Montgomery advanced at twelve miles a day; Patton expected to move at more than four times that pace in Sicily—and he did.

Growing faith in the capabilities of his tank-infantry-artillery teams empowered Patton to seize and maintain the initiative. Before Palermo he wrote, "If the attack . . . works out, it will be a classic example of the proper use of armor. I told [Hugh] Gaffey and Maurice Rose [commanding the lead combat commands] to take chances—to smoke out the enemy and then charge him with tanks. I am sure this will work as the enemy is jumpy and justly so, in the face of the power we can put against him."[196] He later explained his use of tanks: "I held them back far enough so that the enemy could not tell where they were to be used; then when the infantry had found the hole, the tanks went through and in large numbers and fast."[197] Infantry found weak spots, and tanks exploited them—an inversion of official doctrine.

In central Sicily, II Corps captured a report from the Germans who were attempting to defend Agira with superior strength and good defensive terrain. "But after a while it was noticed that the intentions of the enemy were to by-pass the town and to block the routes of approach," the report said. "Here and there, tanks appeared suddenly, light personnel carriers came forward and enemy artillery laid its magic fire closer and closer to our positions. Losses and casualties of men and weapons were noticeable on our side and the situation began slowly to become critical."[198] Such well-drilled combined arms attacks repeatedly unbalanced the Germans. At Agira, as Patton's forces worked their flank, the Germans slowly fell back and then escaped at night.

After Palermo, Patton turned east for Messina. He noted, "Where we are now fighting the country is the worst I have ever seen, really terrible, hills are as bare as babies' bottoms. Omar [Bradley], Terry [Allen] and Manton [Eddy] are having the hardest battle yet fought since last November. Of course we will win but it takes time."[199] To maintain momentum, he turned to combined-service operations. Samuel Eliot Morison reported that when Palermo harbor opened on 27 July, Admiral Hewitt organized Motorized Torpedo Boat Squadron 15, Destroyer Squadron 8, and several minesweepers and a few other warships into "General Patton's Navy" to support Seventh Army.[200] Still, Patton stated, "We are having a good deal of trouble in getting the Navy to go in for amphibious operations east of San Stefano. They appear to have no idea of the value of time or the need for improvisation."[201] He executed three amphibious end runs (over the objections of his own commanders) with combined arms teams that unhinged the enemy line and hastened their withdrawal. Churchill crowed, "I had of course always been a partisan of the 'end run,' as the Americans call it or 'cat-claw,' which was my term. I had never succeeded in getting this maneuver open to sea power included in any of our desert advances. In Sicily, however, General Patton had twice used the command of the sea flank as he advanced along the northern coast of the island with great effect."[202] Like his sweep around western Sicily, Patton's end runs turned the German line and hastened their retreat from Sicily.

Seventh Army conducted detailed after action reviews after Sicily and reported: "The need for sound training of infantry for combined action with tanks, as distinguished from the action of the armored infantry, was again closely disclosed in Sicily."[203] The commander of the 180th Infantry Regiment admitted not knowing how to work with tanks. The 179th Infantry Regiment reported missing many opportunities due to their complete unfamiliarity with working with tanks. Yet the 1st Infantry Division commander, Terry Allen, recounted great success with his attached battalion of light tanks and company of medium tanks. He added, "Tanks were always used *en masse* with all their supporting weapons, and whenever an attack was made the objective was taken."[204] In comparison, 45th Infantry Division commander General Troy Middleton reported to Patton that in his sector "small numbers [of tanks] were employed almost daily, but in general with indifferent success."[205] Patton would not leave Middleton's report alone.

Before his next campaign, Patton determined to fix air-ground coordination. In February 1944 the XIX Tactical Air Command (TAC) under Brigadier General Otto "O. P." Weyland arrived in England to support Patton's Third Army. Weyland said, "Nobody was *really envious* of me, let's put it that way."[206] Not until May did they begin substantial joint training to challenge the Army Air Force School of Applied Tactics assertion that it was "almost impossible" to employ close air support during fast-moving operations.[207] As Bradford Shwedo wrote, "General Patton's forces took a different approach."²⁰⁸ Patton and Weyland abolished bomb lines and allowed fighter-bombers to freely attack targets of opportunity. They increased the number of air liaison officers with the ground troops three-fold over Army standards and gave them tanks with special radios so they could ride at the front and call in air support. They shortened the cycle for air support and improved warning and intelligence by placing all air warning, fighter control, and radio intercept units into a provisional Tactical Control Group under the Advanced Headquarters, XIX TAC.²⁰⁹ Patton's willingness to experiment, to ignore doctrine when required, brought a third dimension to his combined arms columns. Units across the Army would soon adopt the techniques developed by Patton and Weyland.

An air officer recalled, "When the time came for the actual invasion, the Air-Ground Officers who found themselves fifth wheels originally with the ground forces were by then an integral part of the unit upon which the Commanding General relied for maximum help."²¹⁰ The commitment of XIX TAC to the ground support mission was so complete that in October 1944 its 354th Fighter Group became the only outfit to switch back from the advanced P-51 Mustang fighters to the older but better ground attack P-47 Thunderbolts.²¹¹ In December Patton held a correspondence conference jointly with Weyland to highlight their exceptional cooperation. He told the reporters, "Our success has been the results of bringing the air and ground together from the beginning and having them work in consonance. We don't say that we are going to do this and what can you do about it. We say that we would like to make such an operation—now how can that be done from the air standpoint? Then we go on from that basis."²¹²

"For Patton England constituted almost as much of a classroom as the battlefields of North Africa and Sicily," Stanley Hirshson noted. "He was constantly learning and thinking about war."²¹³ Patton ordered Middleton, his VIII Corps commander, to deliver a more complete report on his bad experience with tanks in Sicily and his more recent use of them near Salerno in Italy. In both places Middleton reported the terrain did not support the use of tanks in large numbers.²¹⁴ Reflecting infantry doctrine, he added his belief "that our tank people have been too much indoctrinated with the idea that tanks must be employed in mass and in depth, and not enough thought given to the employment of tanks in small numbers in close support of front line troops."²¹⁵ On 13 April Middleton reported to Patton's headquarters to discuss his thoughts. Three days later Patton issued his third letter of instruction, "Tactical Use of Separate Tank Battalions," with guidance "based largely on the advice of Major General T. H. Middleton."[216]

Patton set conditions for when, as part of an infantry attack, tanks should lead or follow.[217] He encouraged infantry to use tanks at the front and added, "Any weapon which is not actively engaged in killing Germans is not doing its duty."[218] His guidance spelled out how the two arms support each other and what targets they should engage. Even in support, he noted, tanks "must be prepared to take advantage of any break that occurs, particularly to ruthlessly pursue hostile infantry if they attempt to withdraw."[219] Patton lectured his commanders, "The heavy weapons set the pace."[220] He then used Major General Walton Walker's corps to demonstrate proper cooperation in field exercises with the 4th and 6th Armored Divisions flanking defenses and spearheading attacks. Finally, he developed and refined artillery drills—including one he labeled *serenade,* the quick massing of all artillery fires within a corps sector in extreme emergencies.[221]

On 5 May 1944 Patton completed another paper, "Use of Armored Divisions," detailing his doctrine of combined arms columns, leading with armor, fixing the enemy with infantry and artillery, and bouncing around the enemy's flank with mechanized combined arms formations. He outlined his intention to team armor and infantry divisions to create a pool of units from which to form combined arms columns with tactical airpower covering the front and flanks. After reading his paper to his assembled corps and division commanders, Patton said, "Very few officers ever project what they do in training into battle, which is a very sad commentary on our system."[222]

In "Notes on Combat Armored Divisions," Patton published his most advanced thoughts on the organization of combined arms forces. Compared to the previous and existing doctrinal designs, his ideal division differed significantly in its balance of the combat power—armor, infantry and artillery (see figure 4). In the Experimental Mechanized Force designed in 1928, the arms were balanced with four tank companies, four infantry companies (although two were machine gun companies of smaller manpower), and three artillery batteries.[223] The first Armored Division of 1940 placed the ratio at twenty-seven medium and light tank companies, seven infantry companies, and seven artillery batteries. Notably, there was no infantry assigned to the division's strike unit, the single armor brigade. Combat

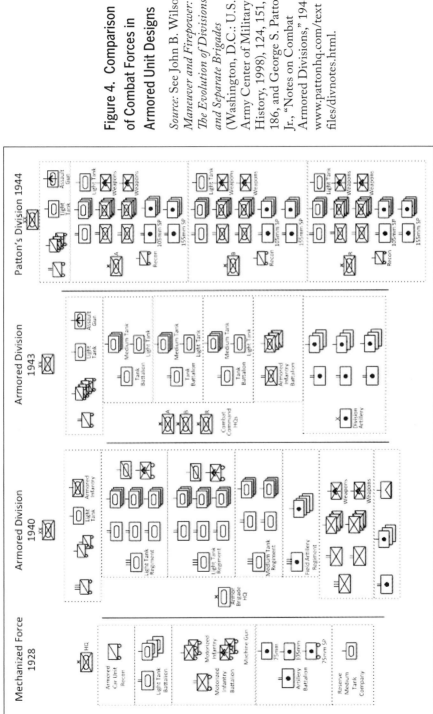

Figure 4. Comparison of Combat Forces in Armored Unit Designs

Source: See John B. Wilson, *Maneuver and Firepower: The Evolution of Divisions and Separate Brigades* (Washington, D.C.: U.S. Army Center of Military History, 1998), 124, 151, 186, and George S. Patton Jr. "Notes on Combat Armored Divisions," 1944, www.pattonhq.com/text files/divnotes.html.

experience led to modifications to this design in 1943 to thirteen tank companies, four infantry companies, and nine artillery batteries. The newest division included three combat command headquarters to which the companies could be assigned as needed for each mission.

Patton's ideal division included a surprisingly large proportional increase in infantry.[224] He wanted thirteen tank companies, eighteen armored infantry companies, six infantry weapons companies, and eighteen self-propelled artillery batteries. Moreover, each combat command would have an assigned strength of four armor companies, eight infantry companies, and six artillery batteries. In the end, therefore, Patton thought the brigade-sized maneuver units required twice as many armored infantry companies as tank companies—belying his reputation as a pure "tank man." While in practice his combat commands mixed companies according to the available forces and mission requirements, Patton's ideal division provided a sense of the kind of mix of combined arms he thought correct. At the ground level he ensured habitual and practiced cooperation by routine association between units of different arms. Within the 4th Armored Division, for example, Creighton Abrams' 37th Tank Battalion and Harold Cohen's 10th Armored Infantry Battalion created a virtually inseparable team at the heart of a combat command.[225]

Using Wood's 4th Armored Division and Weyland's air liaison officers, on 10 May Patton conducted his final tests and demonstrations of his doctrine in the field.[226] It was the culmination of decades of unparalleled thought and practice. He wrote, "I was delighted, and feel that I have at last illustrated the use of marching fire and of tanks and infantry. It strikes me as a sad reflection on our state of preparation for war that I had to personally conduct and drive the rehearsals, but so it is."[227] Where Army doctrine directed commanders to lead with infantry and bring up tanks when needed, Patton trained his units to do the opposite. Doctrine emphasized using preplanned tactical air support as a last resort; Patton incorporated quick-response tactical air as an integral part of his forces. He ordered his mechanized columns and air support to rapidly advance and maintain a pace that would overwhelm the enemy's ability to react. Doctrine said to fight set-piece battles to destroy enemy forces; Patton set out to avoid battles by exploiting weakness and keeping the enemy off balance through his continuous campaign. Doctrine sought attrition; Patton sought shock.

After Patton's large unit rehearsals, Walker's XX Corps reported, "Combined tank-infantry attacks on simulated German pillboxes formed a large part of the exercises. The artillery would lay down a rolling barrage which the men and machines of the combined arms would follow."[228] The corps artillery rehearsed time-on-target massed fires daily and noted, "This type of fire was often used in combat for its tremendous power and shock effect on enemy morale."[229] Patton's teams thus held the enemy by the nose and unleashed combined arms columns around the flanks to kick them in the pants. After the war, Bradley spoke for the traditionalists when he wrote, "Without meaning to detract from his extraordinary achievements, Patton's great and dramatic gains, beginning in Sicily and continuing through Brittany and on across the Seine at Mantes, Melun and Troyes, had been against little or no opposition."[230] He never understood that this was by Patton's design and only made possible by his knowledge of the capabilities of his combined arms columns.

In the breakout from Normandy, Patton unveiled his doctrine with spectacular results. After higher command stopped him in late August and the Germans blocked his path through Metz, he had to revert to that which he tried to avoid: methodical battle. Still, in battles such as Arracourt, his combined arms practices soundly defeated German tank-heavy counterattacks honed on the Russian front.[231] Tank and infantry teams blunted the attacks. Instead of Soviet massed artillery, the Germans faced quick, agile, and accurate American artillery fire. When the fog lifted, XIX TAC air pounced.[232] Finally, Wood's 4th Armored Division's spectacular counterattacks finished off the enemy.

In the counterattack to Bastogne, Patton's Third Army raced north, reorganizing on the move, but always careful to fight as combined arms teams. Units facing east were turned north along the designated routes as soon as they were ready. As they reached the new front oriented on Bastogne, armor, infantry, and artillery battalions were balanced and combined on the fly under new combat commands. Deputy G-3 Paul Harkins wrote, "It was absolutely fantastic, and when we got all straightened out, in two or three days, and the divisions started coming up and taking over and absorbing these little Task Forces. They, the Task Forces, really held the enemy off while the divisions moved up."[233]

The effect of Patton's well-thought-out and rehearsed combined arms operations was electric. A prisoner of war captured along the Saar revealed the common dread among the Germans for Patton's Third Army: "After artillery barrages, which lasted for hours, Americans attacked with tanks and infantry, so we always had to retreat. When he doesn't succeed to pierce our lines with tanks and infantry, he is using his fighter-bombers which we fear very much, and many of our horses and vehicles were hit by these planes."[234] Another captured letter read, "The only thing we have now is the music of American artillery, mud, mire, bad weather, hunger, and thirst."[235] The effect was by design, refined, practiced, and drawn from Patton's long study of combined arms.

Napoleon once observed, "Infantry, cavalry, and artillery are nothing without each other."[236] Patton agreed. He meticulously refined combined arms formations to form columns under responsive tactical air support to be mobile, agile, and hostile. Joined with his vision—his *coup d'oeil*—they became a devastating tool for creating and exploiting chaos. Yet these alone were not enough to achieve decision. Maintaining unbroken continuity in operations, rapidly seizing fleeting opportunities, and beating the enemy to the punch required several additional major departures from official Army doctrine, this time in the realm of command and control.

COMMAND AND CONTROL | 4

> We've been given a wet ball on a muddy field.
> Watch us run with it.
> —Terry Allen, 1st Infantry Division

Patton had a problem. Army doctrine demanded detailed orders and top-down command and control to synchronize all supporting arms with the infantry. *Field Service Regulations 1923* stated: "Distribution of the infantry in depth and in width requires a corresponding width and depth in the general distribution of the means of support."[1] This harmonization constrained operations to meet preconceived plans through pauses after battles to reorganize, plan, and prepare with the inherent unfortunate forfeiture of unanticipated opportunities. Pauses to plan in detail allowed the enemy time to adjust and reinforce weak spots before they could be exploited. Official command and control procedures therefore resulted in temporally sequenced battles—not the kind of operations Patton desired. He needed a better way to execute command and control if he was going to sustain a campaign of serial shocks.

As early as the futile Punitive Expedition in Mexico, Patton recorded his ruminations on the effect of pausing to organize. During practices he noted: "Lack of aggressive enterprise on the part of advance guards, i.e., men would frequently dismount on the mere report of the enemy's presence."[2] In squadron movements he observed: "Lack of offensive spirit on the part of advance guards; these frequently took up defensive positions dismounted, before they had cleared the situation."[3] Such pauses at the first hint of uncertainty, the young lieutenant believed, ceded initiative to the enemy and allowed Pancho Villa and his men to escape.

Patton expanded his thoughts during the Great War. In his tank doctrine he wrote, "When the final objective has been consolidated they must push on at *own initiative* and *seek every opportunity to become pursuit cavalry* [emphasis added]."[4] Changes in organization could enable initiative. In his "Memorandum on Plan for the Use of Tanks," which he sent to

I Corps prior to the Meuse-Argonne offensive, Patton recommended a radical change: one wave of tanks to assist the infantry in breaking the enemy lines, a second to pass through and achieve deep penetration, and a *third* to seize any possibilities for exploitation.[5] Because opportunities rarely arose according to plan, Patton trained and prepared his men to recognize and seize opportunities whenever they emerged.

To instill initiative in his subordinates, Patton practiced it in garrison and in the field. For example, he encouraged and accepted unsolicited recommendations from his soldiers for improvements, such as the suggestion from a Tank Corps private for the inclusion of a "repair tank" trailing each company to enable rapid front-line repairs. As Dennis Showalter wrote, "That the idea came from the ranks, in passing, was not unusual. Patton, recognizing that he had not ever taken a tank into combat himself, began going beyond the old Army caste system by encouraging suggestions from subordinates who had."[6] Moreover, Patton wanted to teach his men to use their imaginations, try things, and not be afraid. In peacetime he instructed his officers, "Don't just sit and think, or just think. There is always something to do. For example, read about war."[7] As with discipline, he instilled habits of initiative in garrison so as to be executed in combat.

Experience convinced Patton that no one could plan in advance for all the chance events that occurred in combat. He described his first battle in World War I as "a great state of perplexity."[8] Smoke and broken terrain obscured the tanks and infantry. He noted, "I could not see my right battalion so went to look for it."[9] One of his messengers later remembered, "It looked as if there were at least six different wars going on instead of one."[10] Tanks broke down, supporting troops refused to move, others went in the wrong direction, and the line fell into disarray. In the literal fog of war, only discipline maintained cohesion and only initiative moved the attack forward. Patton beseeched his tankers: "Your last conscientious effort must be to regain your formation and push on and ever on until there are no more Huns before you and the smiling vineyards of the RHINE open to your eyes."[11] Lieutenant Julian K. Morrison recollected, "His favorite message to his officers was 'Go forward, go forward. If your tank breaks down go forward with the infantry.'"[12]

Study after the war convinced Patton that subordinate initiative was the key to the German *Stosstrupp* tactics in which patrols probed for weak spots to exploit in the Allied lines. Higher headquarters relied on the initiative of low-level leaders to guide the main attack. The Germans provided their shock troops freedom of action through *Auftragstaktik* (mission tactics) in which commanders gave subordinates missions and allowed them to determine how best to carry them out. Patton appreciated this German tradition of subordinate initiative.[13] He would make it a rule: "Never tell people how to do things. Tell them what to do and they will surprise you with their ingenuity."[14] In January 1943 he took issue with the firing of his friend General Jimmy Doolittle in North Africa: "Ike and friends not only told him what do but how to do it."[15] A few months later he instructed his officers, "Plans telling the next lower echelon of command how to do a thing are wrong. They produce confusion and lack of confidence."[16] In England, he ended an instruction, "In this letter, as in those preceding it, I am not laying down inflexible rules. I am simply giving you my ideas. I must and do trust to your military experience, courage, and loyalty to make these ideas tangible."[17] These expressions favoring subordinate initiative, however, conflicted with U.S. Army doctrine on command and control.

Field Service Regulations 1923 only permitted subordinate freedom of action under very specific circumstances: "When the transmission of orders involves a considerable period of time during which the situation may change, detailed instruction[s] are avoided."[18] A full reading of the regulations made it clear that this exception only applied *within* the frontline infantry. All supporting arms—including tanks—had to be carefully planned and controlled. Doctrine instructed, "It is the task of higher commanders to coordinate and direct the action of each arm with a view to the most efficient exploitation of its powers and their adaptation to the ends sought. The coordinating principle which underlies the employment of the combined arms is that the mission of the infantry is the general mission of the entire force."[19] To support this mission, tankers required comprehensive planning and top-down control.

The Army school system fixed in its officers routines for writing detailed plans and the careful execution of command and control. Most lessons were highly scripted, with students expected to find schoolhouse-approved solutions to classroom problems. As Barbara Tuchman noted of the General Service School: "What Leavenworth taught was 'solution of the problem' based on statement of mission, analysis of the enemy, choices of action, solution, decision and plan."[20] To graduate, students had to demonstrate not only mastery of doctrine but conformity to the "school solution."

Patton chafed under such a system. In 1919 at Camp Meade, Ike recalled how Patton secured classroom battle problems from the School of the Line at Fort Leavenworth and said, "Let's you and I solve these together."[21] They compared his new tank tactics with the school solutions. Drawing on experience, Patton would add the kind of unexpected, chance occurrences encountered in war to the problems. Ike recalled, "Every mistake we made, every correction, every scrap of information about the exploitation of terrain was added to the World War I lessons."[22] He added, "These were the beginnings of a comprehensive tank doctrine that in George Patton's case would make him a legend."[23] Patton's writings reveal a growing uneasiness with doctrine that tried to force circumstance to conform to plans.[24] He noted, "[General Joseph] Hooker's plan at Chancellorsville was masterly, its execution cost him the battle. The converse was true [with Napoleon] at Marengo."[25] Contrary to doctrine, Patton came to emphasize execution rather than plans, and execution meant modifying command and control.

Scouring foreign military developments in command theory, Patton came across Hans von Seeckt's 1923 Army Regulation 487, *Leadership and Battle with Combined Arms*, and its emphasis on "the decentralization of operations and the use of judgment and initiative by battlefield leaders."[26] He read American attaché Captain Arthur Conger's report on a German army two-day field exercise in 1922 that recounted how they "pushed forward and continued to push forward" regardless of threats and that "it was proved to be done by intent."[27] Through *Auftragstaktik* a commander defined the mission, but subordinates developed the situation. Patton recognized this as a continuation of Frederick the Great, Helmuth von Moltke, and Alfred von Schlieffen, who all argued that adjustments after the first shot were more important than plans made before the battle.[28]

By 1926 Patton's thoughts had crystalized. Seven years after they worked planning exercises together, he wrote to Eisenhower, "The victor in the next war will depend on EXECUTION not PLANS and the execution will depend on some means of making the infantry move under fire."[29] His opinion only got stronger. After Tunisia, Patton wrote: "It cannot be too strongly emphasized that in importance the issuance of an order in comparison with seeing that it is executed is only 5%."³⁰ Plans set the purpose of operations, but flexible command and control allowed his subordinates to get there.

The Army schoolhouses stressed planning to bring order out of chaos; Patton accepted chaos as an integral part of battle. As Rick Atkinson noted: "Unlike many, he was comfortable with ambiguity; that trait would inform his generalship."³¹ Patton agreed with Clausewitz, who said: "Since all information and assumptions are open to doubt, and with chance at work everywhere, the commander continually finds that things are not as he expected. This is bound to influence his plans, or at least the assumptions underlying them."³² In 1927 Patton delivered a lecture, "Why Men Fight," that debuted what would become one of his maxims: "Battle is an orgy of disorder."³³ In somewhat stilted terms he explained, "The sudden change from accustomed order to utter disorder—to chaos, but emphasizes the folly of schooling to precision and obedience where only fierceness and habituated disorder are useful."³⁴ From chaos emerged opportunities that only *Auftragstaktik* could exploit.

George C. Marshall recalled attempting to challenge Army dogmatism when, as the new assistant commandant of the Infantry School in 1927, he decreed, "Any student's solution of a problem that ran radically counter to the approved school solution, and yet showed independent creative thinking, would be published to the class."³⁵ Yet this encouragement *did not* extend above the infantry regiment level. The hundreds of students and roughly eighty instructors Marshall influenced at the school were taught that operations had to be guided by detailed plans and top-down command and control. The curriculum had consequences. As Carlo D'Este explained: "Schooled in the rigid doctrines of Fort Benning's Infantry School, Bradley was uncomfortable with those who displayed independence and dash, preferring instead the company of more conservative infantrymen who thought in like terms."³⁶ Men such as Bradley went on to the War College for further molding to the homogeneous standards before advancing to high command.³⁷

In 1930 the War Department codified the standards for strict command and control in the *Manual for Commanders of Large Units (Provisional), Volume I (Operations),* drawn largely from French methods of guiding divisions, corps, and armies in "methodical battle."³⁸ As Eugenia Kiesling explained, the French doctrine stipulated "rigidly centralized control" in which infantry would halt for roughly thirty minutes after each 1,500-meter advance to allow artillery to readjust and then halt for even longer periods after a total advance of four to five kilometers.[39] This doctrine of controlled "methodical battle" was designed "to ensure perfectly sequenced commitment of units."[40]

Methodical battle was, in James Corum's words, "essentially a tactical system frozen in time somewhere between Verdun and the autumn offensive of 1918. . . . Battles must be fought by plan, there is little consideration for the 'fog of war,' and individual initiative is not encouraged."[41] While *Field Service Regulations 1923* allowed for initiative in infantry regiments and below, it specified: "Complicated maneuvers are impracticable; efficient leadership and a determination to win by simple and direct methods must be depended upon for success."[42] The new *Manual for Commanders of Large Units* directed commanders to ensure detailed planning and strict coordination of all the arms supporting the infantry. It unequivocally stated: "Orders must be carried out. . . . When a commander has made a decision, he must carry it out and allow no difficulty to stop him."[43]

Patton had other ideas. In his graduate thesis at the War College in 1932, he wrote: "Battle is an orgy of organized disorder. The worst possible preparation for such a situation is one of meticulous order."[44] Classroom battle problems and scripted field exercises that minimized the fog of war taught methods likely to break down in the chaos of battle. The ever-increasing capabilities of mechanized weapons would only magnify uncertainty. Patton concluded: "The present method of controlling units in action depends on detailed voluminous orders and constant communication. . . . To attempt to continue such a system in a war of movement, even if fought with armies as now organized, is doomed to failure."[45]

Doctrine built upon the assumption that the next war would be like the last one. "However," Patton countered, "within the last few years certain signs have appeared which indicate that the tide has turned and that some thought will henceforth be given to fighting wars of maneuver."[46] Observing 1st Cavalry Division maneuvers at Fort Bliss, Texas, in 1929, he identified inadequacies in methodical battle in practice. Umpires routinely punished commanders whenever they maneuvered units beyond the range of radio or wire communications, reasoning that they could not control their subordinates. Exasperated, Patton forwarded to the chief of cavalry: "So far as I can see control and mobility are inimical. We should admit this and . . .

let the two principal elements work independently."⁴⁷ This was a radical and unacceptable proposition in Army circles, but one that indicated the further evolution of Patton's thoughts.

Patton fully realized the value of planning but saw greater importance in granting subordinates freedom to seize fleeting opportunities as they appeared in the chaos of battle. Clausewitz identified two qualities necessary to cope with the "relentless struggle with the unforeseen": the intellect to comprehend and the courage to act.⁴⁸ Patton would use motivation to make certain his men used their initiative. "The secret," he wrote, "lies in the inspiring spirit which lifted weary, footsore men out of themselves and made them march, forgetful of agony, as did Messina's [sic] division after Rivoli and Jackson's at Winchester."⁴⁹ His deliberately constructed mask of command thus served as a vital adjunct to his reliance on subordinate initiative.

In 1935 Patton umpired maneuvers in Hawaii. Command and control was again an issue. He noted, "The operation was conducted as a map problem because our officers are familiar with them, not as a war problem because our officers are not familiar with maneuvers."⁵⁰ He faulted headquarters for its "rigid adherence to methods of procedure current in the World War and applicable, if at all, only to situations involving very large bodies of troops in semi-stabilized operations."⁵¹ Obeying doctrine, officers and umpires repeatedly tried to make the battle fit their plans.

Patton tried to instill initiative in his men by encouraging boldness—a term that linked action to morale. In the 3rd Cavalry Regiment in 1938, he directed that careful planning and top-down control were secondary to his "Golden Rule of War. Speed-Simplicity-Boldness."⁵² He stressed, "BOLDNESS. . . . Speed is more important than the lives at the point. THE ENEMY IS AS IGNORANT AS YOU. . . . BE BOLD. . . . YOU ARE NOT BEATEN UNTIL YOU ADMIT IT, Hence DON'T."⁵³

German success in Poland seemed to prove these maxims. The Military Intelligence Division reported that German columns "*avoided combat* and were *pushed forward as far and as rapidly as possible*, breaking up enemy formations, disrupting his communication, and destroying his establishments and reserve depots of materiel and personnel [emphasis in original]."⁵⁴ German mission tactics and subordinate initiative made the rapid advance possible. Patton wanted the same and instructed his regiment: "As soon as horse cavalry hits opposition contain it in front with minimum force, and get around its flanks. THIS OPERATION MUST BE AUTOMATIC FOR ALL UNITS FROM PLATOON UP."[55]

As the Germans rampaged across Europe, the U.S. Army finally began division, corps, and army level field exercises. As an umpire during maneuvers in Louisiana in May 1940, Patton complained of pauses to facilitate command and control as creating inviting targets for air and artillery. He described an attempted pursuit by IV Corps on 15 May in which planning and preparation caused a three-hour delay in execution. He called for greater attention to the "time factor" in operations. "It also shows," Patton wrote, "that in situations which are somewhat vague and where rapidity of movement is of paramount importance, it will frequently be desirable to employ mission type orders, leaving details to the subordinate commander."[56] His call was not answered. In subsequent maneuvers the Armored Force found itself under men such as Lieutenant General Ben Lear, whom Christopher Gabel described as "a meticulous and methodical soldier, [who] was not conspicuously suited to the conduct of dashing, highly mobile operations."[57] Fourth Corps area commander General Stanley Embrick told his officers, "The maneuvers are not intended as a competitive test of troops or individual commanders."[58] Careful command and control remained the order of the day.

Army leaders felt pressure to demonstrate an ability to stop the kind of massed panzer attacks that the public saw playing on newsreels across the country. McNair, the champion of relatively cheap antitank guns, instructed his two thousand carefully selected umpires, "We are definitely out to see . . . if and how we can crush a modern tank offensive."[59] However, left to his own devices in command of the 2nd Armored Division, Patton proved too quick and agile for antitank defenses. His methods contrasted starkly with those of his doctrinaire peers. During the Tennessee Maneuvers, Secretary of War Stimson observed, "Even at this preliminary presentation of the plans of the respective commanders, I was impressed with the vigor and dash of Patton's plan as compared with the ultra caution and even timidity of the passive defense contemplated by [Seventh Corps commander Frederick H.] Smith."[60] McNair was not pleased, however, and told his umpires before corps exercises in Louisiana, "I want armor used properly in these maneuvers, and Patton must not be allowed to run all over the countryside as he did in the Tennessee Maneuvers."[61] Patton countered with a request:

"I believe it desirable that a member of the Armored Force with considerable rank be present on the umpire staff group whenever Armored Divisions are employed."[62] This request went ignored.

Though placed under a plodding corps commander in Louisiana, Patton probed for weak spots in the enemy lines and oriented his force accordingly, but umpires interpreted these acts as counter to doctrine's dictate: "Command and leadership are inseparable. . . . The commander must be the controlling head."[63] His multiple probes looked like a lack of focus. Doctrine also discouraged sub-unit initiative: "Willingness to accept responsibility must not manifest itself in a disregard of orders on the basis of a mere probability of having a better knowledge of the situation than the higher commander."[64] Patton disagreed.

Patton was in a tough spot: desirous of command in the likely new war, he had to temper his desire to fight his way with the need to find favor with his superiors. With umpires and rule books denying him the ability to find and exploit weak spots, he opted to sweep in mass around the enemy's flanks. Opposing commanders routinely assumed he would take pauses to craft detailed plans and execute top-down command and control, but instead he rapidly seized opportunities and objectives and frequently concluded the maneuvers in about half the expected time.

Some were not amused. McNair wanted free-flowing, unscripted exercise battles but insisted on personally supervising the writing of the umpire manuals.[65] As a sponsor of antitank gun development, he oversaw tank-antitank combat rules perceived as unfair by the armor advocates.[66] Guns as small as .50-caliber machine guns could destroy tanks, but tanks could only destroy antitank guns by physically overrunning their positions. The rules thus compelled tank units into direct assaults. McNair plainly wished to see his economical counter to panzer armies proven in the field.[67]

Umpires criticized Patton for not following the spirit of the rules. His units flowed too freely; he did not appear to exert a firm hand. His deliberate flexibility looked like poor staff work, code for "lack of command and control." His probes for weak spots on multiple routes were interpreted as "too many piecemeal attacks."[68] McNair denounced Patton's methods as "no way to fight a war."[69] In the final exercise, an umpire named Major Harrison critiqued that if Patton had "been faced with a more aggressive and energetic enemy, the wide dispersal of his troops in a double envelopment . . . might have subjected him to defeat in detail."[70] This particularly maddening way of saying "if things had gone differently, he might have lost" failed to take into account that if things had gone differently, Patton could have—and *would* have—adjusted. Traditionalists could not comprehend that he planned to adjust to changes in conditions on the fly. Yet the critics empowered McNair to say of Patton that division command was "probably his ceiling."[71] Marshall received that message and determined not to give Patton more than an army.

Patton knew the great maneuvers were designed to field-test soldiers, equipment, and doctrine, but he wanted something more. He copied and underscored lines from von Seeckt's one-hundred-twenty-page "Observations of the Chief of the Army: Direction of the German Army Training in 1925": "The purpose of exercises and maneuvers is to train the troops and to practice leadership in the field. The idea is to apply in the terrain that which has been learned regarding tactics and to transform the will of the leader into the action of the troops."[72] The means for transmitting the commander's will—"detailed orders and strict control" or "*Auftragstaktik* and subordinate initiative"—was the point of contention between Patton and the umpires. Patton also underlined von Seeckt's argument that subordinate leaders "must besides wake up and occupy their imagination and provoke their own opinion and independent action."[73] He defiantly told his front-line leaders: "Many times the fate of the whole battle, the fate of your Division, the fate of the Nation may depend on your courage, your intelligence, and your initiative."[74]

In a letter to Frank Parker, Patton offered a most cogent metaphor to describe his approach to command and control: "When you are using a saber or a bayonet, you can to a degree control (coordinate) the weapon during the lunge. When you are throwing hand grenades, you can only give them initial impetus and direction. You cannot control (coordinate) these missiles during flight. Armored divisions are of the nature of such missiles."[75] His choice of words was telling: the saber and bayonet were traditional metaphors for the cavalry and infantry. Grenades, on the other hand, suggested both modernity and destructive power. The old weapons were always in hand; the newer ones let loose in the throw. As Patton told Parker, "It is nonetheless noteworthy that in every operation in which this division took part, the several elements (grenades) composing it arrived at the place intended at the time desired."⁷⁶ By training his units to use initiative and devising command and control to provide "impetus and direction," Patton aimed his columns and relied on their initiative to provide forward momentum toward the points he envisioned as most likely to inflict shock upon the enemy.

On 8 July 1941 Patton gathered his division to review lessons learned and offer corrective instruction. He complained that his men had developed "the student complex," stating, "We have a tendency to wait instructions rather than proceed on our own initiative."⁷⁷ Rather than surrender to traditionalist practices of deliberately planned and controlled concentrated blow or successive efforts, he explained his philosophy:

> If the band played a piece first with the piccolo, then with the brass horn, then with the clarinet, and then with the trumpet, there would be a hell of a lot of noise but no music. To get harmony in music each instrument must support the others. To get harmony in battle, each weapon must support the other. Team play wins. You musicians of Mars *must not wait for the bandleader to signal you* . . . You must each *of your own volition* see to it that you come into this concert at the proper place and at the proper time [emphasis added].⁷⁸

Patton modified command and staff procedures to develop, enable, and exploit the initiative of his "musicians of Mars." During the construction of the Desert Training Center in 1942, he told his staff, "I believe the only way to start things is to start, so next week we start. I think we shall just issue canned rations and water, and let nature take its course, taking careful note as to the different methods used by different individuals."⁷⁹ Later, while watching the ships assigned to carry him to Morocco load 700,000 items—including 38 million pounds of clothing and equipment, 22 million pounds of food, and 10 million gallons of gasoline—Patton found a perfect model of his ideal command and control. He asked a quartermaster how they were coming along, and the captain replied, "I don't know, but my trucks are getting on all right."⁸⁰ Patton wrote, "That is the answer; if everyone does his part, these seemingly impossible tasks get done."⁸¹ Everything need not be carefully controlled, just given proper "impetus and direction." Even someone as able as Lucian Truscott needed time to understand. In Morocco, he wrote: "One of the first lessons that battle impresses upon one is that no matter how large the force engaged, every battle is made up of small actions by individuals and small units."[82] If each man used his initiative and pushed on in accordance with the commander's intent, the army would achieve the momentum needed to seize opportunities at the moment they appeared. This philosophy propelled the seemingly impossible breakout from Normandy and the counterattack into the Bulge.

Patton's style of command and control inherently decreased the amount of time required for planning, increased simplicity in orders, and enabled flexibility to grasp opportunity. It *expected* rapid adjustment to changing conditions, something Patton identified as essential in war. In Sicily, he explained: "Perhaps when Napoleon said, *'Je m'engage et puis je vois* [I start the fight and then I see],' he was right."[83] When XII Corps took Bitburg on 26 February 1945, Patton repeated, "The current operation for the encirclement of Trier is the result of that ability to change plans to meet opportunities developed by combat or as Napoleon said, 'I attack then I look.'"[84] Unlike traditionalists who fought according to their plans, Patton fought according to the situation.

To enact his style of command and control, Patton had to attune his staff to his way of war. As early as 1919 he studied and prioritized the characteristics desired in an effective staff: a "personal knowledge of troops, learned by actual command"; "loyalty to the chief they serve"; tact; dependability to "stick absolutely to the facts"; and the effort to "constantly visit the troops to keep in first hand touch with the situation."[85] He remained remarkable steady in these views. Like Napoleon, Patton trained his staff (and commanders) to act in accordance to his ability to quickly see and make sense of the battlefield.[86] He filled his staff with men he trusted and deemed capable to carry out his vision.[87] Throughout the war he retained key men—Geoffrey Keyes, Hugh Gaffey, Hobart "Hap" Gay, Oscar Koch, Kent Lambert, Halley Maddox, and Walter "Maud" Muller—who stayed with him for years.[88] When the "slapping incidents" put his career in jeopardy, he told them, "If you can find a better job, get it and I will help you all I can. You may be backing the wrong horse or hitched your wagon to the wrong star."[89] No one asked to leave.

Patton thoroughly schooled his staff in his way of war. They understood him when he preached: "A good solution applied with vigor *now* is better than a perfect solution ten minutes late. IN CASE OF DOUBT,

ATTACK!"⁹⁰ They also understood his distinction between *haste* and *speed*. "Haste exists when troops are committed without proper reconnaissance, without the arrangement for proper supporting fire, and before every available man has been brought up," he explained. "Speed is acquired by making the necessary reconnaissance, providing the proper artillery and other tactical support, including air support, bringing up every man, and then launching the attack with a predetermined plan so that the time under fire will be reduced to the minimum."⁹¹ His staff, like their boss, believed that "time is more important than coordination."⁹² He explained, "In fact, it is my opinion that coordination is a very much-misused word and its accomplishment difficult."⁹³ His staff turned these thoughts into action.

Patton taught his staff: "There is no approved solution to any tactical situation. There is only one tactical principle which is not subject to change. It is: 'To so use the means at hand to inflict the maximum amount of wounds, death and destruction on the enemy in minimum of time.'"⁹⁴ He wanted simplicity in all orders and plans and wrote to his wife, "All war is simple and we err by allowing its complexities to divert our minds from the few basic truths which fill it."⁹⁵ He often complained that SHAEF's plans were "too complicated."⁹⁶ In 1927 Patton wrote that "one of the chief defects in staff work arises from the fact most recent graduates from the different schools are over impressed with formularism. Their chief concern is to write an order in the nature of an approved solution without regard to the man who must execute it and without considering the [fact] that successful combat depends on energetic and timely execution rather than on wordy paragraphs."⁹⁷ The remedy was to require his staff to spend considerable time at the front.

Patton's first "Letter of Instruction" to Third Army preached that proper command was 10 percent planning and 90 percent execution.⁹⁸ He thus told his staff to produce plans that were "simple and flexible . . . a datum plane from which you build as necessity directs or opportunity offers."⁹⁹ Orders provided direction; leadership and initiative supplied the impetus, "so that if during combat communication breaks down, each Commander can and must so act as to obtain the general objective."¹⁰⁰

Third Army's staff developed an unusually close working relationship with General Weyland and his XIX Tactical Air Command planners. In some sense it was almost a merger. In one telling episode, during a meeting in late 1944 Eisenhower asked his tactical air commanders if anyone could use strategic bombers "to get the ground forces rolling."[101] Encouraged by Patton to "commit the Third Army in my name anytime you want to," Weyland spoke up. "I've got an army that will fight," he said. "If I can get the assistance of all the strategic air—British, American, and some additional help—I will guarantee to cut the Third Army right through the Siegfried line and up to the Rhine River, then cross the Rhine River and slice up there and surround the main part of the German forces. And I think the war will be over."[102] Ike let out a laugh then asked General Carl Spaatz for his thoughts. He agreed to give Weyland a try and when informed of this, Patton was delighted. Weyland's initiative got Spaatz, General Hoyt Vandenburg, and General James "Jimmy" Doolittle to provide "500 to 600 medium bombers, 1,200 to 1,500 heavy bombers supported by fighter bombers, and 600 to 1,000 Royal Air Force bombers" for three to four days beginning on 19 December on the Siegfried Line.[103] Unfortunately, the German assault against First Army aborted this promising operation.

Patton's faith in his staff to act quickly and in accordance with his vision gave him the confidence that he could adjust to changing conditions after an operation was under way. In the Eifel in February 1945, he explained to correspondents, "I think we are going to have to play this part of the war by ear. If we can get a breakthrough, we will be all right."[104] Here was classic Patton: plan to be flexible, create chaos, look for opportunities, and, through simplified staff procedures and subordinate initiative, seize and exploit those opportunities to produce shocks faster than the enemy could react. His rapid, simple, and agile command and control methods made it possible. He presciently wrote, "I am going to be an awful irritation to the military historians, because I do things by sixth sense. They won't understand."[105] Neither did his peers.

Bradley, for one, interpreted Patton's methods as poor planning and wrote, "He was not much concerned with details—logistics were and would remain a mystery to him, and he improvised war plans as he went along—but if you wanted an objective or a favorable headline, Patton was clearly the man for it."[106] All his life Patton kept and reviewed a manual issued to him as a student major in the War College, Colonel O. L. Spaulding Jr.'s *Studies in Applied History*. Spaulding wrote, "It will be evident that as soon as warfare began to take any definite form a leader began to want assistants, to take care of details."¹⁰⁷ Spaulding identified organization and administration of troops, collection of information, planning and conduct of combat operations, and supply as staff functions. Patton agreed that details in these areas should be left to the staff, but he did not ignore them.

After Sicily, Eisenhower stunned Patton by telling him, "You are a great leader but a poor planner."¹⁰⁸ He was echoing Bradley's judgment: "George is spectacular. Does not like drudgery. And planning is drudgery."¹⁰⁹ A more dispassionate review came from Eisenhower's official liaison to Patton's headquarters, Major General John P. Lucas: "George's plans were well drawn up and seemed very complete. He strives to give the impression of doing things in an impulsive and 'on the spur of the moment' manner but in back of all of his actions in war is very careful staff planning and much thought."¹¹⁰ When Ike told Patton he chose Bradley "to form a new Army and plan" the invasion into France, Patton recalled, "I told him I was a pretty good planner but he said I did not like to do it—in that, it seems I am like him, or so he said (compliment?)."¹¹¹ The timing of Ike's comments indicated that he had decided to promote Bradley over Patton independent of the slapping incidents.

In his second memoir nearly four decades after the war, Bradley wrote, "As I have stated often, Patton gave little or no consideration to logistics."¹¹² Historians have long feasted on such opinion. Rick Atkinson commented: "Sloppy loading in Norfolk, and Patton's chronic neglect of logistics—'Let's do it and think about it afterwards,' in his chief engineer's tart phrase—now [in Morocco] cost him dearly."¹¹³ Judged from the evidence of one day into the war, Atkinson's criticism seems premature, unfair, and inaccurate.¹¹⁴ The loss of nearly half of the obsolete landing boats in the first assault was more costly than any errors in loading. Poor inter-service coordination by the Navy—the arbiters of what gets loaded and unloaded first—hurt far more than any lack of logistics. Patton planned to have his three columns converge on Casablanca in seventy-two hours; they did so on schedule.

In his biography of Patton, Stanley Hirshson repeated a curious criticism of Patton in Tunisia by II Corps' artillery executive officer Barksdale Hamlett: "I don't think he was very sound logistically in Africa. He pushed beyond the logistic capability."¹¹⁵ Here again, this complaint makes little sense: logistics were not a problem for Patton in Tunisia. Eisenhower had secured a special delivery of 5,400 trucks and proudly noted that his engineers increased the delivery capacity of the French North African rail line from 900 tons to 3,000 tons of supplies daily.[116] When he assumed II Corps command, Martin Blumenson noted, Patton "expedited the arrival of new equipment, clothing, and mail. He improved living conditions by insisting on better food and well-cooked meals."[117] Supply in II Corps worked so well that Bradley reported, "We not only exceeded the British estimates, we doubled them."[118] As Ladislas Farago pointed out, "In the end, II Corps managed to put in 92,000 troops, and supply them rather liberally throughout the offensive, where the British estimate assumed only 38,000 could be sustained."[119] Patton's operations never ventured beyond his trains because he was ordered not to go so far as to interfere with Montgomery's advance, and so he never "pushed beyond the logistic capability." In Africa, it may well be said, Patton's logistics were more than sound; they were exemplary.

Bradley misperceived the methods of Patton's staff. He wrote that unlike First and Ninth Armies, Patton's Third Army staff "lacked outstanding individual performers" and thought "their performance could be most charitably described as something less than perfect."[120] Bradley recognized Patton's success but not his means. Success in war is impossible without good logistics, and good logistics are impossible without good staff work. Years later General Brenton G. Wallace remembered, "In all my experience I have never worked on a Staff that could compare to that of the Third U.S. Army. . . . Everything was practical and for a purpose. The 'Old Man' hated show and sham. He was interested in one thing only—efficiency; and his spirit permeated the whole organization. You had the feeling that Third Army was going in only one direction—forward."[121] In fact, throughout their careers the members of Patton's staff commonly testified to its special effectiveness.

In late October 1943 Patton met with Ike's chief of staff, General Walter Bedell "Beetle" Smith, who had recently returned from Washington.[122] "He said," Patton noted, "he had told General Marshall that I am the greatest assault general in the world and should lead the attack. General Marshall agreed but said, 'I don't trust his staff.' Smith said, 'Well, they have always succeeded.' General Marshall replied, 'I have been told that in Sicily the supply was not good. I have my own means of knowing.'"[123] Patton immediately—and probably quite correctly—suspected Bradley of passing erroneous impressions (Bradley had visited Marshall earlier on his way to England to take command). "I told Beedle," Patton wrote, "that I would have to stick to my staff as they had stuck to me and that if I fell due to them, it would be too bad."[124] Logistics never constrained Patton's operations in Sicily. His remarkable dash to Palermo and again to Messina would not have been possible without solid logistical support by model staff work. Their performance in Sicily is all the more remarkable considering he did not have a port for supply *until* he took Palermo.

When Third Army's drive across France stalled for lack of gasoline, many historians accepted it as irrefutable evidence of poor logistical planning by Patton and his staff. The historians are mistaken. Beginning 19 May, Third Army chief of supply Colonel Walter "Maud" Muller conducted extensive logistical planning in a series of supply conferences with higher headquarters. Patton's diary indicates his own meetings with Ike's logistics chief, Army Service Forces (formerly known as Services of Supply) commander Lieutenant General J. C. H. Lee. Yet Patton had doubts about Lee and his promises: "What he is doing is putting on a tactical show when he actually does not know the level of supplies in his own SOS. It is very unfortunate that he both commands the SOS and acts as Deputy Theater Commander. He is good for neither."[125] On 2 June Lee promised Muller "supplies on the Continent would be normal after D+41, and that it would be their [SHAEF's] responsibility to maintain supplies without further action on the part of Third U.S. Army."[126] As late as 22 August—while Patton was racing across France—Lieutenant General Brehon B. Somervell, commander of Army Service Forces in charge of the entire Army's logistics, and Under Secretary of War Robert P. Patterson visited Patton and approved Third Army's "supply plan for future combat operations" to ensure rail transportation, "minimum daily tonnages for supply and maintenance" of five thousand long tons per day, and additional truck companies for Third Army.[127] Somervell announced Patton "has no worry about supply."[128] This was at the time when Patton's plans focused on a drive through Metz and into Germany.

SHAEF simply failed to provide the promised support. From the start, the numbered armies had to use organic transportation assets to pull supplies from the depots in Normandy. Once the breakout was under way, this became a burden. Relatively junior officers tried to rectify the problem by forming the ad hoc Red Ball Express, an indication of the lack of effective higher-level usage of assets. Beginning 10 August, however, a large portion of the Red Ball shipping of fuel had to be diverted to carry ammunition to First Army to make up for miscalculated allocations.[129] Engineers did a remarkable job in repairing rail systems out of Normandy, but, as the 12th Army Group G-4 section reported, the communication zone failed to push forward required tonnage by rail due to "operational reasons such as organizational problems."[130] Similar lack of effort and miscalculation of air transport also led to a failure to maximize the push of supplies.

When SHAEF's diversion of trucks and supplies upset Patton's arrangements and crippled Third Army, his staff proved brilliant in their efforts to rectify their circumstances. In Carlo D'Este's words: "Muller and his supply officers resembled Ali Baba and the Forty Thieves. They became the masters at hijacking supplies and sending out raiding parties to relieve First Army supply dumps of whatever was not nailed down."[131] Patton quickly appointed a gasoline rationing board that increased reserve stocks of gasoline to 300,000 gallons.[132] Working with the operations staff to address critical artillery ammunition shortages—especially 8-inch howitzers—they used tanks, tank destroyers, and mortars in indirect fire modes. They employed captured ordnance at unprecedented levels: one mission in XX Corps' zone was fired with German 105-mm howitzers, Russian 76.2-mm guns, French 155-mm howitzers (captured from the Germans), and German 88-mm antitank guns.[133] In the last week of October 80 percent of the rounds fired by XX Corps were German. Captured food, gasoline, fuel cans, and even spark plugs were also used to make up for shortages.[134]

Third Army soldiers built railroads as far to the east as Nancy and then drove the trains.[135] They operated French factories, increasing productivity by 50 percent in everything from coal to dry cleaning.[136] They repaired tanks in the Gnome-Rhone engine works in Paris and used locally procured alcohol for antifreeze. By 8 November, despite receiving no supplies from higher headquarters, Third Army had amassed four days' worth of Class I rations and five days' worth of Class III petroleum supplies.[137] Only heavy artillery shells remained in critical shortage. It was an astonishing performance by any standards—and it was not happenstance. Facing Metz, John Nelson Rickard acknowledged, "Patton proved capable of a measure of detailed set-piece battle planning. . . . Throughout October he spent more time with

Gaffey, Gay, and the rest of his special staff minutely planning each portion of the maneuvers."[138]

SHAEF—not Patton—lacked foresight in logistical planning that hampered operations across the front with chronic shortages of artillery, ammunition, and infantrymen through the fall and winter. Patton's complaints indicated his attention to such matters. In early April 1944, after a dinner with Ike, Bradley, and other top leaders, he wrote, "I had quite a talk with them trying to justify an initial over-strength of 15%."[139] Forecasting manpower needs in France, Patton explained "normal loss from disease and accidents runs about 8%," losses on the first day of battle take time to replace, and "at the crucial point of the battle, usually the third or fourth day, there is a serious shortage."[140] By Patton's calculation, starting with 15 percent overstrength, and assuming 5 percent daily losses, would leave them only 1 percent understrength at the critical point of the fight. He complained, "I can't get anyone to realize this. That is because none of our topflight generals have ever fought."[141] Through autumn manpower shortages became acute, with infantrymen comprising 89 percent of all casualties, many to trench foot. Third Army commented, "Pentagon armchair strategists, from the advanced Ops of their fur-lined foxholes, had omnisciently decided that the war in the ETO [European theater of operations] would end in November. On the basis of the prescient thumb-sucking, troop shipments were drastically cut back."[142] As a remedy, Patton twice drafted 5 percent of all soldiers from his headquarters and support units for reassignment as infantrymen.

Boots that failed in poor weather compounded manpower shortages. Third Army explained: "From 8 November until the end of the month trench foot constituted a serious problem for the Army. . . . During this period 4,587 cases of trench foot were admitted to division clearing stations and it was estimated that 95 percent of the patients would be of no further value for combat duty during the winter months."[143] From 12 to 16 November, Third Army lost an average of 444 soldiers each day to trench foot. Some 46,000 troops throughout the theater were hospitalized. Patton raged, "The Germans have good boots. Why haven't we? Men unable to march cannot fight."[144] In fact, Eisenhower's quartermaster simply had not ordered new winter boots because he believed the war would end before they would be needed.[145] At the end of the month Patton complained, "The shortage of replacements for Third Army is this day, 9,000 and none in sight. I cannot see why Eisenhower could be caught short on both men and ammunition, because after all, these are the two elements with which wars are fought."[146]

Another mythic criticism of Patton, that he ignored higher command, first arose in Morocco. At his headquarters in Gibraltar, Eisenhower thought Patton "ominously silent," leaving some to openly speculate that Patton had deliberately dropped off the radio nets to avoid interference from his superiors.[147] Smith, in London, even reported that Patton was in trouble and withdrawing from the beach under a white flag. "That I do *not* believe," Eisenhower wired back. "Unless my opinion of Georgie is 100 percent wrong, he wouldn't re-embark anything, including himself."[148]

There *were* communication problems, but not with Patton. All communications went through the message center on Admiral H. Kent Hewitt's flagship, where twenty-six radiomen manned eleven receivers and three decoding and encoding machines.[149] They were swamped and fell hours behind. One crew of operators proved so incompetent that they were relieved. Another crew continuously relayed messages to Gibraltar in the wrong code. Some urgent messages were never properly marked and thus went unread. When operators decoded a French message describing preparations to meet the invasion at Casablanca, for example, the crew simply logged and filed it. Concussions from the guns knocked out radios on ships, and weather and distance knocked out radios on land. It all conspired to cut communication between Patton and the Navy, his subordinates, and Eisenhower.

Problematic communication led to tragedy in Sicily associated with Patton. In mid-May 1943 he completed plans for parachute drops by the 505th and 504th Parachute Regiments of the 82nd Airborne Division under Major General Matthew Ridgway. He warned the fleet and Seventh Army of possible friendly airborne operations between 2230 and 2400 hours on any of the first 6 days of Husky. During the initial assault drop on 9–10 July, Ridgway's 3,400 paratroopers were scattered from Ponte Olivo to points as far to the east as Noto in Montgomery's zone and were unable to concentrate. Patton decided to execute his preplanned reinforcement by bringing up 2,500 men of the 82nd Airborne Division to jump on the Farello airfield and radioed his commanders: "Notify all units, especially anti-aircraft, that parachutists 82nd Airborne Division will drop."[150] As evening fell he had second thoughts; that day Allied antiaircraft gunners had faced more than 450 Axis planes.[151] "Went to office at 2000," he recorded, "to see if we could stop the 82nd airborne lift, as enemy air attacks were heavy and inaccurate and army and navy anti-air was jumpy. Found we could not get contact by radio. Am terribly worried."[152] At 2240 hours on 11 July, 50 minutes after another Axis air raid, the first of the paratroopers jumped safely onto the Farello field. As the second flight approached, however, Allied antiaircraft guns opened up, shooting down 23 and damaging another 37 of the 144 American transport planes. Ten percent of Ridgway's paratroopers were killed or wounded, and the rest were badly disorganized.[153] The fratricide was clearly no one man's fault.

Prior to Husky, commanders in Algiers complained of unwieldy air support request procedures.[154] Air commanders refused to provide their naval counterparts with the flight paths to be used by the airborne and glider units.[155] Eisenhower saw the lack of coordination first hand at a meeting on 21 June, but he chose not to get involved.[156] He did agree to take 110 C-47s from Ridgway and give them to the British, leaving too few to deliver both regiments on D-day.[157] Ridgway then clashed with British air and naval commanders and later said, "I probably would have been sent home, or at least sternly rebuked, if General Patton had not articulated and wholeheartedly approved my actions."[158] Not until 6 July did Ridgway finally receive air routes for his initial assault. General Lucas recalled, "They were all disturbed as to the difficulty of getting this information to the troops who were already embarked."[159] Admiral Hewitt complained he put to sea without ever receiving the air plan.[160] As a result, a British naval captain recalled, "Naval ships and merchant ships would in all circumstances be free to open fire on multi-engined aircraft not recognized as friendly."[161] The failure to secure the needed inter-service coordination was simply above the Seventh Army commander's pay grade.

During his upbraiding of Patton on board the USS *Monrovia* off Sicily (unrelated to then-unrealized airborne fratricide), Eisenhower raised the communication issue. Ike's aide Harry Butcher recalled, "Ike spoke vigorously to Patton about the inadequacy of his reports of progress reaching headquarters at Malta. . . . When we left General Patton I thought he was angry. Ike had stepped on him hard."[162] Patton noted, "When I took him to my room to show him the situation, he was not much interested but began to compare the sparsity of my reports with the almost hourly news bulletins of the 8th Army. I have intercepts of many of them and they are both non-essential and imaginary in the majority of cases. Furthermore, they are not fighting, and we are."[163] Ike baffled Patton.

In his memoir, Omar Bradley wrote, "This meeting lasted only forty-five minutes, but I believe it was one of those turning points historians like to pinpoint. I think it marked a distinct cooling of the relationship between Ike and Patton, a sudden loss of faith by the commander in chief in his army commander."[164] But Ike's criticism was off the mark. Patton had indeed sent reports as required to his immediate commander, General Harold Alexander at 15th Army Group, not to Eisenhower, and Butcher reported Ike had received enough of these reports from Alexander to accurately describe Patton's situation while receiving only "numerous fragmentary reports" from Montgomery.[165] Lucas checked Patton's Seventh Army reports at SHAEF and said, "They seemed to me to be as complete as they could well be under the circumstances."[166] Naval historian Samuel Eliot Morison also reviewed the record and concluded that Ike's remarks were "without foundation."[167] Most damning, Butcher reported that while Patton was personally in the battle ashore at Gela, Ike and several of his staff "slipped down to a sandy beach for an hour in sea and sun."[168] It seems incredible that Ike was so anxious for reports as to justify a "loss of faith" in his old friend. In his diary that night, Patton groused, "I think he means well, but it is most upsetting to get only piddling criticism when one knows one has done a good job."[169]

The criticisms charging indifference to communication fed into the image proffered by rivals of Patton as rogue. Writing of Montgomery in February 1945, Norman Gelb said, "He also deplored Patton's practice of ignoring Eisenhower's instructions not to risk exposing his forces to German counterattacks through what seemed to him to be reckless forward thrusts that no general with any understanding of the rules of combat would risk. Advance was supposed to be carefully coordinated clear across the line."[170] The image of Monty preoccupied with a man who was then one of Bradley's subordinates seems odd in retrospect, but in the fall of 1944 Monty was extremely upset with any advance by Patton that seemed to indicate he was not getting priority of supply. It may have looked like Patton was disregarding orders to stop so that all logistics could go to Montgomery, but after all it was Montgomery who told Patton in Sicily, "George, let me give you some advice. If you get an order from [Alexander] that you don't like, why just ignore it. That's what I do."[171]

Patton's command and control methods were unorthodox, but those of his superiors were simply wanting. On the eve of the Kasserine debacle, Eisenhower personally toured the field, leaving II Corps to log: "General disposition of forces was satisfactory to General Eisenhower on 13 February."[172] Ike then spent the next day traveling incommunicado with his entourage, including Kay Summersby, back to his headquarters, stopping for a leisurely lunch among Roman ruins while never realizing the Germans were unleashing their attack.[173] After the debacle Alexander complained, "Real fault has been lack of direction from above [Eisenhower] from very beginning."[174] The British then arranged to have their officers take charge of land, sea, and air operations, each bypassing Eisenhower and reporting directly to London for guidance.

Looking at the plans for Sicily, Bradley opined, "Seldom in war has a major operation been undertaken in such a fog of indecision, confusion, and conflicting plans."[175] When the enemy began his withdrawal to the Italian mainland, Montgomery fretted, "I have tried hard to find out what the combined Navy-Air plan is in order to stop him getting away; I have been unable to find out. I fear the truth of the matter is there is NO plan. The trouble is there is no higher-up grip on this campaign."[176] Even a U.S. Army history added, "The failure of Allied air and naval forces to interdict the Strait of Messina was due in large part to the fact that neither Eisenhower nor his principal air, land, and sea commanders had formulated a coordinated plan to prevent the withdrawal of Axis forces from the island."[177] It seems they could not adapt to changing circumstances.

The Allied campaign on the Italian mainland—conducted without Patton—turned into a slow, bloody affair of attrition. B. H. Liddell Hart concluded: "The root of the trouble is that all our higher leaders, even the best of them, were not only brought up on the slow-motion methods of 1914–1918, but had to go on practicing them for the next twenty years. The few men who were emancipated from these habits of deliberation, by serving with our experimental mechanized forces, have never been allowed a chance to command in the field."[178] As late as 8 October 1944, Montgomery met with Marshall and recalled, "I told him that since Eisenhower had himself taken personal command of the land battle, being also Supreme Commander of all the forces (land, sea, and air), the armies had become separated nationally and not geographically. There was a lack of grip, and operational direction and control was lacking. Our operations had, in fact, become ragged and disjointed, and we had got ourselves into a real mess."[179] Ike was a master at Allied politics, but his command did little to end confusion among the armies.

SHAEF deficiencies in command and control created a failure to coordinate decisive strategic maneuver. In Tunisia, Alexander had used Patton to hold the enemy while Montgomery pushed them back to Tunis. Monty intended to repeat the formula in Sicily and Normandy, but he did not possess the command and control procedures required to execute the driving role. Emerging opportunities were lost on him. In both campaigns, Patton de facto reversed their roles—much to Monty's dismay.

In his memoirs Montgomery described his belief: "A [commander] must ensure from the beginning a very firm grip on his military machine. . . . The firm grip is essential in order that the master plan will not be undermined by the independent ideas of subordinate commanders at particular moments in the battle. *Operations must develop within a predetermined pattern of action* [emphasis added]."[180] He often spoke in encouragement of initiative, the importance of morale, and drive, but he said of the commander: "Many outside influences may attempt to suggest alternative methods, or generally to shake his confidence in his own plan and in his own ability to see it through. But he must have complete faith in his plan and in his own ability; nothing short of this will be of any use. He must then impress his will on his opponent and make him dance to his own tune throughout."[181] When the Axis forces concentrated on Patton in Sicily, Montgomery had an opportunity to push quickly to Messina—but he didn't. He only entered Augusta on 12 July after Patton's sweep around the island forced the Germans to withdraw to a better defensive line. The pattern would repeat in Italy, at Caen and Falaise in France, and during the Rhine campaign.

The unique efficacy of Patton's command and staff procedures was most visible during the Battle of the Bulge. Having detected signs of a German buildup since the end of October, Patton had his staff plan contingencies for a possible enemy assault on VIII Corps in the First Army sector.[182] On the evening of 16 December, after attending the wedding of his orderly to a Women's Army Corps soldier, Eisenhower celebrated his just-announced promotion to five-star rank with champagne and a game of bridge with Bradley. Between hands, reports arrived describing German attacks in the

Ardennes. To the south, Patton began his long-awaited attack due east. Upon the first call from Bradley regarding trouble in First Army, Patton quickly but reluctantly prepared to cancel his drive and execute his previously considered contingency plan for movement due north. Patton thought Bradley might be overreacting to the Germans by taking one of his armor divisions but added: "He probably knows more of the situation than he can say over the telephone."[183]

The next morning, with vague reports from the north, Patton discussed options with his staff.[184] If the Germans were conducting a feint, he had the 4th Armored Division prepared to continue with his breakthrough effort. If it was a diversion in the north for an attack against Third Army, he felt adequately situated to repel them. If it was a main effort attack in the north, he ordered his staff to look for opportunities to swing northeast and "pinwheel the enemy," to "trap their main forces west of the Rhine."[185] He wanted plans to immediately pull Third Army out of its attack, shift zones of operations with Seventh Army, reorient due north, move over one hundred miles without preplanned logistical support, and initiate a hasty attack on the German flank—all in poor winter weather. Amazingly, he felt confident his staff and army could do it all quickly.

Bradley woke late on 17 December at Ike's headquarters before making the rounds. A visiting general wrote, "Brad says the Germans have started a big counterattack toward [General Courtney] Hodges. Very calm about it. Seemed routine from his lack of concern."[186] The poor weather meant Bradley had to endure a long drive from Ike's headquarters at Versailles to his own in Luxembourg. When he arrived, his G-2 briefed him on the extent of the German attack. Bradley was no longer so calm.

The next day at 1030 hours Bradley called for Patton, who arrived at 12th Army Group forward headquarters in the afternoon with his intelligence officer Oscar Koch, his operations officer Halley Maddox, and his logistics officer Walter Muller. The First Army situation had turned critical. Patton recalled that Bradley "then showed that the German penetration is much greater than I thought."[187] The Bulge was by now forty miles deep and thirty miles wide. VIII Corps' divisions were fighting in confused pockets.[188] It was chaos. Asked by Bradley for help, Patton recalled, "I told him that I would halt the 4th Armored and concentrate it near Longwy, starting at midnight, and that I would start the 80th in the morning on Luxembourg.

I also said that I could alert the 26th to move in 24 hours. He seemed satisfied."[189] More than satisfied, Bradley wrote, "His answer astounded me."[190]

Patton spent the rest of the day constantly on the move communicating by radio. He drove under blackout conditions to General Walton Walker's XX Corps headquarters to discuss turning over the entire Third Army zone to Walker. At 2000 hours, Bradley called. "The situation up there is much worse than it was when I talked to you," he said.[191] He wanted Patton's 10th Armored, 4th Armored, and 80th Infantry Divisions to move immediately. He also wanted Major General John Millikin's III Corps in the morning. Fifteen minutes later Patton was meeting with Millikin. At 2300 hours Bradley called back and told Patton to report at 1100 hours the next day to meet with Ike at Verdun.

An unprecedented maneuver was now under way, made possible only by Patton's command, control, and staff procedures. His G-3 section reported: "All possible personnel was concentrated on traffic duty."[192] Third Army dispatched special officer couriers to military police battalions to quickly establish and man 4 "troop movement routes." In just one snapshot of the movement, III Corps had begun moving from Metz to Longwy on 17 December; 2 truck companies left Toul at 2300 hours that night headed for Puttelange to help move the 80th Division; another truck company left Pont-a-Mousson at 0100 on 18 December to join the 80th Infantry Division at Puttelange; and Combat Command B of the 4th Armored Division left Fenetrange at 0200 hours on 18 December for Longwy. According to the Third Army: "These four moves crossed at BARONVILLE at 180330 [3:30 a.m. on 18 December], with Combat Command 'B' having priority. There was a constant flow of traffic during the period of movement, more than 11,800 vehicles passing over the four routes."[193] Third Army G-3 added: "A landslide, a weakened bridge, enemy bombing and strafing, and several wrecks caused detours to be designated, but the troops got through and enabled the Army to make its attack on schedule."[194] Third Army adjusted on the fly.

On 19 December at 0700 hours, Patton met with his principal staff and commanders. An hour later, he convened his entire staff with Weyland and the XIX TAC staff. Patton wrote, "At this meeting I explained the change in plan and told them we would have to make rapid movements, which would depend on them."[195] The chaotic and uncertain situation required flexible command, simple plans, and subordinate initiative. At the map board, Patton recalled, "I then made a rough plan for operations based on the assumption that I would use the VIII Corps (Middleton) [General Troy Middleton of First Army] and III Corps (Millikin) on any two or three possible axes. From the left, the axes of attack were as follows: From the general vicinity of Neufchâteau, against the left nose of the salient. From the general vicinity of Arlon on Bastogne, which is still being held by our troops; and finally, a third attack due north from Diekirch."[196] He preferred the last route, slicing behind the German attack and cutting them off along the Rhine. Patton said, "I made a simple code, one copy of which I left with Gay so that if I was ordered to execute the operation, I could call him on the phone."[197] "When it is considered that [Colonel Paul] Harkins, Codman and I left for Verdun at 0915," Patton wrote, "and that between 0800 and that hour we had a staff meeting, planned three possible lines of attack, and made a simple code in which I could telephone General Gay which two of the three lines we were to use, it is evident that war is not so difficult as people think."[198]

Patton arrived at Bradley's main headquarters at Verdun at 1045 hours to witness one of Eisenhower's finest moments. Ike encouraged his officers to grasp opportunity from the chaos of the Bulge. "The present situation is to be regarded as one of opportunity for us and not of disaster," he ordered. "There will be only cheerful faces at this conference table."[199] Patton replied, "Hell, let's have the guts to let the sons of bitches go all the way to Paris. Then we'll really cut 'em up and chew 'em up."[200] Kay Summersby observed, "Of all the generals, admirals, field marshals, and air marshals I met during the war, only General Patton exuded more consistent, confident optimism than General Eisenhower."[201] It was confidence well founded.

Eisenhower had his G-2, British major general Kenneth Strong, brief the situation and then told Patton he wanted him "to get to Luxembourg and take command of the battle and make a strong counterattack with at least 6 divisions."[202] Ike had talked with Montgomery, who told him his forces could not attack for two months and in fact should pull back first to regroup, plan, and prepare.[203] Patton later heard that only when Monty was told Patton was attacking did he decide to hold fast.

Patton was Ike's only hope for a counterattack. The Third Army commander realized, however, that half of the six divisions mentioned by Ike, those in VIII Corps, by now "existed only on paper."[204] Ike asked General Jacob Devers to hold the line south of Saarlautern. "Bradley," Patton noted, "said little."[205] Patton requested replacements stripped from three newly arrived infantry divisions in theater. Ike declined. Patton then discussed how he would shift his divisions for the counterattack north into the Bulge.

"When can you start?" Eisenhower asked Patton. "As soon as you're through with me," Patton answered.[206] Noticing his host's surprise, Patton explained, "I left my household in Nancy in perfect order before I came here and can go straight to Luxembourg right away, sir, straight from here."[207] "When can you attack?" asked Ike. Patton responded: "On December 22 with three divisions; the 4th Armored, the 26th and 80th."[208]

Codman recalled, "There was a stir, a shuffling of feet, as those present straightened up in their chairs. In some faces, skepticism. But through the room the current of excitement leaped like a flame."[209] Patton had promised to hit the Germans with three divisions in about seventy-two hours, arguing that the time it would take to assemble a larger force would cost him the element of surprise—that is, shock.[210] In fact, Codman confided, "He knew then he would make the attack on the morning of the twenty-first of December."[211] (The difference between the seventy-two hour deadline he promised Ike—Bradley recalled it was forty-eight hours—and the forty-eight hours he pushed his staff toward would remain a point of confusion for many future historians.[212])

Four decades later Bradley recalled the moment: "Ike's initial reaction was extreme annoyance. 'Don't be fatuous,' he snapped. . . . We were facing a potential disaster. Ike did not want any more bravado, but rather careful, reasoned response. Patton's attack was crucial. Three divisions was clearly not enough."[213] Actually, more than the size of the force, it was the speed of movement that gave Eisenhower pause. Ike explained, "If you try to go that early, you won't have all three divisions ready and you'll go piecemeal. . . . I want your initial blow to be a strong one! I'd even settle for the twenty-third if it takes that long to get three full divisions."[214]

Eisenhower's son John wrote, "The prospect of relieving three divisions from the line, turning them north, and traveling over icy roads to Arlon to prepare for a major counterattack in less than seventy-two hours was astonishing, even to a group accustomed to flexibility in their military operations."[215] In Victor Davis Hanson's words, "Patton essentially was being

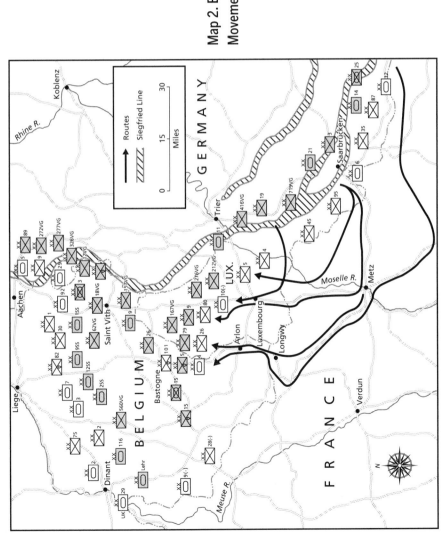

Map 2. Battle of the Bulge Third Army Movement, 19–22 December 1943

ordered to do in a few days what the Germans had taken months to accomplish: to transfer entire armies from their own sectors to another."[216] It was a feat simply incomprehensible to those who failed to understand the effectiveness of Patton's command, control, and staff methods. Wearing his new five-star rank, Ike mentioned how the Germans attacked at Kasserine after he got his fourth star and told Patton after the meeting, "Every time I get a new star I get attacked," to which Patton responded, "And every time you get attacked I pull you out."[217]

It is interesting that Ike turned to Patton and not Bradley for action from the south. Bradley later wrote that Ike's chief of staff Bedell Smith called and suggested Bradley hand over the U.S. forces north of the Bulge to Montgomery because Bradley lacked communication with his two northern armies. Bradley confessed to be "completely dumbfounded—and shocked. . . . There was an Alice-in-Wonderland air about this telephone call. Bedell Smith had been one of Monty's toughest critics and one who had consistently and vehemently opposed Monty's push to promote himself land commander."[218] Bradley added, "I now made one of the biggest mistakes of the war. . . . I knuckled under. . . . 'Bedell,' I interrupted, 'it's hard for me to object. Certainly if Monty's were an American command I would agree with you entirely. It would be the logical thing to do.'"[219] Patton reported being there when "Ike called and he and Brad had a long talk."[220] During the call Eisenhower told Bradley he was giving Monty the First and Ninth U.S. Armies because of 12th Army Group's difficult telephonic communications. Patton noted "communications were all right" and thought Ike had either "lost confidence in Bradley" or given in to British pressure.[221]

Bradley now had to rely on Patton, who in turn was careful to keep him involved. Bradley later wrote: "I do not believe it is generally known, but Patton thereafter temporarily established his Third Army headquarters in Luxembourg and moved into my hotel. . . . We dined together and planned together. We had never been closer or worked in greater harmony."[222] It was actually Patton's advance headquarters that collocated with Bradley. Apparently Patton thought the time was right to reinforce the 12th Army Group staff and Bradley did not disagree—strange, considering Bradley's view of Patton's staff.

Leaving the meeting at Verdun, Patton quickly moved "to place the Third U.S. Army into high gear" with a flurry of orders. During the meeting he had called back to his staff the code word "nickel," indicating Ike's choice of axis of attack.[223] The advance on the Siegfried Line was suspended.[224] Manton Eddy was told to turn over XII Corps' zone and the 87th Infantry Division to Seventh Army, to give the 80th Infantry and 4th Armored Divisions to III Corps, to send the 35th Infantry Division to Metz to regroup before it went to Luxembourg, and to take control of the 5th Infantry Division. Walker was ordered to relieve the 5th Infantry Division in Saarlautern so that it could move to Luxembourg, to assume III Corps' zone, and to take control of the 6th Armored Division and 6th Cavalry Group. Millikin was directed to send the 26th Infantry Division to Arlon and assume control of the 4th Armored and 80th Infantry Divisions. Meanwhile, Weyland was to "vector" the XIX TAC into the First Army area of operations. It was a virtuoso performance. Patton commented, "I have no staff officers [with me] and conducted the whole thing by telephone through Gay and a fine staff in Nancy. . . . This has been a wonderful move on the part of the Third Army. We will attack at 4:00 a.m., December 22nd."[225] He went on to say, "Had anyone proposed such a troop movement at Leavenworth, people would have gone crazy, but here it was being done."[226]

Another unprecedented maneuver was under way. The incredibly complex traffic control involved was again made possible by Patton's command and staff procedures leveraging individual initiative, simple instructions, and flexible execution. There was no stopping to draft plans and orders. All parties involved got to their destinations with little guidance along the way. Patton's G-3 section reported: "Special officer couriers were dispatched to each military police battalion with four troop movement routes."[227] Subordinate units adjusted on the move. Major Albin Irzyk, commanding the 8th Tank Battalion in General Holmes Dager's Combat Command B of 4th Armored Division, recalled, "I was guided and directed by General Dager in a variety of ways: he radioed instructions from his jeep; his staff relayed radio messages; he rode alongside to shout directions at me in my turret; and at tricky intersections, he personally dismounted to point the way."[228] Trained to act in such a fashion, with every soldier doing his part, the vast army moved north.

On 21 December Patton reported, "I had all staffs, except the VIII Corps, in for a conference. As usual on the verge of attack, they were full of doubt. I seemed to always be the ray of sunshine, and by God, I always am."[229]

The logistics concerns were enormous. Almost all the units were without maps. Signal companies had to string 20,000 miles of wire, enough to cross the United States 6 times.[230] Thousands of supply points, field hospitals, and administrative centers had to move. Bradley's chief liaison, Colonel Karl Bendetsen, arrived to coordinate with Patton and recalled, "He wanted to be sure of his supplies of P.O.L. (petroleum, oil, and lubricants), ammunition, ordnance, transport, replacements, rations, etc. He then said, 'Bendetsen, there's something you can do for me and I believe you can do it if you really want to.' I said, 'Sir, anything you request is an order. I will give it all I've got.' He said, 'I need a freight train.'"[231] Patton got his freight train. It was nice to have priority.

Patton issued the order, "Everyone in this army must understand that we are not fighting this war in any half-cocked manner. It's either root hog—or die! Shoot the works. If those Hun bastards want war in the raw then that's the way we'll give it to them!"[232] Third Army transportation officer Colonel Redding F. Perry ironed out the vast movement of vehicles. One officer remembered "Colonel 'Speed' Perry, standing before a map all night and from memory assigning truck and car companies, scattered over hundreds of miles, to move units and supplies equally widely dispersed."[233] Perry did not have to tell the units how to do things in detail, only to provide them with direction and coordinate their movements. In the first 5 days, 37 truck companies moved 61,935 tons of supplies, 18,910 tons of it ammunition.[234]

Incredibly, Dager's Combat Command B from the 4th Armored Division raced the entire 161 miles to Bastogne in twenty-two hours, beating even the Germans to the town.[235] They were then ordered to fall back to join up with the rest of the force until all three divisions were on line in accordance with Eisenhower's instructions at Verdun.[236] When they headed north again the Germans were waiting. What took Dager's men a few hours to travel that first day would take the entire 4th Armored Division several days and hundreds of casualties to traverse.[237] Patton's way of war had once again been undermined by higher command's wishes.

On Christmas Day, as Third Army battled to the outskirts of Bastogne, Bradley shared dinner with Patton. "After supper Brad and I had a talk," Patton recalled, "Monty says that the 1st Army cannot attack for three months and that the only attack that can be made is by me, but that I am too weak; hence we should fall back to the Saar-Vosges Line or even the Moselle to gain more divisions."[238] By traditional command and control doctrine, Montgomery was correct. Patton should have paused for weeks or even months to prepare and plan properly and only then launch his attack guided by a firm hand. But by then Bastogne would have fallen, more men would have died, and the Germans could have strengthened their position. Fortunately for Eisenhower and the men of the 101st Airborne Division, Patton had his own doctrine. At 1845 hours on 26 December, roughly ten days after the German assault into the Ardennes, Third Army's 4th Armored Division broke through, liberated Bastogne, and killed the great German counteroffensive.

The counterattack to the Bulge still stands as a monument to Patton's way of war. Planned flexibility, simple orders, *Auftragstaktik*, and boldness: these were the ingredients of his success. Yet even while his peers confessed amazed appreciation for his accomplishment, they could not comprehend the methods behind it. After the war Bradley wrote, "Until the Battle of the Bulge I did not share George's enthusiasm for his Third Army staff. . . . Indeed, I had once agreed with the observation of another senior commander who said, 'Patton can get more good work out of a mediocre bunch of staff officers than anyone I ever saw.'"[239] Patton's men were in fact as good as any staff officers in the Army, trained to the highest level of proficiency in an unorthodox doctrine. This was especially true of one staff section particularly important to Patton's way of war: intelligence.

5 | INTELLIGENCE

Patton never made a move without first consulting G-2.
—Robert Allen

When he took command of the 2nd Armored Division, Patton told his troops, "Our mission is to attack weakness, and our reconnaissance is what permits us to find that weakness—the soft spot in the line of the exposed flank."[1] To conduct a campaign of debilitating shocks, he needed systems that could quickly find and report enemy weak spots obscured in the fog of war. In essence, he required means for initiating the decision cycle later described by John Boyd: the *observation*, *orientation*, *decision*, and *action* (OODA) loop.[2] Patton demanded intelligence to identify emerging opportunities so that he could orient on the best one, decide on a course of action, and act faster than his foe. By executing faster OODA loops, he could set the conditions for shock by keeping the enemy off balance and uncertain as to both the danger they faced and the next course of action to take. In this Patton intuitively added a step to Boyd's decision cycle—*anticipation*. Through carefully constructed, integrated, and multi-layered intelligence systems, he managed to anticipate opportunities, beat his foes in the observation phase, and win the decision. Patton's unique experience made this use of intelligence possible.

Today the U.S. Army defines intelligence as "information and knowledge about an adversary obtained through observation, investigation, analysis, or understanding."[3] Even this definition falls short; intelligence is the gathering, processing, and use of information that affects decisions about the conduct of operations.[4] It is more than information about an adversary; it includes information about terrain, weather, friendly troops, and anything else that influences decisions on the conduct of operations. Additionally, it encompasses the knowledge base required to understand and filter the information gathered by intelligence systems. Patton, unlike his contemporaries, understood and employed this full definition of intelligence.

Patton's ravenous demand for fresh information on enemy positions and intentions, friendly unit positions, and their relative trajectories exceeded the capabilities of customary intelligence systems. *Field Service Regulations 1923* did not even address "intelligence" per se but talked instead of "military information," which it said was "essential to the efficient preparation and execution of strategical and tactical plans. It constitutes a vital element in the commander's estimate of the situation and decision."[5] While the regulations called for field units to continuously "research information by all available means," schoolhouses and field exercises usually treated such information as a given. Officers therefore failed to learn the need for an aggressive approach to the gathering and use of intelligence. A 1948 study by two Command and General Staff College instructors concluded, "Perhaps the major intelligence weakness of the last war was that commanders were not 'intelligence conscious.' Some were even contemptuous of the assistance intelligence could furnish them."[6] Patton was an exception.

When Patton's statue at West Point was unveiled across from the library, a joke took root that he was holding binoculars so that he could find the building he never visited. Nothing was further from the truth. Despite having been home schooled and possibly hampered by dyslexia, he possessed a remarkably inquisitive and analytical mind that he avidly applied to his lifelong study of military history and theory.[7] He achieved a distinguished record in the military school system, attending the Virginia Military Institute before graduating from the United States Military Academy in 1909 forty-sixth out of a class of 103, despite once failing a math class and being turned back for a year.[8] In 1923 he completed the Cavalry School's Field Officers' Course at Fort Riley, Kansas, with grades high enough to earn him selection to the General Service School (soon to become the Command and General Staff College) at Fort Leavenworth. There, he finished as an honor graduate ranking twenty-fifth of 248 students.[9] In 1931 he entered the Army War College and graduated "superior." His thesis paper, a fifty-six-page essay called "The Probable Characteristics of the Next War and the Organization, Tactics, and Equipment Necessary to Meet Them," was one of only thirty-eight from the class forwarded to the War Department as a "work of exceptional merit."[10] Throughout his life, Patton wrote contemplative essays reflecting his independent philosophies on war. One wonders how much more distinguished his Army school record would have been had he slavishly bought into the tenets of official doctrine.

Patton long collected experience in, and ideas on, intelligence. During the Punitive Expedition into Mexico in 1916, he studied the cost of ignorance resulting from patrols that failed "to report promptly and accurately."[11] He learned the value of good maps, knowledge of terrain, and familiarity with the environment. In the Great War, lessons on terrain became even more important to Patton—his tanks needed dry, crossable ground. As the commander of British tanks commented after the third battle of Ypres, "Nothing can be said in defense of the fatuous employment of machines, weighing over thirty tons, in the liquid mud of what degenerated into a swamp battle, or of the subsequent and equally fatuous condemnation of them for not functioning well under these conditions."[12] Before his battle at Saint-Mihiel, Patton conducted a personal night reconnaissance with a French patrol 1,500 meters into an attack zone said to be an impassable swamp. "The next day," he reported, "we were able to state by our personal knowledge that an attack could be made in this sector."[13] He came away convinced that only first-hand observation provided a true understanding of the situation at the front.

Experience made Patton intensely concerned with the difficulties of knowing the location of his tanks in battle. He did not go gently into the fog of war. He stenciled different large playing cards on the turrets to identify each tank, platoon, and company. When ordered by his commander "not to go into this fight in a tank," he went forward on foot instead.[14] He later explained, "I could not see my right battalion so went to look for it."[15] Accepting the inevitable reprimand, he argued that commanders could only be effective at the front. Not only was this the only way to know what was happening, he also saw that the commander's presence produced a moral effect on men and operations. During an exercise in 1929 he observed, "The value of the commander is most evident. When he is active the maneuvers are fine. When he is slow . . . they are a wash out."[16] During maneuvers in Hawaii in 1935, he reasoned, "If higher commanders would go up and look they would do some good, at least they would inspire the men. . . . The place of the brigade commander is with his men, not with his telephones."[17] Habitual visits to the front became his means for understanding his men and getting them to understand him. After observing his first exercises as the 2nd Armored Division commander, Patton surprisingly concluded, "Division command post should be farther to the front, probably between the main body and the reconnaissance battalion."[18]

Through early assignments from general's aide to tank brigade commander, Patton developed a good feel for the duties and responsibilities of an intelligence staff officer. In 1919 he wrote of the G-2: "He must remember that he is not a historian. He is a journalist. His information must be up to the minute or it will be too old. This will particularly be the case in wars of a less stabilized character than the World War."[19] "Less stabilized character" was code for maneuver warfare. Patton listed a wide variety of questions spanning enemy intentions and capabilities, topography, and infrastructure that a G-2 might have to answer. He attached a litany of sources for answers, including higher headquarters summaries, publications, interrogations and interviews, intercepted communications, photographic reconnaissance, subordinate unit reports, and "reports from independent cavalry."[20] He would employ all these sources in World War II. "To conclude," he wrote, "too much attention cannot be given to assisting the G2 and heeding G2's advice. When G2 is without information, intelligent maneuver is impossible."[21] Patton had identified the foundation of his way of war: intelligent maneuver.

Uniquely, Patton pushed for increased gathering of intelligence *after* operations were under way. Doctrine called for the collection of military information for the vague purpose of "efficient preparation and execution of strategical and tactical plans."[22] For Patton, feedback from reconnaissance and front-line commanders provided essential direction. Koch recalled Patton typically saying, "I'm going to do this—or this—depending upon the situation at that time."[23] He relied on intelligence to clarify that situation and steer him around enemy strength to exploit enemy weakness. In this way Patton fought the battle, not the plan. As he explained: "It may be of interest to future generals to realize that one makes plans fit circumstances and does not try to create circumstances to fit plans. That way danger lies."[24] Few at the time agreed.

Traditionalists insisted on detailed plans and heavy command and control. Doctrine stressed that "the commander must be the controlling head" of thorough planning and control to ensure a focus of effort at the predetermined decisive point.[25] Upon being placed under Montgomery's command, Ninth U.S. Army commander General William Simpson recalled,

"Right from the start he made it very plain that if he had a plan to do anything, he didn't want anybody to do anything to interfere with that plan."[26] Commanders such as Montgomery used intelligence to confirm their plans, not to alter them during execution. Solid intelligence revealing German armor units threatening Market Garden, for example, failed to get Monty to change his plan.[27] During Operation Lumberjack on the German frontier, Patton expressed an opposite view when protesting to Bradley, "We are trying to fight the enemy according to the situation on the ground. Not on a map or by theory. To hit him where he is weak and to keep him on the run until we either kill him or he surrenders."[28]

Twice in his career (1925–27 and 1935–37) Patton served as a G-2 intelligence officer, both times with the Hawaiian Division—one of the few fully formed divisions in the Army between the wars. In these assignments, he concluded, "Surprise is the most ancient and most potent of military methods."[29] "Yet," he added, "the records of all time show that the unchanging ends have been, are and probably shall ever be, the securing of predominating force, of the right sort, at the right place, at the right time."[30] The G-2's job was to find that place and time. Assignments as a G-2 greatly benefited Patton's analytical understanding of the intelligence process, but his peers did not care to share the experience. Bradley spoke for most when he proudly wrote, "Misfits frequently found themselves assigned to intelligence duties. And in some stations G-2 became a dumping ground for officers ill-suited to line command. I recall how scrupulously I avoided the branding that came with an intelligence assignment in my own career."[31] Infantrymen and artillerymen viewed themselves as users of intelligence; for cavalrymen such as Patton, intelligence was *raison d'être*.

As a G-2 in the Hawaiian Islands, Patton also had to consider joint air-land-sea operations. He studied amphibious operations from Sir Francis Drake to the Japanese offensives in 1932 and produced an essay on the failed British operations at Gallipoli in the Dardanelles. In April 1935 he even predicted that "a Japanese attack on Pearl Harbor was both possible and probable."[32] The insight gathered in Hawaii on surprise, leadership, Army-Navy cooperation, fire support, logistics, airpower, and amphibious operations would serve Patton well in North Africa and Sicily.[33]

As mechanization became more advanced, Patton began to put more emphasis on combined arms probes of the enemy line. In 1929 he explained to a friend that he believed mechanization would allow a reserve "to give the knock out punch" *after* units probed the enemy lines to find their weak spot.[34] He rehearsed sequenced reconnaissance to find enemy vulnerabilities, air and artillery to suppress their adjustments, and tanks and infantry to fix and exploit their dispositions.[35] Patton explained, "Years ago I wrote, and I see no reason to change it now, that the whole art of war consisted in catching the enemy by the nose and kicking him in the pants. Try to do that in the maneuvers, and in the war. . . . Make it a principle, to find out where the enemy is, hold him in front by fire, and get around him."[36] Intelligence served as the first step.

At Fort Benning Patton told his 2nd Armored Division troops, "The essential and outstanding difference between the old tank attack and an attack by an Armored Division is the fact that the Armored Division is provided with its own means of reconnaissance."[37] He now had an attached air reconnaissance squadron, a divisional reconnaissance battalion, and regimental reconnaissance companies. By his doctrine, the air located the enemy, the recon battalion verified "negative information" (paths through or around the enemy), and the recon companies developed "the exact location of the enemy and particularly his anti-tank establishments."[38] Patton habitually reinforced companies of the recon battalion with tank platoons and sent them five to ten miles ahead of the main body "to determine the type of terrain and leave guides" for the following units to get around the enemy—a mechanized version of storm troop tactics.[39] To these he added, when necessary, probing attacks by his front-line units. Reminding his men that "a look is worth a thousand words," Patton ordered, "Commanders of each element in the rear of the reconnaissance must be close up to attain full knowledge of what has transpired in front of them."[40] None of this was Army doctrine, but it was Patton's.

The prewar General Headquarters maneuvers put Patton's ideas under Army scrutiny. In Tennessee, his probing had struck umpires as a failure to concentrate forces, and his quick sweeps looked like an unwillingness to close with and destroy the enemy.[41] The Louisiana terrain, broken by swamps, rice fields, numerous rivers, and dense forests, was not "tank country."[42] The terrain prohibited probes across a wide front, channeled attacks, and marginalized intelligence. Even so, when the enemy located Patton's columns sweeping to Shreveport and maneuvered to stop them, his faster recon patrols enabled him to avoid their trap.[43] In the Carolinas, General Hugh Drum boastfully used "military information" to confirm his predetermined plan for using overwhelming force in a carefully scripted steamroller advance against Patton. At the start, however, Patton's fast-moving reconnaissance surprised and captured the highly agitated Drum. Nonetheless, as Bradley noted, "He was criticized by the umpire-generals for his unorthodoxy, for leaving his command post and prowling the 'front line,' for running his division 'roughshod' over the 'enemy.'"[44]

The maneuvers helped Patton refine his use of intelligence. He decided it was more important to know *where* to beat the enemy than *how* to beat them. Patton explained, "The where is learned from a careful study of road, railway, and river maps."[45] At Fort Benning and the Desert Training Center, he experimented with methods of intelligence collection and instructed that "junior officers of reconnaissance units must be very inquisitive. Their reports must be accurate and factual. Negative information is as important as positive information."[46] Significant was this observation:

> Several umpires criticized me for not remaining in my command post. It is patent that for a general officer to sit in the command post during an old time infantry fight was not particularly harmful because while the information appearing before him was from two to three hours old, the slowness of the progress of the fight did not change the situation materially in two or three hours. Were the commanding general of an Armored Division to sit anywhere with information three hours old his units might be from fifteen to twenty-five miles from the point indicated on the maps.[47]

This passage illustrates Patton's unique appreciation for the interrelation of several subtle but profound characteristics of maneuver warfare. Intelligence providing situational awareness was temporal in nature. Perception trailed reality. The time it took to transmit and receive information separated understanding from actual circumstance. In Hawaii, he observed how information relayed from forward lines to the division headquarters by direct telephone communication still took an average of fifty minutes. "This was 45 minutes too long," he reported, "and it was because too many intermediate Gs want to look at it."[48] Patton measured time by the changes in the situation. Once units moved, reports were too late. Conversely, uncertainty—or chaos—could be created through movement. Patton told his soldiers, "Remember that the great advantage possessed by an Armored Division is its ability to produce in the minds of its opponents a fear of the unknown. *To do so you must keep moving* [emphasis added]."[49] Finally, a commander had to take proactive measures to maintain true situational awareness. Patton therefore emphasized movement to create uncertainty in the enemy—the prerequisite for shock—and active intelligence to maintain situational awareness.

In North Africa, a soldier recalled, "George Patton was always on the front lines, never in the rear with the Red Cross. That was one of the secrets to his greatness."[50] His visits allowed him to take stock of the environment and his men. After Kasserine, for example, he found the front "the coldest damn place I have ever seen and it has rained every day . . . it is very hard on the men."[51] He adjusted plans accordingly. Colonel Paul Robinett remembered, "Of all the senior commanders in World War II, General Patton understood best the teachings of one of the very greatest American soldiers, Gen. William T. Sherman: 'No man can properly command an army from the rear, he must be at the front . . . at the very head of the army—[he] must be seen there, and the effect of his mind and personal energy must be felt by every officer and man present with it.'"[52] Patton knew that the power of impression went both ways and explained, "You've got to get the feel of troops to lead them. You've got to know how much is left in them and how much more they can take. I know just how much more by looking in their faces."[53]

Even the first Torch landings would not comport with plans; the Allies lost 556 men killed, 837 wounded, and 41 missing, with Patton losing 142 soldiers.[54] From that point on, circumstance eluded predetermination. The Germans poured into Tunis at the rate of 1,000 men a day, outpacing Allied intelligence intercepts. As one observer noted, "After killing hundreds of American and British soldiers during Torch, the French had failed to so much as scratch a single German invader."[55] Left behind in Casablanca, Patton sifted through intelligence reports and sensed trouble for his peers. He predicted: "I don't think that [Ike] or Clark have any idea of what they are going to do next. I should not be surprised to see the Brit First Army get driven back."[56] On 12 December 1942 Patton visited Algiers and found

"Ike and Clark in conference as to what to do. Neither had been to the front, so showed great lack of decision."[57] A lack of proactive intelligence at the highest levels created uncertainty that caused a drift in operations. Leading the charge east, British general Kenneth Anderson soon reported to Eisenhower an unexpected "nasty setback," stalled, and asked for more troops.[58]

Patton persuaded Ike to let him visit the front "to get a close-up of the fighting," noting, "Something is wrong there. We are losing too many tanks."[59] In the second week of December he flew to Algiers and drove to the line—something neither Eisenhower nor Clark had yet done. Ever the G-2, he gathered intelligence. He visited his son-in-law, Lieutenant Colonel John Waters, whose battalion had lost two-thirds of its tanks in little more than three weeks, to get an unbiased report. Patton was shocked to learn that he was the first general these men had seen. He wrote his wife, "I am very worried about John, as I fear he will be cut off and captured."[60] He reported to Eisenhower his impressions of German advantages in combined arms, air support, tactics, and reconnaissance before dutifully heading back to Morocco. Patton then used what he had learned to prepare for his future operations.

In February the Allies were caught completely off guard by the German attack on Kasserine Pass. As Patton prophesied, his son-in-law was indeed cut off and captured. American operations were piecemeal, reactive movements by commanders lacking situational awareness. One regimental commander delivered a list of complaints to II Corps: there was no coordination in the battle area; no specified areas of unit responsibility; no coordination between units; ad hoc, confused organization; no fire coordination; and no one evacuating prisoners.[61] An army rehearsed in controlled training exercises fell apart on the stage of free-flowing war. Sent by Ike to investigate the disaster, Bradley recalled: "The American army's long neglect of intelligence training was soon reflected by the ineptness of our initial undertakings."[62] After several weeks of searching for others to remedy the situation, on 4 March Eisenhower turned II Corps over to Patton. His limited operations in Tunisia offered little test for his ideas on intelligence, but at El Guettar radio intercepts proved critically important in enabling him to deliver America's first victory over German troops.

After Tunisia, Patton issued his "Notes on Combat," stressing refinements in tactical intelligence. Reflecting his attention to detail, he wrote:

"In mountain warfare reconnaissance is of paramount importance."[63] He called for "vigorous" patrols out before dark to enable night or dawn infantry attacks and wrote, "Without meticulous reconnaissance either form of attack is suicide."[64] He demanded that junior officers in recon units be inquisitive, factual, accurate, and prompt in reports. He instructed, "Troops must not report types of guns or vehicles unless they are certain. The report that three 88's are firing at them may lead to erroneous conclusion."[65] Finally, Patton reminded commanders, "Reconnaissance units should not be used for security missions. Their sole purpose is to get information."[66] In such details, accuracy and timeliness resided.

Prior to Husky, Patton issued another letter of instruction to Seventh Army. He told his men, "Reconnaissance must be well out and must stay out. Contact once gained must be maintained."[67] Reminding them that the initial landings would possibly go in at the wrong locations, he demanded his commanders and platoon leaders "know the general as well as the special plan" and "use their best efforts" to adjust to circumstances and meet the commander's intent."[68] Intelligence systems had to be constantly refined.

Patton often demonstrated his feel for a delicate aspect of intelligence: friendly counterintelligence. When, for example, Montgomery complained that Husky "breaks every commonsense rule of practical battle-fighting and is completely theoretical. It has no hope of success and should be completely recast," Ike granted him permission to form his own plan.[69] Patton entertained his own ideas and while acknowledging his assigned role in the initial invasion, he briefed his superiors that once he had a secure base he intended "to undertake further operations for the complete subjugation of the Island as may be directed by the General Officer commanding Force 141."[70]

One of Patton's favorite books, G. F. R. Henderson's *Stonewall Jackson and the American Civil War,* repeatedly illustrated Jackson's characteristic secrecy in developing his plans.[71] Henderson wrote, "He had not the slightest hesitation of withholding his plans from even his second in command; special correspondents were rigorously excluded from his camps; and even with his most confidential friends his reserve was absolutely impenetrable."[72] After a meeting with Jackson one general complained, "Oh hang him! He was polite enough. But he didn't say one word about his plans. . . . I haven't the slightest idea what they will be. I believe he has no more sense than my horse."[73] Patton signaled his devotion to this example in his

1910 edition of Sun Tzu's *The Art of War*. Next to a particular line about the commander—"He must be able to mystify his officers and men by false reports and appearances, and thus keep them in total ignorance"—Patton wrote in bright red pencil, double underlined, "à la Jackson."[74] In November 1944 Patton prepared an attack at a time when Montgomery wanted him stopped before briefing the war correspondents. "Who is the BBC man here?" Patton began. "You can do me a very great favor by lying for me when we attack by saying we are straightening our line for a winter operation. You know how to lie on this. That may gain us 24 hours."[75] He made a repeated practice of such furtiveness.

When Bradley ordered him to clear the Eifel north of the Moselle and link up with General Courtney Hodges, Patton decided to also send XII Corps east along the north bank of the Moselle from Diekirch through Bitburg and on to Coblenz so as to be positioned to cross the Rhine or turn into the Saar-Moselle triangle. He could then take advantage of whatever opportunity might arise. By this point in the war, however, he feared higher command interference more than the Germans and confided to his diary, "I am trying to keep the impending Bitburg operation secret so that the powers that be will not order it stopped."[76] Several historians have misread Patton's secrecy as impertinence. Charles B. MacDonald, a fierce critic of Patton, wrote, "Aware that Patton was impetuous and that grim, slugging warfare tried his thin patience, Eisenhower and Bradley kept a close rein on the Third Army commander but so unobtrusively that Patton himself often thought he was putting things over on his superiors when they were actually fully informed."[77] This was not quite the case. In the Eifel, as in Sicily and Normandy, Patton kept his plans to himself while taking care to execute the more mundane orders of his superiors. Only after all the conditions were set and the opportunity was ripe would he bring his superior commanders into his plans, certain the advantages presented as a fait accompli would gain their full approval. Of course he did so without concern that this habitual secrecy would confuse chroniclers such as MacDonald.

In Sicily, Patton also demonstrated the interaction between operations and intelligence. By quickly presenting a change in circumstances, he could destabilize the enemy's situational awareness and actually subvert their decision cycles. After repulsing a series of counterattacks in Gela on their first day ashore, Terry Allen's 1st Infantry Division had lost 58 killed, 199 wounded, and 700 missing while capturing 4,265 enemy soldiers in tough fighting.[78] Allen had to commit all his reserves to hold the line. "At the same time," Bradley, then Allen's superior, wrote, "Axis air hit us with full fury, causing chaos in our landing zone."[79] To the east Middleton advanced his 45th Infantry Division inland against lighter opposition, creating a gap between his division and the hard-pressed 1st Division. The enemy detected the gap and, expecting the Americans to consolidate, prepared to attack. Fearing this, Bradley ordered Allen to stretch his thin line even more to fill the gap. Travelling the front lines, Patton met Allen, countermanded Bradley's order, and directed Allen to advance and capture the Ponte Olivo airfield within the next twenty-four hours to reduce the air attacks.[80] Patton wanted to shock the Germans with the unexpected, put them on their heels, and make them susceptible to chaos.

When Allen attacked Ponte Olivo that night as ordered, he noted, "The surprise effect was instantaneous. By 3 a.m. July 12th, the 1st Division attack was rolling along in high gear, with an upsurge of combat morale throughout the entire Division."[81] Captured Germans revealed their ongoing preparations for a coordinated dawn attack and said that Allen's attack caught them completely by surprise. Allen reported, "Before the enemy could 'get set,' the 'Fighting First' had beaten them to the punch."[82] It was exactly the kind of shock Patton desired. Allen got the airfield, crippling Axis airpower over the beachhead, all by doing what the enemy did not expect. If he had followed Bradley's order, the Germans would not have been disrupted and their morning attack likely would have penetrated Allen's perilously thin line. The Ponte Olivo attack set a tone: it made the Germans uncertain about what to expect from Patton and therefore made them hesitant in future operations. They quickly turned their attention to Montgomery's front.

Patton, however, also got a surprise: the attack enraged Bradley.[83] Four decades later Bradley stewed, "In brief, Patton brashly countermanded an order I had given. . . . He did not consult me but gave the order directly to Terry Allen. It soon developed that the order was a mistake and the unit found itself in serious jeopardy."[84] In fact, the attack did not put the 1st Division in jeopardy, and Allen would have been in greater danger if he had obeyed Bradley's order. Ike subsequently conducted his first visit to Sicily, meeting with Bradley before going to see Patton on the USS *Augusta*. Bradley's anger over Ponte Olivo no doubt spurred Eisenhower to deliver his "purple scolding" about communications to the much-astonished Patton. It also played a part in Bradley's criticism of Patton and his staff while visiting Marshall in Washington later that year.

Sicily triggered Patton to again alter reconnaissance methods. He conducted detailed after action reviews with officers of all ranks from his divisions. The 9th Infantry Division reported that they went in with recon units "designed to operate and fight from their vehicles" but learned that in mountainous terrain they needed "foot patrols capable of sustained operations and fighting on foot."[85] The 45th Infantry Division found "the Germans are clever in night sound signals" and after several near-ambushes, "interpretation of night sounds" was added to essential fieldcraft training for recon units.[86] Units also reported, "Because of the rapid enemy withdrawal in some sectors, motor patrolling in ¼-ton vehicles likewise assumed importance."[87] These lessons and more fed constant adjustment to reconnaissance procedures in Third Army.

Elsewhere in Sicily, by D+3 Montgomery had, in accordance with his plan, advanced only twenty miles despite lighter than expected opposition. As in North Africa, he was content to advance apace with the enemy's retreat. Royal Artillery captain D. L. C. Price recalled, "Happily there was little local resistance, but I was conscious that the Army was not fully alive to the absolute necessity to move inland quickly, for our toe-hold would not save us in the event of a counterattack."[88] Curiously, in his published memoirs Montgomery devoted not one paragraph to Sicily *after* the initial landings. General Harold Alexander's memoirs summed up the campaign in one sentence: "Once firmly ashore the two Allied armies set about reducing the island, an operation that went according to plan."[89] In actuality, the British Eighth Army went adrift. Traditionalist commanders not only failed to adapt, they also lacked the intelligence systems required to do so.

In the first days of August, the German 1st Parachute Division and the 29th Grenadiers surprised the Eighth Army and blocked its path toward Catania.[90] Monty then slid the British 30 Corps west across Bradley's front around Mount Etna, effectively cutting the Americans out of the fight. Patton recalled, "They gave us the future plan of operations which cuts us off from any possibility of taking Messina."[91] Bradley wrote, "My staff and I were absolutely outraged. We at once perceived the full import of the decision: that Monty had nominated himself for [the] starring role on Sicily, leaving us in the dust."⁹² Alexander could have shifted his main effort to Patton. As Stephen Ambrose observed, "Patton's Seventh Army was in perfect position to carry out such a maneuver, and Patton was the perfect commander to lead such a drive."⁹³ What Bradley and Alexander did not know was that Patton had *anticipated* this moment and had prepared his secret plans to take Palermo.

"I asked General Alexander permission to advance and take Agrigento," Patton recorded, "which is beyond the line specified for the front of the Seventh Army. He stated that if this could be done through the use of limited forces, in the nature of a reconnaissance in force, he had no objection."⁹⁴ Historians tend to laugh off the "reconnaissance in force" as a Patton ploy, but the reconnaissance was important: if he had found significant resistance, Patton would have modified his plans. In fact, Patton had briefed Alexander on 21 June of his plans to seize Caltanissetta, Enna, and Agrigento as a "pivot" toward the subjugation of the whole island.⁹⁵ As it happened, his intelligence estimate of the enemy in western Sicily was correct. Before the sweep, Patton confided to his diary, "It is my opinion that when the present line of the combined armies is secured, which will probably be around the 19th, it will be feasible to advance rapidly with the 3rd Division and 2nd Armored Division and take Palermo. I will bring this up with Alexander when the time is ripe."⁹⁶ With the trucks secured a month before the invasion and his major units perfectly situated for this mission, Patton executed his historic drive to Palermo and then on to Messina.

Meanwhile, Lieutenant Michael Aldworth of the Royal Marines described the "total failure" of Montgomery's attacks along the Dittanio River: "Poor intelligence, indifferent planning, and almost complete lack of supporting arms (two 3.7 howitzers, which were soon knocked out) were the reasons. The whole of the Army seems to have suffered in the same way."⁹⁷ Monty then set in motion a plan for four divisions to attack at four separate points: Catania, Misterbianco, Paterno, and Adrano. These were not probing attacks, however, as he had not designated a reserve to exploit any success along the axes. He was waging wide-front attrition and wrote to Alexander, "These four thrusts are very strong and the enemy will not be able to hold them all."⁹⁸ Montgomery executed carefully planned operations and hoped for the best; Patton confused the enemy and seized opportunities as they arose. One checked to see if intelligence did not conflict with his plan; the other adapted his plan to changes in the situation revealed by intelligence.

Unfortunately, Montgomery's methods were the methods of higher command. When Ultra radio intercepts uncovered the German plans for withdrawal from Sicily to the Italian mainland, the Allied high command refused to alter operations.[99] As early as 5 August both Patton's and Montgomery's G-2 sections reported that the German withdrawal was under way, but Ike's G-2 disagreed, saying, "There are at present no adequate intentions that the enemy envisages evacuation of MESSINA bridgehead."[100] Monty pressed Alexander and Eisenhower for "the combined Navy-Air plan" to block Messina and concluded, "I fear the truth of the matter is there is NO plan."[101] Ike's staff had presumed different German actions and would not be persuaded to alter their plans. It would not be the last time.

The supreme example of the Allied rigidity came when First U.S. Army captured a bridge intact across the Rhine at Remagen in March 1945. Eisenhower's chief of operations told Bradley, "You're not going anywhere down there at Remagen. You've got a bridge, but it's in the wrong place. It just doesn't fit the plan."[102] Ike instructed Hodges to limit his bridgehead to five divisions and told Bradley not to advance without SHAEF approval.[103] There would be no exploitation. Similar forfeitures of opportunity occurred in Tunis, Caen, Falaise, Aachen, and Market Garden, among other places.

When training Third Army in England, Patton emphasized lessons learned in Sicily and North Africa. He issued instructions stating that "reconnaissance, particularly on the part of the infantry must be stressed."[104] He added, "It is necessary to secure information every night through the capture of prisoners and the observation of hostile actions."[105] Patton listed specifics about radio usage, codes, listening posts, and use of light tanks to draw enemy fire and reveal their locations. He felt the need to add the seemingly obvious statement, "All members of a reconnaissance unit should know what they're trying to do."[106] A month later he summed up: "We must take great and calculated risks in the use of armor, but we must not dive off the deep end without first determining whether the swimming pool is full of water."[107] He was not as reckless and daring as some thought. He followed Helmuth von Moltke's dictum: "First reckon, then risk."[108]

Patton showed special interest in augmenting his intelligence systems with air support. In May 1944 he sent a request to his higher headquarters:

"For some time and based on experiences in the various campaigns in the Mediterranean, including operations involving II Corps in Tunisia, Seventh Army in Sicily, and Fifth Army in Italy, the vital necessity for a Photographic Center on the Army level had definitely been proved."[109] He had been frustrated with the lack of aerial reconnaissance in the Mediterranean theater.[110] His G-2 for air intelligence got an agreement from the 10th Reconnaissance Group to provide daily photographic cover across the Army front.[111] Third Army drew up a table of organization and equipment for the center. Koch assembled a team of photographic interpreters from within Third Army, XIX TAC, and Seventh Army. By the time they hit France, the center had developed photographic reconnaissance of 96 percent of the Third Army's designated area of operations and 93 percent of Brittany.[112] It would remain a key asset, and by the end of the war, the Third Army Photographic Center had processed 1,342,517 air photo prints.[113]

Patton quickly expanded Third Army's G-2 staff beyond normal size and held extra intelligence briefs for his commanders along with daily staff meetings in a specially arranged room in Peover Hall, the Tudor manor that housed Patton's headquarters. Allen recalled, "The War Room was a true reflection of the Third Army and its Commanding General—spectacular and inimitable."[114] It included a 1/250,000-scale situation map of the entire Western Front depicting all Allied and German divisions. (Patton found fault with the first map posted by Koch explaining, "This is fine. But it only goes as far east as Paris. I'm going to Berlin."[115]) At one side stood a 1/100,000-scale map of Third Army's zone showing all units down to battalions. On the other side was a map of the Russian Front. As one staffer recalled, "G-2 reports from SHAEF and Twelfth Army Group were scanned for all information about enemy divisions moving from the Russian front, and from points as far away as Norway and Denmark."[116] A G-2 air subsection gathered and posted intelligence on enemy air forces.[117] Patton's staff also kept a daily casualty chart, the only one in the theater. All the displays could be quickly taken apart and reassembled. The "big picture" context helped frame his expectations in theater.

Recalling his own 1919 advice, Patton adapted an intelligence organization to his method of warfare. He put the 6th Cavalry Group directly under his headquarters, bypassing normal channels, to report on enemy *and* friendly activities along the front. Commonly called "Patton's Household

Cavalry," the 6th was under Colonel Edward Fickett and was sometimes referred to as Task Force Fickett. Patton also instituted plans for his staff officers to routinely visit and monitor regiments, battalions, and divisions. Together, these systems formed Patton's Army Information Service (AIS), which, according to the Third Army staff, "proved invaluable on the Continent by providing the Army Commander with the latest tactical information."[118] Years later John Boyd would cite Patton's Household Cavalry as an example of, in Grant T. Hammond's words, the ability to "direct and shape what is to be done as well as permit one to modify that direction and shape by assessing what is being done."[119] Rapid decision cycles absolutely depended on such intelligence.

As part of the AIS, G-3 liaison officers assisted intelligence collection by maintaining constant contact with front-line units to supply up-to-the-minute tactical information to Patton and his staff.[120] To collect information from civilian sources, Third Army created a new G-5 civil affairs section that grew to 1,200 men and 390 vehicles. Patton wrote, "The sole mission of Civil Affairs Administration is to further military objectives. The exercise of Civil Affairs control is a command responsibility."[121] Third Army also created a publicity and psychological warfare section, the G-6, "to monitor enemy and other radio broadcasts, to originate leaflets and other publications to persuade the enemy that his cause was lost, and to lift the morale of the French citizenship in occupied areas by means of news broadcasts by mobile units."[122] Intelligence was about the perception of the situation; psychological operations affected the enemy's perception. This wide range of intelligence sections demanded senior staff management, under Patton's direct attention.

Another key element of Patton's intelligence system first arrived during Torch when British special liaison units began sharing information from Ultra—the Enigma machine decrypts of the German signals communications—with Allied field commands.[123] An initially rough relationship between the civilian liaisons and Patton led Koch to act as a go-between in Africa and Sicily, where he provided Patton a daily one-page summary of intercepts. Prior to D-day SHAEF assigned to each American field army a U.S. officer to deliver Ultra reports. Major Melvin C. Helfers, a 1937 graduate of the Citadel and the only regular Army officer in Ultra duty, reported to Koch at Third Army. Not until the Germans were about to hit Mortain, however, did Koch introduce him to Patton. Helfers recalled, "I told him that since the Third Army had been operational, I had usually known twenty-four hours in advance what the Germans in front of Third Army units attempted to do."[124] Impressed, Patton immediately directed Helfers to personally brief him every morning at 0700 on all Ultra intelligence of the previous twenty-four hours. He was also authorized to bring any "important intelligence" directly to Patton or his chief of staff at any time. From that day on, Helfers became the only Ultra officer "in all the U.S. armies" who personally briefed his commander every day. As one senior Ultra officer observed, Patton "never failed to use every opportunity that Ultra gave him to bust open the enemy."[125] Some thought Patton lucky or impetuous. With Ultra added to his AIS, he *knew* what he was doing.

In addition to his intelligence systems, Patton insisted on personally interviewing people with knowledge of the front. These ran the gamut from new lieutenants to senior generals and included French partisans, local citizens, and even German prisoners. The records of his separate interviews with German soldiers such as Brigadier General Hans-Georg Schramm, *Schutzstaffel* (SS) major general Anton Dunckern, and Colonel Constantin Meyer reveal a deft touch in varying approaches to provoke responses that not only provided raw intelligence but also confirmed or denied assumptions and suppositions.[126]

All these sources fed into Patton's intelligence system, filtered by his personal knowledge of military theory and history and subject to his trained judgment in decisionmaking. If a scarcity of intelligence information never paralyzed him, it was because he could fill in the gaps with reasonable expectations drawn from a lifetime of study. By the end of his second tour as a G-2, he had collected over 321 military books in his personal library, most heavily annotated.[127] Colonel John S. Wood marveled at Patton's "splendid library of military works" and recalled, "We often sat, glass in hand, arguing loud and long on war, ancient and modern, with its battles and commanders."[128] When in 1930 he suffered from an inflammation of the eyes, his doctor was certain it was from reading into the wee hours every night.[129] Patton deemed reading of military history as essential to his skill as a commander, explaining: "Battles take years to get ready for, and all one's life can be expressed in one little decision but that decision is the labor of uncounted years. It is not genius but memory—unconscious memory—and character, and Divine Wrath which does not hesitate or count the cost."[130]

As early as 1919 Patton wrote: "To be useful in battle, military knowledge, like discipline, must be subconscious. . . . The officer must be so soaked in military lore that he does the military thing automatically."[131] One might argue that Patton's famous belief in reincarnation, and the eerie examples of his personal knowledge of old battlefields, likely resulted from the depth to which he immersed his subconscious in military lore. Patton underlined these lines in Maurice's *Strategikon*: "For battles are not won by weight of numbers, nor by *unreasoning* audacity, not yet by sheer persistence; but rather, by the help of God, by *trained military judgment and tactical skill* [emphasis in original]. Trained judgment utilizes times and places, even unexpected developments and all kinds of opportunities, to outwit the enemy; which may be possible, even without a general action, if a commander be alert and energetic."[132] Patton trained his judgment by mentally reenacting the history through his readings, thus gaining what Jon Sumida would term "synthetic experience" that in turn gave him a veteran's confidence and internal knowledge base.[133]

Through their books, the great masters passed on to Patton the value of intelligence. Sun Tzu taught: "If you know the enemy and know yourself, you need not fear the result of a hundred battles."[134] Napoleon wrote: "In forming the plan of a campaign, it is requisite to foresee everything the enemy may do, and to be prepared with the necessary means to counteract it. Plans of a campaign may be modified ad infinitum according to circumstance, the genius of the general, the character of the troops, and the features of the country."[135] Clausewitz warned that "most intelligence is false," said a "commander must trust his judgment," and added, "If he does not have a buoyant disposition, if experience of war has not trained him and matured his judgment, he had better make it a rule to suppress his personal convictions, and give his hopes and not his fears the benefit of the doubt."[136] Patton agreed and instructed his men, "You can never have too much reconnaissance. Use every available means before, during and after battle."[137]

Third Army reconnaissance, signals intelligence, aerial reconnaissance, civilian affairs, psychological operations, G-3 liaisons, Ultra, Task Force Fickett: they all fed Patton's hunger for information (see figure 5). With

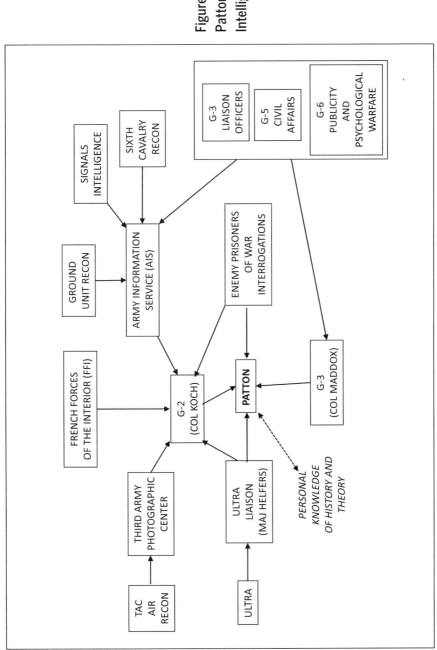

Figure 5.
Patton's Integrated
Intelligence Systems

these resources, he crafted operations to influence the competitive intelligence picture that brought the classical advice to life.

While his systems provided him situational awareness, Patton used operations to confuse his enemy. Through misdirection he clouded the enemy's intelligence picture and unbalanced their decisionmaking. For instance, on 24 January 1945 Bradley directed him to clear First Army's southern flank in the Eifel "without delay" and maintain an "aggressive defense" south of Dasburg to contain "the maximum number of enemy troops."[138] Because only VIII Corps was north of Dasburg, Bradley was in effect halting Third Army. Patton, however, saw opportunity to the south and told his staff, "I'm very anxious to attack in the Palatinate. . . . The bulk of the German forces are up here in the north, particularly their armor. It's the perfect situation for a breakthrough in the south. I have absolutely no doubt that if such an offensive was tied in with attacks by First and Seventh Armies, we could be on the Rhine in ten days."[139]

Two weeks later Patton wrote, "I awoke at 0300 on the morning of the sixth with the complete plan for a break-through by the VIII and XII Corps in my head, when this breakthrough took place, we could use two, possibly three, armored divisions for a re-enacting of the Brest Campaign."[140] As in Normandy, he believed he could break through the Eifel and pivot into the Palatinate. "This was the origin of the Palatinate Campaign," he later confirmed.[141] Patton had determined that when Third Army reached the Rhine on its drive through the Eifel, the Germans would logically expect him to continue northeast across the river, but instead he would turn ninety degrees southeast, jump the Moselle River, cross the Hunsrück Mountains, and cut through the Palatinate to reach the Rhine between Mainz and Karlsruhe—the crossing points he had planned in England a year before. His misdirection caught the enemy by complete surprise and led to the destruction of the German First and Seventh Armies in the Palatinate and the capture of 80,000 soldiers—along with pinching General Alexander Patch's slow-moving Seventh U.S. Army off the Rhine.[142]

While confusing and unbalancing enemy intelligence and decision cycles, Patton displayed exceptional attentiveness to preventing the Germans from doing the same to him. Prior to a directed offensive in November 1944 to "bring the whole pack [of Germans] in on me" and away from the Ninth and First Armies, Third Army exhibited remarkable measures to maintain security.¹⁴³ The 10th Armored Division moved to the south of XX Corps and the 4th and 6th Armored Divisions moved to the north of XII Corps to make the enemy think Patton was concentrating for a breakthrough south of Metz. XX Corps reported that as divisions moved, "all vehicle markings and shoulder patches were changed to correspond with those of the 3rd Cavalry Group, which had been operating for several weeks in that area."¹⁴⁴ Patton altered reconnaissance north of Metz to mislead the enemy. Artillery units moving to attack positions, a sure indicator of a new attack, left some guns behind with increased rates of fire "to match the volume normally fired by all the artillery."¹⁴⁵ All movement was under radio listening silence at night while the 23rd Special Troops maintained false radio nets from the old locations.

Patton then attacked in weather that Robert Grow called the "the worst I have ever seen. I do not see how any operation is possible."¹⁴⁶ Manton Eddy and Grow tried to convince him to postpone his advance but he refused, reasoning that the Germans would not expect an attack. Others were also surprised. Bradley called Patton to ask what he would do now that the weather had cancelled all air support. "I'm attacking, Brad. Can't you hear our guns?" answered Patton. Eisenhower took the phone and told Patton, "I'm thrilled boy! I expect a hell of lot from you, so carry the ball all the way!"¹⁴⁷ Third Army staff reported: "Without benefit of preliminary aerial bombardments, in rain and with unprecedented flood conditions prevailing, the attack, as German prisoners later stated, achieved tactical surprise, for the enemy considered it impossible for Third U.S. Army to launch an offensive under such unfavorable weather and terrain conditions."¹⁴⁸ Similar surprise marked his historic "assault crossing" of the Rhine, an operation that, when compared to Montgomery's crossing, illustrated the vast difference in their methods of warfare.

Perhaps the entry in Patton's diary for 11 January 1945 best illustrates his use of intelligence and belies the legend of his "intuition."¹⁴⁹ Before driving out to meet General Walton Walker and XX Corps, Patton consulted with his G-2 and had the section draw up a map for him "showing the road nets and river lines" in their area. G-2 reported the Germans had river crossing equipment available in XX Corps' zone and located three possible sites. The enemy had pontoons and a serviceable road and railway bridges near Saarburg. Patton thought it unlikely they would cross there because the terrain and the road network were poor. They could attempt to seize Third Army's crossing points near Saarlautern, but it would mean heavy fighting and exposure to American demolitions. "Speed is of such importance to him," Patton reasoned, "that he will not want to attack through here where it will take at least three or four days to cut a road."[150] The Germans also held a bridgehead at Saarbrücken where several standing bridges spanned the river and led to an excellent road network to a point where Patton blocked their path at Saint-Avold. Patton determined that was the most likely place for any German attack. He instructed Walker to prepare demolitions on all crossings on the Nied River "so we can canalize the enemy" and petitioned Bradley for permission to immediately attack the Germans at Saarbrücken to disrupt potential German plans. Bradley ordered him to wait.

Brenton Wallace once said of Patton: "The Old Man apparently made his decision[s] very rapidly, but they were always based on the fullest information and data prepared by his staff."[151] Robert Allen, deputy to Koch, added, "In planning, G-2 always had first say. The usual procedure in other headquarters was to decide what to do and then, perhaps, ask G-2 what was out in front. Patton always got this information first and then acted on the basis of it."[152] Koch merged the intelligence collection systems into a usable product for his boss. Patton then compared the latest intelligence from G-2 with his personal knowledge of military history and theory obtained by his long study of the subjects.

Often the Germans achieved surprise not because of poor Allied intelligence, but because of a lack of judgment by the Allied commanders. On New Year's Day 1945 the Luftwaffe destroyed 180 Allied planes on the ground in Brussels—including Montgomery's personal C-47 Dakota. David Irving noted, "Once again Ultra had given good warning, and once again the Allies were caught with their pants down—in fact, Montgomery's G-2 sent a pair of suspenders to the RAF tactical air commander's G-2."[153] Shortly afterward Bradley ordered Patton to halt and shift divisions to defend the Moselle against a phantom threat. Hirshson noted, "Tracing the origins of the story that the Germans intended to attack southeast of Luxembourg, Koch found it to be the product of the same intelligence officer who, unlike himself, had been caught unaware by the Ardennes offensive."[154] Patton complained, "This is the second time I have been stopped in a successful attack due to the Germans having more nerve than we have—that is, not me, but some of the others."[155] Most errors were not failures of the intelligence system, but rather failures of commanders to use their intelligence.

The importance of intelligence to Patton's operations can be seen in what happened when many of his systems were eliminated. In the Lorraine, one artilleryman noted, "There were no pretty French girls helping us, 'Cherchez les Bouches,' no 'Vin Rouge,' no more 'warm and friendly sunshine,' just plenty of rain."[156] Stripped of divisions, Third Army had only two corps with at most six infantry and three armored divisions; there could be few probes of the enemy lines. SHAEF sent half of the XIX Tactical Air Command to Brittany.[157] Foul weather and gas shortages further halted ground and air reconnaissance, causing Third Army to lose contact with the retreating Germans. As the Germans occupied static defensive positions, they turned to landline communications instead of radios, making Ultra irrelevant. With fuel cut, XX Corps had to withdraw its cavalry from undefended Metz after Koch reported enemy activity in the formerly empty fortifications of de Mousson, Saint-Blais, de Foire, Plappeville, Jeanne d'Arc, Ancy-sur-Moselle, Saint-Julien-lés-Metz, and Queuleu.

Patton tried to probe the Metz-Trier area and was encouraged by reports from Eddy: "None of the Germans in this sector have any fight left in them."[158] When after the pause Walker was able to send a "reconnaissance in force" toward the Moselle River, however, they encountered enemy from Nilvange to Havange to Terville to Uckange. There was no visible weak spot. Patton pushed harder without success. After forty-eight hours, XX Corps reported: "It had become apparent that the German garrison had built up strong defenses in this area and near Thionville."[159] Successive probing attacks finally forced the 553rd Volksgrenadier Division to withdraw from Nancy on 15 September, which, Rickard observed, "proved Patton's point" in that the Germans were "incapable of defending in depth" along the Moselle.[160] But with too few forces, little air cover, and crippled intelligence, and robbed of supply, Patton was unable to achieve shock or exploitation. German chief of staff General Siegfried Westphal recalled, "I have always regarded it as a miracle that we succeeded in halting the eastward flight of our defeated West Army and, after many worrisome weeks, managed to build another, even if only on a very thin front."[161] Actually, the lack of gas and crippled intelligence halted Patton.

When in place, however, the effectiveness of Patton's layered intelligence systems was impressive, never more so than during the months preceding the German offensive in the Battle of the Bulge. Trained to always look beyond the immediate Third Army front, as early as 3 October 1944, Patton's G-2 noticed a suspicious buildup of German armor reserves from panzer units withdrawn from the front line. By month's end Koch identified by name the 130th Panzer Lehr, 90th SS, 12th SS, and 2nd SS reforming in the Paderborn area north of Frankfurt.[162] During a break in the weather in mid-November, he prodded the 12th Army Group to allow XIX TAC to fly night reconnaissance over railroad yards and highway intersections across the Siegfried Line in front of First Army. Within twenty-four hours he had photos indicating that hundreds of trains had been moving into Saarbrücken and the Eifel. By 23 November, Koch estimated five panzer divisions and six parachute divisions were in Westphalia and warned, "This powerful striking force, with an estimated 500 tanks, is still an untouched strategic reserve held for future employment . . . a formidable strategic reserve for coordinated counteroffensive employment."[163] Two days later, after complaining about an unequal distribution of forces, Patton confided to his diary, "The First Army is making a terrible mistake in leaving the VIII Corps static, as it is highly probable that the Germans are building up east of them. The only way to think about these things is to remember that 'What can't be cured must be endured.'"[164]

Busy with his own impending attack, Patton grew concerned the Germans were preparing to interfere with his plans.[165] On 2 December Koch reported that there was a definite enemy buildup of troops and supplies "directly opposite the north flank of Third U.S. Army and the southern flank of First U.S. Army."[166] Two days later he identified eight panzer, three parachute, and three infantry divisions "out of contact in the north," and he said the 5th and 6th SS panzer armies were being held in a powerful mobile reserve "despite the threatening advances into Germany."[167] Would they attack First Army or counterattack against a Third Army breakthrough? On 7 December the Third Army G-2 periodic report reiterated the threat to First Army and noted that the Germans had added the 5th and 8th Paratroops to their reserve despite a chronic shortage of infantry in the front lines.[168] Koch added "that on the basis of this analysis a large build-up of troops and supplies clearly was in progress opposite the southern (Ardennes) flank of First Army."[169]

Patton forwarded Koch's estimate to Bradley's staff. "A few days later," said Allen, "indirect word came back to the effect, 'Mind your own business. We're running this war.'"[170] Koch later explained, "We were minding our own business when we overlapped the armies to the north and south in sufficient depth, intelligence-wise, to protect our flanks."[171] Unknown to Koch, higher headquarters had already been warned. Deciphered radio traffic from the Pacific theater delivered to Eisenhower in September revealed: "The German leader had told the Emperor's ambassador [General Oshima Hiroshi] of his plan to 'open a large scale offensive in the west after the beginning of November.'"[172] Both the SHAEF chief of staff and G-2 had warned Bradley that the Germans would launch a "spoiling attack . . . at the first bad break in the weather."[173] Bradley recalled, "Ike's G-2, Kenneth Strong, at Bedell Smith's suggestion, came to Luxembourg in early December to warn me that, among other possibilities, the German 6th Panzer Army might launch a 'relieving' (or spoiling) attack through the Ardennes against VIII Corps. But at no time did anyone present me with unequivocal or convincing evidence that a massive German attack through the Ardennes at VIII Corps was imminent."[174] Without very rare "unequivocal or convincing" intelligence, the normally cautious Bradley refused to adjust Hodges' lines and dismissed Strong by saying, "Let them come."[175] Hitler's delays had only added to Bradley's false sense of security.

As Carlo D'Este observed, "Koch was the only Allied intelligence officer to anticipate trouble and plan how to deal with it. Thus, where other intelligence officers were lulling their commanders with false optimism and wishful thinking that nothing serious was imminent, the Third Army made plans to deal with what no one else believed would occur."[176] Allen believed this was a result of Patton's unique approach to intelligence. The Allied high command, he thought, "advanced, and acted, on a wishful-thinking theory . . . taught in all U.S. Service Schools, of evaluating the enemy situation based not on the basis of his 'capabilities' but on the British practice of trying to dope out his 'intentions.'"[177] Patton had a unique wide view of intelligence, monitoring all fronts and using all sources, and built his plans upon perceived enemy capabilities.

Years after being caught disastrously off guard, Bradley faulted the Allied "intelligence community" for failing to forecast the German attack in the Ardennes due to its overreliance on "infallible" Ultra, but Ralph Bennett noted there were forty to fifty Ultra intercepts each day indicating such an attack was possible, if not probable.[178] He explained, "The information they contain is not wholly free from ambiguity . . . but when all due allowance has been made it does seem to point much more convincingly towards a coming attack than it was held to do."[179] Those indicators—like Koch's warnings—were disregarded in large part because of Allied commanders' desire to believe otherwise, and the Germans reinforced that belief. A German deception plan, *Abwehrschlacht im Westen* (the Defensive Battle in the West), planted radio communications that portrayed the massing German reserves as a counterattack force aimed at penetrations toward the Rhine.[180] In part the "intelligence failure" was a simple reflection of the Allied habit of forcing circumstance to meet plans; no one planned for a German counteroffensive. Finally, it was also a symptom of a lack of aggressiveness in obtaining intelligence, a further sign that commanders such as Bradley were satisfied to consider intelligence that came to them rather than go see for themselves. Bradley's condemnation of Ultra does not excuse his failure to see what Patton saw.

Patton arranged for additional photo air reconnaissance between 3 and 9 December, the results of which led Koch to estimate "an enemy buildup of six and one-half divisions."[181] The Third Army G-2 found two German buildup areas, one between Düsseldorf and Cologne and the other north of Trier, but noted that movement in the northern one occurred during the day and the southern one only at night. Koch therefore deduced that the northern area was a decoy and the southern area was real, meaning any German attack would most likely hit First Army's VIII Corps in the Ardennes.[182] On 9 December he briefed Patton and his staff that General Troy Middleton's VIII Corps faced more than two and a half times the number of German forces facing the entire Third Army, three and a half more divisions than Seventh Army, and only one less division than the rest of First Army combined. Alarmed, Patton ordered his staff to draw up contingencies to respond to a German assault on VIII Corps or to meet a possible flank attack on his own pending eastward advance and vowed, "We'll be in position to meet whatever happens."[183]

On 10 December Hodges' G-2, Monk Dickson (who had served under Patton in Tunisia and hated him for it), published his estimate of the situation and reported that the Germans would await "the exhaustion of our offensive" before they launched "an all-out counterattack with armor" somewhere between the Roer and the Erft north of the Ardennes opposite Aachen, *after* "our major ground forces have crossed the Roer River."[184] Hodges requested two additional divisions for VIII Corps. Bradley said no.[185] The 12th Army Group commander later explained, "We were thinking in terms of (as a SHAEF intelligence report put it) 'a spoiling attack of considerable power' *after* we crossed the Roer River."[186] Bradley failed to consider that SHAEF might be wrong.

Oscar Koch issued another estimate stating that the enemy maintained a cohesive defensive front "without drawing on the bulk of his infantry and armor reserves."[187] The Germans, he wrote, had "a strong reserve of eight Panzer divisions," along with a possible ninth division from the east, five of which were "available for speedy employment [against] First and Ninth U.S. Armies" in a *spoiling offensive*—not a counterattack. Years later Bradley would acknowledge Koch's "excellent work" since 20 November but argued that Koch only cautioned about "limited" German operations and thus merited little notice.[188]

At the time Bradley's G-2, Eddie Sibert, flatly disagreed with Koch. As late as 12 December in his weekly intelligence summary he wrote: "It is now certain that attrition is steadily sapping the strength of the German forces on the Western Front and the crust of the defense is thinner, more brittle, and more vulnerable than it appears on our G-2 Maps or to the troops in the line. . . . before long he will not only fail in his current attempt to withdraw and rest his tactical reserve, but he will be forced to commit at least part of his Panzer Army to the line."[189] This thinking appeared to be classic mirror imaging: SHAEF embraced a strategy of attrition and assumed the Germans did too, thereby disregarding any idea that the Germans were looking for a chance to execute maneuver warfare. Sibert added, "With continued Allied pressure in the south and north, the breaking point may develop suddenly and without warning."[190] That same day Patton shared his concerns with his staff about a possible enemy attack against First Army and ordered them to make "a study of what Third Army would do if called upon to counterattack such a breakthrough."[191] With foresight gained from intelligence he instructed, "I want you, gentlemen, to start making plans for pulling the Third Army out of its eastward attack, change the direction 90 degrees, moving to Luxembourg and attacking north."[192]

On 14 December Patton drove to Luxembourg to see Bradley, still intending to launch his attack. That same evening a Luxembourg resident reported to Dickson that she had seen many German vehicles, boats, and bridging equipment arriving near Bitburg. In a flash Dickson reported to Hodges, "It's the Ardennes!"[193] He now also believed the Germans would attack VIII Corps; the bridging equipment was for the Meuse. When he reported this to Hodges, Dickson was told to take some overdue leave in Paris. Bradley later rationalized that Dickson was "often a pessimist and an alarmist" and added, "Had I gone on guard every time Dickson, or any other G-2, called wolf, we would never have taken many of the riskier moves that hastened the end of the war"—an extraordinary remark from someone known for avoiding risks.[194] Eisenhower would add, "The commander who took counsel only of the gloomy Intelligence estimates would never win a battle; he would forever be sitting, fearfully waiting for the predicted catastrophes."[195] As Danny Parker noted, Dickson "had developed a reputation as something of doomsayer all through the Normandy Campaign. His peers regarded him as something less than an oracle. An anonymous member of the Washington D.C. based Office of Strategic Services had penned a sarcastic comment under a picture of Hitler that hung in their 12th Army Group office: 'He fools some of the people some of the time, but he fools Dickson all of the time.'"[196]

On 15 December Montgomery published his own signed appreciation of the situation, sending a copy to Bradley—but not to Patton. Monty wrote: "The enemy is at present fighting a defensive campaign on all fronts; his situation is such that he cannot stage major offensive operations. Furthermore, at all costs he has to prevent the war from entering a mobile phase; he has not the transport or the petrol that would be necessary for mobile operations, nor could his tanks compete with ours in the mobile battle."[197] His appreciation reflected supposed German intentions, not German capabilities. About twenty-four hours after he sent out this estimate, the Germans launched their most devastating counteroffensive in the west during the war. Monty's starkly incorrect estimate strangely disappeared from nearly all unit records.

After the war Bradley recalled, "On the morning of December 16, Koch suggested in his report that the reformed and refitted panzers were either 'available for immediate employment in the event of a serious threat of a major [Allied] breakthrough' or were being massed 'in positions of tactical reserve presumably for a large-scale counter offensive.' I, of course, did not see these Koch reports. Even if I had, they would not have unduly alarmed me."[198] Intriguingly, this time Bradley recalled that Koch referred to a "large-scale counter offensive" and not small "limited attacks."

That night Third Army's Signal Intelligence Service noticed that the German reserves north of Trier were breaking up and moving out. Koch was discussing this information with Patton when the intelligence service reported that the Germans had gone to radio listening silence. "I don't know what it means when the Germans go on radio silence," he told Patton, "but when we place one of our units in radio silence it means they are going to move. In this particular case, sir, I believe the Germans are launching an attack, probably at Luxembourg."[199] Patton quickly called in his G-3, Colonel Halley Maddox, to review the contingencies they had prepared.

As they received reports describing German attacks in the Ardennes at Eisenhower's headquarters over champagne and a game of bridge, Bradley recalled, "At first Ike and I were frankly astonished that the *Volksgrenadier* divisions could mount an offensive. However, it gradually became apparent—Ike sensed it before I did—that this was no spoiling attack by *Volksgrenadier* divisions but rather an all-out offensive by three German armies."[200] Remembering Bradley's dismissal of Strong's warnings, Bedell Smith said, "Well, Brad, you've been wishing for a counterattack. Now it looks as though you've got it." "A counterattack, yes," replied Bradley, "but I'll be damned if I wanted one this big."[201]

Patton had finally built up enough supplies to launch Third Army east into Germany. Just as the 25th Cavalry Regiment crossed the border, Colonel Paul Harkins received a call at headquarters from 12th Army Group's G-3 who said Bradley wanted Patton to immediately chop the 10th Armored Division to First Army's VIII Corps. With that division assigned a critical role in his attack Patton called Bradley and pleaded, "Listen Brad, don't spoil my show."[202] Years later Bradley wrote, "Patton's intuition appeared to have deserted him" in that he apparently failed to realize the gravity of the situation.²⁰³ Off the phone, however, Patton turned to Colonel Codman and said, "I guess they're having some trouble up there. I thought they would."²⁰⁴

Koch was often asked after the war if Patton possessed some sort of supernatural intuition that enabled him to foresee enemy actions. He would reply, "If one can call anticipation of enemy reactions based on a lifetime of professional training and on thinking and application 'intuition,' he had it."²⁰⁵ He added, "Anything he had done that would have military application later was stored in his retentive memory, to be applied at the first opportunity. He was a military analyst, always analyzing what the result would be if certain other things happened first."²⁰⁶ With his shock strategy, his combined arms columns, his methods of command and control, and his layered and integrated intelligence systems, Patton created and exploited chaos with revolutionary effectiveness. Nowhere did he more successfully demonstrate his way of war than in the breakout from Normandy.

BREAKOUT: CONCEPTUALIZATION | 6

> Sometimes I wish I had George Patton here.
> —*Dwight Eisenhower discussing Normandy*

The breakout from Normandy is often held up as a prime example of Patton's effectiveness as a commander in action. Left unexamined are the preceding months of preparation that reveal both the genius of the man and the deliberate radicalism of his methods. His remarkable prescience confirmed his unparalleled vision and the inability of his peers to comprehend his unconventional ways. The months of preparation validated Patton's way of war.

After the slapping incidents in Sicily, Patton faced an uncertain future. At 0900 hours on 2 September 1943, he reported to headquarters in Algiers, where Eisenhower lectured him for nearly two hours.[1] Ike announced he would both disband Patton's Seventh Army and send Bradley to England to oversee the formation of the new army for the eventual invasion of France. Patton entered limbo. When the news broke a few days later he wrote, "It is very heartbreaking. . . . I feel like death but will survive—I always have."[2] When his former deputy left for Washington enroute to London, Patton wrote, "Bradley has a chance to help or hurt me with General Marshall. I hope he chooses the former course of action but I did not ask him to."[3] A month later he learned that Marshall had heard that Patton's staff was "not good" in Sicily.[4]

Former Army chief of staff Charles Summerall once told Patton that it was a curse to have a good staff because other commanders always tried to steal them. No one tried to pilfer Patton's men. He commented, "Apparently people have a very low opinion of my staff. Personally, I would not trade them for any other staff officers in Africa or the U.S. and I believe they feel the same way about me."[5] Facing an indefinite stay in the doghouse, Patton offered his staff the chance to leave, but none asked to go.

Otherwise idle, Patton had his staff analyze ongoing operations in Italy and work up contingencies for possible future operations around the Mediterranean and in France. Their work led him to interesting discussions with SHAEF and Armed Forces Headquarters (AFHQ) in early September 1943. "Replacements are the thing," Patton wrote. "I am convinced that some day a serious investigation will take place with respect to the culpable negligence shown by the staff of AFHQ in failing to keep General Eisenhower informed of shortages, and in failing to supply those shortages."[6] As events would prove, his was an astute and prescient evaluation.

At the end of September, Harry Butcher told Patton that Marshall was likely to assume U.S. command in England with Ike as his chief of staff.[7] He said Ike would recommend Patton for command of an army. "I knew that," Patton said, "and can't see how he could have done otherwise."[8] Instead, Patton began to seriously consider operations in France with a new sense of independence. Pondering a potential rivalry with Montgomery, he wrote, "I know I can outfight the little fart any time."[9]

Not until a dinner in Algiers on 27 October did Patton learn for certain—from Smith—that he would receive an army in England. In the meantime, Smith told Patton that he was to use "the prestige of the Seventh Army to draw attention to Corsica."[10] It was the first of many visible deployments over the next two months in which Patton and his staff moved about the Mediterranean to deceive the Germans as to Allied intentions. Hearing in early December that Winston Churchill was "still fooling around about small attacks in the Aegean area," Patton's hopes rose.[11] He then heard that Joseph Stalin dismissed such plans and told Churchill, "This is the last round of a prize fight and it is not the time to dance around the ring but to go in and slug. . . . It is time for you to attack both in the north, and also in the south, of France. I have whittled the enemy down to your size."[12]

Smith called to instruct Patton "to back up AFHQ and make no statement if I was visited by correspondents."[13] Journalist Drew Pearson had ignored Eisenhower's pleas and had broken the story of the slapping incidents. White House adviser Harry Hopkins told Patton, "Don't let anything that s.o.b. Pearson said bother you."[14] As public and political pressure against him swelled, however, Patton confided, "Of course I am worried, but I am quite confident that the Lord will see me through."[15] Assistant Secretary of War John J. McCloy passed the word that Marshall promised

Patton would still get an army. Patton thought, "I should have a group of armies, but that will come."[16] Then another troublesome sign appeared on 7 December when he learned Marshall would remain chief of staff in Washington; Eisenhower would be supreme commander in the European theater.

Finally, on New Year's Day, Patton received orders to move to England. As Seventh Army would remain in Sicily to prepare an invasion of southern France, he had to work to get his staff to follow him to London. "I suppose that I am going to England to command another army but if I am sent there to simply train troops which I am not to command," he worried, "I shall resign."[17] On 3 January Patton saw a copy of a letter written by a British general that said in part: "We don't need worry about being commanded by an American. Ike is only a political General and cannot command, he has never had any experience."[18] Two weeks later he learned secondhand that Bradley would command all U.S. troops in the invasion. Patton again felt keenly disappointed, calling Bradley "a man of great mediocrity" and concluding, "I suppose that all that has happened is calculated to get my morale so that I will say 'What the Hell! Stick it up your ass and I will go home,' but I won't. I still believe."[19] Patton had reached the point at which, if he got another chance, he was determined to do things his way, and damn the consequences.

The London *Daily Express*'s 18 January announcement of Bradley's appointment as the "senior United States Ground commander" left Patton deflated. He wrote, "I had thought that possibly I might get this command."[20] Reflecting common misperception, Marshall wrote: "Patton would be the best man, of course, to lead the invasion, but he is too impetuous. He needs a brake to slow him down . . . and that is why I am giving the command to Bradley."[21] Ike assured Marshall that "in no repeat no event will I ever advance Patton beyond Army command."[22] Both commanders simply failed to appreciate the method behind Patton's façade of impetuousness. By placing Bradley in charge, they seriously challenged Patton's ability to wage his way of war.

On 26 January Eisenhower officially notified Patton that he would command the Third U.S. Army. His days in the wilderness were over. Bradley later admitted, "Had Eisenhower asked for my opinion, I would have counseled against the selection."[23] Bradley later said he dreaded confrontations with Patton and thus determined to make First Army under Courtney

Hodges his main effort. It is likely that Bradley's inability to comprehend Patton's methods made him uneasy. As in Tunisia and Sicily, Patton would be relegated to a supporting role. Privately, he noted, "Not such a good job, but better than nothing."[24] He entered into his diary, "As far as I can remember this is my twenty-seventh start from zero since entering the U.S. Army. Each time I have made a success of it, and this one must be the biggest."[25] He began by meeting with Army Service Forces commander General J. C. H. Lee to talk logistics.

Patton's new command was a closely held secret as he was then being covertly advertised to German spies as the commander of the fictional First U.S. Army Group (FUSAG) for an invasion at Calais. Bradley explained, "Early in the war the British, through Ultra intercepts of Hitler's spy organization, *Abwehr*, were able to find and capture every German spy in England. Most of these spies were 'turned' into double agents, feeding the *Abwehr* disinformation or harmless truth."[26] The British wanted the Germans to believe that Patton would command an invasion at Calais. General Siegfried Westphal, Field Marshal Gerd von Rundstedt's chief of staff, later wrote, "As far as General Patton was concerned, I was of the opinion even then that he was by far the outstanding commander in the [Allied] camp."[27] Rundstedt also believed Pas de Calais was the only sensible place for the Allied invasion.[28] The combination of Patton and Calais, therefore, seemed a likely basis for a readily believable deception plan.

Meanwhile, Bradley worked with SHAEF on the real invasion plans, known as Operation Overlord. On 27 January Patton got his first look at these plans and thought them "bad."[29] First U.S. Army, with six infantry and two armored divisions, would invade on the west side of the landing area on a two-division front, while Montgomery landed to the east on a three-division front. Montgomery's position placed him in the ideal start point toward the open plains beyond Caen and through Alençon toward Paris, the Ruhr, and, hopefully, Berlin. Bradley would take ports in Cherbourg and Brest for logistics bases. On the drive east, Monty would have the sea on his north flank and Bradley's Americans protecting his south flank. While not spelled out, this intention was clear.

According to the initial plan, Patton's Third Army would come ashore some time after the Allies captured a port. He would then help clear Normandy and turn west to take Brittany and the port of Brest before counter-marching east to protect the southern flank of Bradley's forces, which were protecting Monty's southern flank. It was a secondary mission to a secondary mission. Patton noted, "A hell of a lot of things can happen before that time."[30]

According to Farago, when Bradley finished his briefing and asked Patton for his thoughts, the new Third Army commander replied, "I don't know, Brad. I really don't know. It seems to be all right as far as it goes—but I don't think it goes far enough."[31] He then departed to greet his arriving staff in Scotland, leaving Bradley haunted by his comment. Whatever the exact words, the purported conversation accurately captures the essential conflict of vision between the two men. Patton immediately detected a lack of strategy in Overlord. He noted the SHAEF plan simply got troops ashore to build a lodgment "from which further operations can be developed"; he wanted a position that threatened the enemy.[32] Patton commented: "The words 'further offensive operations' indicate to me the intention of halting on a phase line—this is clearly wrong. After we land we must keep on driving, as we did in Sicily. I am very much afraid this operation is going to be conducted in a timid manner. If so, it will not succeed."[33]

Overlord outlined the start of a very linear campaign. While the Germans could only guess where the initial landings would be, once ashore the Allies could be expected to move in a linear direction toward Paris and Germany. Their advance, while likely conducted in a powerful mass, could be easily anticipated. Patton noted SHAEF's only contingencies, "Rankin A and B and C to be put in effect should the Boche cave," and urged another "in the not too unlikely event that the initial landing of the leading armies (First U.S. and First British Army) gets boxed."[34] Patton foresaw the enemy containing Normandy, thus creating ripe conditions for landing a follow-on force (including Third Army) elsewhere to cut behind the German lines and conduct a campaign constructed on a series of shocks. He put together a plan for landing at Calais and submitted it to Bradley on 18 February, saying, "I feel that there is much merit in the plan, as it would disperse the German Reserves and give room for maneuver."[35] He did not mention that by landing in Calais, Patton would also usurp the best approach to Paris from Montgomery. His plan went nowhere. Before the end of the month Patton had his staff prepare contingencies for landing Third Army at either

Saint-Malo, Saint-Brieuc, Morlaix, Brest, or Vannes—all points he would later visit.[36]

Third Army took up residence at the British base near Knutsford, Camp Peover, where it received Weyland and his XIX Tactical Air Command. Some units, such as the 5th and 8th Infantry Divisions, were already in England; others, such as the 4th Armored Division under Patton's old friend Major General John S. Wood, arrived later. For the first time in the war, Patton would train his units in his doctrine before taking them into battle. As Hirshson noted, the fields of England became another laboratory for Patton to test his ideas on the proper conduct of war.[37] It may well be said that France was won on the fields of Knutsford.

Patton fretted over getting his staff in place so that he could form his army in his image.[38] Bedell Smith granted him permission to bring sixteen of his old team from the Seventh Army, including Maddox, Koch, and Muller.[39] Most of his personal staff arrived on 10 February, and his "G" staff followed on 26 February. Patton wrote, "I was delighted to see them."[40] Initially he retained Hap Gay as his chief of staff, but Ike objected strenuously, saying that Gay was unsuited to represent his boss at headquarters. Some felt Ike and his staff secretly held Gay responsible for ignoring orders not to take Palermo. Patton was made to feel that if he did not replace Gay, "I will be superseded myself."[41] He waited until April Fool's Day to replace Gay with Hugh Gaffey.

On 11 February Patton attended a briefing at Montgomery's headquarters. Named the overall commander of the Allied ground forces in the invasion, Monty—whom Patton described as "an actor but not a fool"—outlined updated plans that now placed a division of Third Army, soon followed by a full corps, with Bradley's First Army on D-day. Perhaps thinking he would command these troops, Patton looked at the map and mused, "Possibly two armored divisions via the same route. These will start in on D plus 10, the rest in the Third Army on D plus 25."[42] This—in early February—was the first indication of his conceptualization of the narrow front armored spearhead that six months later would lead the breakout of Normandy. Patton would learn, however, that he would not get command until Bradley officially stood up Third Army. Until then, Bradley would command Patton's lead divisions in a more doctrinally correct, wide-front infantry attack. When Monty finished his brief, Patton thought, "It is not a very critical job for me but things can develop almost any way at any time. One can make his own job. In Sicily, I was destined to cover the rear area of the Eighth Army but I did not."[43] As in Sicily, he entertained his own plans and kept them close to his vest.

Patton seemed fixed on two considerations: where the most advantageous landing positions were and how he could use them to initiate a series of shocks upon the enemy. He began looking anew at ideas for a breakout that would enable a sweep around the enemy rear area. He indicated his thoughts in a letter to his friend in Oahu, Walter Dillingham: "We succeeded in Sicily by those methods which I learned from you in Honolulu—that is, when you get the enemy on the run, keep him there. Had I ever stopped to let myself or the soldiers rest, the Germans would have dug in, and it would have cost many thousands more lives to have moved them out."[44] He now sought to repeat his way of war in France.

On 6 March Patton issued his first "Letter of Instruction" to Third Army, setting to paper many of his long-developed principles. Casting doctrine aside, he wrote that proper command was 10 percent planning and 90 percent execution.[45] Plans were to be "simple and flexible" foundations from which to build operations designed to seize surfacing opportunities.[46] He instructed, "You can never have too much reconnaissance. Use every means available before, during, and after battle."[47] He wanted his officers to visit the front. Above all, he stressed initiative to enable commanders to "act as to obtain the general objective" in the absence of further orders.[48] The Third Army was now enrolled in the school of Patton.

As Allied ground commander, Montgomery continued to polish the Overlord plans. He organized his troops into the 21st Army Group, with Bradley's First U.S. Army on the west and General Sir Miles Dempsey leading the British Second Army on the east. On D-day the British were to seize Caen—the gateway to the plains leading to Paris—while Bradley turned northwest to secure the port of Cherbourg. When the Allies were prepared to advance beyond the initial lodgment area, sometime between D+15 and D+60, Bradley would stand up the 12th Army Group with Patton's Third Army and give First Army to his deputy, Courtney Hodges. Monty would add Henry "Harry" Crerar's First Canadian Army to his now separate 21st Army Group. Patton was to head west, away from Germany, to capture the major port at Brest, and then "be prepared to operate to the east, either in close conjunction with First U.S. Army or by swinging south of the LOIRE if a wider envelopment was feasible."⁴⁹ His mission was to support Hodges' advance.

On 14 March, Patton sent Gay, Harkins, Maddox, and Muller to coordinate with First Army. Patton found Bradley's planning staff "not too clever" and complained, "They plan too minutely on some things and not minutely enough on others. They suffer from not having anyone in command."⁵⁰ Patton objected, for example, to their demand that Third Army advance to take Brittany even if First Army first captured Saint-Nazaire and Nantes and the base of the peninsula: "I think that, if Nantes falls, the peninsula falls too, as it is cut off."⁵¹ The diversion of Third Army into Brittany would become a huge issue.

On 23 March Koch assumed his duties as Third Army G-2 and was immediately summoned to see his boss. Patton had formed his plan for a breakout from Normandy and had now established an objective for his campaign. For at least four months he had been conducting a terrain analysis of the area, corresponding with James van Wyck Osbourne, who authored *The Great Norman Conquest* in 1937. On 29 December 1943, Patton wrote Osbourne, "It is interesting, I think, to realize that in spite of the great change in equipment, the same topographical features which gave strength in 1100 [AD] gave equal strength today."⁵² Terrain formed the skeleton on which Patton fleshed out his plans.

Using a Michelin road map of France and his own intimate knowledge of the French landscape, Patton traced for Koch a series of points north of the Loire River from Nantes on the Atlantic coast through Metz on the German border and directed him to concentrate all of his "G-2 planning" on that path.⁵³ Patton told his staff to look even further, to Oppenheim, south of Mainz, as the place where they would cross the Rhine River.⁵⁴

Patton had circled on his map towns and cities as "the points I then thought I would pass through."⁵⁵ His vision was astonishing, far broader than that incorporated in Overlord, and free from SHAEF's restricted mission dictated for Third Army. The series of points unbound by phase lines and defying enemy anticipation supported the nonlinear advances needed to create a series of shocks. The G-2 had the twofold errand of identifying enemy weak spots while preserving Patton's ability to surprise the enemy. Koch later wrote: "The task facing my intelligence staff was now clear.

Anything which might affect the Third Army mission, from that coast of France all the way to Metz by way of a circuitous route through Brittany, was now of critical concern."[56] Patton intended to use airpower against any threats south of the Loire. His objective was Metz, offering many other possibilities along the way, and he fully wanted to get there before the enemy blocked that ancient gateway into Germany.

Bradley later described his belief that Patton "improvised war plans as he went along."[57] Patton's planning, not revealed to Bradley, demonstrates otherwise. Moreover, it demonstrated a way of war unfathomable to Bradley. SHAEF plans used Leavenworth-taught phase lines to convey a linear perspective; operations were to move deliberately in straight lines to prescribed limits in time and space. Patton's circles—decision points, really—were nonlinear; they prescribed no limits, only possibilities.

Patton understood combat as chaos. Mathematicians and physicists describe chaos as a nonlinear dynamical system highly susceptible to initial conditions and bearing largely unpredictable outcomes.[58] As Alan Beyerchen has noted, Clausewitz connected war to what we now understand as nonlinear chaos and identified friction and chance as its major characteristics.[59] Patton conceptualized his operations within such an environment by translating his intent—in this case, the direction toward his objectives—into a cloud of possible decision points to enable flexibility, simplicity, and adaptability. He put his vision to paper as a plan fit to adjust to circumstances as he found them by leveraging intelligence, command and control, and combined arms columns.

The same day that Patton told Koch his objective was Metz, he sent Muller to submit his first supply request to the European theater of operations (ETO) headquarters. Muller conducted all his supply arrangements with Metz in mind. Seventy-one days later, on 2 June, Ike's headquarters reassured him they still would provide adequate supply to Patton's force after D+41 "without further action on the part of Third U.S. Army."[60] Muller also organized "a Transportation Section to operate and control all motor, rail, water, pack and civilian impressed transportation of Army agencies."[61] Three days later, Patton began daily staff meetings.

On 28 March, Bedell Smith called to say Bradley and Major General Leven Cooper Allen objected to a request Patton had sent to Lee for 15 percent overstrength on personnel because they thought Patton was "trying to rob them."⁶² He added that Patton should have come to him "because General Eisenhower really knew very little about what was going on, and it was up to him, Smith, to fix things up." ⁶³ Patton recalled, "He said, 'Ike often makes mistakes unless I see to it.'"⁶⁴ Patton was suspicious: Bradley was present when Ike had told him to discuss the matter of overstrength with Lee, and fifteen days had passed since Lee had asked Patton to put his request in writing. Patton began to wonder what motivated Smith's interest in his logistics.

On Good Friday, 7 April, Montgomery hosted a historic commanders' conference at St. Paul's School in London.⁶⁵ Before an audience that included Eisenhower, Churchill, and King George VI of England, Monty used a large map depicting three phase lines to summarize his plan for the first ninety days of operations in France. Bradley "objected strenuously," later explaining, "If projected phase lines were not met, it might appear that we were 'failing.'"⁶⁶ During the meeting, however, Patton recalled: "As usual, Bradley said nothing. He does all the getting along and does it to his own advantage." ⁶⁷

Monty announced that the British would seize Caen on D-day and then move another eight miles south to Falaise. Meanwhile the Americans were to drive twenty miles northwest to take Cherbourg by D+8. Bradley's men would then head south and seize the road junction at Saint-Lô for an advance toward Brittany and the port of Brest. Bradley told a correspondent, "I'd gladly sell out for D plus 15—yes, or even D plus 20. The D plus 8 you see here on the map is probably much better than we can do."⁶⁸

The plan now called for the First Canadian Army to join Montgomery's 21st Army Group and Patton's Third U.S. Army to join First U.S. Army to form Bradley's 12th Army Group at about D+20. With Third Army, Patton would receive Lieutenant General Troy Middleton's VIII Corps (initially with Bradley), Lieutenant General Gilbert Cook's XII Corps, Lieutenant General Wade Haislip's XV Corps, and Lieutenant General Walton Walker's XX Corps.

Continuing along a wide front, the Americans were to capture Saint-Malo and Rennes by D+25 and then cut across the base of the Brittany peninsula to Saint-Nazaire by D+35. Third Army would move west and secure the port at Brest before winter weather prohibited resupply across the beaches in Normandy. Meanwhile the British would sweep fifteen miles

George Patton entered the 15th Cavalry Regiment after graduating from West Point in 1909. The Army's doctrine and equipment would still have been familiar to Civil War–era leaders such as Ulysses S. Grant and William Tecumseh Sherman. —*LOC GSP Box 56*

Brigadier General John J. Pershing (center) commanding the provisional division in the Punitive Expedition in Mexico in 1916. Behind the wheel of his car is his driver and aide Second Lieutenant George S. Patton Jr. Significantly, Patton wrangled for himself assignment into the heart of the action in the Army, close to a commander he could both learn from and impress, and to a place from which he could observe and test the latest equipment. —*LOC GSP Box 60*

General Pershing conducts an inspection of lead elements of the American Expeditionary Force in Paris in 1917. Captain Patton, commandant of the force headquarters, is walking just behind Pershing. —*LOC GSP Box 76*

Lieutenant Colonel Patton (center, back turned), America's first tanker, overseeing the instruction of one of his Renault light tank crews at the Tank School he established in Bourg, France, in 1918. —*LOC GSP Box 61*

Patton's 304th Tank Brigade advances during the Saint-Mihiel offensive on 26 September 1918. He was wounded that same day. Note his handwritten comment: "Tanks in action preceding infantry"—contrary to the practice endorsed by high command. —*LOC GSP Box 61*

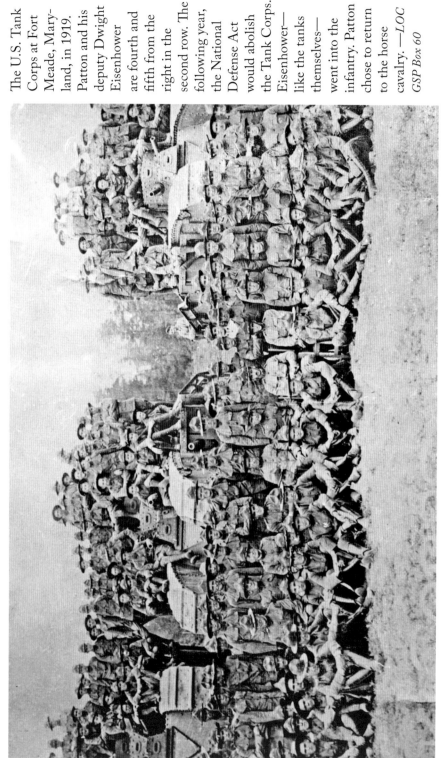

The U.S. Tank Corps at Fort Meade, Maryland, in 1919. Patton and his deputy Dwight Eisenhower are fourth and fifth from the right in the second row. The following year, the National Defense Act would abolish the Tank Corps. Eisenhower—like the tanks themselves—went into the infantry. Patton chose to return to the horse cavalry. —*LOC GSP Box 60*

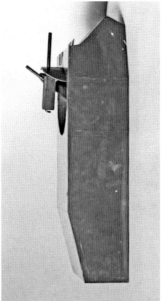

Even while assigned to the Office of the Chief of Cavalry, in 1930 Patton was still absorbed in thoughts on mechanized warfare. Here are two models he created as suggestions for ways to modify a chassis designed by J. Walter Christie into combat fighting vehicles. —*LOC GSP Box 76*

Major Patton (right), G-2 Hawaiian Division, just before takeoff on a reconnaissance flight to Molokai during an exercise in 1925. He made early and extensive investigations of airpower and its relation to ground warfare and even earned a pilot's license. —*LOC GSP Box 60*

Patton (right) riding with the commander of the 13th Cavalry Regiment (Mechanized) in an M1A1 combat car. By the time this vehicle was fielded in 1938, the 15th Cavalry had become part of the experimental 7th Cavalry (Mechanized) Brigade at Fort Knox, Kentucky. Even while serving as the executive officer of the Cavalry School or commanding the 5th and 3rd Cavalry Regiments, Patton seized every chance to investigate the latest tanks and combat cars. —*LOC GSP Box 54*

Brigadier General Patton models one of his designs for an ideal tanker's uniform at Fort Benning, Georgia, in 1940. A similar uniform earned him the nickname "the Green Hornet" from his men. —*LOC GSP 77*

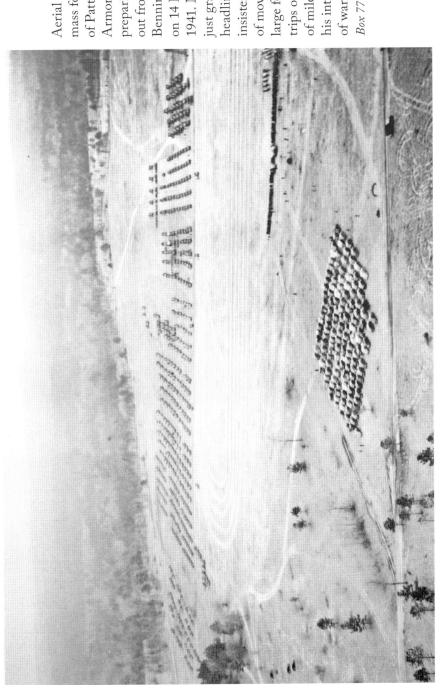

Aerial view of a mass formation of Patton's 2nd Armored Division preparing to move out from Fort Benning, Georgia, on 14 February 1941. More than just grabbing headlines, Patton's insistent practice of moving such large formations on trips of hundreds of miles indicated his intended way of war. —*LOC GSP Box 77*

Patton takes time to instruct exercise umpires on his views of proper tank doctrine during maneuvers in 1941. Maneuver rule books insisted that tanks attack directly into prepared defenses, but Patton taught his men to find, fix, and flank the enemy. —*LOC GSP Box 77*

The beach at Gela, Sicily, 10 July 1943. Patton's Seventh Army fought its way ashore for two days while Bernard Montgomery landed unopposed near Syracuse. It was part of the plan to have the Americans draw the enemy's attention and protect the British left flank. —*LOC GSP Box 64*

Patton's photo of Seventh Army delivering fuel across the beach at Gela reflects his concern with supply. Without a port, he depended on such supplies being brought ashore in small amounts until larger quantities could be delivered through the British port at Syracuse, which gave Montgomery control over Patton's operations.
—*LOC GSP Box 64*

Brigadier General O. P. Weyland and his XIX Tactical Air Command worked closely with Third Army to develop the unique third dimension of combined arms essential to Patton's way of war. Weyland inscribed this picture to Patton: "In years to come the last aviators in the world will toast their comrades of the Third Army—May the spirit of cooperation and comradeship built up by the finest Air-ground teams known to war never die—With the affection of every officer and man of the XIX TAC, Your friend, Opie Weyland. 9 May 1945." —*LOC GSP Box 63*

Patton preparing to conduct an inspection of his front line by air, 29 August 1944. On that day Third Army stretched roughly five hundred miles from Brest to Verdun, and Patton learned Supreme Headquarters Allied Expeditionary Forces had mysteriously failed to deliver 140,000 gallons of gasoline. —*LOC GSP Box 62*

Patton took this photo of an exercise near Fivemiletown, Northern Ireland, 26 March 1944, as the 1st Battalion of the 121st Infantry Regiment, 8th Infantry Division, demonstrated his method of "marching fire," which emphasized initiative, flexibility, and speed. He repeatedly rehearsed this nuanced drill throughout Third Army but noted that he did not feel they got it right until 11 May 1944. —*LOC GSP Box 62*

One of Patton's many instruction sessions with his troops, this one with the 10th Infantry Regiment, 5th Infantry Division, near Kilkeel, County Down, Northern Ireland, on 30 March 1944. By such methods he not only instructed his doctrine and gave his men confidence in his expertise and awareness, he also gained a personal sense of the abilities and morale of his men.
—*LOC GSP Box 62*

Patton and the press, 5 July 1945. As military governor of Bavaria, a duty he was neither suited for nor interested in, Patton gave antagonistic members of the press enough print to erode his legacy and end any chances for further meaningful command. —*LOC GSP Box 62*

southeast from Falaise to Argentan and then ten miles to Alençon. The Americans would then, Bradley wrote, "pivot on the British position like a windlass in the direction of Paris . . . until the Allied line faced east toward the Seine on a 140-mile north-south front . . . where it was anticipated the enemy would hold behind that river bank."[69] In short, the Allies would gain a foothold and then push the Germans east.

If they failed to take Caen, the Allies would struggle to get out of Normandy. Montgomery explained to Churchill, "We must then aim at success in the land battle by the speed and violence of our operations."[70] He even boasted, "I would risk even the total loss of the armored brigade groups—which in any event is not really possible; the delay they would cause to the enemy before they could be destroyed would be quite enough to give us time to get our main bodies well ashore and reorganized for strong offensive action."[71] If history were any indicator, Patton would have been a better choice to take Caen. Monty discussed no plans for any breakout from Normandy.

On 13 April Patton invited Middleton to Peover Hall to have "a little talk on the use of separate tank battalions in support of infantry."[72] He wanted to dig into the VIII Corps commander's lessons learned from Sicily and Italy. Three days later Patton issued his third letter of instruction, with guidance "based largely on the advice of Major General T. H. Middleton."[73] The instructions emphasized combined arms operations and added, "Any weapon which is not actively engaged in killing Germans is not doing its duty."[74] Echoing Ardant du Picq, Patton reminded his commanders, "In battle, casualties vary directly with the time you are exposed to effective fire. Your own fire reduces the effectiveness and volume of the enemy's fire, while rapidity of attack shortens the time of exposure."[75] Turning doctrine on its head, he wrote, "The heavy weapons set the pace."[76] He used Walker's corps to demonstrate his idea of combined arms in field exercises with the 4th and 6th Armored Divisions spearheading attacks and flanking German defenses. Patton paired at least one regiment of infantry to ride on the tanks in his columns—despite the objections of 5th Infantry Division commander Major General Stafford "Red" Irwin. Patton noted, "The professional officer is certainly conservative."[77]

Time was growing short, and Patton's anxiousness increased. On the day of Middleton's visit Patton wrote: "I have a feeling, probably unfounded, that either Monty or Bradley are not too anxious for me to have a command. If they knew what little respect I had for the fighting ability of either of them they would be less anxious for me to show them up."[78] A few days later Undersecretary of War McCloy and Ike's deputy Joseph McNarney met with Patton and urged him to say nothing controversial in the next few weeks lest some in Congress demand his recall.[79]

Patton immersed himself in training. On 22 April XV Corps was alerted for movement with First Army, just as Third Army finally received some large training areas. Patton ran more than thirty artillery, tank, and tank destroyer battalions through gunnery training in thirty days. In May the units refined artillery drills—including *serenade,* Patton's way of quickly massing all artillery fires within a corps sector.[80]

Suddenly, Patton again was the victim of capricious fate. On 25 April he was invited by the British Ministry of Information to attend the opening of a "Welcome Club" for U.S. soldiers at Knutsford. Hirshson noted, "Patton, whose presence in England had been announced, over Ike's objection, just the week before by Bedell Smith, had no inkling a reporter was in the audience."[81] Actually, Patton deliberately arrived fifteen minutes late but quickly noticed reporters and photographers were still present. The club chairperson, Mrs. Constantine Smith, provided the introduction: "General Patton is not here officially and is speaking in a purely friendly way."[82] In an off-the-record address to about fifty ladies Patton said: "Since it is the evident destiny of the British and Americans, and, of course, the Russians, to rule the world, the better we know each other, the better job we will do."[83] He later recalled, "I was asked to stay for supper but felt that I did not wish that much publicity and went home."[84] Subsequent coverage in several papers omitted the mention of the Russians, triggering great protest. Harlan J. Bushfield, U.S. senator from South Dakota, called for Patton's relief.

Possibly the kerfuffle was an intentional ploy by counterintelligence officers to help the Germans confirm Patton's whereabouts and reinforce the FUSAG deception. Through the spring of 1944, as Harry Yeide noted, "Despite detecting false and genuine operational preparations for the mythical operations, the Germans took none of the response measures—including holding divisions in France needed on other fronts—for which the Allies had hoped."[85] Not until 20 March did the Wehrmacht High Command's *Kriegstagebuch* (War Diary) record: "General Patton, who was formerly employed in North Africa and is highly regarded for his proficiency, is now in England."[86] They associated him with "Ninth Army" or "AOK 9," a moniker they hung on Patton even after he came ashore with Third Army. Critics have rightfully noted a sparseness in the German army records referring to Patton at this time that seemingly conflicts with Hitler's and Rundstedt's obsessive concern with Calais. As an Ultra officer wrote thirty years later, "Just how far the creation and carrying out of the brilliant deception plan of Patton's phantom army in Kent, opposite the Pas de Calais, was responsible for reinforcing Rundstedt's views and adding to Hitler's doubts, is still hard to tell."[87] Perhaps Fortitude needed a boost that spring.

Four days after Patton's speech Eisenhower cabled Marshall, "I have grown so weary of the trouble he constantly causes you and the War Department, to say nothing of myself, that I am seriously contemplating the most drastic action."[88] Marshall reminded Ike that Patton's experience in fighting Rommel could be useful in France.[89] The next day Ike replied that he intended to relieve Patton—and that Bradley "fully concurred."[90] Bradley added, "We selected Courtney Hodges to command the Third Army, leaving open, for the time being, my replacement for the First Army.'"[91] Unaware, Patton complained in his journal, "So far as I am concerned every effort is made to show a lack of confidence in my judgment and at the same time, in every case of stress, great confidence in my fighting."[92] On 27 April Smith arrived to tell Patton to keep his mouth shut, that he had cost them promotions, and that Patton might lose his command. Patton recorded, "In consonance with this order I am unable to talk with either the 79th, 80th, 83rd, or 7th Armored Divisions, a restriction that will surely cost lives, yet if I break it I will get relieved and that would mean defeat and a still larger loss."[93]

Patton learned that Eisenhower drafted but tore up a cable to Marshall "saying that he, Ike, had no further need of protecting me and would not resist my being recalled."[94] Marshall cabled Ike: "The decision is exclusively yours. My view, and it is merely that, is that you should not weaken your hand for Overlord. If you think that Patton's removal does weaken your prospect, you should continue him in command."[95] On May Day, Patton recalled, Ike told him "that Marshall had wired him that my repeated mistakes have shaken the confidence of the country and the War Department."[96] Patton answered, "I am not threatening, but I want to tell you that this attack is badly planned and on too narrow a front and may well result in an Anzio, especially if I am not there." He said that Eisenhower replied, "Don't I know it, but what can I do?"[97] Patton left the meeting saying, "I feel like death, but I am not out yet."[98]

Bradley complained, "Patton made his case so persuasively that Ike backed off and decided to reconsider. Without further consultation with me, Ike had made the decision to keep Patton . . . in part because Churchill thought the whole episode a tempest in a teapot."[99] Churchill, who often quizzed Kay Summersby on Eisenhower's thoughts, made it a point to discuss the Knutsford incident with Ike and said "he could see nothing in it."[100] If British intelligence was behind the tumult, Churchill's intervention makes sense. In any event, in May the Germans finally associated Patton with command of the notional FUSAG of Fortitude.[101] A few days later Ike sent orders to Patton never to speak in public without clearing his remarks with him first. He added, "You owe us some victories. Pay off and the world will deem me a wise man."[102] Ike said: "Go ahead and train your Army."[103] Patton did just that.

On 5 May Patton issued a paper, "Notes on Combat Armored Divisions," expanding on his doctrine of reconnaissance, leading with armor, and fixing the enemy with infantry and artillery. He stressed that "our armor must remember to seek the flank, to attack from the rear."[104] Third Army practiced teaming armor and infantry divisions to form pools of units for creating combined arms columns with tactical airpower covering their front and flanks. After reading his paper to his senior commanders, Patton shared his sense of marvel at his opportunity to put into practice his own theories.[105] With Wood's 4th Armored Division and Weyland's air liaison officers, he demonstrated his doctrine in the field.[106] They conducted sand table rehearsals on the afternoon of 8 May with morning and afternoon field demonstrations the next day as Patton raced about in a halftrack making refinements via radio.[107]

Patton's teachings contradicted Army doctrine, which called for leading with infantry and bringing up tanks when needed; he trained his units to do the opposite. Doctrine said to destroy enemy forces; Patton intended to exploit weakness, unbalance the enemy, and push them relentlessly. Doctrine focused on battle; he focused on campaign. Contrary to Army Air Force doctrine, Third Army developed methods to use XIX TAC in place of slower artillery support.[108] Doctrine demanded firm top-down command

and control; Patton preached simple, flexible orders and subordinate initiative. Doctrine was based on attrition; Patton sought shock. A postwar Armored School analysis identified several keys to success for one of Patton's divisions: "mission type orders; no phase lines; keep going until stopped by the enemy; use of secondary roads; close integration of combined arms; boldness in execution; flexibility."[109] This was his doctrine, and it confused traditionalists such as Bradley.

Air-ground liaisons integrated into the ground units worked out new ideas and methods for tactical air support.[110] Patton granted Weyland autonomy over his air assets, and Weyland promised in return to provide all the support he could muster. It was subordinate initiative in the third dimension. Patton wrote, "To accomplish this happy teamwork two things are necessary: first, intimate confidence and friendship between air and ground; second, incessant and apparently ruthless driving on the part of the ground commander."[111] In First Army, by contrast, Bradley complained, "As a result of our inability to get together with air in England, we went into France almost totally untrained in air-ground cooperation."[112] This was not the case with Patton's Third Army.

In large unit rehearsals Walker's XX Corps reported, "Combined tank-infantry attacks on simulated German pillboxes formed a large part of the exercises. The artillery would lay down a rolling barrage which the men and machines of the combined arms would follow."[113] The corps artillery rehearsed time-on-target massed fires daily and noted, "This type of fire was often used in combat for its tremendous power and shock effect on enemy morale."[114] On 10 May, on West Down range before an assembly of all Third Army regimental and battalion commanders, the 4th Armored again demonstrated Patton's tactics. Patton commented, "I was delighted and feel that I have at last illustrated the use of marching fire and of tanks and infantry. It strikes me as a sad reflection on our state of preparation for war that I had to personally conduct and drive the rehearsals, but so it is."[115] Wood's report on the demonstration carefully noted the expenditure of ammunition "appears to be well within the possibilities of re-supply."[116]

Finally, to make his system work, Patton organized his unique Army Information Service consisting primarily of Colonel Edward Fickett's 6th Cavalry Group to report enemy *and* friendly activities directly to Third Army headquarters. Patton tasked staff officers, line units, and supporting air forces to conduct reconnaissance.[117] "You can never have too much reconnaissance," he repeated. "Reports must be facts, not opinions; negative as well as positive. Do not believe intercepts blindly: cross-check—sometimes messages are sent out to be intercepted. Information is like eggs; the fresher the better."[118] At army level, Koch stitched together the layered intelligence systems into an unparalleled machine. Clausewitz wrote that most intelligence reports were invariably false; Patton would try to make it otherwise.

On 1 June Third Army's 253,500 soldiers assembled in 275 camps for the move to France. Patton was still concerned that Overlord was on too narrow a front; he again suggested three landings on a ninety-mile-wide area to give chance for maneuver.[119] It was not to be. He went with Bradley to see Monty and noted, "Montgomery was especially interested in the operations of the Third Army and it was very fortunate that, two nights ago, I had rehearsed the whole thing for General Simpson, so I was very fluent."[120] Montgomery twice said, "Patton should take over for the Brittany campaign, and possibly for the Rennes Operation."[121] At dinner with his army commanders, Monty expressed his belief the war should be over by November.[122] He offered a toast, and when no one replied, Patton announced, "As the oldest army commander present, I would like to propose a toast to the health of General Montgomery and express our satisfaction in serving under him."[123] As to Monty's plan, he thought, "It never does go as planned."[124] The next morning Patton said goodbye to Montgomery who responded, "I had a good time and now we understand each other."[125]

D-day was 6 June 1944. First Army met tough resistance. Remaining at sea that day, Bradley wrote, "Our communications with the forces assaulting Omaha Beach were thin to nonexistent. . . . I gained the impression that our forces had suffered an irreversible catastrophe, that there was little hope we could force the beach. Privately, I considered evacuating the beachhead."[126] The next day Eisenhower arrived. "What ensued," Bradley recalled, "was an almost exact replay of Ike's D-plus-1 visit with Patton at Sicily. He jumped all over me for not sending him progress reports on D-Day. He'd been in the dark again, unable to brief the Combined Chiefs. I was stung—and inwardly boiled—because I had faithfully reported to Ike almost hourly."[127] Bradley reported no sense of whether he thought Ike had lost confidence in him.

Montgomery failed to take Caen on D-day. Bradley complained, "In sum, the British and Canadian assault forces sat down. They had Caen within their grasp and let it slip away."[128] Montgomery later explained, "Of course we did not keep to the times and phase lines we had envisaged. . . . Of course we didn't. I never imagined we would."[129] Overall, in the first 24 hours the Allies suffered 5,000 casualties but had 80,000 men ashore—about 20,000 fewer than planned—and unloaded only 4,000 of 14,500 planned tons of supply and about 7,000 of 14,000 vehicles.[130] Historians seem unconcerned with this case of "poor logistical planning."

On D-day Patton wrote: "I have horrible feelings that the fighting will be over before I get in but I know this is not so, as destiny means me to be in."[131] Two days later he observed, "Apparently things are not going too well and one gets the impression that people are satisfied to be holding on, rather than advancing."[132]

The *bocage*, small farm plots bordered with thick earthen walls and edged by sunken roads, stifled progress. One aerial photograph showed more than 3,900 such plots in less than 8 square miles.[133] Bradley said, "I hadn't visualized it at all as much as I had studied photographs and maps before I went in."[134] VII Corps commander Joe Collins deemed it "as bad as anything he had encountered during the fighting he had experienced on Guadalcanal."[135] Bedell Smith added, "You cannot imagine it when you have not seen it."[136] The Army frantically searched for terrain studies on Normandy. They found a 1913 "reconnaissance" report in the Cavalry School files discussing the suitability of roads from Cherbourg to Saumur for military traffic. The report's author was Lieutenant George S. Patton Jr., who wrote it while on vacation with his wife.[137]

Montgomery broke past Caen at Villers Bocage with the British 7th Armored Division but, lacking combined arms infantry support, was driven back. Combined arms operations were not a British strength. Monty wired Alan Brooke that he intended to assume an "aggressive defensive posture" to "pull the Germans on to the Second British Army and fight them there, so that First U.S. Army can carry out its task the easier."[138] Yet Eisenhower recalled, "On June 18, Montgomery still felt that conditions permitted the early capture of Caen. . . . He gave the following instructions to the British Army, 'The immediate task of this Army will be to capture Caen.'"[139]

A three-day storm wrecked the beachhead and pushed the Allies further behind schedule.[140] With the capture of Cherbourg now imperative, Bradley said, "Our best opportunity lay in driving north at such speed as to prevent a consolidation of their defenses."[141] (He would apparently think differently in Brittany.) When the Germans stopped Collins outside Cherbourg on 21 June, Bradley hit the city with a thousand bombers, and although the bombs killed many American soldiers, the effort "encouraged" Bradley "to think about saturation bombing as an effective tactical weapon."[142]

By the end of the month the Allies had nearly 850,000 men, 150,000 vehicles, and 500,000 tons of supplies in Normandy while suffering 8,500 killed and more than 50,000 wounded.[143] The Germans suffered nearly 100,000 casualties. Normandy had become a battle of attrition. Ike remembered, "Late June was a difficult period for all of us. More than one of our high-ranking visitors began to express the fear that we were stalemated and that those who had prophesied a gloomy fate for Overlord were being proven correct."[144] Desperate to find a way through the enemy, Ike met with Bradley on 24 June to decide, recalled Bedell Smith, "that the full weight of the U.S. strength should be used to breakout into the open on [the] right."[145] Bradley ordered Middleton's VIII Corps to attack "down the west coast Cotentin road from La Haye du Puits through the moors of Lessay to Coutances."[146] That attack failed. Montgomery again attacked Caen, telling Ike, "I will continue to battle on eastern flank until one of us cracks and it will not be us."[147] The Germans held.

Though Cherbourg finally surrendered, in the south Bradley had no luck. The Allies were not close to their expected line of Avranches, Mortain, and Argentan. Butcher observed, "Ike is considerably less than exuberant these days."[148] Bradley grew concerned that the buildup was exceeding the dimensions of the lodgment and warned, "G-4 [Major General Robert W. Crawford] had repeatedly stressed the necessity for capturing the Brittany ports before the September gales knocked out our beaches and left us totally dependent on Cherbourg."[149] Ike explained to the combined chiefs that since Monty "had been unable to break out toward the Seine," he had ordered Bradley to "smash out" from the west.[150]

Despite the stalemate, SHAEF crafted plans labeled Lucky Strike for operations after Normandy to close the Paris-Orleans gap before halting along the Seine. Lucky Strike B called for Patton's Third Army to exploit *south* of the Loire *after* enemy resistance collapsed in Brittany.[151] Carlo D'Este wrote, "It was essentially the LUCKY STRIKE plan which was later implemented after COBRA."[152] Actually, Patton diverged noticeably from Lucky Strike. He would head east long *before* resistance collapsed in Brittany and stayed *north* of the Loire. Instead of guarding the Allied flank, he would spearhead their advance. As one of Bradley's planners noted, "There wasn't anything clearly defined from the standpoint of a breakout" in Lucky Strike.[153]

As directed by Eisenhower, Bradley began a new attack to smash forward all along his front. He explained: "My plan was bold, ambitious and optimistic. I would employ four corps (V, VII, VIII, IX) composed of about twelve divisions through the crust of enemy defenses."[154] He wrote to Ike, "I am very much anxious that when we hit the enemy this time we will hit him with such power that we can keep going without any appreciable halt until we turn the corner at the base of the [Brittany] Peninsula."[155] It was a repeat of Montgomery south of Etna in Sicily, a broad front advance without a designated exploitation force to seize any opportunities that might arise. On 2 July Bradley accompanied Ike on a visit to see Monty, whom they found "quite pleased with himself" and insisting that everything was "going according to plan."[156] Eisenhower had expected Montgomery to be on the road to Paris by now and resented the change to plans resulting from Monty's failure to take Caen.[157] Bradley recalled, "So scrupulously did we conceal our irritation with Monty that I doubt he was even aware of it."[158]

Montgomery was also irritated. As Stephen Ambrose noted, "He thought Bradley should have done more. He told Brooke that he had tried to get Bradley to drive south towards Coutances at the same time as he was moving on Cherbourg, 'but Bradley didn't want to take the risk.'"[159] Monty implied that it was Bradley's reluctance that had led to stalemate. With Ike's support, he directed Bradley to continue south as far as Avranches while Collins cleared the Cherbourg peninsula. Meanwhile, he directed Miles Dempsey to capture Caen "as opportunity offers—and the sooner the better."[160] Unfortunately, simply issuing orders did not equate to results. Bradley recalled, "Ike was moody. Later, privately, he groused about Monty's lack of progress on Caen."[161] Major General Everett Hughes heard Ike lament, "Sometimes I wish I had George Patton here."[162]

On 2 July Third Army received a call from the Build Up Command Office Headquarters instructing Patton to depart for Normandy three days later. That same day, sitting in England with his Michelin road map, Patton sent Eisenhower a new plan for breaking the stalemate.[163] With the Germans still holding Calais against the expected landing of his fictional army group, and much of Third Army already committed under Bradley, Patton proposed a landing in Brittany at Morlaix with one armored and two infantry divisions to capture that port and provide a springboard for enveloping the Germans in Normandy from the west.[164] The shock of such a landing would force the Germans to react by either falling back from Normandy or risk attack from the rear. Either way, Patton envisioned "driving on to the line Alençon-Argentan, and thereafter on Evreux or Chartres, depending on circumstances, we will really pull a coup."[165] This projected advance would pose a series of threats to the Germans. Unfortunately, as Farago stated, "To see and understand what he had so brazenly sketched, the men for who he had prepared it would have needed—but woefully lacked—his kind of imagination."[166] "I dressed my paper up with the names of Scharnhorst, Clausewitz and Moltke," Patton wrote, "so as to catch Ike's eye. I hope he reads it."[167] Ike ignored Patton's "reverse Schlieffen" plan.

Patton's typed transcription of his diary discussing the 2 July proposal, cited by Blumenson, included a statement: "It is a good paper. However, the same thing could be effected by placing one or two armor divisions abreast and going straight down the road, covering the leading elements with air bursts. I am sure that such a method, while probably expensive in tanks, due primarily to mines, would insure our breaking through to Avranches from our present position in not more than two days."[168] These comments undermined Bradley's claim to ownership of the scheme used in executing Operation Cobra, but they do not appear in Patton's handwritten diary.[169] Charles Codman habitually typed the handwritten pages at the end of each week and would not likely have added a breakout plan without Patton's instruction.[170] Beatrice Patton used the typed pages in editing *War as I Knew It*, but she could have only added such comments if she had retyped the entire page. A close examination of the typed manuscript, however, shows that on the page in question just below the comments for 3 July appears a handwritten annotation referring to "movements" and "G-4" written in Patton's unmistakable scrawl.[171] It seems inescapable that he had overseen the inclusion of the passage into the typed manuscript weeks before Bradley drafted Cobra.

By 2 July Patton had formed his ideas of breaking out of Normandy to Avranches and beyond with two armored divisions abreast on a narrow front under air cover. This was the idea he considered at the 11 February briefing at Montgomery's headquarters.[172] It was also precisely the mission and method for which Patton trained the 4th and 6th Armored Divisions in England. Avranches was an advantageous position from which Patton could clear Brittany, isolate that peninsula, or cut behind the Germans in Normandy. It offered a starting point for inflicting a series of shocks upon the Germans in a number of directions along to the points he had drawn on his Michelin map. From Avranches roads led west toward Brest, south to Quiberon Bay, and east across France.

Traditionalist methods in Normandy, as in Tunisia, Sicily, and Italy, had produced slow, bloody struggles of attrition. On 3 July Bradley conceded, "The VIII Corps attack failed to crack the enemy crust and give us a breakout. . . . The VII Corps attack likewise failed to provide the breakout."[173] He fired the commanders of the 90th and 8th Infantry Divisions. The next day Montgomery again attacked Caen and again faltered. Eisenhower returned to London "smoldering over the whole business."[174] He went to see Patton, who later remarked that Ike seemed "a little fed up with Monty's lack of drive."[175] Patton also met with Hughes, who warned him that he "would not be wanted" in France.[176]

At 1025 hours on 6 July Patton landed in France at an airfield near Omaha Beach. He wore a subdued helmet, field boots, and a single sidearm; Bradley had ordered him not to wear his ivory-handled revolvers. Troops rushed to get his picture and cheered as he drove in an open jeep to Bradley's command post south of Isigny, less than four miles from the front lines. "Bradley could not have been more polite," Patton said, "and we had a long talk until supper."[177] Hodges presented a detailed analysis of the German tactics that exposed U.S. troops to costly machine gun and mortar fire in the *bocage*.[178] Patton outlined the plan he had sent over four days earlier for a two armored division attack to Avranches.[179] Bradley declined it.

The next day Bradley attacked again, this time with Major General Charles H. "Cowboy Pete" Corlett's XIX Corps paralleling VII Corps toward Saint-Lô. Bradley reported, "We met fierce enemy resistance, and as a consequence the XIX Corps attack likewise failed to punch the crust."[180] This time he fired the 3rd Armored Division commander. Leo Daugherty observed, "In any analysis of the opening round to take St. Lô, it becomes clear that part of the problem lay with General Bradley's unrealistic expectations that a solitary reinforced tank battalion could exploit any breakthrough amidst two of the best German armored divisions in Northwest Europe."[181] The doctrinal, infantry-centered approach to combined arms practiced by Bradley and his commanders simply failed in Normandy.

Patton went with Bradley to Montgomery's headquarters. "Here," Patton noted, "Montgomery went to great length explaining why the British had done nothing."[182] On 8 July Monty launched Operation Charnwood against Caen with 460 bombers dropping 2,300 tons of explosives in a 4,000-by-1,500-yard area to open a path for 3 British divisions. The British also fired 80,000 artillery rounds; the Germans could respond with only 4,500.[183] After 2 days British troops occupied the north half of bombed-out Caen, but the Germans still held. Bradley confessed, "By July 10, we faced a real danger of a World War I–type stalemate in Normandy. . . . My own breakout had failed."[184]

Montgomery gathered his commanders at his headquarters near Bayeux. Bradley was pessimistic. Dempsey recalled, "Monty told him not to worry and not to hurry and—without Bradley realizing it—got across to him the idea that he must concentrate his forces for a solid punch at one point. Bradley probably now thinks that he thought of this himself because Monty was careful to put the suggestion very tactfully."[185] Of course Patton had already made such a suggestion to Bradley. Forty years later Bradley reported, "By July 10, I had conceived a new plan for a breakout. Rather than mount the second attempt across a broad four-corps front, I would focus the breakout on a very narrow front in the St. Lô area, spearheaded by Joe Collins and his aggressive VII Corps."[186]

The next morning Montgomery began Goodwood, a 750-tank attack through Caen to reach the Falaise plain. Again lacking adequate combined arms, it failed. Monty later explained, "Many people thought that when Operation GOODWOOD was staged, it was the beginning of the plan to break out on the eastern flank towards Paris, and that, because I did not do so, the battle had been a failure. But let me make the point again at the risk of being wearisome. There was never at any time any intention of making the break-out from the bridgehead on the eastern flank."[187] Afterward Bradley observed, "If Ike had a free hand, I am certain that he would have sacked Monty then and there."[188]

That night Montgomery issued orders for the Second Army to pivot at Caen and extend to Le Bény Bocage. From there Bradley was to extend the line south to Mortain and Fougeres. Monty wanted a solid front before wheeling south and east.[189] D'Este commented, "This was one of the strangest directives ever issued by Montgomery, for it directed both armies into the worst of the bocage where casualties were bound to be high and the going slow."[190] Even so, Bradley approved the move, reasoning, "We've got to stand here and slug it out with him. Afterwards we can make the breakthrough and run deep."[191] The Allied strategy, as was the norm, had openly embraced attrition.

On 12 July Bradley gathered his commanders, including Patton, to reveal his narrow-front plan, Operation Cobra. The plan outlined three phases: breakthrough, exploitation, and consolidation.[192] It included no mention of breakout. After repeated failure to get to the Saint-Lô–Coutances road, Bradley now aimed for the closer Saint-Lô–Périers road in the breakthrough phase.[193] The plan stated: "Operation 'COBRA' has the object of effecting a penetration of the enemy's defenses West of ST. LO by VII Corps and exploiting this penetration with a strong armored and motorized thrust deep in the enemy's rear toward COUTANCES."[194] This was an advance of about twelve miles.

Bradley—like Monty in Charnwood—would begin his attack by using strategic bombers to replicate the massed artillery of World War I, this time blasting a hole in the German lines at Marigny and Saint-Gilles. He explained: "The employment of air power in a carpet bombing to break a path for COBRA was no more novel than the use of artillery in preparation for a conventional attack."[195] He later recalled, "Then to make certain the blitz would get off to a fast start, I called on the Big Red One [the 1st Infantry Division] to pace it."[196] The order stressed the "momentum of the attack must be maintained until Phase I objectives have been reached."[197] The Phase I objectives were the creation of solid flanks to the hole blasted by the bombers.

In Phase II exploitation, Bradley wrote after the war, "a motorized infantry and two armored divisions would lunge through that hole in the line. The motorized infantry would push on to Coutances, 15 miles to the southwest, in hopes of bagging the remnants of seven German divisions blocking Middleton on his front. Meanwhile the armor would dash toward Avranches and turn the corner into Brittany."[198] In the Cobra order, however, there was no mention of Avranches or Brittany. VII Corps would pass the two armored divisions with an ad hoc motorized division ("motorized by such transportation as is available to VII Corps") through the hole. VII Corps' mission was to "seize COUTANCES and crossing of the SIENNE [sic] River to the Southwest. In addition, it will seize BREHAL and prevent any movement of enemy reinforcements to the North."[199] The Seine River lies about two and a half miles south of Coutances. At Brehal, about ten miles south of Coutances and twenty miles north of Avranches, VII Corps would complete Cobra by assuming the defensive.

In the final consolidation phase, V, VIII, and XIX Corps were to increase pressure on the enemy in their sectors, "exploiting every advantage gained from his state of disorganization."[200] VII Corps was to "continue the mission outlined in Phase II."[201] This was essentially a preplanned halt. Collins recalled only modest objectives in Cobra: a breakthrough at Marigny–Saint-Gilles, the 1st Infantry Division and 3rd Armored Division driving on Coutances, and the 2nd Armored and the 30th Infantry Divisions covering their movement.[202] No one could mistake Cobra for a breakout operation.

Collins decided that instead of driving through Coutances to cut off the Germans facing VIII Corps, he would halt east of that city.[203] He would not drive to Brehal. Cobra's deepest objective would therefore be about twelve miles—roughly thirty miles north of Avranches. The operation would not gain any advantageous position against the enemy. Bradley did not designate any pursuit or exploitation force.

As he listened to Bradley explain Cobra, Patton thought the plan as written was "a very timid operation," but he saw opportunity.[204] He wrote, "I could break through in three days if I commanded. They try to push all along the front and have no power anywhere. All that is necessary now is to take chances by leading with armored divisions and covering their advance with air bursts. Such an attack would have to be made on a narrow sector, whereas at present we are trying to attack all along the line."[205] Patton advised Middleton and Collins to lead with their armor but, with Bradley's support, they declined; it was infantry country, after all.[206] Collins explained, "The only doubtful part of the COBRA plan, to my mind, is that we shouldn't count too much on fast movement of armored divisions through this country. If we make a breakthrough it is OK but until then, the tanks can't move any faster than the infantry."[207]

Patton asked Bradley to activate Third Army as an exploitation force to be ready to seize any opportunities that might arise. Bradley declined. "Brad says he will put me in as soon as he can," Patton noted. "He could do it now with much benefit to himself if he had any backbone."²⁰⁸ One the eve of the attack Bradley suggested to Patton only that he might "utilize XIX Corps" for advance southwest of Coutances after "the COBRA operation is finished."²⁰⁹

Finally, Patton urged Bradley to aim for Avranches as his objective, but Bradley again declined. Patton revealed to Bradley an ulterior motive for his urgency. "I told him that Monty sent me an order that I will not go in until we reach Avranches. Brad said he had never seen the order, so I will send him a copy."²¹⁰ That night a somber Patton wrote in his diary, "Neither Ike or Brad has the stuff."²¹¹

In his autobiographies, Bradley repeatedly referred to Cobra as a "plan for breakout."²¹² This description, reinforced by the version Bradley oversaw portrayed in the movie *Patton*, led many historians to routinely refer to Cobra as Bradley's plan to break out of Normandy, keeping the myth lingering on the pages of history.²¹³ The evidence clearly shows Cobra was not a breakout plan. As Blumenson noted, "The word *breakthrough*, frequently used during the planning period, signified a penetration through the depth of the enemy defensive position. The word *breakout* was often employed later somewhat ambiguously or as a literary term to describe the results of COBRA."²¹⁴ Even if Cobra produced a rupture, Bradley—a stickler for control—had designated no exploitation or pursuit force, certainly not Third Army. Cobra was only intended to take a chunk out of the German lines. It was a doctrinal battle, to be followed by a pause to plan and prepare the next battle as part of a chain leading toward national strategic objectives. D'Este observed: "It cannot be over-emphasized that both before and after D-Day the Allied commanders were not thinking in terms of a 'breakout' except as it pertained to the seizure of Brittany."²¹⁵ Only Patton envisioned something more for Cobra, if he got a chance to take part in it.

Meanwhile, attacks across the front continued to falter. The 2nd Infantry Division seized a critical hill on 12 July and then halted. The Germans, one historian noted, "were relieved. . . . Most German commanders felt that if the 2nd Division had continued its attack towards the south, the Americans would accomplish a clean breakthrough."²¹⁶ First Army was able

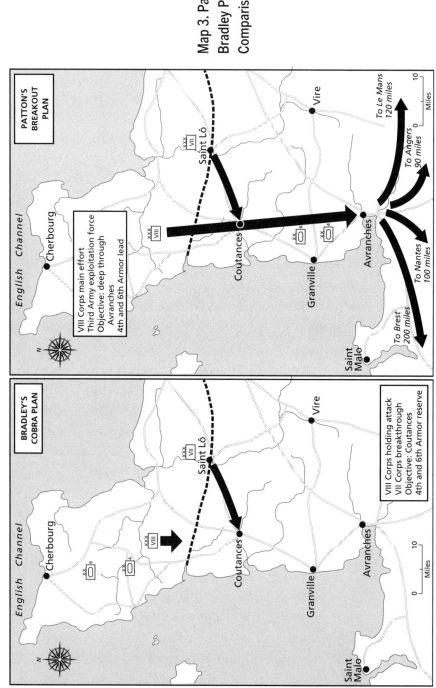

Map 3. Patton/Bradley Plan Comparisons

to neither spot nor exploit such an opportunity. By 14 July VIII Corps had completed "a gain of 12,000 yards in 12 days" and was still far short of its objectives when Bradley ordered it to halt and regroup.[217] Patton griped in his diary, "Half of July is gone and no progress, but only casualties."[218]

When First Army finally captured Saint-Lô on 18 July, Bradley halted to regroup for Cobra.[219] Frustrated, Ike prodded Bradley "that every chance should be taken to win the battle, to border on the reckless, and not to get stopped."[220] It was not for lack of trying: to date Montgomery had taken almost 35,000 casualties and Bradley 62,000.[221] Coincidentally, there was a notable and growing shortage of ammunition across the front.[222] Caution had neither reduced casualties nor gained ground. Something else was needed.

Ike's thoughts turned to Patton. Seeing twenty-one American divisions on First Army's situation map, he asked Bradley when he intended to "bring Group into the picture."[223] Standing up the 12th Army Group meant activating the Third Army. Bradley demurred. He wanted to restrict Cobra to First Army "for ease in control."[224] Bradley later candidly explained, "I was apprehensive in having George join my command, for I feared that too much of my time would probably be spent in curbing his impetuous habits. But at the same time I knew that with Patton there would be no need for my whipping Third Army to keep it on the move."[225] Bradley innately preferred a docile command environment. Failing to move Bradley, Ike wrote to Montgomery, "Time is vital. We must not only have the Brittany Peninsula—we must have it quickly. . . . Now we are pinning our hopes on Bradley's attack."[226] Bradley finally relented and suggested 1 August as a possible activation date for Third Army.

Meanwhile, Patton quizzed Bradley on his plans after Cobra. There were none. Bradley was focused on battle, not campaign. Bradley opined that Patton might be able to use XIX Corps and its two divisions (5th and 35th Infantry) "for a further advance to the southwest"—away from the main line of the Allied advance.[227] Frustrated, Patton wrote that he was "nauseated" by commanders like Bradley and Hodges who insisted that "all human virtue depends on knowing infantry tactics."[228] Patton wrote: "The tactics belong to the battalion commanders. If Generals knew less tactics, they would interfere less."[229]

The United States had been at war for 964 days; Patton had been in combat for 80 of them. He had been in danger of being sent home at least three times. He watched less capable commanders struggle while he felt constantly repressed. If he were ever to prove his way of war, he would have to do it soon. On 22 July he wrote his wife, "When I start I am going to employ tanks to get the show rolling. I know it can be done if we only show guts, and select one point of attack instead of being all along the front."[230]

Bad weather on 24 July led to delaying the start of Cobra, but 400 strategic bombers failed to get the word and dropped bombs that killed 25 American soldiers and wounded 131 more. Bradley explained, "One reason for the error was that the planes flew a course perpendicular to our lines rather than parallel to it as I was assured they would. I have seldom been so angry. It was duplicity—a shocking breech [sic] of good faith."[231] Allied Air Forces commander Vice Marshall Trafford Leigh-Mallory overruled Bradley's initial request to fly perpendicular to the lines and insisted on a parallel approach, but Lieutenant General Jimmy Doolittle had his Eighth Air Force fly according to Bradley's wishes.[232] Even so, Doolittle had protested the mission, arguing that "2,500 bombers could not drop thousands of bombs accurately" in a target area obscured by smoke from the first bombs.[233] Lieutenant General Carl "Tooey" Spaatz, commanding the Allied Strategic Air Force, reported, "It had been previously explained to Bradley that in a large-scale operation of this kind, placing a heavy concentration in a small area in the proximity of our front lines would inevitably result in some casualties."[234] In Sicily, Bradley blamed Patton for similar fratricide. Now he blamed the pilots.

Late that night Patton met with his staff and corps commanders with Bradley's chief of staff, Major General Lev Allen, in attendance.[235] He unilaterally informed them that when Third Army was activated he would place Middleton's VIII Corps—with the 4th and 6th Armored Divisions in the lead—on his west and Haislip's XV Corps on his east.[236] Patton surprised his audience by announcing Avranches—not Coutances—as his immediate objective. He then stunned them when he said that from Avranches he would send VIII Corps west 70 miles to Saint-Malo and then on a hundred miles more to Brest. XV Corps would drive south 160 miles to Quiberon Bay. XX Corps would advance southeast 110 miles to Rennes—at the center of the neck of Brittany—and be prepared to drive east another 160 miles to the Seine.[237] From his years of experimentation and practice, he realized these distant locales were suitable objectives for his combined arms columns. His objectives were the advantageous positions that would sustain successive shocks, threatening the enemy with the isolation and reduction of Brittany, the envelopment of forces in Normandy, the loss of Paris, and the penetration of the open German frontier. These were some of the points he had circled on his map months earlier.

It was astonishing. Bradley had planned a twelve-mile breakthrough; Patton intended a breakout of hundreds of miles.[238] Traditionalists were flummoxed. The 6th Armored Division commander, Major General Robert Grow, said Middleton admitted to him "that he had great reservations about using armor in exploitation . . . It was evident that Middleton lacked confidence in armor."[239] The veteran doughboy was out of his element.

On 25 July just after 0930 hours, Cobra began in earnest. More than 2,400 bombers dropped 4,000 tons of bombs. A unit history reported: "Wave after wave of big bombers flew in. . . . Each bomb drop was felt at Fourth Armored positions four miles away."[240] Among those killed in the bombing this time were 111 American soldiers, including General Lesley J. McNair; an additional 490 soldiers were wounded. This time Doolittle flew overhead in a P-38 fighter to ensure compliance with Bradley's orders but watched helplessly as unexpected winds again obscured the target area and front lines from the bombardiers: "It was one of those harrowing moments that you sometimes dream about, but in dreams you are relieved to awaken and find it is not real."[241] Bradley complained that air commanders again misled him about their route. Even after the previous day's fratricide, First Army had failed to employ adequate control measures.[242] Eisenhower declared he would no longer authorize the use of heavy bombers against tactical targets.[243]

When at about 1100 hours the 9th, 4th, and 30th Infantry Divisions "charged" into the gap made by the bombers, Bradley recalled, "All were shocked to meet heavy resistance. The assault bogged down. I was dismayed."[244] The rate of advance failed to overwhelm the Germans. Depressing reports arrived: "'The enemy artillery,' one stated, 'was not touched by our bombing.' Another declared, 'The effect of the bombing on the elimination of infantry resistance was negligible.'"[245] VII Corps advanced just over two thousand yards for the day. Ike flew back to London "glum, even depressed."[246] Bradley remembered, "When Eisenhower took off for

England that evening, the fate of COBRA still hung in doubt. . . . The attack looked as though it might have failed."[247]

The day before, Eisenhower had encouraged Monty to conduct an attack simultaneously with Cobra, and Monty reluctantly decided to send Harry Crerar's First Canadian Army toward Falaise. They were repelled and suffered more than one thousand casualties. Frustrated, Montgomery complained to Brooke that it was "clear that Ike knows nothing about strategy."[248] Still, Monty's attack met Ike's intent: the Germans scrapped plans to pull back their panzer divisions from the British sector to use against Bradley.

After a day of slow crawling, Collins brought tanks from the 2nd and 3rd Armored Divisions forward to lead his attack, just as Patton had suggested.[249] With tanks in the lead, the attack gained steam. That afternoon the 2nd Armored Division broke through to Saint-Gilles, west of Saint-Lô, on the road to Coutances. The 3rd Armored hit that road, turned west, and bounced a strongpoint at Marigny. The 1st Infantry Division, after being held up to clear Marigny, headed west toward Coutances. Bradley recalled, "Slowly it came to me that COBRA had not failed. It had succeeded; we had broken through."[250] He wired Ike optimistic forecasts. Before midnight Ike dispatched a message to Bradley: "You have got the stuff piled up and we must give the enemy no rest at all until we have achieved our objective. Then we will crush him."[251] It is not clear if Ike and Bradley had the same objective in mind, but now Bradley began to think of Avranches—just as Patton had urged him to do.

Suddenly an opportunity arose. An ill-timed repositioning by the German forces between Saint-Gilles and Coumont opened a path southeast to Paris-Orleans. Unfortunately, neither Bradley nor Montgomery was prepared or able to exploit this development. Had Bradley activated Third Army as an exploitation force as Patton had suggested—or had he even been able to deviate from his plan—he might have turned this opportunity into a historic turn. Bradley stuck to his plan. The opportunity passed.

In the first forty-eight hours Middleton's VIII Corps attack advanced two miles to the Lessay–Saint-Lô road while Collins' VII Corps covered about ten miles to the eastern side of Coutances. As Bradley intended, the Germans facing VIII Corps were in danger of being cut off by VII Corps, but the enemy did not sit still and began repositioning elements of the 2nd

SS Panzer Division and the 17th SS Grenadier Parachute Division against the halted Collins. Bradley had not anticipated this development.

Behind Middleton's corps Third Army had set up headquarters in Néhou, much closer to the front than the headquarters of either 12th Army Group or First Army. That evening Patton hosted SHAEF G-3 Major General H. R. "Pink" Bull, soon-to-be 12th Army Group chief of staff Major General Lev Allen, and new First Army chief of staff Major General William Kean, and he sensed that they were anxious to get him into the fight.[252] Undoubtedly, Patton discussed his ideas on leading with two armored divisions to break through the front. At that moment VIII Corps continued to press forward with the 79th Infantry Division at Lessay, the 8th Infantry Division west of Periers, the 90th Infantry Division east of Periers, and the 83rd Infantry Division holding the east flank south of the Taute River, all still more than seven miles from Coutances. Middleton had the 4th and 6th Armored Divisions in reserve.

Bradley met with Patton the next morning, 27 July, to discuss the operation, and at 1200 hours he optimistically redirected his forces to Avranches.[253] Collins ordered the 1st Infantry and 3rd Armored Divisions toward that city twenty miles to his south while Bradley instructed VIII Corps to assume VII Corps' objectives around Coutances.[254] Unfortunately, Bradley's top-down command and control trumped lower unit initiative. By redirecting the 2nd Armored Division from blocking positions around Saint-Denis-le-Gast and Villebaudon west to join the attack against the Coutances-Avranches corridor, Bradley actually turned Collins away from an enemy weak spot into stronger enemy positions. Holding VIII Corps with minefields and roadblocks, the Germans completed their reorientation to contain VII Corps. Collins hit Germans positioned on the Coutances-Avranches corridor covering withdrawal from the Cotentin. Momentum waned. The official Army history noted: "The result of the main COBRA effort produced disappointment. 'Generally, we are not able to push very fast,' the VII Corps G-3 admitted."[255] Six U.S. and three German divisions competed for space on the two roads converging on Coutances, while a disorganized but effective German resistance held Collins' troops. It was not quite chaos, but VII Corps paused to reorganize. The Germans got the break they needed.

Bradley faced another disappointing end to a promising start. Having already wired his optimistic forecasts to the long-frustrated Eisenhower, he desperately wanted to reinvigorate this attack. Bradley went to see Patton, who had already hosted planners and operations staff from Ike, Bradley, and Hodges in the previous twenty-four hours. Soon after Bradley conferred with Patton, Middleton did something uncharacteristic: he ordered the 4th and 6th Armored Divisions forward to lead his attack. It was *the* critical decision of Cobra. In the early morning hours of 28 July, the 6th Armored Division weaved its way forward through the 79th Division at Lessay.[256] The 4th Armored Division reported moving forward at 0945 hours that morning, with Combat Command B under Brigadier General Holmes Dager leading through the 90th and 83rd Infantry Divisions.[257]

Was Middleton's decision to lead with armor the result of Patton's influence? The official Army history states: "That evening, as orders from Bradley shifted First Army from COBRA into exploitation, Patton manifested his influence by substituting armor for infantry. Two armored divisions were to spearhead the attack to the south."[258] Yet Hirshson for one argues against such an "unwarranted assumption."[259] He cites comments Wood made to Basil H. Liddell Hart in 1948 claiming, "Patton, of course, had no part in the Avranches break-through."[260] From Wood's perspective with 4th Armored, this seemed accurate. On the other hand, the official U.S. Army history, written by Blumenson, suggests: "Though Patton remained in the background of command to the best of his ability, his presence on the operations that developed was as visible as his shadow on the wall of the operations tent."[261] Considering Middleton's past actions and writing, it was clear he was uncomfortable leading with tank divisions.

Fortunately for historians, Middleton himself clarified the role Patton played in turning Cobra into a successful breakout from Normandy. In 1974 Frank J. Price published *Troy H. Middleton: A Biography*, based on his personal interviews with the general, who subsequently read, proofed, and approved the manuscript. Middleton described how he and his staff planned five contingencies for possible exploitation scenarios in Normandy, but when the Germans failed to act as expected, he had to play it "strictly off the cuff."[262] When Bradley turned Cobra toward Avranches on 27 July, Middleton began adjusting his plans. However, he stated: "Before the final steps of the plan could be executed, there were some small hitches. *At Patton's direction*, the infantry spearheads of the VIII Corps were replaced by the Fourth Armored Division under Major General John S. Wood and the Sixth Armored Division under Major General Robert W. Grow [emphasis added]."²⁶³ The exact moment and method of how Patton made this direction remain unclear, but beyond a doubt Middleton credited Patton with the decision to lead with the armored divisions.

The combined arms columns of VIII Corps tank divisions busted through the German lines and ended nearly two months of frustration in Normandy. Dennis Showalter noted that Cobra had turned into an operation frequently "described as uncharacteristic of Bradley in particular and the U.S. Army of World War II in general."²⁶⁴ Bradley had employed Patton's ideas for leading with two armored divisions and aiming for Avranches. Now, Bradley reasoned, "Because VIII Corps was to become part of Patton's Third Army once the latter was committed, I ordered George to trail Middleton's columns and aid in unscrambling them should they become entangled."²⁶⁵ In effect, he created space for Patton to use VIII Corps as the lead of Third Army as an exploitation force for turning the battle of Normandy into the campaign for France. Patton had finally reentered the war.

7 | BREAKOUT: EXECUTION

> George is such a pushing fellow that if we don't stop him he will have Monty surrounded.
>
> —Anonymous British general

Bradley tried to keep Patton out of France until victory in Normandy was well in hand, and even then sought to restrict him to a supporting role. As events developed, however, victory required Bradley to invite Patton's participation. Historians may still debate Patton's influence on the breakout from Normandy, but the record is clear. Patton not only delivered the breakout, he also orchestrated the historic exploitation across France. Moreover, he was the only Allied general who could have done so because he was the only one to have crafted the doctrine and means necessary to accomplish the feat.

The morning of 28 July saw slow going for the 4th and 6th Armored Divisions as corps engineer teams had to part a sea of mines, many of new design. The official Army history noted, "General Bradley, after conferring with General Patton on 27 July, had already ordered General Middleton to disregard COBRA limit of advance north of Coutances and infantrymen of the VIII Corps were streaming south as quickly as engineers could clear the paths for them through the mine fields."[1] The limited road network was choked with vehicles, combat detritus, and German resistance. VII Corps had not yet attained its objective and VIII Corps was beginning an unexpected change of mission, as Bradley now wanted it to get behind the Germans holding Collins' VII Corps. The circumstances prevented Middleton from entertaining any thoughts of exploitation. "To assure control and balance while the armored divisions passed to the front," the Army history noted, "General Middleton instructed the troops to halt for further orders after capturing Granville and Cérences."[2] Middleton therefore planned to stop the 6th Armored halfway between Coutances and Avranches near Granville, and the 4th Armored Division one-third that distance near Cérences. Concerned by the rising chance of chaotic developments, Bradley sought help.

That afternoon Bradley called Patton's headquarters. The Third Army commander was out inspecting a fuel depot and did not return the call until 1645 hours. Bradley told Patton to "take over the VIII Corps and put in the XV Corps at the left at once. The official change will be effective at noon on 1 August."[3] Bradley would not yet activate Third Army, but he still needed Patton. He gave Hodges supervision of his four corps to the east and asked Patton to serve as a "Deputy Army Commander" supervising VIII Corps— and to keep quiet about it.[4] Bradley later explained, "Because VIII Corps was to become part of Patton's Third Army once the latter was committed, I ordered George to trail Middleton's columns and aid in unscrambling them should they become entangled."[5] He reasoned Patton's role had to remain secret so as not to compromise his continuing role in the Fortitude deception plan holding the Germans in Calais.[6] Patton was Third Army commander preparing for action and FUSAG commander in the great deception, but now also unofficial First Army deputy commander. He gladly accepted, interpreting Bradley's words as an immediate appointment of command of Third Army.[7]

Grabbing several members of his staff and XV Corps commander Haislip, Patton headed to Middleton's command post "but conducted everything very casually so as not to get people excited at the change."[8] Middleton briefed VIII Corps' dispositions: the 79th Infantry Division at Lessay, the 8th Infantry Division at Periers, the 83rd Infantry Division south of the Taute River, and the 90th Infantry Division on the Sevre River, all still more than five miles from Coutances. These were the dispositions displayed on the First Army situation map as late as 2400 hours that night. Patton asked, "Where's your armor?" He was aware that Middleton now had both Wood's 4th and Grow's 6th Armored Divisions. Patton told Middleton, "I want Wood and Grow to lead the advance."[9] The two armored divisions were in fact working their way south by the time Patton met Middleton, but as Blumenson noted, "The columns were strung out and backed up through the countryside."[10]

Patton's comfort with overturning doctrine unsettled Middleton. Instead of tanks supporting infantry, he was going to form his combined arms columns led by tanks as trained in England. Patton then tipped his intentions. He called Bradley and asked for an airborne operation to seize the dams on the Selune River, about four miles south of Avranches.[11] If the Germans blew these dams, they would flood the roads leading into the Brittany peninsula and south toward Nantes. Not even considering pausing at Granville and Cérences, Patton was now aiming past Coutances, past Avranches, deeper into France. Bradley told Patton it would take too long to plan, prepare, and execute a paratroop operation to seize the dams.

Ordered by Middleton to "seize the corps objective northwest of COUTANCES," the 6th Armored Division's Combat Command A (CCA) under Brigadier General James Taylor headed south on the western Lessay-Coutances road with the 79th falling in behind them.[12] A few miles to the east, the 4th Armored Division's Combat Command B (CCB) under Holmes Dager advanced down the Periers-Coutances road with the 8th Infantry Division in tow.[13] As trained, the divisions paired battalions of different arms. Patton reassured Middleton, "You know Troy, such an operation would certainly get us unsatisfactory marks at Leavenworth. But this is War!"[14]

With combined arms formations, Patton's "bounce around them" tactics, and rapid tactical air support, the armored columns began to pick up momentum. His command and control techniques would ensure they maintained it. The 4th Armored Division reported: "The tanks lurched through the rubble of Periers and by nightfall swarmed into Coutances, first city to fall to CCB and the division. The division was 18 miles through the German lines. American armor was rolling everywhere. . . . It was like old home week at Fort Knox."[15] Patton's acceleration of VIII Corps inverted Cobra: with the Germans now holding Collins' VII Corps, he sliced behind them with Middleton's long-stifled VIII Corps. Dager's CCB secured Coutances—the Cobra objective—despite heavy German artillery fire and dense minefields that killed the commander of Combat Command Reserve, Colonel Louis J. Stork. Wood went forward on foot with the 4th Armored and sent back a message: "General Dager, send the infantry through after me."[16] With that, he was off for Avranches.

Patton went forward after lunch on 29 July. After stopping at the VIII Corps and 79th Division headquarters, he found troops digging in at Coutances and ordered them to move out.[17] He discovered the 6th Armored Division's CCA stopped at the Seine River. "Grow was not showing any life," Patton reported, "so I lit a fire under him."[18] Grow and Taylor explained that division reconnaissance found all bridges destroyed and that they were searching the map for a ford. "I told them I had just waded across it, that it was not over two feet deep, and that the only defense I knew about was one machine gun which had fired inaccurately at me," Patton recalled. "I repeated the old Japanese proverb: 'One look is worth one hundred reports,' and asked them why in the hell they had not gone down to the river personally."[19] Furious, he told Grow "that unless he did something, he would be out of a job."[20] CCA forced a crossing at Pont de La Roque. Patton went on to Periers but could not find 8th Division headquarters. "I did find a battalion of the 90th Division, miles behind the front," he noted, "digging tomb-like slit trenches. I told them to stop it, as it was stupid to be afraid of a beaten enemy."[21]

At Bradley's headquarters spirits soared and the staff happily adjusted plans, later reporting that operations were unfolding "somewhat differently from what had been intended in the 'COBRA' plan itself."[22] Bradley sent a note to Eisenhower: "To say that personnel of the First Army Headquarters are riding high tonight is putting it mildly. Things on our front look really good. I told Middleton to continue tomorrow toward Avranches and go as far as resistance will permit. As you can see we are feeling pretty cocky."[23] He made no mention of Patton. Bradley now set Avranches as his endpoint; Patton still envisioned it as his start point. Bradley told Ike, "I can assure you that we are taking every calculated risk and we believe we have the Germans out of the ditches and in complete demoralization and expect to take full advantage of them."[24]

At 1400 hours on 29 July Bradley caught up with Patton to discuss new plans. Patton thought, "They are getting more ambitious but are just what I wanted to do, as I set down the other day, so I am very happy."[25] The attack was rolling with the 4th and 6th Armored Divisions in the lead and Weyland's air support overhead. In just one example, on 30 July, the 6th Armored Division ran into a German roadblock at Brehal. They paused just long enough to allow XIX TAC's overhead P-47s to pounce on the defenders. Doctrine dictated that airpower was not to be used against anything that the artillery could hit. Weyland said, "Well, time was of the essence. So I said to hell with that. . . . Hell, it might take them an hour or two, I'd have fighter-bombers out in front and we'd try to take care of anything out there. . . . They'd be there in three minutes. Wham! Wham! They'd keep rolling."[26] XIX TAC had adopted Patton's command and control style.

Weyland explained, "In support of Gen. Patton, Nineteenth TAC would find its targets in the field, and would plan as it flew."[27] By 1345 hours Brehal was secured. The next morning the 6th Armored columns reached Granville another ten miles farther south, where Middleton intended to stop.

In the first hour of 31 July Rundstedt's replacement as commander of the German forces in the west, Field Marshal Günther von Kluge, reported, "It's a mad house here. . . . Commanders are completely out of contact."[28] In reaction to the breakthrough he authorized the German Seventh Army to fall back to a new line from Granville or Troisgots.[29] This would have perfectly matched Middleton's planned halt—but Patton intended to sustain the shock. He had already asked for nine infantry and three tank divisions to balance his columns for fast, prolonged movement but knew Montgomery needed American forces, so he would have to make do with less.[30] He quickly tried to trade some self-propelled tank destroyers and truck-drawn infantry to the Army Service Forces for four armored cavalry regiments, arguing, "I think we can clear the Brest peninsula very fast. The thing to do is rush them off their feet before they get set."[31]

At 1500 hours on 31 July Patton ordered Grow to ignore Middleton's halt plan and push his division through Le Point Gilbert, northwest of Avranches. Wood, unaware of this change in boundaries, was already on the road to be used by Grow. Without pausing the two commanders arranged to share the narrow route and kept moving. CCB of the 4th Armored Division "battled into" Avranches at 2000 hours and reported heavy fighting.[32] The 704th Battalion's tank destroyers under Lieutenant Colonel Delk Oden knocked out several German tanks in the town before the German Seventh Army command scampered south, leaving two thousand soldiers to surrender with the city.

A month earlier when Patton had first proposed this drive on Avranches, he said, "I don't care if I don't get any credit for the idea as long as they allow me to carry it out."[33] Now he wrote to his wife, "Brad has really pulled a great show and should get credit for it."[34] Though Bradley did not share credit with Patton, observers could still guess. At SHAEF headquarters Butcher noted, "Among comments heard about the current battle is the rumor that Patton must be 'in there' because our armor is racing ahead so effectively. Patton, of course, is there personally, though he is not yet in command, but he may have influenced the battle tactically."[35] Paul Harkins, on Patton's staff, described how Patton even personally directed traffic at a road junction in Avranches for nearly an hour and a half to ensure the forward movement of his army.[36]

Patton had been pushing the advance for three days. Bradley was now ready to halt and actually stopped his four eastern corps to regroup. Patton, however, saw emerging opportunities. He noted, "Bradley simply wants a bridgehead over the Selune River [at Avranches]. What I want and intend to get is Brest and Angers [southeast at the junction of the Mayenne, Loir, and Loire Rivers]."[37] Patton had his enemy off balance and fully intended to maintain his series of shocks and turn this battle into a campaign. Here was the second critical decision, the one that turned breakthrough into breakout, and it was unequivocally Patton's decision.

Middleton, out of contact with Bradley and out of objectives, halted.[38] The VIII Corps commander told Patton that "he did not know what to do next and could not get ahold of Bradley."[39] Hearing this, Patton flew into a fury and instructed him to move south at once and secure Pontaubault, a few miles south of Avranches, where several bridges crossed the Selune River. Patton wrote, "I told him that throughout history it had always been fatal not to cross a river, and that while I did not officially take over until tomorrow noon, I had actually taken over on the 28th, and therefore, he was to get over now."[40] If left alone, the Germans might reestablish their defense by destroying dams upriver to flood the crossing points. Patton's advanced intelligence systems informed him that a bridge at Pontaubalt was still passable and that the 4th Armored had captured the dams. "On getting this news," he recorded, "I told Middleton to head for Brest and Rennes, with the 79th [Infantry] and 6th Armored for Brest and the 8th Infantry and 4th Armored for Rennes."[41] Middleton was getting a crash course on Patton's way of war.

Patton held one last staff meeting that night. He studied the situation map while puffing a cigar and reminded his officers, "The harder we push the more Germans we kill, and the more Germans we kill, the fewer of our men will be killed. . . . Flanks are something for the enemy to worry about. Not us. . . . We are advancing constantly and we are not interested in holding anything, except onto the enemy. We're going to hold onto him and kick the hell out him all the time."[42] He finished, "Our basic plan of operation is to advance and keep on advancing regardless of whether we have to go over, under, or through the enemy. We have one motto, '*L'audace, l'audace, toujours l'audace!*'"⁴³

After 4th Armored Division, which was well schooled in Patton's tactics, secured the crossings on the Selune River in the predawn hours of 1 August, Middleton asked Patton, "What do we do now?" It was the second time the old infantryman was ready to halt. "Keep on going across the river. Get a bridgehead at once," Patton instructed. "Never sit on a river when the enemy is on the run."⁴⁴ He told his staff to keep VIII Corps moving west into Brittany toward Brest and to prepare the newly arriving XV Corps to move southwest to Quiberon Bay to isolate the Brittany peninsula, and following XX Corps south to Rennes, where he could head west toward Metz or north to bag the Germans. As the situation developed, he would decide on his courses of action.

Bradley, now 12th Army Group commander, arrived at Patton's headquarters at 1500 hours and revealed a new boundary between First and Third Armies. "These are rather cramped as far as Third Army is concerned," Patton observed, "as we have to slide through a very narrow bottleneck between Avranches and St Hilaire."⁴⁵ Bradley wanted more room for First Army and wrote, "Published regulations suggested that an army group should direct but not conduct operations, confining itself to broadly stated 'mission orders.' But these regulations were not binding. . . . I would exercise the very closest control over Hodges and Patton."⁴⁶ Just as Marshall and Ike expected when they placed him as a brake on Patton, Bradley rejected the kind of command and control Patton instituted as necessary to seize opportunities. Yet before he could fully grasp the reins, Patton was off and charging.

Koch informed Patton, "The heavy stripping of the Brittany Peninsula has reduced its garrison to a crust of two divisions and the immobilized elements of three others."⁴⁷ It would not require a full corps to clear Brittany. Ultra intercepts of German radio traffic also indicated the enemy at Laval, forty miles east of Rennes on the road toward Paris, was critically short on supply, and at LeMans fifty miles farther east the garrison was requesting vehicles to evacuate.⁴⁸ Patton saw the weak spot. Without waiting for Haislip's XV Corps to pass through Avranches, he instructed Middleton to split his corps and send the 6th Armored and 79th Infantry Divisions to Brest and the 4th Armored and 8th Infantry Divisions to Rennes—one corps to two points 130 miles apart, freeing XV Corps for central France.⁴⁹

Middleton, who had confessed his uneasiness with armored exploitation, was now ordered to conduct one. At 0600 hours the 4th and 6th Armored Divisions began sweeping to their separate destinations with little more than overlays indicating their routes.[50] Bradley worried: "As Middleton's VIII Corps carried Patton's colors around the corner at Avranches to head for the Brittany ports, I ordered George to post a strong force on guard in the center of the Brittany neck."[51] Knowing VII Corps' 30th Infantry Division was closing in on Mortain twenty miles east of Avranches, Patton redirected the 90th Infantry Division to reinforce them. He thought, "This is an operation which, at Leavenworth, would certainly give you an unsatisfactory mark, as we are cutting the 90th Division through the same town and on the same street being used by two armored and two other infantry divisions. However, there is no other way of doing it at this time."[52] He sent officers to manage traffic, including Haislip at Avranches.

In all the scrambling of units, Patton was remarkably careful to maintain his combined arms columns. Learning that Middleton, "despite what I had already told him," did not send infantry with the 4th Armored Division, Patton cut a motorized combat command team from the 8th Infantry Division to follow the 4th Armored toward Rennes.[53] He also ensured that the 79th Infantry Division stayed with the 6th Armored Division into Brittany. He organized a task force under Brigadier General Herbert L. Earnest with the 15th Cavalry Regiment, an infantry battalion, and a self-propelled tank destroyer battalion, to secure the railroad around Moralix. When Koch reported a German strongpoint at Dinan, Patton ordered Grow to bypass it and dispatched a special task force of 3,500 men to deal with it. He felt Middleton should have done this and wrote, "I cannot make out why Middleton was so apathetic, or dumb—I don't know what was the matter with him."[54]

The time invested in air-ground training in England paid dividends. The 4th Armored Division reported: "XIX TAC Air Support Parties swung their radio vehicles into the Fourth Armored's leading columns and were on the spot to call the P-47s when they were needed to bomb and strafe ahead of the tanks. . . . Roaring over the armored spearheads, the fighter planes provided almost continuous air cover."[55] The air controllers quickly oriented the planes with identification panels and gave awaiting aircraft direction and distance to targets over radios. Columns fired signal smoke for better identification when needed as aircraft announced how many runs they would make and with what kind of ammunition.⁵⁶ Patton later explained: "We have seen the attempts of air and ground to work together for years but it was only on the 1st of August that it really worked."⁵⁷

To the east, Montgomery planned to attack Caumont with six divisions on 2 August. "But because of the unexpected speed of the American advance," he wrote, "with Dempsey's agreement I advanced the date to 30th July."⁵⁸ For forty-eight hours his attack floundered, but now as Germans shifted toward Patton, the British VIII Corps broke through at Le Bény Bocage, giving Monty an open road south to Vire, twenty-five miles east of Avranches and fifteen miles north of Mortain. An attack there would disrupt German actions against the breakout, but Monty decided he had met his objectives, halted, and redrew boundaries so as to place Vire in the American sector. Another opportunity was lost. Montgomery noted, "From that time onwards there were always 'feelings' between the British and American forces until the war ended."⁵⁹

Ultra revealed that German troops were to "begin at once" the destruction of Rennes.⁶⁰ Realizing that the enemy was not prepared to defend that city, Patton spurred Middleton. CCA under Colonel Bruce C. Clarke, the 4th Armored Division recorded, "plunged 54 miles to Rennes, ancient Breton capital. Smacking nests of emplaced heavy antitank and flak guns north of the city the morning of August 2, the tanks wheeled wide to the west and south."⁶¹ Bypassing enemy strength, Wood sent CCA west to Bain de Bretagne, CCB to Redon, and the 2nd Cavalry Group around Rennes. After a tough fight the Germans retreated and surrendered the city.⁶² Patton now had Brittany by the neck.

Wood was at a literal and figurative crossroads. Given the mission to go southwest to Saint-Nazaire on Quiberon Bay to seal off the Brittany peninsula, he grasped that the deterioration of the German defenses created the opportunity for a decisive sprint east toward Paris. As Hanson Baldwin noted, "It already seemed clear to him that the main action in Western Europe would take place not in Brittany but in central France. Few enemy forces remained in Brittany, so why proceed westward to the Atlantic Ocean and a dead end?"⁶³ Without coordinating with Middleton or Patton, Wood turned east.

In London, an elated Eisenhower looked at the SHAEF operations map and told his aide, "If the intercepts are right, we are to hell and gone in

Brittany and slicing 'em up in Normandy."⁶⁴ He thought, "All else could wait upon [Bradley's] exploitation of this golden opportunity, in the certainty that with the enemy destroyed everything else could quickly be set right."⁶⁵ Ike wanted to throw everything at the Germans, but Bradley hesitated and said he assumed the German armies "would make a gradual withdrawal to the Seine River . . . But the Germans were not following the textbook."⁶⁶ Bradley worried, "Since this opportunity had not been anticipated in the Overlord plan, it required some hasty and rather radical revisions in our thinking."⁶⁷ He was unprepared to grab opportunity out of an uncertain situation.

Pulled by Patton and pushed by Ike, Bradley wrote, "Over the period August 2 to August 6, I began to develop an idea for a vast encirclement—or long envelopment—of the German forces in Normandy."⁶⁸ He envisioned an operation to encircle the Germans, but only *after* securing Brittany, getting his armies on line, and building up supplies. Then he envisioned sending six armored divisions leading motorized infantry in a controlled "long envelopment" around the southeast of Paris as three airborne divisions dropped between Paris and Orleans. It was a large, cumbersome operation. Bradley explained, "This long and vast wheeling movement and envelopment would trap all the Germans in Normandy, prevent a withdrawal to the Seine, block any efforts of the German Fifteenth Army to move toward the Seine and isolate Paris. . . . I viewed my idea as nothing less than a war-winning drive."⁶⁹ It was a maneuver that should have been a planned, rehearsed, and prepared sequel to a breakout from Overlord, but no one at SHAEF anticipated such an opportunity. It still might have been possible through rapid maneuver on the heels of the current developments. Unfortunately, in the time needed to plan, coordinate, and execute Bradley's plan, the situation could—and did—change.

Meeting at VIII Corps headquarters without Patton on the afternoon of 2 August, Middleton drew Bradley's attention to his flank at Fougères. "I'm wide open here," he said, "nothing to fend with if he [the enemy] hits me when my stuff is turned the other way. Hate to attack with the enemy at my rear and with my rear exposed the way it is."⁷⁰ Bradley fumed. He recalled, "Patton had ignored the Group order to establish a strong force in the Brittany neck and instead had ordered Middleton to race on toward

Rennes and Brest."⁷¹ Patton had placed the 90th Division on that flank, reinforced by XIX TAC, confident they could hold any possible attack long enough for him to react. Unappreciative of Patton's methods, Bradley convulsed, "Dammit, George seems more interested in making headlines with the capture of Brest than in using his head on tactics. I don't care if we get Brest tomorrow—or ten days later. . . . But we can't take a chance on an open flank."⁷²

Bradley's comment on headlines is interesting, given that he still kept Patton's presence in France secret. There were as yet no headlines for Patton. Even at SHAEF, Butcher thought the breakout "sounds very much like Patton. . . . In the war room, I was asked by a cheerful RAF [Royal Air Force] officer as to whether the arrow toward Rennes should be labeled 'Patton' and another halfway to Saint-Malo should be marked 'Patton's aide.'"⁷³ Several days later Butcher was still asking, "Wouldn't it be great for Patton if his name could be printed? I suggested to Ike release of his name, this being a good time to prove to Ike's critics that he was right in keeping Patton, but Ike said, 'Why should I tell the enemy?'"⁷⁴ As late as 7 September, Patton began a conference with correspondents: "Before starting the inquisition, I wish to reiterate that I am not quotable, and if you want to get me sent home, quote me, God damn it."⁷⁵ In the meantime, Bradley got the headlines.

Those arrows in Brittany masked contention. Bradley approved a reduced commitment there but insisted Patton clear that peninsula *before* driving east. He explained, "There was one reason why I sent Patton and Middleton to Brittany: logistics. . . . Without ports and facilities we could not supply our armies. . . . Beyond that, simply ignoring Brittany and 'sealing it off' appeared to be militarily imprudent."⁷⁶ Events would prove Bradley mistaken. He instructed Patton to seize, in sequence, Rennes, Saint-Malo, Quiberon Bay, and Brest.⁷⁷ Patton had a different idea.⁷⁸ He already had Rennes and Wood was sealing off Brittany at Quiberon Bay while Grow swept the peninsula. The rest of Third Army would drive east toward the Seine River. As D'Este noted, "However, during these crucial days, Patton was dealing from a position of weakness when it came to challenging the authority of Bradley and Eisenhower. . . . Patton was painfully aware that another serious misstep might be his last."⁷⁹ Patton walked a razor's edge determined to finally do things his way while not giving grounds for removal.

Told by his G-3 that Patton was violating orders requiring him to "establish a firm front before turning into the Brittany peninsula," Bradley pulled the 79th Infantry Division out of Brittany to guard Fougères, leaving the 6th Armored Division without enough infantry to take Brest.[80] Patton recalled how he had made Bradley irate when he had redirected the 1st Infantry Division in Sicily. When Bradley informed him of his orders to the 79th Division, Patton smiled, put his arm around him and said, "Fine, fine, Brad, that's just what I would have done. But enough of that—here, let me show you how we're getting on."[81] Privately Patton feared Bradley "was getting the British complex of over-caution" and mused, "It is noteworthy that just about a year ago to the day I had to force him to conduct an attack in Sicily. I do not mean by this that he is avengeful, but he is naturally super-conservative."[82] Patton redirected the 83rd Infantry Division to join the 6th Armored Division and ordered Grow to move rapidly on Brest.

Middleton quickly sent a courier to reverse Patton's instructions and caution Grow: "Do not by-pass DINAN and ST MALO for we are getting too strung out. We must take DINAN and ST MALO before we can proceed."[83] Grow sent two liaisons back to protest. On 4 August Patton visited Grow, saw Middleton's order, and said quietly, "And he was such a good doughboy, too."[84] Grow complained that the order had cost him twenty-four hours. Patton replied, "Don't take any notice of this order, or any other order telling you to halt, unless it comes from me. Get going and keep going till you get to Brest."[85] The twenty-four hours likely eliminated any chance to rush what had been a lightly defended port and resulted in a tough siege that did not end until 18 September, when it took three infantry divisions ten days and ten thousand dead and wounded to capture the city in an assault.[86] Traditionalist control proved costly.

Third Army accelerated the movement of XV and XX Corps to the front. Pausing to look at how Patton was rapidly pushing 200,000 men and 40,000 vehicles through the "straw" at Avranches, Bradley marveled: "Every manual on road movement was ground into the dust. He and his staff did what the whole world knew couldn't be done: it was flat impossible. . . . Yet out of the other end of the straw came divisions, intact and ready to fight. If anybody else could have done it, no one ever got that man's name."[87] He still could not comprehend the methods of Patton's staff and felt more comfortable with doctrinaire procedures. Bradley praised the "steady, undramatic, and dependable" First Army commander Courtney Hodges, saying, "Whereas Patton could seldom be bothered with details, Hodges studies his problems with infinite care and was thus better qualified to execute the more intricate operations."[88] It is hard to understand how any operation could have been more intricate than Patton's breakout from Normandy.

Patton looked ahead. The Germans could fall back to a new defensive line, most likely along the Seine River, or they could counterattack against the American breakout. Koch thought there were four unlocated German panzer divisions in front of First Army that threatened "to rupture the jugular supply vein" at Avranches.[89] Patton drew up countermoves. If the Germans fell back, he would race across the Seine and flank them from the south. If the Germans attacked Avranches, he would turn against their flank. Meanwhile, he would advance. Patton leveraged uncertainty.

Once south of Avranches, Haislip's XV Corps received the 79th and 90th Infantry Divisions and the 5th Armored Division and headed east. Bradley approved an attack toward LeMans but instructed Patton to halt between Mayenne and Laval to allow First Army to close up, in keeping with his long envelopment.[90] Patton, however, feared any halt that would allow the Germans to regroup and told Haislip, "Don't stop."[91] He wanted to maintain his series of shocks. Yet anticipating a possible German attack toward Avranches, he added, "Don't be surprised if you get orders to move to the northeast or even to the north."[92]

On 4 August Eisenhower, after consulting with Marshall, approved the ongoing swing east. He also endorsed economy of force in Brittany to send the "great bulk of forces to the task of completing the destruction of the German Army . . . and exploiting beyond that as far as we possibly can."[93] Montgomery agreed. Still the overall land force commander, he now sent word to Brooke, "I have turned only one American corps westward into Brittany as I feel that will be enough."[94] Unfortunately, the concern with Brittany would pin down two of Patton's best armored divisions.

Edward Fickett's fast-moving reconnaissance platoons of the 6th Cavalry Group were by now sending a blizzard of reports to Third Army. Part of the Army Information Service, they kept Patton and his staff better informed of the situation across the front than any single corps or division, better informed than Bradley's G-2, and better informed than the Germans.[95]

The Germans were busily reorganizing under Kluge. As Yeide noted, "Nearly ignorant of Third Army's activities, Kluge and his staff fought the battle they could see, against First Army and 21st Army Group. German commanders began to realize how powerful a force the Americans squeezed through the gap only when, on 5 August, XV Corps' 90th Division was in Mayenne and the 70th Division appeared at Laval, which was held by two reinforced infantry battalions and a battalion of 88s, and probable mechanized cavalry units were spotted near the Loire."[96] This was uncertainty by design, the product of Patton's unrelenting movement, and it created opportunities to exploit chaos.

Patton wrote his old cavalry mentor Kenyon Joyce, "We are having one of the loveliest battles you ever saw. It is a typical cavalry action in which, to quote the words of the old story, 'The soldier went out and charged in all directions at the same time, with a pistol in each hand and a sabre in the other.'"[97] The faster he advanced, the more confused the enemy became, the less able their command and control became, and the less effective their operations were. Increased speed of operations therefore increased Patton's decision cycle advantages. Decreases in German morale were sure to follow.

Suddenly Patton's scouts spotted a rogue: Wood on his way east toward Paris instead of southwest to Quiberon Bay as ordered. Patton politely reminded Middleton to make certain that Wood was on his way to Quiberon Bay. Middleton went to Wood and asked, "What's the matter, have you lost your division?" "No," replied Wood, "but they [higher command] are winning the war the wrong way."[98] "Maybe he was right—I am inclined to believe he was," recalled Middleton, "but those weren't the orders we had had from Bradley."[99] Middleton ordered Wood to assume the defensive south of Rennes and to send reconnaissance to the southwest. Unaware that Patton was about to send the XV and XX Corps east, Wood "got bull headed" and ignored Middleton.[100] Third Army deputy chief of staff Colonel Paul Harkins wrote, "When General Patton found out about this, he exploded."[101] He ordered Wood southwest to Vannes and Lorient, adding, "You nearly got tried for that." Wood responded "that someone should have been tried but it certainly was not I."[102] Patton did not bother explaining his reasons; he encouraged initiative but would not tolerate insubordination. He fumed that Wood's "over-enthusiasm wasted a day."[103] For his part, Wood never forgave Patton for diverting him from the decisive drive in France.

Anger propelled Wood. Between 1400 and 2100 hours on 5 August, his CCA drove seventy miles to Vannes at the mouth of Quiberon Bay and cut off Brittany. Meanwhile, Grow's 6th Armored Division continued to Brest, and Haislip's XV Corps closed on Mayenne and Laval. Patton now sent Walker's XX Corps (the 5th Infantry and 35th Infantry Divisions and the 2nd French Armored Division) to Angers where the Loire met the Mayenne, Sarthe, and Loir Rivers.[104] From there they would gain unbroken ground into the Paris-Orleans gap. Walker's staff reported, "A fleeting opportunity now existed for a major Allied victory and it was necessary to grasp this tactical advantage before the bewildered enemy recovered from the initial shock of the breakthrough."[105] Patton went to Bradley's headquarters, later recalling, "I succeeded in getting the boundary Bracey-St Hilaire-Mayenne-Le Mans all to Third Army. This is exactly the boundary I desire as it keep me on the outside—on the running end."[106]

Just as XII Corps under Lieutenant General Gilbert Cook prepared to join the fray, the Germans played their hand. Late on 6 August, Third Army Ultra liaison Major Melvin Helfers relayed intercepts warning of a heavy German attack to cut off Patton. Helfers was alarmed by Hitler's words: "The outcome of the Battle of France depends on the success of the attack," and he recalled, "When I first saw this message, I immediately felt that if General Patton doesn't get this message immediately—I'd be court-martialed."[107] He awoke Koch, who took him to see the chief of staff. "We'll go see the commander," Hap Gay decided.[108] Patton asked his G-2's opinion of the source.[109] Koch said it was consistent with his estimate of the enemy. Patton noted, "Personally, I think it is a German bluff to cover a withdrawal, but I stopped the 80th, French 2nd Armor, and the 35th in the vicinity of St. Hilaire just in case something might happen."[110] He called Walker, who sent the 35th Infantry Division to Mortain.[111]

At 0100 hours on 7 August four German armor divisions, drawn from Montgomery's front and supported by the Seventh and Fifth Panzer Armies, attacked toward Avranches and ran into the 30th Infantry Division of Hodges' First Army near Mortain. Ike later wrote, "We had sufficient strength in the immediate area so that if we chose merely to stand on the defensive against the German attack he could not possibly gain an inch. However, to make absolutely certain about our defenses at Mortain, we would have to diminish the number of divisions we could hurl into the enemy's rear and so sacrifice our opportunity to achieve the complete destruction for which we hoped."[112] With Ultra intelligence, massed artillery, good defensive positions, and priority air support, the 30th Infantry Division heroically stopped the German attack at Mortain.

Meanwhile, Churchill visited Bradley's headquarters in Normandy. Noticing Third Army's 6th Armored and 83rd Infantry Divisions in Brittany, Churchill asked if this was not a waste. He suggested isolating Brest instead, saying, "The garrison here will die like flowers cut off at their stems."[113] His comments echoed those Patton had made during the planning of Overlord. Bradley declined to pull Patton's divisions out of Brittany.

When the Germans launched their attack on Mortain, a detachment of French Forces of the Interior (FFI) arrived at Patton's headquarters with an American pilot downed three weeks earlier at Angers. They reported no large German units between Angers and Châteaubriant. "They saw German signal detachments taking up wire while moving east," Patton noted. "The French say the Germans are steadily drifting east, north, and west of the Loire River."[114] Patton asked the FFI to guide a combat team of the 5th Division with a tank battalion and recon troop to seize Angers.

On 8 August Third Army captured Le Mans, about seventy miles south and east of the German spearhead at Mortain. Patton now had nearly twelve divisions south of Avranches, four not yet committed. Bradley debated options to "play it safe on the hinge" by using those four divisions to strengthen Hodges at Mortain or sending them with Patton "in an effort to destroy the German Seventh Army."[115] Prodded by Ike, he decided: "If the Canadians could push into Falaise and beyond into Argentan, and if I turned Haislip due north from Le Mans toward Argentan, there was a good chance that we could encircle and trap the whole German force in Normandy in a matter of a few days."[116] Bradley dropped his "long envelopment" for this "short envelopment," turning Patton ninety degrees north from Le Mans and hoping to "strike for annihilation of the German Army in the west."[117] Monty endorsed Bradley's plan without denying him the authority to cross the inter-army group boundary to complete the envelopment. In fact, when they met at Monty's headquarters on 13 August, Monty again made it clear: "So long as the Northward move of Third Army meets little opposition, the . . . leading Corps will disregard inter-army boundaries."[118] As he had demonstrated in Sicily, Monty could be very flexible with boundaries when the situation demanded. Ike was confident that "in Patton ... we had a great leader for exploiting a mobile situation."[119]

Patton was now fighting in many directions at once. As Grow battled toward Brest, another battalion task force seized Nantes farther west on the Loire. Gaffey arrived with the 5th Armored Division at Angers to secure the pivot to the east. "I am doing this without consulting Bradley," Patton noted, "as I am sure he would think it is too risky. It is slightly risky, but so is war."[120] The risk was somewhat mitigated by Ultra intercepts on 8 August that revealed the German effort against Mortain left little to threaten Third Army.[121] Patton also knew from the FFI that there was no enemy threat south of the Loire; XIX TAC could guard that flank. He had the enemy ready for the kill. German Seventh Army chief of staff Christian Gersdorff later reported: "The American breakthrough at St. Lô-Avranches, led by General Patton, was carried out with operational genius and unprecedented dash. It developed into a deep thrust in to the flank and rear of [Army Group B], which gave the German High Command the choice of either crossing the Seine as quickly as possible, or facing the danger of utter annihilation of the bulk of the German army in the West."[122] Patton had achieved shock, but he had to keep it going. The Germans were stopped at Mortain to the west, had Patton to their south, and the rest of the Allies to the north, leaving a single door open for retreat to the east at Falaise. Patton could slam that door shut.

Bradley went to the Third Army headquarters to show Patton his plan for sending XV Corps north from Le Mans toward Argentan. Bradley recalled, "He was curiously cool to the idea. He leaned toward my idea of the day before—the deeper and wider envelopment along the Seine—perhaps because it was more dramatic, perhaps because the success of my proposed shorter envelopment was heavily dependent on the Canadian army closing the gap from the north. Typically, the fact that logistical considerations argued for the shorter envelopment carried no weight with Patton."[123] Bradley did not see what Patton saw. Patton commented, "I would rather head for Chartres or Dreux but Bradley won't let me. This axis of attack is, in my opinion, too close in."[124] He had already considered a "short hook" to Alencon, Argentan, and Falaise, and had even warned Haislip not to be surprised if he was suddenly ordered north. He then decided that a deeper envelopment along the Seine, after crossing the Eure through Chartres or

Dreux, was more certain to bag the Germans in Normandy.[125] It would also better support a rapid drive into Germany through Metz. Patton, however, diverged from Bradley's "long envelopment" in that he would not wait for First Army to come on line, he would not wait for airborne drops, and he would not wait to build up logistics. As he was to prove, he could easily advance to the Orleans-Paris gap with extant "logistical considerations."

As Patton ordered Haislip north toward Falaise, Bradley intervened. "We'll go as far as Argentan and hold there," he said. "We've got to be careful we don't run into Monty coming down from Falaise."[126] After the war, Bradley offered, "Falaise was a long-sought British objective and, for them, a matter of immense prestige. If Patton's patrols grabbed Falaise, it would be an arrogant slap in the face at a time when we clearly needed to build confidence in the Canadian Army."[127] Building confidence in the Canadian army was, of course, Monty's job, not Bradley's. When Haislip raced past Argentan, one historian reported Montgomery told his chief of staff, "Tell Bradley they ought to get back."[128] Blumenson wrote that Monty's staff urged him to overrule Bradley's stop order, but he declined. Bradley later admitted, "But Monty had never prohibited, and I had never proposed that U.S. forces close the gap from Argentan to Falaise. I was quite content with our original objective and reluctant to take on another one."[129] Bradley added, "In halting Patton at Argentan, however, I did not consult with Montgomery. The decision to stop Patton was mine alone; it never went beyond my CP [command post]."[130] Whatever his reasoning, Bradley had Patton pull back XV Corps reconnaissance elements after they had nearly reached Falaise.[131]

An exasperated Patton wrote to his wife, "I am the only one who realizes how little the enemy can do—he is finished. We may end this in ten days."[132] Yet British code breakers Alan Pryce-Jones and Peter Calvocoressi recalled that Bradley told them "that the German army was no longer a factor with which we need reckon, and the only brake on our advance was our supply problem. He explicitly said that the Allied armies would clear France within 3 weeks, and be in Berlin within 6 weeks."[133] Bradley told his staff, "We'll shoot the works and rush east with everything we've got."[134] He even released Walker's four divisions from backstopping Mortain—but he still kept the two superb armored divisions in and around Brittany.

The rapidity of Patton's breakout turned August into what the 12th Army Group G-4 described as a period of "frantic supply."[135] Almost immediately, the SHAEF Communication Zone (COMZ) proved unprepared to push forward sufficient supply and in turn forced the numbered armies to use their organic transportation to draw stores from the Normandy area. By the second week, supply was "governed entirely by the transportation available."[136] Meanwhile, the Corps of Engineers began busily repairing the damage done to regional rail systems by SHAEF's interdiction bombing campaign and a pipeline for fuel.

By 9 August Crerar's First Canadian Army was clearly losing momentum halfway to Falaise. For nearly two days Montgomery considered sending the Second British Army to reinforce Crerar but decided against it. The Falaise gap remained open. Meanwhile, with Haislip's XV Corps halted facing north, Patton could not renew his drive east until Walker's XX Corps got into position. He was losing time in getting to undefended Metz. Bradley's interference threatened to unravel Patton's exploitation.

Patton swiftly sent the 5th Armored to La-Ferte–Bernard near Fourges and the 80th Infantry Division to Lavalle to block possible German spoiling attacks; then he gave Walker the just-arrived 7th Armored Division. On 10 August he called Middleton to release CCA of the 4th Armored Division from Vannes, and it raced 80 miles southeast in seven hours to relieve the 5th Armored Division at Nantes. The next day Patton's staff found him particularly ill tempered at finding that Middleton had not released the rest of Wood's division. He ordered Middleton to send enough of the 6th Armored Division to Lorient to relieve the 4th Armored Division for the Paris-Orleans gap to join Cook's newly arrived XII Corps. Grow left a force holding Brest—the self-named "Brassiere Boys"—and sped off to relieve Wood. "I drove up to his CP," he recalled, "just as it was moving out to go east. Our relief was the most informal and brief I have ever heard of in military history. He said words to the effect: 'We're off, it's all yours,' and he was gone."[137] Never have flexibility, initiative, and mission orders been better demonstrated.

The 4th Armored Division's CCB drove an astonishing 264 miles to Prunay in 34 hours while CCA raced 120 miles to Saint-Calais in 22 hours, refueled, and then drove 60 more miles to Orleans.[138] Overhead Weyland covered the loping columns. Wood said, "Outsiders could never understand what made us so different or how we operated."[139] He listed guiding principles that might have come from Patton himself: audacity, indirect approach, "direct oral orders—no details, only missions," depth, carrying supply in "rolling reserves," personal communication "only possible by plane now," the Patton motto of "never take counsel of fears," and "trusting people in rear to do their part (a trust sometimes misplaced, but not generally)."[140] Dager recalled one of Wood's order's briefings: "'P' would pull the map out of his shirt, spread it and point . . . 'here's your boundaries, the units left, right and following us and the first, second and third objectives—let's get at it now!'"[141]

As Wood galloped east, XV Corps reached Beaumont and Patton asked for First Army help in protecting Haislip's left flank. Bradley denied the request.[142] To the north, 12th Army Group reported "the British effort [toward Falaise] . . . appears to have logged itself in timidity and succumbed to the legendary Montgomery vice of overcaution."[143] Sensing opportunity slipping away, Bradley said, "If the other fellow will only press his attack for another 48 hours, he'll give us time to close at Argentan and there completely destroy him. And when he loses his Seventh Army in this bag, he'll have nothing left with which to oppose us. We'll go all the way from here to the German border."[144] Unfortunately, circumstances refused to abide by Bradley's plans. By 12 August as XV Corps swung around Forêt de Perseigne and cut east of Alençon, LeClerc's French 2nd Armored Division disobeyed orders, took the wrong road, and caused a delay in refueling operations. Three panzer divisions beat Haislip to Argentan.

The British were still eighteen miles from Argentan as the Germans began escaping through the Falaise gap. Four days earlier Patton had warned Bradley that Montgomery would not reach the city. Now he sent Haislip instructions: "Upon the capture of Argentan push on slowly [in] direction of Falaise. . . . Continue to push on slowly until you contact our allies."[145] Hearing this, Bradley became "furious."[146] Patton joked, "Let me go on to Falaise and we'll drive the British back into the sea for another Dunkirk."[147] Bradley answered, "Nothing doing. You're not to go beyond Argentan. Just stop where you are and build up on that shoulder."[148] On 13 August Patton wrote, "I am sure that this halt is a great mistake, as I am certain that the British will not close on Falaise. As a matter of fact, we had reconnaissance parties within a few miles of it when we were ordered back."[149]

As overall ground commander, Montgomery should have overseen the proposed linkup operations between 12th Army Group's Third Army and 21st Army Group's Canadians near Falaise. His chief of staff, Freddie de Guingand, faulted his boss for not specifically inviting Bradley to drive across the inter-army group boundary to close the gap.[150] Yet Monty *had* given Bradley a green light when they first discussed the short envelopment and again at their midday meeting on 13 August.[151] Bradley claimed he stopped Patton because he was worried about a possible fratricidal collision between the Americans and the Canadians.[152] This excuse made little sense when communications were good, liaisons had been exchanged, and air reconnaissance existed—and a common headquarters was available to coordinate the linkup. Ike, then collocated with Bradley, later said, "I completely supported Bradley in his decision that it was necessary to obey the orders, prescribing the boundary between the army groups, exactly as written; otherwise a calamitous battle between friends could have ensued."[153] In the end, rigid command and control forfeited a once-in-a-century opportunity.

Bradley also expressed fears that XV Corps' four divisions could not hold a forty-mile sector against nineteen "stampeding" German divisions and said, "I much preferred a solid shoulder at Argentan to the possibility of a broken neck at Falaise."[154] He not only discounted the airpower that had stopped the Germans at Mortain, he also ignored the British and Canadian divisions that could have strengthened the neck upon linkup. Most important, as Patton recognized, the fleeing enemy was too damaged and disorganized to stage an effective attack; chaos would play to the Allies' advantage. The 90th Infantry Division's Brigadier General William Weaver explained, "German units were depleted, disintegrated and mingled with the full normal unity of command gone with the wind. George was so firmly convinced that the odds were in his favor that it would not even be a gamble."[155] Bradley, the traditionalist, was uncomfortable with any operation that was not well planned and controlled and so booted the chance for an envelopment at Falaise that may well have ended German resistance in France. Moreover, he had no plan ready to address failure at Falaise.

Pausing Haislip allowed the Germans to assemble defensive positions to his north and south of the stalled British and Canadians. In time Butcher observed, "General Ike is a bit disappointed that because of the extraordinary defense ring created by the Germans north of Falaise, which has taken so long to break, our bag of prisoners in the pocket will not be as great as he first thought."[156] Though they suffered terribly at the hands of Allied air attacks, losing 50,000 men captured and roughly 10,000 killed, some 40,000 veteran German troops escaped to fight again.[157]

Incredibly, Bradley later wrote, "A golden opportunity had truly been lost. I boiled inside, blaming Monty for the blunder."[158] He added, "If Monty's tactics mystified me, they dismayed Eisenhower even more. And at LUCKY FORWARD where a shocked Third Army looked on helplessly as its quarry fled, Patton raged at Montgomery's blunder."[159] However, Bradley had halted Patton forty-eight hours *before* the Germans began their withdrawal. There was still time to bag the German Seventh Army and Fifth Panzer Army. Patton told Hugh Gaffey: "The question why XV Corps halted on the east-west line through Argentan is certain to become of historical importance. I want a stenographic record of this conversation included in the History of the Third Army."[160]

In the United States, stories began to surface in the press that the Normandy breakout was the work of "Old Blood and Guts." On 12 August the *Washington Star* reported: "According to the Nazi news agency Transocean, they believe he is in France commanding 'the Third American Army.' The news agency respectfully adds that he is 'an exponent of mobile warfare.'"[161] The article went on to say that the Germans "know a good commander when they see one and are mauled by him," and added, "and since General Patton is most certainly 'an exponent of mobile warfare' and since our forces are spreading and racing like a prairie fire right up to the environs of Paris, the Nazi agency's report is at least logical and may yet be confirmed as true."[162] At the same time Hitler finally authorized a retreat from Mortain to avoid envelopment; little could he expect that Bradley would stop Patton for him.

Patton started shuffling forces on the move as he received new troops in the line and got back the 80th Division from Mortain. "This will give me five armored and four infantry divisions on the marching flank," he wrote, "the XX Corps moving on Dreux and the XII Corps on Chartres, the XV remaining where it now is."[163] There was no need to pause, reorganize, and plan. He explained his thoughts: "In this formation I can turn from north to southeast without crossing columns and can shift divisions between corps at will; as I have no Corps administration it is all from division directly to Army. It should be a very great success, God helping and Monty keeping hands off."[164]

Uncertain what to do next, Bradley went to Patton's headquarters. He wrote, "George helped settle my doubts when on August 14 he called to ask that two of Haislip's four divisions on the Argentan shoulder be freed for a dash to the Siene. With that . . . I sided with Patton."[165] With the 80th Infantry, French 2nd Armored, and 90th Infantry Divisions to Argentan, Haislip could take the 5th Armored and 79th Infantry Divisions fifty miles east to Dreux. XX Corps headed to Chartres on the Eure River and XII Corps to Orleans on the Loire River. From Dreux, XV Corps would cross the Eure, turn north, and cross the Seine thirty-five miles north of Paris at Mantes-Gassicourt. These movements would enable Patton to complete his desired encirclement of the Germans along the Seine. Thirty years later Bradley wrote that this plan was his idea and that Patton only suggested sending XX Corps to Dreux and XII Corps to Chartres—a plan Bradley said required complete revision.[166] Bradley may have considered the operations a variation of his earlier "long hook" idea. In his diary at the time, however, Patton explained, "It is really a great plan, wholly my own, and I made Bradley think he thought of it."[167] Patton had all corps moving by 2030 hours "so that if Monty tries to be careful, it will be too late."[168] Almost immediately Bradley had second thoughts. Decades later he wrote, "To this day I am not yet certain that we should not have postponed our advance to the Seine and gone on to Chamblois [near Falaise] instead."[169]

That day the Associated Press reported the formation of the 12th Army Group, making it appear that Bradley had been promoted co-equal to Montgomery. Bradley wrote, "It was a harmless story that erred only in anticipating by two full weeks the full parity that was to come our way once Eisenhower crossed to France."[170] The British press, however, was not amused—and neither was Monty.

The bill for the lack of strategic vision in Overlord now came due. Ike believed "the enforced hold-up of our advance which eventually must occur while we improve maintenance facilities and prepare for a further offensive" should occur on the German border.[171] He intended to reach the border with all armies on line along a broad front. "However," explained Butcher, "General Montgomery feels that if his Army Group is given practically all the maintenance available to both the Americans and British, his 21st Army Group could rush right on into Berlin."[172] Ike argued that such a narrow advance was "impractical," risking German counterattacks and immobilizing the rest of the front. Curiously, Montgomery used a Patton phrase to describe his plan: "In its simplest terms this was the German 'Schlieffen Plan' of 1914 in reverse, except that it would be executed against a shattered and disorganized enemy."[173] The problem was, unlike Patton, Montgomery had not proved capable of conducting such a daring thrust.

On 15 August Jake Devers' Seventh U.S. Army landed almost unopposed on the Mediterranean coast of France. That night the 7th Armored Division of Patton's XX Corps reached Chartres, the "Gateway to Paris."[174] A fierce four-day battle ensued. The 5th Infantry Division entered Chartres only after the corps artillery arrived following a seventy-two-mile march in twenty-four hours. The capture of Chartres on the Eure compelled Hitler to pull his Army Group G facing Devers north to stop Patton.

Meanwhile, Montgomery called Bradley and asked if XV Corps had enough strength to hold Argentan against the large number of German forces still in the Falaise pocket.[175] Hearing that five panzer divisions were closing on Argentan, Bradley went to Patton's headquarters "fit to be tied," and though acknowledging that Patton was completing "some of the most astonishing wide-open sweeps of the entire war," he was again afraid he had erred in allowing Patton to move east.[176] He ordered Third Army not to advance to the Seine.[177] A frustrated Patton thought Bradley was "suffering from nerves. . . . His motto seems to be, 'In case of doubt, halt.'"[178] Patton saw an opportunity to drive north and cut the Germans off along the Seine. He asked Bradley that "since he was already to the Seine River, in fact had pissed in the river that morning, what would he want him to do—pull back?"[179] Bradley reluctantly relented and authorized Patton to kick out to the Seine south of Paris.

The next day the Germans conducted a forceful attack on the 90th Infantry Division near Argentan. Patton quickly sent Gaffey with a provisional corps headquarters to command his three divisions there. When the Canadians finally captured Falaise, he again requested permission to close the remaining fifteen-mile gap, but Bradley vacillated before ordering him to "halt on the line and consolidate."[180] Meanwhile, Montgomery complained to Brooke, "Patton is breaking straight for Paris and is determined to get there and will probably do so."[181] He then asked Bradley to close the Falaise gap at a point seven miles northeast of Argentan at Chambois. Bradley sent First Army's new V Corps headquarters under Lieutenant General

Leonard Gerow to take charge at Argentan.¹⁸² Blumenson mused, "Why Bradley sent Gerow to take charge in an area and a situation Gerow knew nothing of is difficult to understand. . . . Bradley counted on Marshall's and Eisenhower's pleasure for Gerow's participation in a pivotal action, for Gerow was a favorite of both."¹⁸³ Over Patton's objections, Bradley then took Third Army's three divisions at Argentan and gave them to Gerow and First Army, shifting the inter-army boundary south of Argentan. Patton had counted on using those divisions.

Meanwhile, the rest of 4th Armored Division joined XII Corps and at first light on 16 August attacked Orleans. After hard combat along mined streets, they handed the city to the 35th Infantry Division.¹⁸⁴ Patton now had forces due south of Paris prepared to pivot north. While First Army's XIX Corps worked its way along Third Army's northern boundary to Evreux, Bradley allowed Patton to push XV Corps reconnaissance to Mantes-Gassicourt, fifteen miles northwest of Paris on the Seine. Bradley proclaimed, "If the Germans had any hope of organizing a defensive line on the east bank of the Seine, Haislip's maneuver dashed it."¹⁸⁵ Patton noted, "Our chief success was due to the fact that we cut the armored divisions loose and did not tie them to the infantry."¹⁸⁶ To cap the day, Ike finally revealed to the press Patton's presence in France.

With XV Corps centered at Dreux west of Paris, XX Corps at Chartres southwest of Paris, and XII Corps at Orleans south of Paris, opportunities abounded. Patton was positioned to take Paris, or to pivot north to bag the Germans west of the Seine, or to punch through the Paris-Orleans gap and drive to the empty German border at Metz. He preferred to take all three corps up the banks of the Seine River to bag all the Germans. Blumenson noted, "Unfortunately, only Patton had his eyes fixed and focused on the proper military objective, destroying the enemy forces. To Montgomery and Bradley, getting to Germany took precedence over trapping and liquidating the Germans west of the Seine."¹⁸⁷ Actually, the Allied leaders were less than certain as to what to do next.

Montgomery had advanced less than 30 miles in the 70 days since D-day, while Patton spanned nearly 400 miles from Brest to the Seine River in about 2 weeks. When Patton entered the fight, the Allied campaign was 45 days behind schedule; in 30 days he advanced the Allies 15 days ahead of schedule.¹⁸⁸ The press, however, began focusing on reports that at least 20,000 Germans had escaped through the Falaise gap. A *Washington Times-Herald* editorial stated, "It is generally recognized in congressional circles and common gossip in military circles that General Eisenhower is merely a figurehead and the actual command of the invasion is in the hands of the British General Staff."[189] Marshall cabled Ike, "The Secretary [of War] and I and apparently all Americans are strongly of the opinion that the time has come for you to assume direct exercise of command of the American Contingent."[190] The British chief of the imperial staff complained, "We considered Eisenhower's new plan to take command himself in Northern France on Sept 1st. This plan is likely to add another 3 to 6 months to the war!"[191] Despite those worries, Ike needed to look like he was in charge.

As Patton raced about in light aircraft and jeeps visiting his far-flung units, Eisenhower and Montgomery met with Bradley with orders to get across the Seine. On 19 August Bradley took a "new plan" to Patton to move Third Army "north along the west bank of the Seine" to block the remaining German forces.[192] Patton asked Bradley for permission to take Melun-Fontainebleau and Sens. "By getting these, in addition to the crossing at Mantes, the line of the Seine becomes useless to the enemy," he wrote. "Bradley said it was too risky, but eventually I talked him into letting me try Monday, the 21st, if I do not receive a stop order by midnight, Sunday, the 20th."[193] Patton added ominously: "I also asked for a plan of future operations and an inter-Army boundary, extending well to the front so I can plan supply—to the present time the boundary has always stopped at the front line."[194] He was completing contingency planning for his goal, to get through Metz before the Germans occupied its formidable defenses.

XV Corps crossed the Seine against little opposition and reported: "Often the book of rules went out the window and any expedient was adopted to speed the advance . . . while all the might of the corps was directed against the tottering German defenses with an intensity and single mindedness that disheartened the foe and gave him no rest."[195] In a steady rain at daybreak on 21 August, XX Corps reached Melun and Montereau.[196] Ike then pulled the 2nd French Armored Division from Third Army to lead the First U.S. Army in the liberation of Paris. Instead of receiving reinforcement for his success, Patton had now four divisions taken from him. Patton lamented, "Bradley also declined to let me withdraw the 6th Armored from Brittany for fear of a possible attack from the south. In my opinion, such an attack is impossible."[197]

XII Corps commander Gilbert Cook suffered from such debilitating high blood pressure that he could not continue in command. Patton had to choose a successor. Even though Wood had been acting in Cook's place for several weeks, Bradley and Patton chose the more pliable Manton Eddy. After his new staff briefed him on operations, Eddy exclaimed, "What in hell kind of war is this? I've been fighting for two months and have advanced five miles. Now in one day you want me to go 50 miles?"[198] Eddy immediately called Patton with concerns about his flanks and speed. Patton said, "I told him to go fifty and he turned pale."[199] Patton told him, "If you worry about your flanks you could never fight this sort of war. Our air can spot any group of enemy large enough to hurt us and I can always pull something out of the hat."[200]

Third Army galloped another seventy miles and seized crossings over the Seine at Sens, Montereau, and Melun before the enemy could react and blow the bridges. After XII Corps seized Sens, Eddy called Patton: "General, had a lovely drive. I'm in Sens. What's next?" to which Patton replied, "Hang up and keep going."[201] Bradley's plan for a large airborne assault in the Paris-Orleans gap was now moot, and he had been proven wrong in his concerns over logistics requirements for the move. On 21 August Patton wrote, "We have, at this time, the greatest chance to win the war ever presented. If they will let me move on with three corps, two up and one back, on the line of Metz-Nancy-Epinal, we can be in Germany in ten days."[202] He was certain the road network would support an advance of six infantry and three armored divisions. "It is such a sure thing," Patton said, "that I fear these blind moles don't see it."[203]

Hirshson wrote: "The speed with which Patton was able to move from Argentan to the outskirts of Paris indicated two things. First, he had enough gas for the movement. Second, he was meeting but scattered resistance from the Germans. And, according to the *New York Times*, when he did encounter opposition, he often went around it."[204] As the four-day fight for Chartres proved, this was not entirely true. Patton attacked weakness and avoided strength, but his columns *did* encounter resistance, the kind that would stop other units. XX Corps reported: "Numerous minefields and road blocks defended by strong rear guard detachments slowed the advance near Limour . . . strongly entrenched enemy forces in front of Etampes . . . heavy artillery fire from commanding ground east of the Seine . . . several attempts to push through the constant barrages proved useless and costly."[205] Others would have paused, enabled the enemy to organize, and wound up fighting battles. On 23 August the Germans waged fierce counterattacks against bridgeheads on the Seine, but Third Army would not pause. Armor slipped around strongpoints, artillery quickly opened up, XIX TAC pounced, and infantry "held them by the nose" while armor "kicked them in the ass." The enemy was constantly outgunned, outflanked, and outpaced. In the end Patton's advance presented the enemy with threats exceeding the time-space constraints of any single battlefield. The Germans were compelled to retreat from the front of the First U.S. Army and the British 12th Army Group. Patton explained his units to the press: "There was little resistance because they had moved so fast that they had broken through."[206] As long as he kept moving—maintained his series of shocks—the exasperated Germans could not muster effective reactions.

With the enemy appearing defeated, Montgomery now stepped up efforts to get overall command of a "single thrust" into Germany. He wanted nothing less than twelve American divisions added to his 21st Army Group and all other armies halted so that their supplies could be sent to him. On 22 August he dispatched his chief of staff, Major General Sir Freddie De Guingand, to win Ike's approval for this plan. De Guingand may not have had his heart in the presentation as he later confessed, "This was the only major issue over which I did not agree with my chief."[207] Bradley countered with a plan closely resembling Patton's.[208] Montgomery invited Eisenhower to his headquarters and Ike agreed to come. Early the next day Monty made a rare visit to Bradley's headquarters and wrote, "I found to my amazement that Bradley had changed his mind; on the 17th August he had agreed with me, on the 23rd he was a whole-hearted advocate of the main effort of his Army Group being directed eastwards on Metz and the Saar."[209] Bradley later replied, "I had not changed my mind. I had *never* agreed to the main features of Monty's plan."[210]

Bedell Smith flew from England with Eisenhower to Montgomery's headquarters but Monty insisted—and Ike agreed—that he remain outside the meeting tent. Smith fumed, "What makes me so Goddamn mad is that Monty won't talk in the presence of anyone else. He gets Ike into a corner alone."[211] Perhaps Monty did not want to lecture Ike in front of others, as he later explained, "I gave him my views about the immediate need for a firm and sound plan. I said we must decide where the main effort would be made and we must then be so strong in that area that we could be certain of decisive results quickly."[212] David Irving wrote, "Montgomery then heaped criticisms on Eisenhower's broad-front strategy; he demanded that Hodges' First Army should be given to him for the big northern offensive into Germany he was planning, and that all supplies for Patton should be cut off in his favor."[213] Monty stressed, "To adopt my plan [Ike] must stop the man with the ball: Patton, and his Third American Army."[214] Monty also bluntly advised Ike against involving himself in operations and warned, "The Supreme Commander must sit on a very lofty perch in order to be able to take a detached view of the whole intricate problem—which involves land, sea, air, civil control, political problems, etc. Someone must run the land battle for him."[215]

Ike faced a critical decision: should he support Monty in the north, Patton in the south, or Bradley's compromise favoring both? Patton was the right man, at the right place, at the right time to spearhead into Germany. He had demonstrated his ability to craft unprecedented drives. He had pushed nearly 400 miles from Normandy in about 3 weeks. His 4th Armored Division had just raced 328 miles in 12 days.[216] Metz was about 120 miles away, the Siegfried Line 20 miles farther. The German border was open. Beyond it was the Rhine, the Ruhr, and Berlin. All Patton needed was support. Ike chose to compromise—with priority given to Monty. He stuck with his "broad front" but gave Monty "operational direction" over First Army in coordination with Bradley. "Monty and Hodges would get the lion's share of supplies and gasoline," Bradley recalled, "but Patton's drive on Nancy and Metz would be supported, albeit minimally."[217] He added, "This was a clear-cut victory for Monty and a stinging defeat for me—and Patton."[218]

Patton remained focused on Metz. As he had foreseen in February, the city was empty, but with so much of VIII Corps still in Brittany and four divisions taken for First Army, he had only four divisions left, and one had to remain north of Orleans.[219] It was not enough. On 23 August he went to ask Bradley for two more divisions. Patton recalled, "He was quite worried, as he feels that Ike won't go against Monty and that the American armies will have to turn north in whole or in part. Air Marshal Leigh-Mallory had been with him all day, trying to sell him this idea. Bradley was madder than

I have ever seen him and wondered aloud 'what the Supreme Commander amounted to.'"²²⁰ Patton would get no more divisions.

It suddenly occurred to Patton that Third Army "must go north, the XX Corps from Melun and Montereau and the XII Corps from Sens can do it faster than anyone else."²²¹ He prepared contingencies. If Ike authorized him to go north, he formed "Plan A" to send XX, XII, and XV Corps toward Beauvais along the Seine River to "open that river to the British and Canadians, and have our supplies come across at Mantes, thereby reducing the present haul by 50 percent. This is the best strategical idea I have ever had."²²² In this scheme Patton expected to regain the 4th Infantry Division, 79th Infantry Division, and 5th Armored Division along the route. Patton sold his idea to Bradley's G-3 before leaving 12th Army Group headquarters, arranging that "if Bradley approves he has only to wire me, 'Plan A' by 1000 tomorrow."²²³ If he did not hear from Bradley, however, he would continue Plan B and go east. Liddell Hart would note, "Patton had a keener sense than anyone else on the Allied side of the key importance of persistent pace in pursuit. He was ready to exploit in any direction—indeed, on August 23rd he had proposed that his army should drive north instead of east."²²⁴ That evening Patton wrote, "I am having the staff put both plans in concrete form now. This may well be a momentous day."²²⁵

That same day SHAEF G-2 Kenneth Strong declared, "The August battles have done it and the enemy in the West has had it. Two and a half months of bitter fighting have brought the end of the war in Europe within sight, almost within reach."²²⁶ It was time to form a broad Allied front to share the final march into Germany. With Montgomery in the north, Bradley in the center, and Devers in the south, Ike prepared to advance on line to victory. Only much later would Bradley say, "We were all wrong, of course—tragically and stupidly wrong."²²⁷ Yet the German condition *was* desperate. Rundstedt's chief of staff, General Siegfried Westphal, recalled, "The overall situation in the West, [for the Germans,] was serious in the extreme. The Allies could have punched through that any point 'with ease' until mid-October, and would have been able to cross the Rhine and thrust deep into Germany unhindered."²²⁸ The SHAEF G-2 was accurate at the moment, but moments came and went.

Despite Strong's optimism, Patton sensed difficulties ahead. The Marne, Meuse, and Moselle Rivers cut across the path to Germany. Koch predicted possible German counterattacks by 4 divisions released from Calais. Additionally, logistical issues arose from Ike's decision to divert Third Army's supplies to Montgomery. Patton's staff reported: "Gasoline shipments were short daily requirements and a critical situation began to develop. No appreciable reserves of rations had been accumulated."[229] Muller began to beg, borrow, and steal gas wherever he could. At Sens, Third Army used 37 captured train cars carrying over 100,000 gallons of German fuel.[230]

Third Army *had* arranged for logistical support. Just two days earlier Muller outlined for Lieutenant General Brehon Somervell, commander of the Army Service Forces, and Under Secretary of War Robert Patterson his "supply plan for future combat operations" including "minimum daily tonnages for supply and maintenance" of five thousand long tons per day and additional truck companies for Third Army.[231] The commander of U.S. Army supply approved the plan. Somervell clearly understood Patton's intentions and said, "The job now is swift pursuit. Patton has the right idea—straight ahead, and let the air forces take care of the flanks."[232]

The next day Muller reported, "Communications Zone was notified that tonnage scheduled for this Army had not been delivered and was requested to extend the airlift allotment for ten days after 25 August to meet a critical supply situation."[233] The "tonnage scheduled" was not delivered. Scarcities included individual equipment, construction and obstacle materials, and medical supplies. The stocks were in theater but not delivered to Patton. Butcher noted, "Ike has already assigned General Montgomery great numbers of trucks, temporarily withdrawn from supplying American divisions, to help him reach the Rhine in the north and to threaten the Ruhr."[234] Only twenty-four hours after Ike promised priority to Monty, the flow of supplies went away from Patton.

Undaunted, Patton pressed on according to his doctrine. On 24 August he wrote to Geoffrey Keyes, "To attack with the limited forces I have now left available—since I occupy a 300-mile front—I am taking chances, but I am convinced that the situation in the German Army warrants the taking of such risks, and I am sure that if we drive him hard enough now, we will cause the end of the war in a very few days."[235] Without approval to turn north, Patton put his Plan B into action. XII Corps crossed the Seine at Melun and Mandara. XX Corps received orders "to continue straight east in pursuit of the stricken enemy."[236] To Monty, Third Army's advance belied

Ike's promise that Bradley would only "be prepared" to move on Metz; Ike, however, had issued no such orders.

The next day Bradley gathered his commanders in the cathedral at Chartres to issue new orders. He was not happy. Hodges would take First Army's 9 divisions across the Seine at the bridges captured by Third Army at Melun and Mantes and orient northeast to Lille in support of Montgomery.[237] Bradley complained, "It occurred to me that the command picture was developing exactly along the lines Monty had offhandedly suggested on July 2. . . . Monty's plan sprung from his own megalomania."[238] Bradley's irritation grew as he spoke. As Norman Gelb explained, "The war was coming to an end and he did not wish to play a lesser role in the windup."[239] Left basically with only Third Army, Bradley authorized the advance on Reims and told Patton to "be prepared to continue the advance rapidly in order to seize the crossings on the Rhine River from Mannheim to Koblenz."[240] Patton sent XII Corps (4th Armored, 35th Infantry, and 80th Infantry) and XX Corps (7th Armored and 5th Infantry) toward Metz-Strasbourg, noting, "The direction is part of my plan."[241] He hoped to have XV Corps (French 2nd Armored and 90th Infantry) soon follow. Despite several days of rain—and a diversion of XIX TAC to Brittany—Third Army advanced, even as gasoline deliveries fell 190,000 gallons, about 20 percent, short of requirements for the next 2 days.

That day the French 2nd Armored and U.S. 4th Infantry Divisions entered Paris. When Patton could have taken the city earlier, Ike said he hoped to avoid it altogether. Pressured by Charles de Gaulle, he gave the honor to Jacques-Philippe LeClerc—after officially taking this division away from Patton and giving it to Hodges. The BBC announced, however, that Third Army had liberated Paris. "Poetic justice," wrote Patton.[242]

Fatigue began to set in. XX Corps reported: "The men were worn and empty-eyed, covered with dust, and dead tired; but the pursuit of the battered enemy went on at a quickened pace. The narcotic of exhaustion dulled the feelings."[243] Yet the troops were anxious to keep going. Grow drove 312 miles from Lorient to Patton's headquarters northeast of Orleans to beg for his 6th Armored Division to get into the fight. He explained, "It is maddening to be left here by stupid orders which I have done everything honorable to get revoked."[244] Patton quietly told Grow to "slip" a combat command toward Orleans and he would get the rest out of Brittany as soon as possible.

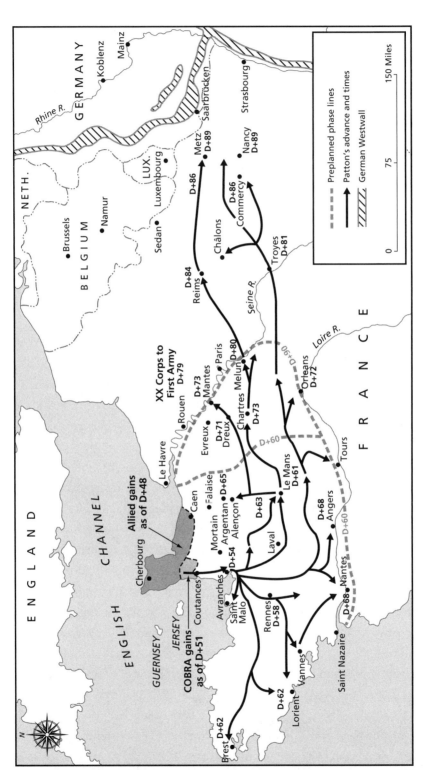

Map 4. Third Army Breakout, 28 July–2 September 1944

On 26 August Patton received ambitious orders from Bradley to cross the Seine and Yonne Rivers in zone, advance to Troyes, Challons-sur-Marne, and Reims, and "be prepared to continue the advance rapidly on order to seize crossings in Germany of the RHINE River from MANNHEIM to KOBLENZ, to protect the south flank along the LOIRE River, and, employing VIII Corps, to complete reduction of the BRITTANY Peninsula."[245] The 4th Armored Division reached Troyes, eighty miles southeast of Paris, and stormed two thousand defending enemy troops in a "desert formation" not used since they left Patton's desert training center.[246] The stunned 51st SS Brigade tried to escape in a twelve-truck column only to be cut down by waiting tanks. Over one thousand Germans were killed or captured. Thunderbolts of the XIX TAC and 4th Armored tanks chased the rest. When XII Corps commander Eddy was quickly told to resume the offensive at 0600 hours on 28 August, Patton noted, "He is not used to our speed yet, so was a little surprised."[247]

As he tried to scrounge together more forces, Patton chafed at having to still keep forces in and around Brittany. Under orders, he also had to leave the 35th Division covering the area south of the Loire, something he did under protest. His intelligence systems told him the situation allowed for greater economy of force. Cryptically referring to Ultra on southern France, for example, he wrote, "Studied the 'black market' dope intently and could see no hazards there."[248]

On 27 August XX Corps took Nogent. Lieutenant Colonel Creighton Abrams' 37th Tank Battalion of the 4th Armored Division bridged a canal at Saint-Germain and swung north and east around Châlons-sur-Marne. The next day the old World War I battlefield of Chateau Thierry on the Marne River fell. Patton wrote, "Bradley came in at 10:30 and I had to beg like a beggar for penetration to keep on to the line of the Meuse. What a life."[249] Bradley arrived at Third Army headquarters to tell Patton that he was further reducing Third Army's daily rations from "seven days and seven units" to "five days and three units."[250] Patton had not outrun his supplies; they were deliberately being sent elsewhere.

On 28 August Third Army received 140,000 fewer gallons of gasoline than it was allocated, even though large stocks of gasoline sat in Normandy.[251] By this time the "major system" of Class III distribution had moved from La Haye to Alençon. Rail lines delivered 3,875 tons daily to Nogent le Rotreau.

First Army supply dumps in the forests at La Loupe supported Third Army, and the Red Ball express was delivering 10,000 tons daily.[252] Four days later a single track extended 20 miles farther, delivering 500 tons daily to Chartres.[253] Advanced airfields opened at LeMans on 19 August and at Orleans and Brest a week later. Still, as 12th Army Group reported, "Class III supplies began to dwindle to a point where serious effect upon tactical decisions was almost certain to result. This was due to inadequate facilities for forward movement rather than to lack of supplies on the continent. The progress of the pipeline was almost negligible."[254] The scramble to established forward delivery nodes meant little without a priority of supply.

Despite logistical limitations, the 4th Armored Division's CCB captured Châlons-sur-Marne and CCA took Saint-Dizier. Third Army now had a solid bridgehead across the Seine River. Koch reported to Patton, "Indications pointed to a marked decline in the battle-worthiness of enemy personnel and it was evident that the enemy was facing a serious manpower problem, this being partially borne out by the increasing employment of low grade units in front-line fighting."[255] Patton noted: "Went carefully over the situation. There is no real threat against us from anywhere as long as we do not let imaginary dangers worry us."[256] Here was a decisive moment; the enemy was near his breaking point. Patton wrote, "If they would give me enough gas, I could go anywhere I want."[257]

Bradley went to see Ike and protested against placing First Army in support of Monty. Eisenhower issued a new directive by which Monty was "authorized to effect" through Bradley "any necessary coordination between his own forces" and First Army.[258] Monty was surprised to see that "the term 'operational direction' was cut from the directive."[259] He was also perplexed by Patton's continued drive to the east. Bradley recalled, "As Patton continued to push on in the face of a gasoline shortage that theoretically should have stopped him somewhere on the Meuse, Montgomery accused me of having hedged on Ike's orders to grant top priority to Hodges."[260] Monty believed Ike had broken promises to give him First Army along with Patton's supplies.

Without supplies from SHAEF, Third Army had to drag about 350,000 gallons of fuel across a 500-mile-long supply line stretching from the beaches of Normandy, where SHAEF still kept 90 to 95 percent of all its stored supplies.[261] The distance strained but did not break Patton's supply.

Now, however, SHAEF also ordered Patton to divert another 3,000 tons of supplies each day to the citizens of Paris, which had been liberated by First Army. Then higher headquarters took more trucks from Third Army.

The British Army reported "problems of the greatest complexity. Not one of the Tn [Transportation] units was fully mobile."[262] The 21st Army Group's administrative history explained, "A major fault occurred in the engines of K-5 4x4, three-ton Austins, 1,400 of which, as well as all the replacement engines, were found to be defective and to have piston trouble."[263] British industry had produced defective engines for their trucks. Ike quietly transferred 1,500 U.S. trucks from Patton and Bradley to Monty. These trucks could carry about 800 tons per day, tonnage equal to about 40 percent of Third Army's authorized total after its supplies were cut to 2,000 tons daily.[264] When Ike chopped First Army to Monty, Bradley stripped Third Army of even more transportation assets to restore First Army's allocation of trucks *and* to supply the British. It was this diversion of trucks that halted Patton.

Two officers at COMZ tried to fix things. On 25 August chief of the motor transport brigade Lieutenant Colonel Loren Ayers and Major Gordon Granville scrounged up as many trucks as they could for an ad hoc priority truck supply line.[265] They began with 67 truck companies, many from idle units in Normandy, totaling 3,385 trucks, to ferry supplies 125 miles to Chartres. They had a rough start. The G-4 history reported, "At any rate, even ADSEC's [Advanced Section of COMZ] G-4 didn't know until the afternoon of 27 August what the full Red Ball route was. First reports reaching him caused TCP [Traffic Control Point] personnel to be placed at Verneuil on Route N24, where they waited three days for trucks to come along consigned to Third Army. None came, and only seven trucks from First Army."[266] Third Army caught on fast. Soon the famed Red Ball Express *consumed* 300,000 gallons of gasoline every day—about the same as a field army. The gallant experiment lasted 81 days.

Beyond the diversion of support to Monty, SHAEF simply mismanaged logistics. The deputy theater commander and chief of Army Service Forces, J. C. H. Lee, was a difficult man who exasperated field commanders. When Ike banned soldiers from Paris, for instance, Lee seized 665 of the city's best hotels and other buildings for his headquarters. He also employed an armada of vehicles and consumed 25,000 gallons of gas daily in his empire, "routinely sending a bomber to North Africa to fetch fresh oranges for his breakfast table."[267] Because Lee notoriously punished complaints from the field, commanders turned directly to Eisenhower. Bedell Smith urged his boss to replace Lee, but Ike declined to move against a man he knew was strongly supported by Marshall. Ike decided instead to delegate logistics to his chief of staff.

Smith quickly learned that whereas Lee automatically pushed supplies forward in France, his counterpart in Italy, Lieutenant General Humphrey Gale, routinely used supply priorities to *influence* operations.[268] Smith opted to similarly influence operations in France on Ike's behalf. He set out to deliberately manipulate the supply of fuel to bring about Ike's desired broad front—restraining Patton in the process. As Crosswell noted, "Smith calculatedly used logistics as a means for directing operations at the front. Recognizing Patton's 'ardor for glory,' and fearing he 'might stick his neck out too far in the wrong direction,' Smith limited 3rd Army's supplies."[269] In this Smith was supported by the estimates of logisticians who "continued to insist that what Patton and Hodges were doing was impossible."[270]

Many historians criticize Patton for not heeding the logisticians, but as Martin van Creveld explained, the logisticians had "a very pessimistic view indeed of logistic capabilities."[271] They consistently found reasons why decisive maneuver could *not* be carried out. By 25 July (D+49), for example, with the Allies about thirty-four days behind schedule, SHAEF G-4 General Robert W. Crawford produced a study for Eisenhower that concluded the Allies could not possibly reach the Seine River on schedule "for a deficit of no less than 127 quartermaster truck (GTR) companies was to be expected on D+90 [6 September] and serious logistics difficulties encountered as early as D+80."[272] Patton then put them on that river eleven days *ahead* of schedule. By D+80 COMZ delivered supplies to points near the German border they thought could not be reached until D+330 (May 1945).[273] Again and again, the logisticians were mistaken, yet historians have used their work to critique Patton while mostly ignoring how he proved them wrong.

In setting supply priorities, Smith was influenced by the prevalent belief that the Germans had been defeated and the Allies needed to prepare for their lockstep march into Germany. He wanted to ensure Patton did not charge ahead and spoil Ike's "broad front" advance to victory. Even though Smith deemed Montgomery's single thrust "the most fantastic bit of balderdash ever proposed by a competent general," Monty still had to be brought up toward Antwerp to get online.[274] Smith therefore approved the transfer of supplies and vehicles to Monty without concern about Patton's opportunities. As Liddell Hart observed, "The best chance to finish quickly was probably lost when the 'gas' was turned off from Patton's tanks in the last week of August, when they were 100 miles nearer the Rhine, and its bridges, than the British."[275]

On 29 August Third Army reported: "The supply situation for gasoline as well as certain other Army requirements was by this time alarming. All gasoline supply points reported no gasoline received during the afternoon. Delivery of Class III supplies was 100,000 gallons short of requirements."[276] They tried to adapt. The 4th Armored Division was making nearly fifty miles a day with fuel delivered by aircraft.[277] Wood's chief of staff, Hal Patterson, later explained, "Every kitchen truck was stripped of its mess equipment and loaded with gas or ammunition. Rations were carried on combat vehicles. Every supply truck was loaded to more than 100% overload, and indeed some trucks carried as much as seven to eight tons of supplies."[278] Still Monty fumed.

Third Army did not go dry slowly, as one would expect if they were outrunning their supplies; they were simply cut off. Patton ordered Eddy to advance to Commercy on the Meuse and Walker to Verdun with what gas they had. The extent of the opportunity before him created by his unique way of war became clear when XX Corps captured German documents revealing they "intended to organize a strong defense on the line of the Meuse, but that the speed and power of the Corps' lighting advances gave him no chance. The enemy still had large forces but was stunned and bewildered by the large tactics of the XX Corps which would by-pass towns and strong points and then wheel to attack from the east."[279] Patton's "series of shocks" was having its intended effect—if only he could keep them up. On 30 August he went to Bradley's headquarters "to present my case for an immediate advance to the east and a rupture of the Siegfried Line before it can be manned."[280] He was told the gas would go to Monty. "It is a terrible mistake," Patton claimed, "and when it comes out in after years it will cause much argument."[281]

Returning to his headquarters, Patton found that Gaffey had authorized Eddy, the new XII Corps commander, to halt at Saint-Dizier on the

Marne rather than to press on to the Meuse at the risk of running out of fuel. Irate, he instructed Eddy to drive on until he ran out of gas and then to advance on foot. Patton noted, "It is terrible to halt, even on the Meuse. We should have the Rhine in the vicinity of Worms and the faster we do it, the less lives and ammunition it will take. No one realizes the terrible value of the 'unforgiving minute' except me. Some way I will get on yet."[282]

Despite his best efforts, Third Army ground to a halt. Patton had swept a span of nearly 700 miles only to be stopped 70 miles from the German border for lack of gasoline. His staff recorded: "Twelfth U.S. Army Group notified Third U.S. Army that there would be no gasoline available for it in appreciable amounts until 3 September."[283] Out of 400,000 gallons requested for the day, only 31,975 were received. All supply points were dry, and unit loads were fast disappearing. Patton went to Bradley's headquarters and found H. R. Bull, Ike's chief of staff for operations. Patton quarreled, "Look at the map! If I could only steal some gas, I could win this war."[284] He told anyone who would listen that, if pressed home, the shock of the advance would collapse the German resistance: "You can't have men retreating for 300 or 400 miles and then hold anything—the psychological result in long retreats."[285] "Bradley was sympathetic," Patton noted, "but Bull—and I gather the rest of Ike's staff—do not concur and are letting Montgomery over-persuade Ike to go north."[286]

Butcher recalled asking Eisenhower if he could continue the advance into Germany and Ike replied, "Port capacity is not what it should be, the roads are already clogged with our transport, bridges are out, signal communications are bad; yet these deterrents are overshadowed by the frequent headlines of victorious battles."[287] Like the logisticians, Ike was focused on factors that *could* cause a supply problem, not factors that *were* causing a supply problem. He had simply predetermined to halt on the border to reorganize and prepare before continuing into Germany, and he was sticking to his plan.

From his study of German records, Harry Yeide calculated that Patton had a window of possibly forty-eight hours when "the Germans could have interposed no coherent military formations in Patton's way."[288] On 1 September the entire German First Army had nine infantry battalions, two artillery batteries, ten antitank guns, and ten tanks blocking Third Army;

forty-eight hours later the German First Army controlled roughly five divisions.[289] On 2 September Patton met with Ike and Bradley and told them Third Army "had patrols on the Moselle near Nancy and Metz" and begged for support to attack.[290] Ike would not allow it until "the Calais area was stabilized." "He kept talking about the future great battle for Germany," Patton later recalled, "while we assured him that the Germans have nothing left to fight with if we push on now. If we wait, there will be a great battle of Germany."[291] Without gas, the 2nd Armored Regiment patrols on the Moselle were recalled.[292] Twenty-four hours later, German Army Group G commander Generaloberst Johannes Blaskowitz had assembled 106,700 infantry and 78,000 panzer troops, supported by more than 200,000 reserve troops, in and around the Metz fortifications.[293] Autumn had come for Patton.

Sadly, priority to Montgomery did not pay dividends. His effort was supposed to open the port at Antwerp as a major supply base as soon as possible. On 10 September, however, Eisenhower approved Monty's Operation Market Garden plan aimed at crossing the Rhine. The doomed diversion meant Montgomery failed to clear the Scheldt until 9 November, and shipping to Antwerp did not begin until 26 November.[294] Moreover, to support Monty's airborne plans, vital aircraft were withdrawn from supply operations. As 12th Army Group reported: "Had the planes not been withdrawn at this time, and air supply continued, an average of 1,200 tons per day could have been achieved during the subsequent four or five weeks, equal to requirements of five divisions of Third U.S. Army spearhead units' gasoline requirements, thereby enabling these divisions to proceed at least to the Rhine."[295] When stopped for fuel, Patton's army had been averaging 30 miles a day and stood roughly 100 miles from the Rhine. Given any logistical support, he could have blitzed into Germany and upended Hitler's plans for the Ardennes, thereby saving perhaps 100,000 lives—perhaps producing shock enough to hurry the end of the war.

Envisioning all the lost possibilities, Patton could only commiserate with trusted friends who understood what he saw. Hap Gay recalled, "Patton and Wood were often together, particularly so when the shortage of gasoline grew critical. One evening, just at dusk, I saw them standing alone, facing to the East, with tears in their eyes as they foresaw the awful waste of life—lives of our boys being sacrificed, unnecessarily so, by the lack of fuel for their armor."[296] Patton, now supremely confident in his way of war, was absolutely convinced of the ineptitude of those commanding above him. If only they understood.

When the press asked Patton to explain his "overwhelmingly successful" drive across France, he replied, "We have always gotten to each defensive line, not through my efforts, but through the glory of God 3 days before the Germans thought we would."[297] The speed of advance essential to his way of war conflicted with traditional doctrine. Privately Patton complained, "Ike is all for caution, since he had never been at the front and has no feel for actual fighting."[298] Ike's enforced halt was unforgivable; it ceded the initiative to the enemy, granted them time to organize defenses in Metz and along the Siegfried Line, and even gave Hitler a chance to craft a counterattack, which he chose to do in the Ardennes. The denial of gas to Patton not only cost many casualties, however; it pointed to the future path of Army doctrine.

DEATH AND RESURRECTION | 8

> In the context of America's World War II,
> George Patton was a hero out of his time.
> —*Dennis Showalter*

The end of World War II ended Patton's opportunities to prove the validity of his way of war and began an erosion of his reputation. It also heralded a change in the Army's outlook on proper doctrine. Where the post–World War I Army moved forward under the assumption that the next war would look like the last one, this time the Army advanced under the notion that it would not and should not ever fight the same kind of war. The Army carefully developed a future generation of political generals as the previous generation fought over blame and credit for World War II combat operations. The decades would find the Army in conflict over both warfare and legacies, with Patton figuring prominently in both.

Germany surrendered on 7 May 1945, signifying the end of World War II in Europe and the beginning of the end for Patton. He wrote in his diary, "There is going to be a tremendous let down unless we watch ourselves."[1] With no more combat, Eisenhower, now commander in chief of U.S. Forces, European Theater, had no further need for his fighting general's particular skills. For reasons not entirely clear, Ike appointed Patton and Third Army to administer the eastern portion of the American Zone (minus Berlin); Patton had little to offer aside from his habit of causing headaches for his commander. The two had sparred over the conduct of operations in North Africa, Sicily, France, and Germany. Then there were the slapping incidents and the Knutsford speech. Patton got into more trouble when he ordered "a censorship stop on the discovery" of over $100 million of Nazi gold in his sector and then fired a censor who broke the story.[2] He warned Ike it was a mistake to leave Berlin to the Soviets. Asked by reporters why he did not take Prague, Patton replied slowly, "I can tell you exactly why. Because we were ordered not to."[3] Setting up headquarters in Munich, he told correspondents, "What the tin-soldier politicians in Washington and

Paris have managed to do today is another story you'll be writing for a long while if you live. They have allowed us to kick hell out of one bastard and at the same time forced us to help establish a second one as evil or more evil than the first."[4]

Three days after the German surrender, the victorious Supreme Allied Commander assembled his senior commanders at 12th Army Group headquarters. "After lunch," Patton reported, "General Eisenhower talked to us very confidentially on the necessity for solidarity in the event that any of us are called before a Congressional Committee. . . . It is my opinion that this talking cooperation is for the purpose of covering up probable criticism of strategical blunders which he unquestionably committed during the campaign."[5] Ike issued other guidance: "It should be brought home to the Germans that Germany's ruthless warfare and the fanatical Nazi resistance have destroyed the German economy and made chaos and suffering inevitable and that the Germans cannot escape responsibility for what they have brought upon themselves."[6] The Army set out to remove all Nazis and "militarists" from positions of influence. Patton bluntly told his staff, "Eisenhower is running for President."[7]

On V-E Day Third Army occupied a zone of 7 million residents, 460,000 displaced persons in 238 camps, 28,376 civilian internees, and 282,003 disarmed Axis troops, 52,293 of whom were in hospitals.[8] Patton was ill suited to be their governor and even less inspired by the job. He repeatedly asked for another assignment, but Ike insisted he stay in place. This made the Soviet allies uncomfortable, as Patton belligerently opposed their desire to punish the Germans. When a Soviet general arrived at Third Army headquarters demanding the handover of German prisoners, Patton stood up, slammed a pistol onto his desk, and shouted to his chief of staff, "Gay, goddammit! Get this son-of-a-bitch out of here! Who in hell let him in? Don't let any more Russian bastards into this headquarters. Harkins! Alert the 4th and 11th Armored and 65th Division for an attack to the east."[9] As the flustered Russian fled, Patton laughed. Later, after hosting a hard-drinking banquet for the commander of the Soviet 4th Russian Guards Army on 12 May, Patton observed: "They are a scurvy race and simply savages. We could beat the hell out them."[10] After being decorated with the Order of Kutuzov medal, first degree, by commander of the third Ukrainian front Marshal Fyodor Tolbukhin two days later, he reported:

"The officers, with few exceptions, give the appearance of recently civilized Mongolian bandits. The men passed in review with a very good imitation of the goose step. They give me the impression of something that is to be feared in future world political reorganization."[11]

Patton openly shared such thoughts with Eisenhower and Bradley: "In my opinion, the American Army as it now exists could beat the Russians with the greatest of ease, because while the Russians have good infantry, they are lacking in artillery, air, tanks, and in the knowledge of the use of the combined arms; whereas we excel in three of these. If it should be necessary to fight the Russians, the sooner we do it the better."[12] His audience was not amused. A few weeks later Patton talked with Ambassador Robert Murphy, Eisenhower's diplomacy adviser. An alarmed Murphy recalled, "He inquired with a gleam in his eye whether there was any chance of going on to Moscow, which he said he could reach in thirty days, instead of waiting for the Russians to attack the United States when we were weak and reduced to two divisions."[13] Patton advocated rearming the Germans for war with the Soviets. As D'Este wrote, "Coming from Patton, the warnings seemed like the rambling of a warmonger."[14]

Sent to the United States to sell bonds and give speeches, the emotional Patton again got himself into trouble when he tearfully said, "It is a popular idea that a man is a hero just because he was killed in action. Rather I think a man is frequently a fool when he gets killed."[15] The Associated Press reported he had insulted the honored dead. Relatives of the deceased were aghast. The *Stars and Stripes* responded with an imaginary letter from a "Private X, one of 30,000 who died under Patton's command," which included the line, "It is no fun to die, particularly when the general you followed turns to the homefolks and tells them you died in vain."[16] Critics included popular cartoonist Bill Mauldin, who called Patton overly controlling, and the president of the United Auto Workers, Rolland Jay Thomas, who labeled him "anti-union."

In Washington, Patton learned he would not be going to China to fight the Japanese. That job went to Courtney Hodges. Depressed, Patton visited Walter Reed Army Hospital where daughter Ruth Ellen was a volunteer in the double amputation ward. She recalled that while talking with the wounded soldiers "suddenly, he whipped out a large white handkerchief and burst into tears. He looked around and said, 'God damn it, if I had been a better general, most of you wouldn't be here.'"¹⁷ Before returning to Germany in early July, he told his daughters—out of earshot of his wife—"Well, goodbye girls. I won't be seeing you again. Take care of George [his son]. I'll be seeing your mother, but I won't be seeing you again." When they protested, he explained, "No, I mean it. I have a feeling that my luck has run out at last."¹⁸

Back in Germany, reporters were lying in wait. When pressed on denazification efforts, Patton used an analogy of an occupied America: "Denazification would be like removing all the Republicans or all the Democrats who were in office, who had held office, or who were quasi Democrats or Republicans and that would take some time."¹⁹ His remarks were reported as stating, "SS means no more in Germany than being a Democrat in America."²⁰ On 31 May Victor M. Bernstein in the left-wing New York daily *PM* had accused Patton of allowing Bavarian minister president Fritz Schaeffer to keep Nazis in important positions.²¹ Privately, Patton complained, "It is very evident that anybody who was in business, irrespective of his real sentiments, had to say he was a Nazi and pay his dues. . . . We are certainly in a hard position as far as procuring civil servants is concerned."²² He collected notes and articles on the adverse impact of occupation policies—for example, noting that "De-Nazification has removed nearly 95 percent of experienced officials from public health positions and, in some areas, more than 50 percent of the private doctors."²³ With these notes Patton waged an unwinnable fight with higher headquarters.

The Army in Europe began drawing down quickly. Ordered to send his most experienced men home first, Patton complained, "This so-called re-deployment [is] really [a] vote catching program."²⁴ He tried to begin training his men for war against the Japanese—or other threats—but the men's interests were elsewhere. As he traveled about, still peppering his speeches with stunning profanities, Patton sensed that his once-devoted troops were drifting away. Victor Davis Hanson observed, "That Patton enjoyed killing enemy soldiers because he felt them to be agents of evil and a danger to a democratic society was less important to an increasing number of Americans, who were bothered by his candor and imagery far more than they appreciated the thousands of their sons and husbands that he had saved."²⁵ The soldiers just wanted to go home.²⁶ The atmosphere of victory was not conducive to military discipline. The chief of the information and education of special services, renowned eugenicist Brigadier General Frederick Osborn, met with Patton to argue his belief that the barriers between officers and men in the U.S. Army had to come down, they needed to "talk more freely." Patton responded, "I think he is a man whose education has surpassed his mental capacity."[27] Osborn's ideas, however, were the future.

Patton was an odd man out in the postwar Army. His friend Jimmy Doolittle insightfully noted, "I have often thought Ike used Georgie as one would use a pit bulldog. When there was a fight, he would tell Georgie to 'sic 'em.' But when the fight was won, he would have to put him in isolation somewhere until the next scrap."[28] Left unsaid was what happens to attack dogs when they are no longer wanted. Once Patton was considered the finest trainer in the Army and given the responsibility for creating and commanding the Desert Training Center. Now when Bradley rated his generals, he placed Patton "Number 1 as a commander in combat and Number 5 of 10 generals he knew with comparable experience for all around duty."[29] People close to Patton reported that he had aged noticeably.[30] Ike selected Jake Devers to head the Army Ground Forces, McNair's old position as chief Army trainer. Disappointed, Patton wrote, "Another war has ended, and with it my usefulness to the world. It is for me personally a very sad afterthought. Now all that is left to do is to sit around and await the arrival of the undertaker and posthumous immortality."[31]

With his future uncertain, Patton immersed himself in the past. He began a series of interviews with assemblies of commanders down to platoon level in three of his armored divisions, three infantry divisions, and three cavalry groups. "Then," he wrote, "taking an algebraic sum from each type of unit, I will get a solution to the method of warfare."[32] He presciently noted, "Of course, the horrid thought obtrudes itself that, in spite of my efforts—which will probably be filed and forgotten—the tactics of the next war will be written by someone who never fought and who acquired his knowledge by a meticulous study of the regulations [i.e., doctrine] of this and the last World War, none of which were ever put into practice in battle."[33]

Patton recognized that the Army leadership had little understanding of his methods and a diminishing appreciation for his accomplishments. He complained, "In this war we were also unfortunate in that our high command in the main consisted of staff officers who, like Marshall, Eisenhower and [Joseph T.] McNarney, had practically never exercised command. I think it was this lack of experience which induced them to think of, and treat, units such as divisions, corps and armies as animated tables of organization rather than as living entities."[34] In other words, lack of front-line combat command bred a mindset prone to attrition warfare. A lack of future combat would only further institutionalize this tendency. After his visit to Washington, he wrote, "I was particularly depressed with the attitude in the War Department where everyone seems to place emphasis on what they call 'planning' and no emphasis at all on fighting."[35]

Any interest in Patton's methods vanished with the detonation of the atomic bomb on Hiroshima on 6 August 1945. Three days later the second bomb fell on Nagasaki. On 10 August Japan surrendered. Two months earlier Patton had been one of the few people Marshall had told of the atomic bomb. Bradley noticed, "Curiously, Ike, almost alone among senior military men, opposed using the bomb. He believed Japan was already defeated, that dropping the bomb was 'completely unnecessary' and that we should avoid 'shocking world opinion' by dropping such weapons on people who were at that very moment attempting to seek surrender with minimum loss of face."[36] As president, however, Ike would make nuclear war the cornerstone of his defense policy. Patton feared "ill-informed people" would think the bomb made armies obsolete and stated, "It is simply, as I have often written, a new instrument added to the orchestra of death, which is war."[37]

Two days after Hiroshima, Patton debated with McGeorge Bundy, who was then traveling with Secretary of War Henry Stimson. Hearing the heated discussion, Stimson advised Bundy, "Haven't you learned not to take this man seriously?"[38] The jest stung Patton, who shortly afterward again asked for reassignment as either superintendent at West Point or commandant of the Army War College. The War College went to Ike's friend Leonard Gerow and West Point to Maxwell Taylor—either of whom would have made a much better choice as governor of Bavaria.

On 26 August Third Army asked to be allowed to discontinue arresting persons in the lowest category of Nazi party officials.[39] As Farago wrote, "By then the German was no longer the Hun. Patton had begun to regard him as his future ally in a joint crusade against the Bolsheviks."[40] Third Army had removed all those identified by G-2 as Nazis and awaited processing of others. Patton argued that "if he just indiscriminately threw all these people out at one time, a vacuum would be created that would probably result in the death of many children."⁴¹ He believed he needed experienced administrators in hospitals, transportation, and other essential industries if the people were to survive the winter. Ike warned him to remove the Nazis and Patton agreed but showed little interest. He wanted out, but there was no place to go. Frustrated, he wrote to his wife, "I am going to quit the army when I leave here or so I think now. . . . Ike and George [Marshall] and some others of the union know where people are going but they never tell me. I see no job that I could take. But I have been at a dead end before and have gotten out O.K. Something may turn up."⁴² He did not know the walls had ears.

A staffer recalled, "General Patton, to his own detriment, frequently was not tactful."⁴³ On 11 September he was at a victory parade in Berlin next to Soviet marshal Georgii Zhukov watching massive new heavy tanks roll past. Unable to suppress his pride, Zhukov asked Patton how he liked the latest Russian war machine. "I said I did not," recalled Patton, "and we had quite an argument. Apparently I was the first person to ever disagree with him."⁴⁴ Zhukov boasted that his new tanks could fire shells seven miles. "Indeed?" replied America's oldest tanker. "Well, my dear Marshal Zhukov, let me tell you this, if any of my gunners started firing at your people before they had closed to less than seven hundred yards I'd have them court-martialed for cowardice."⁴⁵ Zhukov was stunned into silence.

By this time Patton had received numerous reports on Soviet brutality. Lieutenant General Bishop Gowlina of the Polish army told him how the Russians had beaten an innocent girl nearly to death in front of a captive bishop to compel him to sign a "false certificate" against two priests.⁴⁶ Gowlina described shootings, hangings, and torture in Soviet-occupied Poland, where over two million men had been hauled off to Russia as slave labor. General Wladyslaw Anders of the 2nd Polish Corps told him he was certain that "the Russians had deliberately murdered quite a few thousand Polish officers."⁴⁷ Patton concluded: "In addition to his other amiable characteristics, the Russian has no regard for human life and is an all-out son of a bitch, barbarian, and chronic drunk."⁴⁸

As complaints against Patton boiled, Eisenhower sent Murphy, accompanied by a Dr. Walter Dorn, to investigate his denazification efforts and received two internal reports that indicated Patton was not fully implementing the program.⁴⁹ Murphy distrusted Dorn as a radical academic.⁵⁰ Patton wrote of Dorn, "He is a very slick individual. I think pure German, and very probably a Communist in disguise."[51] On 12 September Ike wrote to remind Patton that there was no compromise on denazification. Patton rationalized, "It is very evident that anybody who was in business, irrespective of his real sentiments, had to say he was a Nazi and pay dues."[52] He could not see how he could keep the government, economy, and social order operating without some of these people.

Four days later Ike had dinner with Patton and, talking until 0300 hours, revealed that he would soon replace Marshall as chief of staff of the Army and that his deputy, General Joseph McNarney, would assume supreme command in Europe. Patton told Ike he preferred not to serve under McNarney "because I thought it unseemly for a man with my combat record to serve under a man who had never heard a gun go off."[53] Asked what job he wanted, Patton suggested that his grade and experience left open only two appropriate positions, president of the Army War College or commanding general of the Army Ground Forces—positions given to Gerow and Devers. The writing was on the wall. Ike had no place for him. Patton wrote, "Therefore, at present writing, it would seem the only thing I can do is go home and retire. However, Eisenhower asked me to remain at least three months after he left so as to get things running quietly. I tentatively agreed to this."[54] All things considered, it was a strange request from Ike.

President Truman forwarded to Eisenhower complaints about Patton. On 20 September, when Stimson resigned as Secretary of War and was replaced by Robert Patterson, Patton saw a powerful ally replaced by a man he offended. That same day the *New York Times* ran a story by Raymond Daniell stating that "Nazis still hold some of the best jobs in commerce and industry" and quoting Patton as asking a subordinate "if he did not think it 'silly' to try to get rid of 'the most intelligent' people in Germany."[55] The article posited that Patton flatly disobeyed Ike.

McNarney called Patton to relay a Russian complaint that he was too slow in disbanding some German units. Patton exploded, "Hell, why do you care what those Russians think? We are going to have to fight them sooner or later. . . . Why not do it now while our Army is intact and the damn Russians can have their hind end kicked back into Russia in three months? We can do it ourselves easily with the help of the German troops we have. . . . In ten days I can have enough incidents happen to have us at war with those sons of bitches and make it look like their fault."[56] Horrified, McNarney warned Patton to shut up, for the Russians might have tapped the line and such comments could trigger a new war. The line *was* tapped—by Ike. His G-5, chief of civil affairs Major General Clarence Adcock, had secretly ordered Signal Corps personnel to tap Patton's phone and even had microphones hidden in his quarters.[57] His men personally delivered transcripts of Patton's conversations directly to Eisenhower.

On 22 September Patton agreed to talk with reporters, including Pierre Huss of the International News Service, Nora Waln of the *Atlantic Monthly*, and Kathleen McLaughlin of the *New York Times*. McLaughlin invited her *Times* colleague Raymond Daniell, who came with his wife and fellow *Times* correspondent Tatiana Long, Carl Levin of the *New York Herald Tribune*, and Edward Morgan of the Chicago *Daily News*.[58] Farago noted, "The reporters knew that Robert Murphy was in Munich with Dr. Walter Dorn, his deputy, to investigate Patton's controversial handling of the Nazi problem."[59] They did not know that Dorn and Adcock had secretly sent a psychiatrist disguised as a supply officer to report on Patton's sanity.[60] One correspondent, Blumenson noted, "later said he overheard the three of them [reporters] plotting at breakfast that morning before the press conference, to needle the General and make him lose his temper."[61]

When Patton began to depart the weekly staff briefing, Daniell, Levin, and Morgan stopped him and quizzed him on denazification. Evidence uncovered by Dorn indicated that Patton's headquarters no longer prevented the Bavarian minister from employing former Nazis.[62] Privately Patton believed, "If we let Germany and the German people be completely disintegrated and starved, they will certainly fall for Communists, and the fall of Germany for Communists will write the epitaph of Democracy in the United States."[63] The reporters did not have a problem with such an outcome. Patton told the reporters that Third Army was enforcing higher command's policies and that no known Nazis were holding government offices. Hap Gay reported that Daniell, Levin, and Morgan tried to put words into Patton's mouth, "making use of only partial truths, construed the answers to their questions to suit their own purposes and . . . tried to bring discredit upon General Patton."[64] Again trying to explain the difficulty in rooting out Nazis, Patton said it was like trying to remove members of the Republican and Democratic parties from a government in the United States.

Former president of the International News Service Frank E. Mason was in Europe as a correspondent and a confidant of Herbert Hoover. Mason believed that correspondents from the *New York Times* and *Herald Tribune* were running "interference for a Red government in Germany" by making certain that "only those Germans who were acceptable to the Russians and to the German Communists were appointed to local government posts in the American zone. To this end, he felt, radical journalists attacked general officers who named anti-Communists German officials."[65] Mason reported, "Victor Bernstein of *PM*, came to Bavaria to eliminate [ardent anti-Communist Catholic Cardinal Michael Ritter von] Faulhaber. He devoted himself to a smear campaign on the cardinal. He tried to assassinate Faulhaber's reputation."[66] Mason noted that Daniell and Levin rapidly worked over Patton with condescending, leading questions. At one point Patton snapped, "You are so smart. You know everything. Why do you ask me?"[67]

Most correspondents reported nothing remarkable about the press conference. Carl McArdle of the *Philadelphia Bulletin* reported that no story emerged.[68] However, on 23 September the *New York Times* noted several former Nazis in high positions in the Bavarian government and again quoted Patton, "The Nazi thing is just like a Democrat-Republican election fight."[69] The story appeared in newspapers across the country. Two days later Bedell Smith called and said Patton caused him more headaches than anyone else he knew. Patton remembered, "He then read me extracts from headlines in the United States covering the remarks I was alleged to have made on Saturday. I told him now that the war was over, I did not propose to be jumped on any more by the press, and if they did not like what I said, I would resign so I could be in a position to talk back. He urged me not to do this and said there were going to be many changes soon and that both he and I might be out of jobs."[70]

Resignation was a particularly strong threat: retirement came with restrictions on behavior but resignation did not—something Eisenhower well knew. Discussing his prospects for replacing Marshall, Butcher wrote, "Ike thought he might be of greater use to his country if he could resign, not merely retire, from the Army and write and speak in support of proper military preparedness of the United States. He wants to be in a position to speak freely without even the trace of restriction that might be present if he were simply a retired rather than resigned officer."[71] Smith relayed an order from Ike instructing Patton to hold another press conference.[72] On 24 September Patton apologized to reporters for having nothing exciting to say and regretted the "startling headlines" that had appeared back home. As ordered, he read verbatim portions of Ike's earlier letter on denazification. "My point," he told the reporters, "is that some of these things alleged to have been said by me might possibly reflect on my commanding officer, General Eisenhower. That would be very unjust."[73] Still, when asked to repeat his original inflammatory statement, he did. That night Eisenhower sent a telegram saying Patton stood accused by the press of varying from the denazification program and summoned him to a meeting. Patton wrote to his wife, "If Ike etc. don't like what I do, they can relieve me. Then I will resign, not retire, and can tell the world a few truths which will be worth having."[74] He told confidants, "It was too damn bad I wasn't killed before the fighting stopped."[75]

On 25 September Eisenhower issued Military Law No. 8 banning the use of ex-Nazis from anything but "ordinary labor."[76] Smith briefed a gaggle of reporters that included Daniell, Morgan, and Levin. Asked directly whether Patton was "temperamentally and emotionally" capable of carrying out Ike's denazification program, Smith told the reporters that he too was worried about "ultraconservative" Germans placed in power and assured them that Patton was a good soldier who would carry out his orders. The reporters' use of rumors, innuendos, and misquotations caused Smith to question the veracity of their information. One reporter told Smith that Patton had expressed "views in direct contradiction to everything he was asked to carry out."[77] Smith blurted, "His mouth does not always carry out the functions of his brain."[78] Saying Ike had summoned Patton to "give an account of his stewardship," Smith asked the reporters to "slip" him any information they had on Patton's recalcitrance.

Daniell, Morgan, and Levin questioned Smith on the lack of official support for the Bavarian People's Party and other "social democratic and left wing parties."[79] Smith, a Catholic, became uneasy with their criticism of Cardinal Faulhaber and his efforts to prevent Communists from making gains in Bavarian politics. The reporters described Patton and Faulhaber as obstacles to promoting certain palatable persons to important positions in the German government. To this end they insinuated that Patton was not loyal to Eisenhower. Smith asked them to wait a week until after Ike met with Patton before they drew conclusions. They would not. The next day a Morgan article appeared in newspapers across America such as the *Des Moines Tribune* saying Patton had been "called on the carpet" for saying "he saw no need for a sweeping de-Nazification program in Germany."[80] Patton never made such a statement. Morgan and others repeated invented stories that Patton denounced Ike's policies, or refused to carry them out, and that there were universal calls for his relief. The current of events contributed to the impression among people who never understood Patton's methods that he was simply a loose cannon, disloyal, and irrational.

On 29 September Patton drove to see Eisenhower, worrying, "It may well be that the Philistines have at least got me."[81] With press clogging the corridor outside his office, Ike berated Patton for his failure to shut up, but Patton seemed unfazed. Eisenhower reminded him that complete denazification was the order of the day, no matter the repercussions on Germany. He said that world public opinion demanded it. Ike had Adcock present a list of faults found in Patton's administration. Adcock brought in Dr. Dorn, whom Ike had never seen before and did not know. D'Este noted, "Dorn skillfully and surgically destroyed Patton by painting Minister President Schaeffer, an ultraconservative, longtime Catholic politician, as an intriguer whose administration was rife with former Nazis."[82] Patton noted that he stood accused of allowing a total of 16 former Nazis—none in the "mandatory arrest category"—to remain in the regional secretariat while Third Army had to date processed 251,074 suspects and removed 49,882 former Nazis from various positions and jobs.[83] On Adcock's and Dorn's recommendations, however, Patton agreed to remove Schaeffer. Dr. Dorn specifically recommended Social Democrat Dr. Wilhelm Hoegner to replace the anti-communist Schaeffer.[84] Informed that he was putting a minority party in office, Ike said he did not care. (Hoegner would lose his reelection bid in December 1946. Schaeffer, banned from politics by the U.S. Army for two years, would serve as German minister of finance and minister of justice in the Bundestag from 1948 until his retirement in 1961.)

In a sense, the things that made Patton's way so effective in war caused him problems in peace. Regarding his suspicions of Ike's policies, Patton reported "that while I would have never expressed these views to my Staff, they had absorbed them from me in the same way they had absorbed my battle system."[85] As the two-hour meeting wound down, Eisenhower wished aloud that he had another command to give Patton so that he could remove him as the military governor of Bavaria. It then occurred to him that he could transfer Patton to Gerow's old Fifteenth Army, now devoid of troops but still an active headquarters. Patton remarked, "I told him in my opinion I should be simply relieved, but he said he did not intend to do that and had had no pressure from the States to that effect."[86] Ike wanted Patton to remain in Europe. Their business complete, Ike had a train waiting to take Patton back to Bavaria.

Patton left bitter and tired. He had agreed to the transfer, he explained, "because I was reluctant, in fact, unwilling, to be a party to the destruction of Germany under the pretense of de-Nazification. Further, that the utterly un-American and almost Gestapo methods of de-Nazification were so abhorrent to my Anglo-Saxon mind as to be practically indigestible. Further, that I believe Germany should not be destroyed but rather rebuilt as a buffer against the real danger, which is Bolshevism from Russia."[87] Feverishly sensing a vile plot, Patton wrote to his wife, "The noise against me is only the means by which the Jews and Communists are attempting and with good success to implement a further dismemberment of Germany."[88] To his imagination, both groups had natural reasons for revenge against the Germans.

Reporters waiting in the hall pressed Ike, but he refused to take the bait. When asked for a statement Ike replied, "I have conferences with my Army Commanders whenever I feel like it—period."[89] He added, "General Patton and myself remain the best of friends."[90] Ike then dealt with Dr. Dorn by ordering Adcock to "get rid of that goddamn professor."[91] Patton returned to Bavaria while newspapers stateside churned out stories of his being in hot water for failing to support Ike. Finally, at the end of the month Eisenhower quietly directed Lucian Truscott to replace Patton as the head of Third Army and as military governor of Bavaria. The story leaked quickly in Berlin, forcing Eisenhower to make a public announcement (Patton first suspected Smith before concluding that Ike leaked the news for his political benefit).[92]

The press in America roiled in pro and con commentary. For every editorial glad to see Patton go, there was another like that in the *Cincinnati Times-Star*: "The drastic penalty inflicted upon General Patton . . . will shock most Americans, though it will probably delight those leftist commentators who have lately been hounding the great tank commander with all the venom of a Goebbels. . . . Without blaming Eisenhower, it must be said that the drastic punishment of Patton, in view of the occupation mess in Germany, has the effect of making the man a scapegoat."[93] Patton told Murphy, "Ike wants to be President so much you can taste it."[94] In his diary he wrote, "Everyone seems to be more interested in the effects which his actions will have on his political future than in carrying out the motto of the United States military academy, 'Duty, Honor, Country.'"[95]

On 7 October a teary George Patton handed over Third Army to Truscott, telling his assembled men, "All good things must come to an end. The best thing that has ever come to me thus far is the honor and privilege of having commanded the Third Army."[96] He even lost his faithful orderly and driver, Sergeant William George Meeks, who rotated home. Weyland wrote to Patton, "I feel that the Third Army has died. To me, the Third Army meant Patton."[97] The next day Patton told a United Press writer off the record, "I felt that perhaps I had not had quite a square deal because I believe it will be proven that Bavaria is more de-Nazified and more reorganized than any section of Germany."[98] A few days later, the secretary of war announced his satisfaction that denazification was nearly complete in the American zone. Dorn later wrote: "The impact of the Patton affair upon the administration of the U.S. zone can scarcely be exaggerated. . . . The Russians dealt more quickly and ruthlessly with the top echelon Nazis, but the scale of the purges was much smaller than the American."[99]

Within twenty-four hours Patton reported to Fifteenth Army headquarters to assume command of the sections turning battle histories into volumes on "the strategy and tactics of the war to see how the former conformed to unit plans and how tactics had changed."[100] Patton wrote his wife, "We are writing a lot of stuff which no one will ever read."[101] Ike's son John, a member of Patton's new headquarters, found "Old Blood and Guts" had a surprisingly "generous nature."[102] The work gave him hope for influencing future doctrine. "I am convinced," wrote Patton, "we should avoid the error we made at the end of the last war of taking this war as an approved solution for future unpleasantnesses. We must use this account simply as a datum plane from which to annually build a new set of jigs and dies."[103]

Ike visited on 13 October and during the evening encouraged Patton to run for Congress—"I presume in the belief that I might help him."[104]

Others also sent feelers to Patton about political possibilities, but he always declined. Patton told Gay, "I have given this a great deal of thought. I am going to resign from the Army. Quit outright, not retire. That's the only way I can be free to live my own way of life . . . to say what I want to."[105] He later wrote, "Ike is bitten by the presidential bug and is also yellow. . . . I will resign when I have finished this job which will be not later than December 26. I hate to do it but I have been gagged all my life, and whether they are appreciated or not, America needs some honest men who dare to say what they think, not what they think people want them to think."[106]

Suddenly, Patton was widely praised in editorials across the nation. The *New York Times*, for example, editorialized, "He was obviously in a part which he was unfitted by temperament, training, and experience to fill. It was a mistake to suppose a free-swinging fighter could acquire overnight the capacities of a wise administrator. His removal by General Eisenhower was an acknowledgement of that mistake. . . . He reaped no laurels from the peace, but those he won in war will remain green for a long time."[107] He went to Paris to be decorated and praised by Charles de Gaulle. He spent the better part of a week touring France and receiving thanks from the people he greatly admired. The king of Belgium decorated him as a grand officer of the Order of Leopold. Admirers sent flattering press clippings. He toured Denmark and Sweden and received honorary citizenship of many of the cities he had liberated. His sixtieth birthday came and went quietly. He wrote, "It is rather sad to me to think that my last opportunity to earn my pay has passed. At least, I have done my best as God gave me the chance."[108]

Eisenhower left and handed over temporary command to Patton, the senior officer in theater, who endeavored to make no changes. He avoided Bedell Smith but finally got distinguished service medals for his former staff. He wrote, "I think it is amusing that no one trys [*sic*] to get any for me. I got nothing for Tunisia, nothing for Sicily and nothing for the Bulge. Brad and Courtney [Hodges] were both decorated for their failures in that operation."[109] Patton seemed to mellow. A letter to a confidant indicated that Patton's ire had passed and he likely would not speak out against Ike. On 3 December, after attending ceremonies for McNarney's assumption of theater command, Patton wrote, "The whole luncheon party reminded me of a meeting of the Rotary Club in Hawaii where everyone slaps everyone else's back while looking for an appropriate place to thrust the knife."[110]

He pointedly noted, "I had a good deal of fun at luncheon, quoting from recent articles on the Military Government of Germany, which I had the forethought to take with me, and which removed the appetite from [new U.S. ambassador to Germany] Bob Murphy and the new CG [commanding general] of the ETO [McNarney]."[111]

Patton prepared a long holiday vacation at home, planning to depart Europe aboard the battleship *New York* out of South Hampton on 14 December. He sent word to his wife, "I have a month's leave but don't intend to go back to Europe. If I get a really good job I will stay in [the Army], otherwise I will retire."[112] The day before he was to leave for home, however, he was on a pheasant hunt with Hap Gay when his Cadillac staff car was hit by a 2½-ton Army supply truck at thirty miles per hour. Patton alone suffered injuries: a gash three inches above his eyebrow and a broken neck.

Taken by ambulance to the 130th Station Hospital in Heidelberg, Patton learned that he was paralyzed from the neck down. Despite the work of British brigadier Hugh Cairns, professor of neurosurgery at the Oxford University School of Medicine, and U.S. Army expert neurosurgeon Colonel R. Glen Spurling, there would be no recovery. Beatrice Patton flew in from the States to hear her husband say, "I am afraid, Bea, this may be the last time we see each other."[113] Ike did not visit his old friend but sent heartfelt concerns and promised Patton would still have a job in the Army.

As the days passed Patton suffered bouts of confusion, tried hard to clear his lungs, and grew tired. Although cheerful in the presence of visitors, he confessed to the nurses his depression. Word came that the White House ordered Patton home, even though doctors advised against such a move.[114] Scheduled to fly back to America on 30 December, doctors encased Patton in a plaster body cast. Ten days short of departure, he took a turn for the worse with a probable embolism in his lung. For two days his wife read to him at his bedside. Throughout 21 December, the first day of winter, he was weak and could hardly breathe. He feared death was near. In the morning he whispered to Bea, "It's too dark . . . I mean, too late."[115] At 1730 hours he was sleeping when Beatrice slipped out to eat dinner with Dr. Spurling. Their meal was interrupted with a summons to Patton's room. When they got there, he was dead.

Stating that "I know George would want to lie beside the men of his Army who have fallen," Beatrice had her husband buried in the American military cemetery at Hamm, Luxembourg—the final resting place of so many of the Third Army soldiers from the Ardennes campaign.[116] Representatives from all the major commands plus delegations from Britain, France, Luxembourg, Belgium, Sweden, and the Soviet Union attended his funeral service in Heidelberg on 23 December. Eisenhower, Bradley, and Montgomery could not find time to attend. Patton's casket moved by train to the cemetery in Luxembourg to rest among his men, his grave marked by the standard government-issued plain white cross but embossed in gold with his name, rank, serial number, and four stars. The *New York Times* wrote, "History has reached out and embraced General George Patton. His place is secure. He will be ranked in the forefront of America's great military leaders. . . . Hot in battle and ruthless, too, he was icy in his inflexibility of purpose. He was no mere hell-for-leather tank commander but a profound and thoughtful military student."[117] Forces were already moving to define Patton in history.

Some felt relief. Bradley said, "It may be a harsh thing to say, but I believe it was better for George Patton and his professional reputation that he died when he did. The war was won; there were no more wars left for him to fight. He was not a good peacetime soldier; he would not have found a happy place in the postwar Army. He would have gone into retirement hungering for the old limelight, beyond a doubt indiscreetly sounding off on any subject any time, any place. In time he probably would have become a boring parody of himself—a decrepit, bitter, pitiful figure, unwittingly debasing the legend."[118] Of course, Patton would never have the opportunity to prove him wrong.

If the new Army leadership posted a sign, it might have read "fighters need not apply." Germany and Japan lay in ruins, the Soviet Union was an ally, and the United States had a monopoly on the atomic bomb. Another war seemed unthinkable. Americans were tired of war. With the Army's remaining ten divisions on occupation duty, old warriors stepped aside for a new generation of officers marked by diplomatic and political skills. For his deputy Ike selected his old friend Thomas Handy, who had spent the war in Washington. Handy would keep the job until Collins was ready. Ike's replacement in Europe, McNarney, had also spent most of the war in Washington. Like himself, Ike described McNarney as an administrative type "possessed of an analytical mind and a certain ruthlessness in execution which was absolutely necessary to uproot entrenched bureaucracy and streamline and simplify procedures."[119] In 1947 Lucius D. Clay replaced McNarney. Bradley described Clay as "an engineer in peacetime, during the war he had been Marshall's chief of procurement, an awesome job with horrendous political ramifications, which he carried out brilliantly. . . . He had a keen political antenna and was an ideal choice for this international hot spot."[120] These men became the role models and mentors for future generations of officers. Pattons were out; Ikes were in.

Six days before Patton's fatal accident, Eisenhower replaced Marshall as chief of staff. First U.S. Army commander Courtney Hodges and Ninth U.S. Army commander Alan Simpson had already retired for medical reasons. Seventh U.S. Army commander Alexander Patch died of pneumonia in November. The 6th Army Group commander, Jake Devers, whom Ike did not like, received command of the Army Ground Forces, an organization soon to be extinct. The Fifteenth Army commander, Leonard Gerow, whom Ike did like, received command of the Command and General Staff College. Ike left Mark Clark in command of a now-skeletal 15th Army Group in Italy. The ever-loyal Bedell Smith begged Ike for another position somewhere in the Army, even if it meant a reduction in rank, but Ike arranged for his appointment as ambassador to Moscow. Smith served there for three years before becoming director of the Central Intelligence Agency and later assistant secretary of state in the Eisenhower administration.[121]

Though MacArthur remained untouchable in his fiefdom in Japan, Bradley observed, "Ike turned to the 'younger' officers—many of them corps or division commanders from the ETO—to help him run the postwar Army."[122] Rumors spread that Ike had drafted a "rocket list," a roster of promising young officers he would groom for leadership assignments.[123] These were steady men, mostly infantry, whom Ike knew, liked, and trusted. Maxwell Taylor assumed duties as superintendent of West Point. Matthew Ridgway got his third star and command of the Mediterranean theater in November 1945 before moving to the new United Nations (UN) Military Staff Committee in January. Bradley's favorite, J. Lawton Collins, became director of information for the War Department, fighting the Army's legislative battles on Capitol Hill, while he was groomed for better things.

"Patton's boys" did not fare so well. Hobart Gay would spend the better part of the next six years commanding various skeletal divisions without promotion. Troy Middleton retired. Manton Eddy went stateside to staff jobs until 1948 when he became commandant of the Command and General Staff College before moving on to command Seventh Army in the occupation of Germany. Walton Walker received command of the 8th Service Command, a logistics and services organization based in Dallas, Texas. Wade Haislip became president of the Secretary's War Personnel Board. Hard-charging Ernest Harmon remained on constabulary duties until named deputy commander of Army Ground Forces in 1947 before retiring the next year. The brilliant but mercurial John Wood commanded the Fort Knox Armor Replacement Training Center until his quick retirement in 1946.

Only at Fort Knox did Patton's influence take root. Hugh Gaffey assumed command there (until being killed in a plane crash in June 1946) and rescued former 4th Armored Division colonel Creighton Abrams from a desk in the Pentagon to make him the Armor School deputy director of tactics from 1946 to 1948. Patton had said, "I am supposed to be the best tank commander in the Army, but I have one peer—Abe Abrams."[124] In his assignment at Fort Knox Abrams sowed seeds that helped institutionalize many of Patton's—and Wood's—tactical methods. Still, Abrams' record should have earned him greater assignments. As Lewis Sorley noted, "He was subsequently sent to Fort Leavenworth for schooling at the Command and General Staff College, although many others were given constructive credit for that level of education based on their wartime experience. And then he was sent to command another tank battalion, a job he had already performed with enormous distinction over a matter of years."[125]

Official diminution of appreciation for fighters mirrored other changes of taste in the Army. In March 1946 the secretary of war appointed a board under Jimmy Doolittle to investigate officer-enlisted relations. Many interpreted the board's recommendations as a mandate to lower standards of professionalism.[126] Rules governing behavior fell, the saber and Sam Browne belt were no longer to be worn, and officers were to "pay-as-you-go" in commissaries and post exchanges where once their word was good enough. It was common to find officers in Germany and Japan going unpunished for participating in the black market, trading rations for the valuables of destitute and desperate local citizens. On seeing one officer's ill-gotten heirloom silverware, Abrams called the officer a "goddamn crook" and stormed out of his residence. As Dupuy recalled, "The fine edge of the officer's honor was blunted."[127] Patton's high standards in dress and discipline had no place in the postwar Army.

Congress's push for "unification" of the Department of War and the Department of the Navy increased demand for tactful generals skilled in political infighting.[128] The Army now had to fight the other services for budgets, weapons, and missions while it shrank from 10.4 million to 1.5 million soldiers in the twelve months from late 1946 to late 1947.[129] The Army budget withered to about $10 billion (compared to the new budget for veterans' benefits of $8 billion). Overall military spending fell as a percentage of the national budget from nearly 38 percent in 1944 to 3.5 percent in 1948.[130] Bradley decried the "helter-skelter demobilization" that by 1948 left the Army with only 560,000 men, half dedicated to noncombat occupation duties.[131] Years later Marshall recalled, "I thought the disintegration of '46 and '47 was the most amazing thing. I was out of the country most of the time in China, and I didn't realize how complete it was until I went over as Secretary of Defense [1950] and I found literally nothing."[132] Lieutenant General Phillip B. Davidson recalled, "We couldn't even keep track of who we had and where they were; we had to hold musters for the first time since the Revolutionary War."[133] As chief of staff, Bradley lamented Truman's orders to contain the Russians while cutting the Army. Only years later would he say, "From this distance, I must say that this decision was a mistake, perhaps the greatest of Truman's presidency. My support of his decision—my belief that significantly higher defense spending would probably wreck the economy—was likewise a mistake, perhaps the greatest mistake I made in my postwar years in Washington."[134]

The drastic cuts in manpower and budgets left hollow divisions, with many regiments and battalions missing at least one-third of their strength. Weigley noted, "These reductions were serious handicaps in a tactical system that assumed three-battalion regiments; in combat, a regimental commander would have to fight with a single battalion if he desired a reserve, or put both battalions into line and fight without a reserve. Furthermore, the divisions generally lacked their organic armor."[135] The instruments of Patton's way of war were no more.

By choice and circumstance, the Army returned to a doctrine that emphasized the primacy of tactical infantry-artillery attrition battles over decisive operational maneuver. Uncertainty reigned as to the role of tanks. A Command and General Staff College history noted, "In the years between World War II and Korea, the Army carefully considered its tactical doctrine, but its methods remained essentially those of World War II."[136] The General Board of the European Theater announced, "The uniformly better performance of infantry, in any operation, when closely supported by tanks is probably the biggest single tactical lesson of the European campaign."[137] To that end, tanks were again subordinated to the infantry: the War Department adopted a recommendation by the board to place armor in the triangular infantry division. This decision spurred the retrenchment from Patton's methods in the budget-restricted postwar atmosphere. As Jonathan House wrote, "Even if the tank was the best anti-tank weapon, using it to defeat enemy armor might not be the best employment of available tanks, which found themselves tied to their own infantry instead of attacking and exploiting enemy vulnerabilities."[138]

Patton's doctrine of combined arms columns, spearheaded by tanks and under tactical air support, faded away. A U.S. Army history noted, "There was no intention to form large armored formations, and, if an armored division was employed, it would be within an infantry-heavy corps in which there was one armored division and two or three infantry divisions. The tank had demonstrated its potential in World War II, but infantry remained the 'queen of battle.'"[139] Scant resources made large-scale maneuvers impossible and air support for training nonexistent—not that the Army envisioned any use of armored spearheads. Phillip L. Bolté wrote, "The Army's contribution to the strategic reserve was little over two divisions—a forty-thousand-man force that included one armored combat command. The Armored Force component in Europe was the U.S. Constabulary, consisting of three brigades. . . . The four infantry divisions on occupation duty in Japan each had only one company of light tanks. It was at the time the postwar low point of the Army's Armored Force."[140]

Faith in America's monopoly of atomic weapons mitigated any worries Truman and his advisers had about the decline of the Army. The certainty that the Navy and Air Force could destroy large formations of hostile soldiers guided Army Chief of Staff Bradley's plan "Halfmoon," which prescribed how the Army would fight the next war. Although the Command and General Staff College would later claim, "The third and final phase would be a large-scale ground assault to defeat the enemy," the plan was more nuanced.[141] Bradley explained, "If Russia launched all-out war, its huge Army overrunning Western Europe (as we assumed), we would respond by dropping atomic bombs on the Soviet homeland. . . . The Army's role in Halfmoon was to support the strategic air offensive. . . . Much later, following a World War II–type mobilization, the Army would occupy Western Europe and Russia in order to help restore law and order and stable governments."[142] There was no actual assault, only occupation of an atomic wasteland. The Army tailored doctrine to this occupation mission.

When a Soviet-supported insurgency threatened Greece in 1947, the State Department reported, "Unless urgent and immediate support is given to Greece, it seems probable that the Greek Government will be overthrown and a totalitarian regime of the extreme left will come into power."[143] Bradley wrote, "Our Army was so weak and already spread so thin worldwide that even if the [Joint Chiefs of Staff] deemed it strategically advisable to send appreciable numbers of ground troops to Greece we could not have done so."[144] Instead, the United States sent a military advisory group under Lieutenant General James Van Fleet that soon stabilized Greece. This success suggested that President Truman's strategy to "contain" the Soviet Communists would not require great investment in the Army. Truman later sent one thousand troops under General David Barr to Chiang Kai-shek in his fight against Mao Tse-tung but, as Bradley recalled, "In contrast to Van Fleet's role in Greece, the Barr advisory group was specifically instructed to stay away from the battlefields, lest the Chinese blame us when the inevitable defeat came."[145]

The U.S. Army's worst-case expectations involved a defensive war against the Soviets in Germany.[146] When in June 1948 the Soviets closed down all approaches to Berlin despite agreements to the contrary, General Clay immediately asked Bradley for permission to "shoot our way into Berlin." Bradley recalled, "Had I enough hair on my head to react, this cable would probably have stood it on end. . . . We were far from ready to fight a general war with Russia then, and owing to the frank and public discourses we were compelled to make on the Hill [Congress] in defense of our military budgets, the Russians knew precisely how weak we were."[147] Patton's belligerent alarm about the Russians must have haunted Bradley. "Indeed," wrote D'Este, "the folly of failing to heed the warnings of Patton, Churchill and others in the aftermath of the war was starkly demonstrated barely three years later during the Berlin blockade of 1948, which resulted in the creation of NATO the following year to counter the growing Russian threat in Europe."[148] Only a heroic ad hoc air bridge kept Berlin supplied until the Russians backed down.

A serious debate began regarding ground armies. It was assumed, as Halfmoon attested, that the maneuver of large forces toward strategic objectives no longer applied. Any new "blitzkrieg" would simply be a target for atomic weapons. Bradley told Congress in 1949, "I am wondering whether we shall ever have another large-scale amphibious operation. Frankly, the atomic bomb, properly delivered, almost precludes such a possibility."[149] Bradley was off the mark again; within a year, MacArthur would lead the invasion at Inchon.

The Army's inadequacies were dramatically brought to light on 25 June 1950, when communist North Korea invaded South Korea. Despite some Central Intelligence Agency warnings, the attack caught the United States and its allies by surprise. South Korea's forces collapsed. Truman appointed MacArthur as commander in chief Far East and ordered him to lead American troops into the battle. However, MacArthur possessed only four undermanned, undertrained, and underequipped divisions in Japan. The Army scraped together Task Force Smith—one battalion of two infantry companies and supporting artillery under the command of Lieutenant Colonel Charles B. Smith—but the North Korean tanks quickly surrounded and wiped out the ineffective team. Follow-on units fared little better. An Infantry School study in 1954 observed, "Withdrawals were mob movements rather than military movements, and men were cut to pieces."[150] New Army chief of staff General Joe Collins went to Tokyo and told MacArthur, "General, you are going to have to win the war out here with the troops available to you in Japan and Korea." MacArthur replied, "Joe, you are going to have to change your mind."[151]

On 25 July the Joint Chiefs of Staff started sending troops from the United States, including the 1st Marine Division, as the North Koreans pushed southward virtually unimpeded. Just a few days into the war, while standing on a hill near Seoul watching the invaders, MacArthur formulated plans for holding the North Koreans by the nose with a strong defensive perimeter around the southern port of Pusan and then kicking them in the ass far behind the front with an amphibious assault at Inchon. The Joint Chiefs of Staff argued that such a maneuver was too risky, but MacArthur brushed aside their worries. Appropriately enough, the Pusan perimeter was given to Patton's reliable "old fighter," Lieutenant General Walton Walker, in command of the newly formed Eighth U.S. Army. The landing at Inchon on 15 September caught the North Koreans completely by surprise. As they tried to reposition, Walker charged out of his perimeter and sprinted north. The shocked North Koreans, unable to react effectively, collapsed. In ten days Seoul was recaptured. In less than two months MacArthur swept to the Chinese border. As Ernest and Trevor Dupuy wrote, "The Inchon landing was one of the great strategic strokes of history, in conception, execution, and results. MacArthur's genius had transformed into a stunning victory a desperate defense seemingly doomed to disaster."[152]

Unfortunately, MacArthur's success was soon eclipsed by the Chinese intervention. Hundreds of thousands of Chinese troops crossed the Yalu River in the bitter winter weather and shocked the overextended Allied forces. MacArthur—unlike Patton—failed to look beyond his area of operations and did not anticipate a potential Chinese intervention. The contrast between MacArthur in North Korea and Patton before the Bulge could not be more dramatic. To be fair, Truman had forbidden MacArthur to fly air reconnaissance over China or to bomb the bridges over the Yalu. Only skillful retrograde operations aided by air and naval power prevented complete defeat. Tragically, Walker, like Patton, died in a car crash. Lieutenant General Matthew Ridgway assumed command of Eighth Army.

As the Chinese and North Koreans drove south, Ridgway turned to traditional firepower-based attrition warfare. In March he launched Operation Ripper, a four-week battle calculated principally to impose casualties through massed firepower and to relieve Seoul.[153] Korea was now a war reminiscent of Grant in the Wilderness or Bradley at Hürtgen Forest, predicated on the infantry-artillery team. To MacArthur, the most decorated American officer of World War I, this was unacceptable.[154] His belligerent insistence on maneuver warfare contributed to his relief by President Truman on 11 April 1951. Ridgway replaced MacArthur; Van Fleet, the former leader of the Greek advisory mission, assumed command of Eighth Army.

As an Army history noted, in Korea "the Army experienced difficulties with its doctrine. The combination of terrain, weather and enemy tactics tended to hamper employment of much of the tactical doctrine and equipment of the Army which were oriented toward another world war that would be fought primarily in Western Europe."[155] Planners believed that the mountains made decisive maneuver impossible, but the same had been said in Sicily, where Patton had proved otherwise. In Korea, however, there were few commanders who understood maneuver warfare. No one anticipated, recognized, or exploited opportunities for decisive movement. As a result, Army operations degraded into a positional war of attrition.

MacArthur and Patton were uniquely alike in their strategic use of ground forces and their eccentric masks of command; it is little wonder that they both suffered repression and removal. Their brilliance in generalship seemed to include the price of unwanted individualism. As Bradley complained, "Like Patton and Monty, MacArthur was a megalomaniac."[156] Eisenhower, a former longtime MacArthur aide, once said, "I wouldn't trade Marshall for fifty MacArthurs. My God! That would be a lousy deal."[157] The new Army would not tolerate such leaders again.

The culture of attrition returned with Ridgway. "His tactical system," wrote Weigley, "called for the maximum exploitation of firepower, including air and artillery, to soften up the enemy in methodical attacks, in place of the swift but vulnerable movements of mechanized columns that had approached the Yalu. In the idiom of his troops, he introduced the tactics of the meat grinder, to chew up Chinese manpower at a rate even the Chinese could not afford."[158] Traditional doctrine now dominated the infantry school and guided the other combat arms. It was a future drawn from the past.

Ridgway ordered his commanders to "direct the efforts of your forces toward inflicting maximum personnel casualties and material losses on hostile forces," but he also tasked them to "maintain the offensive spirit . . . and retain the initiative, through maximum maneuver of firepower."[159] He used frontal pressure to fix the enemy while he swung other forces against the enemy's flanks—but unlike Patton's, Ridgway's "hammer and anvil" only applied within the tactical battlefield.[160] As before World War II, the Army encouraged initiative only at lower levels of command. Maneuver supported firepower. Of course, Ridgway had little need for operational maneuver, because in Korea there was no place to go. He was forbidden to drive deep and so could only bash the enemy on the nose. The dictates of politics and the threat of nuclear arms eliminated all thoughts of far-ranging maneuver and produced a war of limited objectives but unlimited carnage, much as the debut of airpower, massed armies, and machine guns had ended thoughts of strategic maneuver in World War I. Yet as Patton had warned, morale is linked to movement. In Korea, soldiers began to chant, "I'll fight for my country, but I'll be damned if I can see why I'm fighting to save this hell hole."[161] With its invisible link to discipline, the degradation of morale would have far-reaching consequences for the Army.

The final years in Korea recalled World War I's trenches, but Jonathan House noted differences: "Instead of a defense-in-depth along relatively narrow frontages, U.N. units in Korea formed a very thin line of strongpoints on high ground. Centralized fire control and artillery proximity fuses gave the U.N. defenders unprecedented firepower in the defense, while the attacking communists often had only limited fire support."[162] Defensive terrain, modern communications, and airpower magnified the impact of attritional doctrine of massed fires. A Command and General Staff College study noted, "Throughout the latter phases of the war, tactical air continued to play a key role even though some argued that aircraft were often used when artillery would have been sufficient."[163] This was not surprising considering that the Far East Air Force had been placed under General Otto P. Weyland, Patton's air commander.

The ground commanders in Korea resisted Weyland's advice on effective air-ground coordination. Wood wrote to Liddell Hart, "O. P. Weyland, the Far East Air Force commander, with whom I developed a murderous combination of air-armored action in France, says all that hard-bought experience has been lost."[164] The Air Force was not interested in tactical air support either and preferred interdiction missions; it put in place a unwieldy process for close tactical air support requests.[165] New Eighth Army commander Maxwell Taylor argued, "An outstanding impression from the operations in Korea had been the ineffectiveness or incapability of many of our modern weapons to the requirement of the Korean type of limited war. I refer particularly to the weapons of the Air Force, the Navy and the Armor, to which certain other Army weapons and equipment may be added."[166]

Tanks, few in number at first, gradually increased in Korea but operated strictly in support of tactical infantry operations.[167] Doughty noted a "subtle but important" change in doctrine: "The Army had become accustomed to massive amounts of firepower which came at the expense of mobility.

The Army had also perfected its techniques of employing firepower and the defense to inflict huge losses on an attacker. Thus, the Army focused upon attrition at the expense of maneuver and its offensive spirit."[168] Patton's achievement was inverted: in Korea, campaign became battle.

Although Patton's way of war fell into the shadows, his legacy still ate at Eisenhower. Throughout the presidential campaign of 1952, rumors spread of newspapers about to print criticism of Ike from Patton's diary. Despite Mrs. Patton's refusal of offers to publish the diary, sections secretly copied by Sergeant Joe Rosevich made their way onto the pages of the *New York Times*. Once Patton's acerbic comments on Eisenhower and Bradley became public, neither man would forget or forgive. Passing Patton's statue during a reunion at West Point, someone remarked to Ike, "General Patton was quite a legend." He loudly responded, "Yes, mostly a legend!"[169]

As president, Eisenhower installed a "New Look" national defense policy. Taylor called it "little more than the old air power dogma set forth in Madison Avenue trappings" and explained, "Its implementation assumed the preponderant use of air power and avoidance of the bloody, exhausting battle on the ground. . . . Army forces would be kept small lest we be tempted to use them to fight another Korea by conventional means."[170] "Determined to avoid spending the country into defeat," Edgar F. Raines Jr. and Major David R. Campbell explained, "Eisenhower accepted massive retaliation as the optimal national strategy for the United States. For the president, like the Army, the lesson of Korea was 'never again,' but in his case it was never again fight a limited war where the enemy had the advantage in manpower."[171] Massive firepower—even nuclear firepower—elevated attrition strategy to new heights.

Efforts to improve the million-man Army in Korea included the expansion of the Armored Force from one combat command to four armored divisions by 1956.[172] This did not mean an embrace of Patton's doctrine. To the contrary, the Army turned further toward defensive, positional warfare emphasizing firepower over maneuver. Firepower superiority rested on traditional infantry-artillery teamwork augmented by tactical airpower.[173] Instead of using fire to achieve maneuver, the Army firmly returned to using maneuver to enable fires. Armor had no operational or strategic role. Where once Patton had used infantry to open holes for decisive combined arms drives, now the tanks only supported infantry.[174]

When the Soviets detonated an atomic bomb in 1949, the United States lost its nuclear monopoly. In 1954 General Taylor, Lieutenant General Bruce C. Clarke, and Major General James Gavin led a series of studies and tests that called for changes in organization and doctrine to better enable the Army to defend against a Soviet tactical nuclear attack. Their efforts led to the "Pentomic Division," which changed the basic three-regiment "triangular" division to a five-battlegroup "penta" configuration designed to be less vulnerable to a single nuclear bomb.[175] As Doughty explained, "Combat units must be dispersed and must be organized in 'checkerboard' fashion with considerable gaps between units. . . . An atomic strike might damage a battle position or cause some disruption, but it would not result in a complete 'fracturing' of the entire position."[176] It was akin to the pillbox defenses Ridgway employed in Korea. If a Soviet spearhead entered one "checker-board square," the surrounding battle groups were to close on it.

In the pentomic design, armor divisions formed a mobile reserve to counterattack Soviet spearheads. This concept sprung from recently published Army studies on German and Soviet combat methods on the Eastern Front during World War II.[177] However, the redesign tossed aside the flexibility and maneuverability of the triangular divisions. It caused greater difficulties in command with more units to control. It also had neither enough transport nor artillery for breakthrough or exploitation. Combined arms columns were forgotten along with offensive warfare. Such concerns were alleviated by the expectation embedded in war plans that the Army was only to defend behind the Rhine while airpower and missiles defeated the Soviets. The effort to increase battlefield firepower and survivability cast aside operational maneuver.

Anyone in the Pentagon thinking of protesting these designs would not find a receptive ear in the Eisenhower administration. Ike's lack of patience with military dissent resulted from more than just his experience with Patton. Just before the Korean War, Truman felt betrayed by the "revolt of the admirals" in which senior Navy officials actively undermined executive decisions favoring the Air Force. Chairman of the Joint Chiefs of Staff Bradley denounced the admirals as "dishonest" and told Congress they were a bunch of "fancy Dans who won't hit the line with all they have on every play, unless they can call the signals."[178] Then there was MacArthur.

Later, when Chief of Staff Ridgway argued against the New Look, Taylor observed, "His courageous opposition, which he felt obliged to maintain against the majority view, eventually brought him into official disfavor and led to his retirement two years later in 1955."[179] Taylor replaced Ridgway after promising the president not to speak out against administration policies. In 1956 there was a "revolt of the colonels'" against the New Look. As Ernest Dupuy wrote, "A small coterie of ill-advised Army staff officers courted publicity with an open challenge to the Air Force doctrine asserting that national security lay mainly in air power."[180] The administration cracked down, moving some missile programs from the Army to the Air Force and placing a greater emphasis on selecting officers who would support the team.

As the Eisenhower administration entered its final year, the commander of the U.S. Continental Army Command, Bruce Clarke—formerly of Patton's Third Army—produced a study, "Modern Mobile Army 1965–1970," that argued for a more flexible force. He called for better firepower and mobility through armored vehicles than those found in the pentomic division.[181] Clarke's ideas were rejected, but, with John F. Kennedy's embrace of Taylor's call for a "flexible response" military, they spurred other studies that led in 1961 to the "Reorganization Objectives Army Division [ROAD] 1965."

ROAD recommended a return to triangular divisions built on three brigades, each with interchangeable or building block battalions. Jonathan House explained, "The unique aspect of the ROAD division was the ability to 'task organize' and tailor structures at any level."[182] These brigades offered the potential to form true combined arms columns. ROAD also increased armored personnel carriers and aviation assets, especially helicopters, in divisions. The design returned flexibility, extended frontages in defense, and erased the cumbersomeness of the pentomic division. Changes in doctrine embraced mobile and area defenses.[183] However, as Doughty wrote, "the doctrine for the employment of tank forces was the least affected by these changes. . . . The formation of mechanized infantry units forced the infantry to adopt many of the practices and thinking of armor and irrevocably linked a significant portion of its resources and intellectual energies to the mechanized battle. Tactical doctrine, nevertheless, stressed continuity rather than change."[184] Infantry-focused doctrine ensured firepower still trumped maneuver.

The new emphasis on linear defenses minimalized counterattacks against enemy penetrations. In the doctrine, "offense was no longer considered the primary means of destroying the effectiveness of the enemy forces," even though the ROAD units were more capable of offensive action.[185] The dominant culture was of strategic defense, attrition through firepower, limited objectives, and restricted initiative—all of which would come to light in Southeast Asia.

President Kennedy sent Taylor to devise a strategy to contain communism in South Vietnam. One historian explained, "Despite the President's call for 'a whole new kind of strategy,' the military recommendations were remarkably reminiscent of the familiar limited-war prescriptions of the 1950s, including General Taylor's own, which had little to do with unconventional war but reflected the frustrations of the conventional war in Korea and proposed how such a war might have been won."[186] Taylor called for tactical airpower and helicopters to shuttle South Vietnamese forces to the battlefields. He called for eight thousand American troops to assist the Vietnamese. When Army chief of staff General George H. Decker warned that "we cannot win a conventional war in Southeast Asia," the administration forced his early retirement.[187]

Following the Gulf of Tonkin incident, President Lyndon Johnson increased U.S. ground forces in Vietnam to 320,000 soldiers and Marines by 1966. They were there not to *win* the war, but to prevent South Vietnam from *losing* it. The geopolitical context dictated a limited strategic defense with attrition by tactical mobile offensive operations to search and destroy the elusive enemy.[188] Colonel Hoang Ngoc Lung of the Army of the Republic of Vietnam observed, "The Americans had designed a purely defensive strategy for Vietnam. It was a strategy that was based on the attrition of the enemy through prolonged defense and made no allowance for decisive offensive action."[189] The Army knew no other way.

The strategy of limited warfare produced desultory operations. In *Armored Combat in Vietnam,* General Donn Starry recalled that the Army staff "concluded that while tanks for the support of dismounted infantry might be required, there was no possibility for independent large-scale combined arms action by armored forces such as those of the World War II armored divisions."[190] They had forgotten Patton's advice: "There is no such thing as 'tank country' in a restrictive sense. Some types of country are better than others, but tanks have and can operate anywhere."[191] Both the North Korean and North Vietnamese armies used tank spearheads in decisive drives, at the beginning of the Korean War and the conclusion of the Vietnam War.

American military planners hoped to force the enemy to quit in Vietnam through a purely defensive strategy. Weigley wrote, "Specifically, they hoped to succeed where the French had failed by drawing on the immense logistical apparatus of the American Army for superior intelligence, superior mobility, and tremendously superior firepower."[192] Tactics were built around the infantry, supported by tactical air, helicopters, and artillery—"massive artillery and air firepower"—applied in limited tactical battles.[193]

The stagnant front in Vietnam cultivated detrimental doctrinal practices. To coordinate operations with intelligence collection and massive firepower, the Army increasingly valued precise planning and heavy command and control—symbolized by ground commanders in helicopters directing units from above the battle. In a 1966 study, Major General Arthur L. West Jr.—one of Patton's former battalion commanders in the 4th Armored Division—reported, "Currently, most battalion commanders and all brigade and division commanders command and control from the relative safety of a helicopter. We are teaching many bad habits that could cost us dearly in a war of the future where we do not have absolute control of the skies. Also, Vietnam looks just a bit different from the air than it does from the ground."[194]

A corporate management attitude developed. This was partly Eisenhower's postwar legacy of politically attuned generals, a trend taken to a higher level by Secretary of Defense Robert McNamara. The former president of Ford Motors relied on "statisticians and systems analysts" to provide data for measuring success in the absence of victory.[195] He chose compliant generals such as Army chief of staff General Earle G. Wheeler, a man described as "primarily a staff officer who spent nearly half of his post–World War II career in Washington" and who was "particularly adept at working within the Washington bureaucratic maze and was talented at creating compromises between parties otherwise disinclined to reconcile their differences."[196] Eisenhower's legacy of Bradley, Taylor, Wheeler, and a host of similar subordinates created a management culture throughout the Army. The emphasis on "team play" created leaders who not only failed to challenge the Vietnam policy, they also abetted it.[197]

Abandoning decisive maneuver, the U.S. Army settled down in Vietnam in numerous firebases. Colonel Harry Summers Jr. recalled, "Base camps were constructed that were even more elaborate than the training camps constructed in the United States during World War II and attempts were made to provide all the amenities of home. The effect was an inordinate number of soldiers tied down in base camp operations and a reduction in our ability to rapidly redeploy our forces."[198] The U.S. commander, General William Westmoreland, lamented "firebase psychosis," an excessive concern with protection over offensive operations. Political aversion to casualties stifled any desire for maneuver and offense.[199] But this was an illusion of the short term: over the duration of the war, 58,000 U.S. soldiers died in Vietnam. Patton had argued that maneuver reduced casualties and brought victory to boot. He urged, "A violent pursuit will finish the show. Caution leads to a new battle. . . . Find the enemy, attack him, invade his land, raise hell while you are at it. Ride the enemy to death."[200] This was the way to defeat the enemy's will. In Vietnam, the enemy accepted the static war of attrition, negotiated pauses and adjusted when necessary, and outlasted the American will to stay.

The link between morale and maneuver became clear in Vietnam. Patton explained how moving forward created an "interesting psychological situation" in which the officers and men "feel that they are on the winning side."[201] He deplored the "stop, build up, and start" methods of war as morally draining, saying, "The shorter the battle, the fewer men will be killed and hence the greater their self-confidence and enthusiasm."[202] Pursuit instilled a feeling of defeat in a retreating enemy, while failure to pursue transferred that feeling to one's own troops. Vietnam proved that sitting on the defense too long could indeed destroy an army's esprit de corps.

General Colin Powell wrote of his first trip to a firebase in 1968: "I had not expected to find stateside spit and polish. Still, what I discovered jolted me. As I stepped out of the helo, I practically stumbled over rusted ammo left lying around the landing site. Sanitation was nil, weapons dirty, equipment neglected, and the troops sloppy in appearance, bearing, and behavior. . . . The end was nowhere in sight, and deterioration of discipline and morale was obvious."[203] After about four years in strategic defense, General Hamilton Howze reported, "Some units turned against their officers, in some cases trying to kill them; drug abuse and racial difficulties became widespread and units rapidly lost combat efficiency."[204] Patton had warned, "Officers who fail to correct errors or to praise excellence are valueless in peace and dangerous misfits in war."[205] Patton was long dead.

Desperation led President Johnson to appoint a Patton man, Creighton Abrams, to succeed Westmoreland—but only after Deputy Secretary of Defense Cyrus Vance endorsed Abrams as someone with "total and affirmative loyalty to his civilian superiors."[206] Abrams made several immediate changes: eliminating body counts as a metric of success, reorienting the Army on defending populations instead of "search and destroy" sweeps, and turning operations over to the South Vietnamese through the process termed "Vietnamization." There was little else Abrams could do. Even after the 1968 Tet offensive, "a resounding tactical failure" for the North Vietnamese, the United States would not attempt to seize the offensive.[207] As the Richard Nixon administration came to power, frustrations in the military reached an all-time high. Good men left and were replaced with poor-quality draftees. Leaders compromised their integrity in attempts to motivate their men and themselves.

In the summer of 1970 Walt Ulmer and Mike Malone, both lieutenant colonels at the Army War College, reported to a Pentagon conference room to present to the Army senior leaders a report commissioned by the chief of staff entitled *Study on Military Professionalism*. It was not well received. Among a litany of morale issues, they found the Army dominated by "selfish behavior" and preoccupied with "the attainment of trivial short-term objectives even through dishonest practices that injure long-term fabric of the organization."[208] Army leadership had incorporated structures of statistical measurements that substituted self-interests and promotions in place of efforts to win a war. As James Kitfield explained, "To the rank and file, it seemed as if nothing was too sacred to be sacrificed on the altar of numerology, whether the statistics tracked enemy killed, miles trekked, villages 'pacified,' or soldiers reenlisted and AWOL [absent without leave]. And the senior leadership present in that conference room had stood by for five years, seemingly oblivious to the rampant corruption that the system produced."[209] Absenteeism was rampant, officer careerism reached manic levels, and a climate of deceit and fraud pervaded everywhere. Ulmer and Malone blamed the senior Army leaders. Westmoreland ordered their report buried.

Suddenly, at this dark hour, Patton reappeared. With a brilliantly iconic portrayal by George C. Scott in the title role, the movie *Patton* packed theaters in 1970. Admonitions from Old Blood and Guts jolted American audiences mired in Vietnam and the Cold War. His opinions about the Russians sounded prophetic. BBC journalist Trevor Royle noted, "So powerful was its message that Richard Nixon, the U.S. president of the time, was rumored to view the film repeatedly while looking for inspiration to deal with setbacks during Vietnam."[210] Some have said Nixon decided to invade the North Vietnamese refuges in Cambodia after seeing the film—an effort to grasp decisive maneuver.

There were notable inaccuracies in the film despite the efforts of George C. Marshall's former executive officer Frank McCarthy as producer and of Omar Bradley serving as senior technical adviser. D'Este noted, "It was ironical that Bradley received a considerable sum of money, including a percentage of the gross receipts, for his professional consultation on a film about a comrade-in-arms he despised and never understood."[211] The movie overemphasized Patton's rivalry with Montgomery without hinting at Bradley's obsessive enmity with the field marshal. It lacked the subtext of British disregard for American abilities and concern for maintaining British prestige. It ignored Eisenhower's and Bradley's errors in Tunisia, Sicily, France, and the Ardennes. Absent are Patton's designs to close the Falaise gap, race to Metz, clear the Palatinate, and rush across the Rhine. Not only is Eisenhower above criticism; he never even makes an appearance. Most regrettably, Bradley's role is inflated, especially in Patton's Normandy breakout. Royle noted, "Bradley is seen as the even handed and realistic professional who brought sense to the battlefield; Patton as the profane hard hitting soldier who fought his battles by preferring intuition to military logic. Bradley is down-to-earth and decent; Patton is bloodthirsty and vainglorious."[212] John Eisenhower believed that the belittling depiction of Montgomery in the movie resulted from Bradley's "hatred" of the field marshal.[213] In all this the movie created an unfortunate tutorial: it explicates Patton's success as a product of a fiery temper, desire for glory, and sense of history. Countless future officers inspired by the film failed to gain an appreciation of his true methods.

Coincidentally, in 1972 Nixon elevated Patton's former point man Abrams to again succeed Westmoreland, this time as chief of staff of the

Army. Here was a tough man for a tough job. The Soviet army was bigger and better armed than the U.S. Army in Europe, which had been plundered to support the war in Vietnam. Drugs, racism, and poor-quality draftees threatened the Army's new all-volunteer force. The officer corps was a shambles; most of the best had left. Honesty and ethics throughout the ranks were lacking. Most important, Americans appeared to be turning their backs on their military. There were no parades for this returning Army. Abrams set his priorities to rebuild the Army morally, materially, and professionally despite limited available resources.[214] Like Patton after Kasserine, he was determined to change the climate. He dug out Ulmer's and Malone's report and used it to tell his generals that their junior officers resented careerism, falsified reports, and misguided leadership.[215]

Abrams faced another challenge: doctrine. The Army conditioned to the infantry-artillery attritional warfare of Korea and Vietnam had to refocus on the possibility of conventional war against superior Soviet forces in Europe.[216] A study noted, "The training base of the Army and its institutional experience in warfare focused entirely on the infantry-intensive combat and counterinsurgency effort in Vietnam. Whatever combat experience the Army had gained in Vietnam seemed likely irrelevant to war in Europe where U.S. forces would decidedly not have the overwhelming advantages in firepower and air power that they enjoyed in Vietnam."[217] Although the Army doctrinal Field Manual 100–5, *Operations*, included occasional accents on seizing and maintaining the initiative through continuous offensive operations, it generally stressed defense and deterrence. It specified, "The fundamental purpose of U.S. military forces is to preserve, restore, or create an environment of order or stability with which the instrumentalities of government can function effectively under a code of laws."[218] There was no mention of grasping opportunity out of chaos; chaos was the enemy. The ultimate objective was "the defeat of enemy's armed forces"; nowhere did the manual mention "victory."[219] To change this mindset, Abrams decided to begin anew.

The path to changing both doctrine and ethics ran through the Army school system, but it remained split among the branches. In 1973 Abrams united the branch schools under one roof with the creation of the Training and Doctrine Command (TRADOC) with a four-star general at the helm who outranked the two-star branch chiefs. To command TRADOC,

Abrams selected his vice chief of staff, General William E. DePuy, who had served in Third Army with the 90th Infantry Division. That unit had underperformed as part of First Army, and Bradley had relieved the first two commanders before sending it to Third Army in exasperation. Patton then worked closely with new commander Major General Raymond McClain to turn the unit around.[220] By the time they reached the Bulge, Patton found the 90th "very clever," "in splendid form," and "a very inspiring sight."[221] Like others in the division, DePuy claimed to have internalized Patton's way of war. One report noted, "DePuy carried out of World War II a clear impression of the potential of armored forces to conduct rapid operations across varied terrain while employing both fire and maneuver. . . . The key to success that lingered in DePuy's memory was the concentration of fire against the enemy to suppress him while other elements maneuvered to take him in the flank or rear."[222] DePuy thus carried Patton's ideas to TRADOC.

DePuy—and Abrams—also agreed with Patton on simplicity in operations and encouraging initiative in subordinates, a marked departure from the strict control required in existing doctrine. Paul Herbert explained, "DePuy was not impressed with the initiative and aggressiveness of American soldiers. He perceived them as inherently reluctant to take risks and, because of inadequate training, unable to take charge in the absence of orders from a superior."[223] Echoing Patton, DePuy set out to erase the corporate management culture in the officer corps and reinstill the principles of leadership, initiative, and offensive spirit.

Just as DePuy got under way at TRADOC, a watershed event unfolded in the Middle East: Egypt and Syria, supported by a number of other countries, suddenly attacked Israel. The Egyptians crossed the Suez Canal with more than 500 tanks, seized limited objectives, and repulsed hasty and unsupported Israeli armored counterattacks. In the Golan Heights 5 Syrian divisions with 45,000 men and 1,400 tanks furiously attacked the Israeli 7th and 188th Armored Brigades. The Israelis held, adjusted, and turned the tide against great odds. DePuy immediately saw this war as a laboratory for examining potential U.S.-Soviet conflicts in Europe where the equipment and doctrine were much the same. As George Knapp stated, "In many ways, the battle for the Golan Heights mirrored the U.S. Army's image of how it would have to fight a war in Central Europe. American doctrinaires viewed the all-out assault model of Syria, a Soviet client, as a reflection of Soviet Doctrine."[224]

General Donn Starry, then chief of the armor branch, was visiting British Army training facilities in January 1974 when he got a phone call from the Army chief of staff. "Send your wife and staff home," Abrams told Starry, "Take one man with you. You're going to Israel."[225] Starry had not served in Europe during World War II, but it might be said that he was a second-generation Patton man. He had served under Abrams and George Patton III in the 63rd Tank Battalion in Germany in the 1950s and the 11th Armored Cavalry Regiment in Vietnam, an outfit that included other Third Army alumni such as Jimmie Leach and Wallace Nutting.[226] Serving as DePuy's eyes and ears, Starry began searching for lessons learned in Israel.

Moshe Dayan had become chief of staff of the Israel Defense Forces in 1953. His predecessors, Major Generals Yigal Yadin and Mordechai Mackleff, routinely dispersed tanks to support infantry, but Dayan hoped to better use his armor.[227] He was intrigued with the German use of armor in World War II but for obvious reasons was reluctant to emulate Nazis. There was another example to follow. On a visit to the United States he had a chance meeting with Abe Baum, commander of Patton's raid on Hammelburg. Listening to Baum's explanations of the 4th Armored Division's tactics emphasizing speed, mobility, and leadership, Dayan decided to explore American armor doctrine.[228] He expanded Israel's armor force from a single brigade to a full corps (drawn from a hodgepodge of tanks) and endorsed Patton-style operations. A decisive victory against Soviet-equipped Egypt in 1956, noted Robert Citino, "proved to Israel that their armored forces were the most important element of modern warfare."[229] In 1967, however, the success of their sweeping armor and air attacks bred overconfidence.

By 1973 the Soviets were providing their Arab clients surface-to-air missiles to negate Israeli airpower and new antitank Sagger missiles to blunt their armor. They almost succeeded. Caught off guard and not appreciating the lethality of these new weapons, the Israelis, like Montgomery at Caen, repeatedly launched disjointed attacks without sufficient infantry into the teeth of defenses with devastating results. A Leavenworth study noted, "When the fighting ended, total tank and artillery losses for both sides together exceeded the entire tank and artillery inventory of the U.S. Army, Europe. Captured Arab equipment, supplied by the Soviets, showed that the Soviets were well ahead of the United States in combat vehicles technology."[230] Kitfield added, "Though Israel eventually prevailed, in just over two weeks of fighting it lost the equivalent of three years' worth of U.S. tank production."[231] DePuy concluded, "If we lost tanks at that rate in a war we might fight in Europe with the Seventh Army, we would run out of tanks almost immediately. We do not have the kind of war reserves which could support a war with losses that high."[232] It was a scary realization—the Soviets could well win an attrition war through sheer numerical advantage.

In gratitude for the critical support offered by the Nixon administration during the war, the Israelis provided Starry complete access to their battlefields. He saw firsthand the obvious effects of guided missiles and improved tank cannons. The tactical blunders of failing to fight as combined arms elements or committing reserves at the decisive place and time were slightly harder to notice. The greatest lesson was only visible to one schooled in Patton's way of war.

Starry's guide was Israel's 146th Armored Division commander, General Moshe "Musa" Peled, who had taken a reserve tank division to the Golan Heights at the most desperate hour. In 1963 Peled had become the first Israeli graduate of the U.S. Armor School at a time when Albin Irzyk, a 4th Armored Division veteran who spearheaded the initial drive to Bastogne, commanded the school. Peled learned the methods Abrams had instilled in the tactics curriculum when he returned as chief of staff of the Armor Center between 1954 and 1957. Peled guided Starry through the battlefield on the Golan, which reminded Starry of the Fulda Gap in Germany where an outnumbered U.S. Army might have to repel Soviet forces, just as the Israelis had turned back the Syrians. Peled's experience was invaluable.

At Starry's prodding Peled explained that when his division first arrived at the Golan Heights, he was ordered to reinforce the Israeli weak spot. He argued that this would fail to obtain victory. As Heidi Toffler and Alvin Toffler related, "Instead Peled—supported by General Chaim Barlev, a former chief of staff, who was then a top military adviser to Prime Minister Golda Meir—decided to use his reinforcements to attack. In the midst of general defeat, a tactical attack was ordered, and instead of directing it at the main point of the Syrian strength, it would strike at them from an unexpected direction."[233] That attack, including a second pincer by a division under General Dan Laner, turned defeat into decisive victory. The line on the Golan held the Syrians by the nose while Peled's counterattack kicked them in the ass. When the Syrians broke, the Israelis pursued—all the way to the outskirts of the Syrian capital, Damascus. The Syrians had been knocked off balance and ridden down to defeat.

Peled could not have better illustrated the relevance of the Patton doctrine he learned at Fort Knox: *L'audace, l'audace, toujours l'audace!* Patton preached, "Battles are won by frightening the enemy.... You must hold him by frontal fire and move rapidly around his flank."[234] Peled had done just that: he boldly attacked around the flank, shocked the enemy by inducing fire from the rear, and continued shock until breaking the enemy's will to fight.

Starry and subsequent teams of officers, such as the Special Readiness Study Group under Brigadier General Morris J. Brady, delivered findings to DePuy and Abrams from which TRADOC identified 162 recommendations for reforming the Army. Everything from antiaircraft weapon designs, methods for repairing knocked-out vehicles, and platoon movements on modern battlefields had to be addressed. DePuy drew up his own report to Abrams, drawing attention to what he believed was the most immediate concern: transforming the U.S. Army into an organization that could fight and defeat modern, combined arms mechanized forces quickly anywhere in the world.[235]

Just a year earlier an article in the U.S. Army's *Armor Magazine* heralded "The Death of the Tank": "Though it has many obvious advantages, it has evolved to the stage of imminent extinction because it has become increasingly inefficient in an age which demands more of machines than ever before."[236] Many believed the lethality of guided missiles made the tank obsolete. DePuy, echoing Patton, countered, "The fact of the matter is, the tank today is the single most important weapon on the mechanized battlefield. There is no doubt about it. The Russians think so, the Germans think so, the British think so, we think so. However, the tank can't do it alone.... The tank carries the battle to the enemy."[237] For the first time since World War II, the Army's doctrinal infantry-artillery focus was to be challenged.

More than a year before the start of the October War, Abrams and DePuy chaired a meeting of the Army senior brass to discuss plans for a new tank. Abrams endorsed the use of the nearly impenetrable British Chobam armor over the objections of chief of armor Major General William

Desobry, who worried about the armor's tremendous weight. Desobry would later admit that DePuy and Abrams were right.[238] Abrams and DePuy well remembered going up against mammoth Tiger tanks with what Patton called "quail hunting" tanks.

DePuy preached, "Tanks are designed to break through the enemy's defenses and get into his rear where they can attack his communications, his reserves, his artillery, his maintenance units, and his supply stocks. Tanks can go around the flank, too, particularly, if there's an open flank."[239] How familiar this sounded. Patton had taught: "The enemy's rear is the happy hunting ground for armor. Use every means to get it there."[240] DePuy emphasized "close supporting suppressive fires" during the attack to "cause the defender to take cover and thus stop the delivery of defensive fires against the attacker," echoing Patton's emphasis on marching fires.[241] He also reiterated Patton's views on combined arms tactics, coordinated tactical air support, an emphasis on intelligence, simplicity in plans and orders, and initiative at the lowest levels of command. Paul Herbert noted that DePuy's doctrine "had its roots firmly in his earlier experiences. . . . His World War II experience with the 90th Infantry Division had convinced him to do that by avoiding enemy strengths and attacking enemy weaknesses to gain a decisive advantage over that force."[242] Paul Gorman added, "General DePuy had much in common with George S. Patton, indeed, in 1945, after a session with the 90th Division's commanders on World War II's 'lessons learned,' Patton asked DePuy to become his aide-de-camp."[243]

With Abrams' support, DePuy decided to completely rewrite the Army's doctrine from top to bottom—all in eighteen months. He chose Starry and the Armor School to take the lead. Herbert observed: "DePuy was not always pleased with his Pattonesque apostle of tank warfare, but DePuy knew that Starry was a self-starter who would spare no effort to get things done."[244] Patton had complained of being "reduced to the speed, physical and mental, of the Infantry."[245] DePuy recalled, "I wanted the Infantry School to get away from the 2½ miles per hour mentality but they were in the hands of the light infantrymen. . . . They didn't understand it."[246] He therefore used the Armor School to bring the infantry into mechanized dimensions of time and space. Tragically, Abrams was lost to cancer in September 1974, leaving DePuy to continue the fight to change the Army.

When the Armor School discussed its draft doctrine with the Infantry School, disagreement arose. Reminiscent of McNair's antitank gun philosophy, the Infantry School argued for static lines built on reinforced antitank missiles positions in a "strongpoint defense" concept. But this ceded the initiative to the enemy, and Starry argued that he who seized the initiative, "whether he is outnumbered or outnumbering, whether he is attacking or defending," would win.[247] Clearly, in any war against the Soviets, the United States would fight outnumbered. Starry added: "The defense should be designed to lure or canalize the enemy onto ground of our choosing—preferably a reverse slope, where a brisk tank counterattack wipes him out."[248] The infantry favored a means to inflict attrition on the enemy; Starry wanted to "hold them by the nose and kick them in the ass."

In 1975, two years after the U.S Army had withdrawn from Vietnam, the North Vietnamese Army launched an all-out four corps conventional attack against the South. After a brief fight, the unsupported South Vietnamese army collapsed. North Vietnamese tank columns—operating where the U.S. planners said armor had little utility—sliced south to Saigon and crushed all resistance. The secret to their success, said North Vietnamese general Van Tien Dung, was "lightning speed, more lightning speed; boldness, more boldness," leading Summers to note, "Dung's comments echoed the words of General George S. Patton, Jr., thirty years earlier as he raced his Third Army across Europe. But such sentiments were out of fashion in the American Army during the Vietnam War."[249]

The next year TRADOC published a new version of Field Manual 100–5, *Operations*, containing a doctrine called "Active Defense" that carefully prescribed tactics on how to use terrain to canalize the enemy. It detailed the use of kill sacks for massing fire. It described methods for calculating force ratios to determine opportunities for counterattacks. It also described how to correctly use combined arms, how to maximize battlefield intelligence collection, and how to suppress enemy fires. There was, however, something lost in the translation from Starry's ideas: the manual had too much explanation of how to hold the enemy by the nose with massed fires and had too little discussion on how to kick them in the ass with maneuver.

Detractors rose up throughout the Army. Gabel explained, "Critics charged that Active Defense was a doctrine based on weapons systems, not soldiers. . . . Others asserted that the doctrine overstressed defense at the expense of offense."[250] Most important, the manual did not address Soviet second and third echelons of forces in an attack. "I must admit I simply hadn't . . . an answer to [that] in the '76 edition," Starry said much later. "We tackled the tactical problem up forward [but] we kind of brushed aside the operational level considerations, the theater-level considerations."[251] Conditioned by doctrine, Starry had focused on battle, not campaign. Strategic vision was by now a strictly national-level consideration. As Doughty observed, "The new doctrine stressed maneuver predominantly in the sense of moving to deliver firepower or to increase combat power. Using maneuver to strike at the enemy's will to fight was not an inherent part of the doctrine."[252] As Patton might have said, Active Defense was fine as far as it went, but it did not go far enough.

Criticism of Active Defense moved reform to a second phase just as Starry succeeded DePuy in command of TRADOC. Kenneth Allard explained, "Rejecting the firepower attrition models in favor of movement to gain tactical leverage, maneuver theorists argued that enemy forces should not be met head-on, but should be allowed to penetrate and engage infantry defenses. At the same time, friendly armor-heavy forces would circle to the enemy's rear to attack his vulnerable supply trains, lines of communications, and command and control centers."[253] This echoed Patton's call at Bastogne to let the Germans "shoot the works all the way to Paris" so as to open a flank for deep penetration. Doctrine was moving closer to the German model of operational maneuver to achieve decisive battle but still missed Patton's concept of maneuver to create a series of shocks that would paralyze an enemy's ability to react and defeat his will to continue.

On 20 August 1982 TRADOC issued its new Field Manual 100–5 announcing the "AirLand Battle" doctrine that called for using airpower to find and attack follow-on enemy echelons. The new manual embraced a reliance on subordinate initiative, tactical and operational offensives even as part of a strategic defense, surprise counterattacks aimed at weak spots, and moral dimensions of war.[254] Initiative, offense, attack weakness not strength, leadership, training, air-ground cooperation, and operational art: these tenets of Patton's way of war were now Army doctrine.

Kitfield wrote, "In many ways the 1982 version of FM 100–5, the official designation of the Army's doctrine manual, was a direct repudiation of the dogged, 'pile on and slug it out' doctrine of attrition that had dominated

Army thinking. . . . Instead, the 1982 version of FM 100–5 admonished commanders to 'move fast, strike hard and finish rapidly.'"[255] Its aggressive, offensive doctrine was not surprising considering its roots. As Orr Kelly explained, "While other commanders would slug it out with the enemy mile after mile, priding themselves that heavy casualties demonstrated aggressiveness, Patton looked for the breakthrough. . . . Through Abrams and those he influenced, such as DePuy and Starry, this aggressive spirit, with its reliance on a tank-heavy armored force, became the key component of the doctrine that eventually emerged."[256]

A new debate arose over the proper balance between commander initiative and unity of action across the front. Should commanders have the leeway to drive deep, or should certain deep areas be reserved for airpower, long-range artillery, and intelligence-gathering assets? In *Forward into Battle*, Paddy Griffith said of the new doctrine: "Not even the most gutsy disciple of Patton wanted to dispense completely with long-range ET [emerging technology] weapons, electronic surveillance aids or airmobile assaults, although there was a considerable debate about just how far ahead of the fighting troops one should try to look, shoot, or fly helicopters."[257] With his "household cavalry" and dedicated air reconnaissance, Patton had found ways to keep such assets *ahead* of his rapidly advancing columns.

Patton was noted for saying, "Our basic plan of operation is to advance and to keep on advancing regardless of whether we have to go over, under, or through the enemy."[258] When forced to assume the defensive he complained, "It is my earnest effort to keep it from becoming static because that is a poor way of fighting. The best way to defend is to attack, and the best way to attack is to attack."[259] Starry similarly constructed the new doctrine: "The offense is the decisive form of war. . . . The attacker concentrates quickly and strikes hard at an unexpected place or time to throw the defender off balance. Once the attack is under way, the attacker must move fast, press every advantage aggressively, and capitalize on each opportunity to destroy either the enemy's forces or the overall coherence of his defense."[260] Continued movement to seize opportunities and destroy the enemy's coherence: Starry channeled Patton.

After his retirement DePuy noted, "General George S. Patton, Jr. would be pleased to know that maneuver doctrine has taken hold of the U.S. Army of the 1980s."[261] Patton might have been even more pleased to learn that the Army decided to create a vast training area for mechanized brigades to practice the tenets of AirLand Battle. That training area, called the National Training Center (NTC), was in the same California desert where he had established his Desert Training Center nearly forty years earlier. It was a tough environment where, as Patton would say, an ounce of sweat could save a gallon of blood. Using high technology, visiting "blue" brigades would fight the resident "red" opposing force (OPFOR) and its Soviet-styled equipment and doctrine. The OPFOR mission was simple, Kitfield wrote: "Find any structural weakness in a visiting Blue Force unit and pry into that fissure relentlessly until you either crack the brigade wide open or the Blue Force patches up the problem."[262] After each exercise a team of observers/controllers would conduct an after action review with the Blue Force leaders to discuss what they had done, why they had done it, and how they could do it better—a computer-aided version of Patton's post-training reviews with his oversized maps and loudspeakers. He once famously said to his assembled division, "I have showed you . . . briefly . . . the big picture of what the division did. This will enable each of you to insert yourself into the picture and know why it was that at that or this place on that or this day you were particularly tired, particularly hungry, or particularly choked with dust, and why the enemy invariably withdrew. Before I tell you how good you are, I want to again emphasize certain tactical errors of which we were guilty."[263] These words could serve as a mantra at the NTC.

As the name suggests, AirLand Battle relied heavily on airpower to disrupt the enemy in depth and prevent his concentration at the decisive place and time on the battlefield. Yet Patton, with Weyland's XIX Tactical Air Command, had developed unprecedented air-ground cooperation for a purpose different from that included in AirLand Battle. The new doctrine mirrored Eisenhower's use of airpower in Normandy to block possible German reinforcements. Patton used airpower to cover the flanks and front of his advancing columns. Even at war's end, Patton noted, "The effectiveness of air-ground co-operation is still in its infancy."[264] Forty years later, cooperation was still lacking. Air Force historian Robert Frank Futrell noted, "The name AirLand Battle implied that there was cooperation and agreement between the Army and the Air Force but in fact the doctrine was a unilateral development in the Army."[265] That changed somewhat in 1983 and 1984, when successive Army chiefs of staff and the Air Force chief of staff signed agreements to train, improve, and execute the methods of AirLand Battle doctrine.

In 1986 the Army released an updated version of Field Manual 100–5. This version contained five references to Patton sprinkled throughout the volume. (There were also three to Bradley and one to MacArthur, but none to Eisenhower.) Under "Major Operations Planning" was a reference to Patton in the Bulge. "Deception" mentioned his role in deceiving the Germans as to the location of the D-day invasion. The section "Lines of Operation" discussed the failure to support either Patton or Montgomery for a decisive drive to the German border. On page 122 the manual cited Patton's definition of the difference between *haste* and *speed*. Yet perhaps most striking was this passage:

> Audacity has always been a feature of successful offenses. More attacks have been defeated because of a lack of audacity than for any other reason. To the overly cautious around him, General George S. Patton, Jr., warned, "Never take counsel of your fears. The enemy is more worried than you are. Numerical superiority, while useful, is not vital to successful offensive action. The fact that you are attacking induces the enemy to believe that you are stronger than he is." In short, the key tenets of AirLand Battle doctrine—initiative, agility, depth, and synchronization—also apply to any successful attack.[266]

As General Wesley Clark noted five decades after Patton's death, "The spirit of maneuver warfare, and the use of combined arms, including airpower, as taught by Patton, became hallmarks of army war-fighting doctrine."[267] The Army had finally accepted the principles of Patton's way of war, but key tenets of his vision eluded doctrine. DePuy, for one, cautioned that the 1983 doctrine had to take care to ensure "concentration of actions in time via synchronization."[268] The 1986 edition of Field Manual 100–5 specified, "Synchronization is the arrangement of battlefield activities in time, space and purpose to produce maximum relative combat power at the decisive point. . . . So defined, synchronization may and usually will require explicit coordination among the various units and activities participating in any operation."[269] This synchronization implied detailed, top-down planning and control to ensure all elements played their part at the right place and time. It was aimed at decisive battle. As noted previously, Patton looked for something else.

Patton saw subordinate initiative conducted in accord with the commander's intent through *Auftragstaktik* as superior to enforced synchronization.[270] As he explained to his "musicians of Mars," each of his own volition had to "come into this concert at the proper place and the proper time."[271] He sought harmony, not synchronization. Detailed planning and control would not be able to keep pace with changing conditions. Commanders who pause to plan ceded the initiative to the enemy. Patton wanted leaders to develop the situation, to recognize and respond to fleeting opportunities through initiative using intelligence and fluid command and control. He urged commanders to "fight the battle, not the plan." The new Army doctrine did make an allowance: "Synchronization need not depend on explicit coordination if all forces involved fully understand the intent of the commander, and if they have developed and rehearsed well-conceived standard responses to anticipated contingencies."[272] Doctrine seemed to still seek to bring order to the chaos of battle; Patton sought to develop an Army that could find opportunity in chaos. Moreover, Patton sought to avoid battle, to shock the enemy with unexpected and threatening maneuver, and to repeat such shocks as to overwhelm the enemy's ability to react effectively and thus erode his morale and break his will. This was not AirLand Battle.

In February 1990 *Time* magazine ran a cover story calling for massive cuts in the defense budget. Stating that with "each passing day" the need for a mechanized army designed to fight in Europe was fading, the article said of the M-1 tanks: "These 60-ton behemoths will be eliminated from future military budgets."[273] Less than a year later AirLand Battle would employ thousands of tanks against twice their number when Saddam Hussein's Iraqi army invaded Kuwait. In September 1990 an Allied coalition led by the United States responded by massing forces to protect Saudi Arabia and demanding Iraq's withdrawal from Kuwait. When Saddam refused to comply, on 17 January 1991 the coalition forces initiated Operation Desert Storm to evict the Iraqi forces. In the first 24 hours, the Allied air forces had achieved uncontested control of the skies. For the next 38 days the coalition airpower pounded 38 Iraq divisions—consisting of 545,000 men, 4,300 tanks, and 3,100 artillery pieces—in Kuwait and Iraq. This immense bombing campaign not only isolated the Iraq front line, it also decreased critical Iraqi troop strengths by nearly 50 percent, more in specially targeted locations.

Once the force ratios reached desired levels, on 24 February the coalition forces under U.S. general Norman Schwarzkopf attacked. Along the Kuwait–Saudi Arabia border where the Iraqis expected an attack, the 1st Marine Expeditionary Force, reinforced with an Army tank brigade, and Arab forces conducted a steady, deliberate advance designed to hold the Iraqi lines in place. Meanwhile, two corps that had earlier moved to positions some five hundred miles west of the Iraqi lines launched a long, rapid envelopment referred to as the "Hail Mary," sweeping through Iraqi territory and hooking east to cut off the Iraqi army in Kuwait. It looked for all the world like an operational-level "hold them by the nose and kick them in the ass" maneuver.

The long air campaign decimated Iraqi command and control and logistically starved their front-line units. Assisted by a wide variety of intelligence-gathering assets, the U.S. command could literally see and target Iraqi movements as they unfolded throughout the theater of operations. Schwarzkopf applied operational-strategic vision in securing an advantageous position off the western flank of the Iraqi lines and sweeping around the enemy army to accomplish the political objective of securing Kuwait. The fixing attack into Kuwait encountered less resistance than anticipated and was allowed to push on through to Kuwait City. The envelopment around Kuwait also moved faster than hoped. Schwarzkopf told the press: "When you stop and consider that our tanks and armor traveled 200 miles in a period of two days, O.K., I was confident that we could travel those great distances before the enemy could react."[274] The racing Allied forces almost completely trapped the vaunted Iraqi Republican Guard divisions in Kuwait. With a few exceptions, the U.S. forces destroyed the Iraqi army at the cost of just over one hundred casualties in one hundred hours.

The victory was astonishingly one-sided. Heidi Toffler and Alvin Toffler explained the application of AirLand Battle doctrine in the Gulf War: "Destroy the enemy's command facilities. Take out its communications to prevent information from flowing up or down the chain of command. Take the initiative. Strike deep. Prevent the enemy's backup echelons from ever going into action. Integrate air, land, and sea operations. Synchronize combined operations. Avoid frontal attack against the adversary's strong points. Above all, know what the enemy is doing and prevent him from knowing what you are doing."[275] The emphasis on frustrating enemy reactions reflected the core of Patton's doctrine.

The influence of Patton, passed down through men such as Abrams, had again found expression on the fields of battle. The importance of DePuy in this lineage cannot be overstated. Colin Powell, who worked directly for DePuy as a young officer, recalled other graduates of the "DePuy School": "They included Max Thurman, the soldier par excellence, a thinker and leader before whom we all stood in awe, who became commander in chief of Southern Command [and orchestrated the invasion of Panama]; Lou Menetrey, who became commander of the U.S. Forces in Korea; Fred Mahaffey, on his way to becoming Army Chief of Staff until felled by a brain tumor at the age of fifty-two; and Carl Vuono, who did become Army Chief of Staff."[276] Norman Schwarzkopf had worked for and been greatly influenced by Brigadier General Willard Latham, who, he recalled, "brought with him a new approach to training that had been developed by General DePuy at TRADOC."[277] He was also a close longtime friend of DePuy protégé Carl Vuono.

Even the "Patton persona" made something of a return in the style of Schwarzkopf. In describing "Stormin' Norman," Rick Atkinson noted, "Flamboyance could be a useful element in the general's art: a George Patton packing his ivory-handled revolvers, or a Lucian Truscott in his bright leather jacket, visible to all the troops at the front."[278] Schwarzkopf's persona greatly alleviated public doubts as to whether the United States could evict the Iraqis.

It is important to note, however, that there were real differences between AirLand Battle practiced in the Gulf and Patton's way of war. For thirty-eight of its forty-one days, the Gulf War was strictly a battle of attrition. If artillery substituted for airpower, this phase would have been a replay of a World War I offensive. (Still, some airmen found guidance from Patton. The aircraft carrier USS *John F. Kennedy* ship's newspaper headlined Patton's first principle of warfare: "To use the means at hand to inflict the maximum amount of wounds, death, and destruction on the enemy, in a minimum amount of time."[279]) Patton would likewise have taken issue with Schwarzkopf's direction to his commanders and planners: "We need to destroy—not attack, not damage, not surround—I want you to *destroy* the Republican Guard. When you're done with them, I don't want them to be an effective fighting force anymore. I don't want them to exist as a military organization."[280] Patton would likely have sought decisive maneuver to *defeat* the enemy—to crush his will to fight—through a campaign to create sustained and repeated shock. Schwarzkopf sought this destruction by envelopment, in essence creating a German operational maneuver to develop a decisive battle. It might be said the "Hail Mary" was designed to use maneuver to bring fire on the enemy. This was not Patton's series of shocks. Knowing the political demands and limitations in this case, however, Patton may well have endorsed Schwarzkopf's directive.

Finally, one key moment in the Gulf War stands in contrast to Patton's example. Schwarzkopf recalled that when he first showed his envelopment plan to VII Corps commander General Fred Franks, he responded, "The plan looks good, but I don't have enough force to accomplish my mission."[281] On the second night of the attack—reflecting the concern for top-down coordination still prevalent in Army culture—Franks feared that he was fast approaching the Iraqi Republican Guard without enough massed armor. He queried his commanders and then issued instructions: "Halt, refuel, ensure formation postured to achieve mass when attack recommences at [first light]."[282] The pause was noticeable. The next day Chairman of the Joint Chiefs of Staff Powell called Schwarzkopf and asked, "Can't you get Fred Franks moving faster?"[283] Schwarzkopf had been trying to "light a fire under VII Corps" all along but finally said to his deputy, "Okay, we'll have to do it his way."[284] It is impossible to imagine Patton saying such a thing to Ward in Tunisia, or Truscott in Sicily, or Middleton in France. Inevitably, VII Corps failed to close the trap fast enough to prevent some of the elite Republican Guard from escaping back into Iraq.

Despite these points, the Gulf War marked a monumental shift from the massed fires, attrition, and infantry-oriented doctrine embraced at Cold Harbor, Belleau Wood, Aachen, and in Korea and Vietnam. The Patton flame was reignited by Abrams, fanned by DePuy, and set roaring by Starry. It burnished a new doctrine, fed by new weapons and leaders and demonstrated in the Gulf War. The best example of this change was the most obvious. During the planning for Desert Storm, Schwarzkopf told his leaders, "Forget the defensive bullshit, we are now talking offensive. And we're going to talk offense from now until the day we go home."²⁸⁵ There was Patton's spirit manifested. Its impact was expressed by Harry Summers Jr.: "The offensive was once again the American way of war. Patton would have been proud."²⁸⁶

Patton's way of war, as reasserted in the Gulf War, enjoyed an unfortunately brief renaissance. With the end of the Cold War and victory in a hot war, overconfidence and new challenges eroded its impact on doctrine in many ways—some obvious, some subtle. Change, however, is always unsettled, and perhaps the wheel will again turn. Before it can, let us examine where it stands.

THE LIMITS OF LEGACY | 9

> I want to say my job and your job is not over.
> —George S. Patton Jr.

In the wake of the Gulf War and the collapse of the Soviet Union, the U.S. Army stood down from many forward positions it had occupied since World War II. In subsequent years the Army withdrew from the Patton principles embraced in AirLand Battle doctrine. A new generation of Army leaders facing new challenges around the world and at home searched for new solutions, which have brought us far from Patton's way of war.

The retreat from force structures and missions brought new questions. In December 1989 *U.S. News and World Report* ran a cover story titled "Does America Need an Army?" in which Representative Barney Frank declared, "We're going to cut the hell out it."[1] U.S. force strength in Europe quietly fell from 350,000 soldiers in 1990 to roughly 28,000 in 2015.[2] The Army withdrew from hundreds of buildings, barracks, and bases—many bearing Patton's name. The annual Return of Forces to Germany exercises ended in 1992, ending the Army's premier deployment practice.

Ironically, instead of bringing a peace dividend, the end of the Cold War saw an increase in violence around the world. Analysts at the International Monetary Fund observed, "Between 1989 and 2000, more than 4 million people are estimated to have died in violent conflicts, while international terrorist attacks increased from 342 a year between 1995 and 1999 to 387 between 2000 and 2001."[3] The U.S. Army switched focus, first to intervention and peacekeeping operations in places such as Somalia, Haiti, and Bosnia, and then to counter terrorists and insurgents. These manpower-intensive operations challenged America's military supremacy. In June 1993 the Army issued a new edition of Field Manual 100–5 that, while maintaining precepts of AirLand Battle (without using that name), emphasized joint operations, the integration of advanced technology, and "operations other than war." Interestingly, the new manual mentioned Patton only once:

as an example of failure to plan and arrange logistics.[4] The attacks on 11 September 2001 justified a focus on operations other than war. In the counterattack against the terrorists in Afghanistan, smart bombs and Special Forces aided indigenous forces in defeating the terrorist-allied regime, only to see al Qaeda forces escape to sanctuaries in Pakistan from which to carry on seemingly interminable operations.

In 2003 U.S. forces initiated a more conventional Operation Iraqi Freedom campaign that, in some aspects, echoed Patton's way of warfare. General Tommy Franks promised a "campaign unlike any other," characterized by speed and layered and integrated sources of intelligence, with subordinates "given an extraordinary latitude to make their own decisions."[5] Reporters noted how he accepted risks associated with "deviations from standard military procedure" in which "the war plan deviates from traditional doctrine."[6] As correspondents Evan Thomas and Daniel Klaidman noted, "To an unusual degree, Operation Iraqi Freedom is relying on psychological warfare, or 'information operations.'"[7] Much like Patton, Franks set out to break Saddam Hussein's will to resist by attacking his morale. The initial attack plan sought to create "shock and awe" in an opening salvo of pyrotechnic-enhanced bombing and then maintain it through a rapid ground assault. The three-division drive into Iraq featured integrated satellite, aircraft, and ground operator intelligence along with tactical precision airborne weapons substituting for artillery support to make faster-moving columns. In the end, the Army advanced more than two hundred miles to Baghdad in nine days in what General Barry McCaffrey described as "a blitzkrieg of historic importance."[8] Franks sought to frustrate the Iraqis by demonstrating their inability to react against his attacking forces.

There were problems, however. Shock and awe failed, as concern to avoid noncombatant casualties forced planners to focus destruction on targets divorced from the populations. As psychiatrist J. T. MacCurdy explained in *The Structure of Morale*, the experience of surviving direct exposure to violent threat may traumatize populations, but near and remote misses inure them to threat.[9] In other words, to be effective, shock must convey convincing threat, which requires demonstrated lethality. Paradoxically, the more precisely airpower is tailored to prevent collateral damage, the less effective it is on defeating popular morale. The presence of rampaging armor columns in the enemy's rear area, on the other hand, proved effective in undermining enemy army morale.

As to military intelligence, Franks enjoyed abilities exceeding Patton's wildest dreams. Yet where Patton's systems primarily pulled intelligence up to determine where and when to seize opportunities out of the chaos of war, the Army in Iraq used intelligence at all levels to support a straightforward push against the enemy according to plan. What seemed to enhance subordinate initiative had the unfortunate side effect of creating subordinate reliance on a not always reliable external support for decisionmaking. In one unit, Third Infantry Division operations officer Colonel Peter Bayer reported: "The network we had built to pass imagery, et cetera, didn't support us. It just didn't work."[10] Subordinate initiative slaved to high-tech intelligence sources counterintuitively risked speed and continuity in decisions.

Unlike Patton's unpredictable maneuvers, the advance in Iraq was rapid but linear. Its predictable axis allowed the Iraqi leaders to simply get out of the way and change strategy. The attack less resembled Patton's drives across Sicily or France than Napoleon's march on Moscow, in which seizing the enemy capital did not end the fighting. With the enemy disappearing rather than surrendering, and a power vacuum accelerated by a "de-Baathification" effort similar to the earlier denazification program in Germany, a chaotic patchwork of insurgents, guerrillas, criminals, and terrorists arose to carry on resistance. By April the ground forces commander, Lieutenant General William Wallace, told reporters, "The enemy we're fighting is different from the one we war-gamed against."[11] The U.S. forces now had to fight the enemy and not the plan. In September 2003 *Time* magazine quoted an anonymous "U.S. official closely involved in Iraq" as saying: "This is asymmetric warfare all the way, and in asymmetric warfare you can't win. There isn't a military solution, and I'm not alone in saying that."[12]

In the United States, the war in Iraq became a contest in the moral dimension that editorials described as "distant and never ending."[13] Each day forces suffered one to three attacks, out of more than ten thousand daily convoys. The Army increasingly turned to search and destroy missions against elusive opponents, within the context of a larger nation-building effort. Frustration rose. Comparisons to Vietnam grew. Military leaders were trying to bring order out of chaos in the absence of better ideas. *Time* magazine commented: "Even now, more than four years after invading Iraq, the Pentagon seems to be investing much of its current $606 billion budget in an effort to fight the wrong war."[14]

As the war dragged on, arguments arose over how to best conduct operations. In 2004 Victor Davis Hanson presented a lecture entitled "What Would Patton Say About the Present War?" Among his thoughts: Patton would recognize it as a war on Islamic fascists; he would see the need for aid and reconstruction; he would attack the enemy morale with boldness and speed; and he would make certain that he defeated the terrorists and their supporters "in such damaging fashion that none in the Middle East might find such a repugnant cause at all romantic, bringing as it did utter ruin as the wage of the wrath of the United States."[15]

In the midst of wars in Iraq and Afghanistan, the U.S. Army opted to conduct the most major reorganization of forces in over half a century.[16] In the 1930s Daniel Van Voorhis and Adna Chaffee Jr. demonstrated the superior tactical flexibility of the German-designed triangular division. After a few years in the new wars, the Army adopted unit-of-action and unit-of-employment designs that sacrificed flexibility in order to gain more boots on the ground for counterinsurgency operations. The Army shifted back to square divisions of four brigades and reorganized brigades into two combat battalions (one tank, one infantry) and one reconnaissance battalion (mounted in four-wheeled Humvees). Some armored battalions received eight-wheeled Stryker combat vehicles and Humvees instead of M-1 tanks. Subsequent reforms to recreate triangular brigade combat teams have been incomplete and hampered by budget limitations.

Changes in organization reflected changes in doctrine. General David Petraeus spearheaded several years of cooperative effort to produce Field Manual 3–24, *Counterinsurgency*, in 2007. Much of what the new doctrine emphasized suited Patton's way of war: subordinate initiative, flexibility in approach, rapid decisionmaking, an emphasis on intelligence, and a focus on the enemy's will rather than his physical destruction.[17] Still, it described counterinsurgency as strategically defensive in nature, lacking maneuver, and without discussion of advantageous positions. Patton emphasized tactical killing to allow decisive operational maneuver; the new counterinsurgency doctrine substituted moral approaches for killing at the tactical level with a vague connection to winning popular support. Patton's calculus connected maneuver to shock, shock to frustrate enemy decision cycles, frustration to undermine morale, and undermined morale to defeat enemy will. The counterinsurgency doctrine focused on winning popular support to deny sustenance to insurgents.

The new field force structures and doctrine began taking effect during a time of rising casualties and declining U.S. political will. As in Vietnam, when the Army ceased moving, it risked moral momentum. In March 2006 President George W. Bush appointed a bipartisan panel of distinguished veteran policymakers to the Iraq Study Group and tasked them to review and determine the best course forward in Iraq. They submitted a final report in December that included seventy-nine recommendations, all pointing to withdrawal.[18] In January 2007 skeptical pundits reported, "Rather than reversing course, as all the wise elders of the Iraq Study Group advised, the Commander in Chief is betting that more troops will lead the way to what one White House official calls 'victory.'"[19] Following the advice of Frederick Kagan and Jack Keane, the President "surged" an additional 20,000 troops to Iraq. Three of the five brigades arrived by March without improving the situation. On 23 April Senate majority leader Harry Reid declared, "This war is lost and the surge is not accomplishing anything as indicated by the extreme violence in Iraq yesterday."[20] Casualties in 2007 numbered 23,600, a drop from 34,500 the previous year, then fell rapidly and bottomed out by 2012 at 1,317—before climbing as the United States began withdrawing from Iraq.[21] No similar trend appeared in the attrition battle of Afghanistan. As battalion commander Lieutenant Colonel Brett Jenkinson said in the Korengal Valley in April 2009, "We are not going to kill our way out of this war."[22]

In 2010 the U.S. Army took a major step in dismantling Patton's legacy when it closed the Armor Center at Fort Knox, Kentucky, and moved the Armor School back to Fort Benning, Georgia, the following year. In January 1933, at the direction of Chief of Staff MacArthur, Van Voorhis moved his 175 men and 35 light tanks of the Experimental Mechanized Force to Fort Knox to form the 1st Cavalry (Mechanized) Regiment with orders to field "a second type of cavalry (mechanized) in which the horse and mule shall have disappeared entirely."[23] The War Department deliberately kept the unit away from the chief of cavalry at Fort Riley, Kansas, and the chief of infantry at Fort Benning so that it might develop independently in order to realize mechanized armor's full potential.[24] Maintaining this independence had been essential in both keeping Patton's doctrine alive after World War II and enabling the eventual development of the AirLand Battle doctrine. Now, with tankers just as likely to be assigned to Stryker wheeled vehicles or Humvees as to tanks, the Army submerged the entire armor branch into a Maneuver Center of Excellence based at the home of the infantry. Army vice chief of staff General Peter Chiarelli noted the "bittersweet occasion" by telling worried attendees at the 2010 Armor Warfighting Conference, "Some of you are concerned that the Armor Branch is dead, but I assure you that Armor Branch is alive and well."[25] The commander of Fort Benning, Major General Bob Brown, announced, "We've been waiting a long time to merge armor and infantry and get the folks down here from Knox."[26] Tankers understandably felt betrayed and saddened.

This turn of events stirred Patton's ghost. In March 2012 his grandson, Ben Patton, author of *Growing Up Patton*, posted an editorial on the Huffington Post blog answering the question: "What Would General Patton Do in Iraq and Afghanistan?" He concluded that the general would follow his own advice: "Weapons change, but the man who uses them changes not at all. To win battles, you do not beat weapons, you beat the soul of the enemy."[27] That task seemed ever more difficult against the fanatical forces of the Islamic State of Iraq and Syria (ISIS) that began defeating U.S.-trained Iraqi forces and taking territory once hard won by U.S. forces. On a Sunday morning talk show in September 2014 Bill O'Reilly, television host and author of *Killing Patton*, told George Stephanopoulos, "If George Patton were alive today he would be saying to President [Barack] Obama, 'Give me the Third, I'll go into Syria and I'll wipe them all out.'"[28]

But Patton is not alive today. Neither is an understanding of his methods. Many, like O'Reilly, misread Patton's success as a simple result of determined attack. Forgotten is his use of intelligence systems to find and exploit enemy weaknesses so as to avoid battle and to target and defeat morale. The website *Defense One* stated: "The key to defeating ISIS must be a systematic and sustained drone air campaign in support of Kurdish and Iraqi forces—in effect a high-tech upgrading of a proven battlefield strategy first employed by George Patton's Third Army during World War II and by U.S. Marines in Korea."[29] Of course, Patton rejected such attrition strategy. He developed and employed flexible tactical air support, the kind executed by today's superb A-10 Warthog, not drones. Yet the Air Force has decided to get rid of the A-10, a decision Air Force chief of staff General Mark Welsh defended to lawmakers in March 2015 by saying, "We have priced ourselves out of that game."[30] Without the right tools, the Army loses the third dimension of cover for Patton's fast-moving combined arms columns. The future once again belongs to firepower-based attrition warfare—something not suited to all occasions. When your only tool is a hammer, all problems look like nails.

The fact is that Patton's way of war was tailored to the particular circumstances of conventional land warfare, not counterinsurgency. His methods might apply against ISIS ground units, but such forces remain a "protean enemy," in Jessica Stern's brilliant phrase.[31] Defeat their conventional forces, and they transform into guerrilla and terrorist operations. However, just because Patton's ideas might not apply does not mean attrition strategy serves as an appropriate default. Americans traditionally fight a style of warfare that mirrors football: huddles to plan, violent action, and measurable progress toward a physical goal. Insurgents employ a Greco-Roman wrestling paradigm: no clocks, grapple for leverage, and induce the opponent into a sudden fall. Different styles of warfare require different counters. In the final analysis, Patton proposed a revolutionary approach to conventional warfare, and that is enough.

NOTES

Chapter 1. Legends and Lies

Epigraph: Harry Yeide, *Fighting Patton: George S. Patton, Jr., Through the Eyes of His Enemies* (Minneapolis, Minn.: Zenith Press, 2011), 420.

1. George S. Patton Jr., diary, September 6, 1944, box 3, Papers of George S. Patton, Library of Congress, Washington, D.C. (hereafter GSP LOC).
2. *Life Magazine*, cover, 7 July 1941, 13.
3. Omar Bradley, foreword in Fred Ayer Jr., *Before the Colors Fade: A Portrait of a Soldier, George S. Patton, Jr.* (Boston: Houghton Mifflin, 1964), viii.
4. George S. Patton Jr., "Success in War," *Cavalry Journal* (January 1931), in George S. Patton Jr., *Military Essays and Articles, 1885–1945*, ed. Charles M. Province (San Diego, Calif.: The George S. Patton Jr. Historical Society, 2002), 338 (hereafter GSPHS). See also Stanley P. Hirshson, *General Patton: A Soldier's Life* (New York: HarperCollins, 2002), 201.
5. For firsthand impressions of his men toward Patton's speech, see D. A. Lande, *I Was with Patton: First-Person Accounts of World War II in George S. Patton's Command* (St. Paul, Minn.: MBI Publishing, 2002), 116.
6. George S. Patton Jr., letter to Walter Dillingham, 4 March 1944, box 28, GSP LOC.
7. Albert C. Wedemeyer, *Wedemeyer Reports!* (New York: Henry Holt, 1958), 222.
8. Eisenhower memorandum on Patton for personal files, 11 June 1943 (A472, Eisenhower Library, Abilene, Kansas), cited by Carlo D'Este in *Patton: A Genius for War* (New York: HarperPerennial, 1996), 501, and Omar Bradley and Clay Blair, *A General's Life* (New York: Simon and Schuster, 1983), 139.
9. Forrest C. Pogue, *George C. Marshall, Interviews and Reminiscences* (Lexington, Va.: George C. Marshall Research Foundation, 1991), 547.
10. Andy Rooney, *My War* (New York: Times Books, 1995), 187.
11. Patton, letter to Major J. M. Scammell, 4 October 1943, box 27, GSP LOC. In a previous letter, Scammell recalled Patton making a toast long before the war at the German attaché's house in Washington, D.C., in which he wished for another war.
12. Patton's method of motivation led to victories but "also caused problems for himself and for his senior commanders. It brought about the slapping incident, the abortive speeches, and quarrels with American and Allied commanders." Edgar Puryear Jr., *Nineteen Stars: A Study in Military Character and Leadership* (New York: Ballantine Books, 1971), 287.

13. Samuel P. Huntington, *The Soldier and the State: The Theory and Politics of Civil-Military Relations* (Cambridge, Mass.: Belknap Press, 1985), 8.
14. See the overview of U.S. Army interwar doctrine presented in Kenneth Finlayson, *An Uncertain Trumpet: The Evolution of U.S. Army Infantry Doctrine, 1919–1941* (Westport, Conn.: Greenwood Press, 2001), 78–79.
15. See Martin Blumenson, ed., *The Patton Papers, Volume I: 1885–1940* (Boston: Houghton Mifflin, 1972), 831.
16. Finlayson, *An Uncertain Trumpet*, 160.
17. U.S. Army, *Field Service Regulations 1923* (Washington, D.C.: Government Printing Office, 1924), which stood unchallenged until 1939, cited by William O. Odom, *After the Trenches: The Transformation of U.S. Army Doctrine, 1918–1939* (College Station: Texas A&M University Press, 1999), 50.
18. See George F. Hofmann, "Army Doctrine and the Christie Tank," in *Camp Colt to Desert Storm: The History of U.S. Armored Forces*, ed. George F. Hofmann and Donn Starry (Lexington: University Press of Kentucky, 1999), 92–93.
19. David E. Johnson, *Fast Tanks and Heavy Bombers: Innovation in the U.S. Army, 1917–1945* (Ithaca, N.Y.: Cornell University Press, 1998), 73.
20. See Bradley's uses of Mobile Strategy in Bradley and Blair, *A General's Life*, 66, compared to Patton's concept in "Mobile Strategy," 2 July 1944, box 46, GSP LOC.
21. James W. Rainey, "Ambivalent Warfare: The Tactical Doctrine of the AEF in World War I," *Parameters, The Journal of the U.S. Army War College* XIII, no. 3 (September 1983): 34–46.
22. Pershing cited by Finlayson, *An Uncertain Trumpet*, 35.
23. David Chandler, ed., *The Military Maxims of Napoleon* (London: Greenhill Press, 1994), 61.
24. Russell F. Weigley offers this definition of strategic maneuver as the Army's pre–World War II popular counterpart to strategy as expressed by Clausewitz. See Russell F. Weigley, *The American Way of War: A History of United States Military Strategy and Policy* (Bloomington: Indiana University Press, 1973), xviii.
25. See Eisenhower's Overlord objective in Appendix A in Gordon A. Harrison, *The European Theater of Operations, Cross Channel Attack* (Washington, D.C.: U.S. Army Center of Military History, 1989), 450, compared to Patton's ideas for the same operation in "Mobile Strategy," 2 July 1944.
26. Bliss believed the size of modern armies and their vulnerability to air reconnaissance made surprise impossible below the level of grand strategy. See Tasker H. Bliss, draft article in January 1923 cited by Weigley, *The American Way of War*, 203–5.
27. George S. Patton Jr., *War as I Knew It* (Boston: Houghton Mifflin, 1947), 358.
28. Malcolm Gladwell observed, "In the military, brilliant generals are said to possess '*coup d'oeil*'—which, translated from the French, means 'power of

the glance'; the ability to immediately see and make sense of the battlefield. Napoleon had *coup d'oeil*. So did Patton." Malcolm Gladwell, *Blink: The Power of Thinking Without Thinking* (New York: Little, Brown, 2005), 44.

29. See Carl von Clausewitz, *On War* (1882), ed. and trans. Peter Paret and Michael Howard (New York: Alfred Knopf, 1993), 118–19.
30. William Duggan, *Napoleon's Glance: The Secret of Strategy* (New York: Nation Books, 2002), 147–48.
31. Ladislas Farago, *Patton: Ordeal and Triumph* (New York: Ivan Obolensky, 1963), 381–82.
32. Victor Davis Hanson, *The Soul of Battle: From Ancient Times to the Present Day, How Three Great Liberators Vanquished Tyranny* (New York: Anchor Books, 2001), 338.
33. Hirshson draws his conclusion from Bradley's misguided criticism of Patton's staff. See Hirshson, *General Patton: A Soldier's Life*, 701.
34. Bradley and Blair, *A General's Life*, 99.
35. Harry Semmes, *Portrait of Patton* (New York: Paperback Library, 1970), 73. See also Hanson, *The Soul of Battle*, 268.
36. Hirshson, *General Patton: A Soldier's Life*, 694.
37. James S. Corum, *Roots of the Blitzkrieg: Hans Von Seeckt and German Military Reform* (Lawrence: University Press of Kansas, 1994), 49.
38. Infantry Journal Incorporated, *Infantry in Battle* (Richmond, Va.: Garret and Massie, 1939), 138. Emphasis in original.
39. Helmuth von Moltke, "On Strategy" (1871), in *Moltke on the Art of War*, ed. Daniel J. Hughes (Novato, Calif.: Presidio Press, 1993), 45. See also Jay M. Shafritz, *Words on War: Military Quotations from Ancient Times to the Present* (New York: Prentice Hall, 1990), 474.
40. Patton, letter to Eisenhower, 9 July 1926, in Blumenson, ed., *The Patton Papers, Volume I*, 801–2.
41. From the facsimile of Patton's annotations in *Infantry in Battle* as presented in Roger H. Nye, *The Patton Mind: The Professional Development of an Extraordinary Leader* (New York: Avery Publishing Group, 1993), 100.
42. See Patton, *Military Essays and Articles, 1885–1945*, GSPHS, 255.
43. George S. Patton Jr., speech to 2nd Armored Division at Fort Benning, 6 July 1941, box 45, GSP LOC. See also Martin Blumenson, *The Patton Papers, Volume II: 1940–1945* (Boston: Houghton Mifflin, 1974), 39–41.
44. Infantry Journal Incorporated, *Infantry in Battle*, 169.
45. Bernard Law Montgomery, *The Memoirs of Field Marshal Montgomery* (New York: Collins, 1958), 80–81.
46. Bradley and Blair, *A General's Life*, 199.
47. See Omar N. Bradley, *A Soldier's Story* (New York: Henry Holt, 1951), 355. See also Duggan, *Napoleon's Glance*, 169, who cites Bradley as saying after Sicily he thought Patton "a shallow commander."

48. Dwight D. Eisenhower, *Crusade in Europe* (Garden City, N.Y.: Doubleday, 1948), 215–16. Ike promised Marshall, "In no repeat no event will I ever advance Patton beyond Army command." See Hanson, *The Soul of Battle*, 277.
49. Bradley and Blair, *A General's Life*, 353.
50. Oscar W. Koch with Robert G. Hayes, *G-2: Intelligence for Patton* (Philadelphia: Whitmore Publishing Company, 1971), 71.
51. Hirshson, *General Patton: A Soldier's Life*, 683.
52. Terry Brighton, *Patton, Montgomery, Rommel: Masters of War* (New York: Three Rivers Press, 2008), 393.
53. See Eisenhower, *Crusade in Europe*, 81, 281–86.
54. Bradley, *A Soldier's Story*, 51–52.
55. Brighton, *Patton, Montgomery, Rommel*, 394–95.
56. Charles Whiting, *Patton's Last Battle* (Havertown, Pa.: Casemate, 1987), 22–23.
57. Michael Lee Lanning, *The Military Top 100* (Secaucus, N.J.: Citadel Press, 1996), 348.
58. Marshall wrote to Admirals Hewitt and King: "Patton is indispensable to Torch." See D'Este, *Patton: A Genius for War*, 421.
59. Stephen Ambrose, *Ike: Abilene to Berlin: The Life of Dwight D. Eisenhower from His Childhood in Abilene, Kansas, Through His Command of the Allied Forces in Europe* (New York: HarperCollins, 1973), 229.
60. Erwin Rommel in *The Rommel Papers*, ed. B. H. Liddell Hart (New York: Harcourt, Brace, 1953), 523.
61. Yeide, *Fighting Patton*, 419.
62. Rundstedt's opinion cited by Cornelius Ryan as noted in Albin F. Irzyk, *Gasoline to Patton: A Different War* (Oakland, Calif.: Elderberry Press, 2005), 159.
63. Martin Blumenson, *Patton: The Man Behind the Legend, 1885–1945* (New York: William Morrow, 1985), 296.
64. See Yeide, *Fighting Patton*, 419–20.
65. D'Este, *Patton: A Genius for War*, 463.
66. Irzyk, *Gasoline to Patton*, 77.
67. Lande, *I Was with Patton*, 103.
68. Hanson, *The Soul of Battle*, 270.
69. "The World Wars," History Channel miniseries, premiered 26–28 May 2014.
70. Google.com search conducted 10 March 2015.
71. Amazon.com book search conducted 10 March 2015.
72. Brighton, *Patton, Montgomery, Rommel*, 403.
73. D'Este, *Patton: A Genius for War*, 811.
74. Bradley termed the Hammelburg raid "a foolhardy operation." See Hirshson, *General Patton: A Soldier's Life*, 623.
75. D'Este, *Patton: A Genius for War*, 815.
76. Ibid., 378.

77. Hubert Essame, *Patton, as Military Commander* (London: B. T. Batsford, 1973; Conshohocken, Pa.: Combined Publishing, 1998), 258–59. Citations refer to the 1998 edition.
78. Trevor Royle, *Patton: Old Blood and Guts* (London: Weidenfeld and Nicolson, 2005), 209.
79. Alan Axelrod, *Patton: A Biography* (New York: Palgrave Macmillan, 2006), 178.
80. Bradley and Blair, *A General's Life*, 218.
81. Lande, *I Was with Patton*, 291–92.
82. See Eisenhower, *Crusade in Europe*, 181, 215. See also Ed Cray, *General of the Army: George C. Marshall, Soldier and Statesman* (New York: Cooper Square Press, 1990), 444.
83. D'Este, *Patton: A Genius for War*, 622.
84. Ibid., 818.
85. Essame, *Patton, as Military Commander*, 259.
86. Ian P. Hogg, *The Biography of General George S. Patton* (New York: Gallery Books, 1982), 157.
87. Hanson, *The Soul of Battle*, 304.
88. John Nelson Rickard, *Advance and Destroy: Patton as Commander in the Bulge* (Lexington: University Press of Kentucky, 2011), 304.
89. Charles R. Codman, *Drive* (Boston, Mass.: Little, Brown, 1957), 159.
90. See John Nelson Rickard, *Patton at Bay: The Lorraine Campaign, 1944* (Washington, D.C.: Brassey's, Inc., 2004).
91. Hirshson, *General Patton: A Soldier's Life*, 701–2.
92. Patton, letter to Brigadier General P. F. Gallagher, commandant of the United States Military Academy, 16 July 1943, box 27, GSP LOC.
93. Dennis Showalter, *Patton and Rommel: Men of War in the Twentieth Century* (New York: Berkley Caliber, 2005), 422.
94. "Up to Front Go Re-Inforcements," *Life Magazine*, 7 July 1941, 79.
95. Ibid.
96. Badsey wrote, "Patton, a cavalryman who had joined the tank corps as a personal career move and would leave it in 1920 for the same reason, was anything but a theorist." Stephen Badsey, "The American Experience of Armour, 1919–1953," in *Armoured Warfare*, ed. J. P. Harris and F. H. Toase (New York: St. Martin's Press, 1990), 125.
97. See D'Este, *Patton: A Genius for War*, 63.
98. Nye, *The Patton Mind*, x.
99. Hanson, *The Soul of Battle*, 275.
100. Patton diary, April 4, 1944, box 3, GSP LOC.
101. Paul D. Harkins, *When the Third Cracked Europe: The Story of Patton's Incredible Army* (Harrisburg, Pa.: Stackpole Books, 1969), 57.
102. See Patton's intention in Rickard, *Patton at Bay*, 205.

103. "Interview Between General Patton and Captured German Colonel Constantin Meyer (Metz Area)," 22 November 1944, 1000 hrs., box 52, folder 18, GSP LOC.
104. Bradley and Blair, *A General's Life*, 317.
105. See Izyk, *Gasoline to Patton*, 27.
106. Patton diary, August 30, 1944, box 3, GSP LOC.
107. Hanson Baldwin, *Tiger Jack* (Fort Collins, Colo.: Old Army Press, 1979), 137.
108. Duggan, *Napoleon's Glance*, 187.

Chapter 2. A Series of Shocks

Epigraph: Robert Coram, *Boyd: The Fighter Pilot Who Changed the Art of War* (New York: Little, Brown, 2002), 336.

1. See Koch, *G-2: Intelligence for Patton*, 42.
2. Baron Henri de Jomini, *The Art of War* (Westport, Conn.: Greenwood Press, 1974 [1862]), 306. See also Duggan's discussion of *coup d'oeil* in *Napoleon's Glance*, 4.
3. Edward Mead Earle, "Introduction," in *Makers of Modern Strategy: Military Thought from Machiavelli to Hitler*, ed. Edward Mead Earle, Gordon A. Craig, and Felix Gilbert (Princeton, N.J.: Princeton University Press, 1943), viii.
4. U.S. Army Field Manual 3–0, *Operations* (Washington, D.C.: Department of Defense, 27 February 2008), 6-2.
5. Ibid., 6-3.
6. Ibid., 6-4.
7. U.S. Army Field Manual 100–5, *Operations* (Washington, D.C.: Government Printing Office, 15 June 1944), 3.
8. See, for example, Walter E. Piatt, "What Is Operational Art?" (thesis, School of Advanced Military Studies, U.S. Army Command and General Staff College, 1999).
9. Richard Simpkin, *Race to the Swift: Thoughts on Twenty-first Century Warfare* (London: Brassey's, 1985), 37–54.
10. Richard Simpkin, *Red Armour: An Examination of the Soviet Mobile Force Concept* (London: Brassey's Defence Publishers, 1984), Appendix A, 229.
11. Robert M. Citino, *Blitzkrieg to Desert Storm: The Evolution of Operational Warfare* (Lawrence: University Press of Kansas, 2004), 8.
12. Weigley, *The American Way of War*, 147.
13. As John Antal noted, "There are two distinct styles of operational warfighting: attrition and maneuver." John F. Antal, "Thoughts about Maneuver Warfare," in *Maneuver Warfare: An Anthology*, ed. Richard D. Hooker Jr. (Novato, Calif.: Presidio Press, 1993), 61.
14. Alan Brooke, *War Diaries, 1939–1945* (Berkeley: University of California Press, 2003), 575.
15. Montgomery, *The Memoirs of Field Marshal Montgomery*, 235.

16. Ibid.
17. Rickard, *Advance and Destroy*, 308.
18. Stephan D. Skelenka, "General George S. Patton: Operational Leadership Personified," (thesis, Naval War College, 4 February 2002).
19. Robert Leonhard, *The Art of Maneuver Warfare: Maneuver—Warfare Theory and AirLand Battle* (Novato, Calif.: Presidio Press, 1991), 40.
20. Codman, *Drive*, 174.
21. See Thomas E. Griess, ed., *Ancient and Medieval Warfare (The West Point Military History Series)* (Wayne, N.J.: Avery Publishing Group, 1984), 4.
22. Sergeant Thomas Morris, 71st Regiment, cited by John Keegan, *The Face of Battle: A Study of Agincourt, Waterloo, and the Somme* (London: Penguin Books, 1976), 156.
23. Jomini, *The Art of War*, 286.
24. Ibid.
25. Ibid.
26. George S. Patton Jr., letter to Mrs. J. E. Johnston, United Daughters of the Confederacy, 30 December 1943, box 27, GSP LOC.
27. See Hirshson, *General Patton: A Soldier's Life*, 24.
28. Patton in a draft Letter of Instruction (undated), page 3, folder 10, box 46, GSP LOC.
29. Kept out of school until he was nearly twelve years old, young Patton favored "anything and everything about Napoleon." See D'Este, *Patton: A Genius for War*, 39.
30. Weigley, *The American Way of War*, 145.
31. Patton in "Notes on some faults of the Advance Guard of a Squadron of Cavalry," undated (1916), box 25, GSP LOC.
32. Farago, *Patton: Ordeal and Triumph*, 70.
33. Weigley, *The American Way of War*, 201.
34. Robert B. Bruce, *A Fraternity of Arms: America and France in the Great War* (Lawrence: University Press of Kansas, 2003), 121.
35. Odom, *After the Trenches*, 50.
36. Bruce, *A Fraternity of Arms*, 123.
37. Steven J. Zaloga, *The Renault FT Light Tank* (London: Osprey Publishing, 1998), 10.
38. Dale E. Wilson, *Treat 'Em Rough! The Birth of American Armor, 1917–1920* (Novato, Calif.: Presidio Press, 1989), 39.
39. Blumenson, *The Patton Papers, Volume I*, 537.
40. Ibid.
41. Here Napoleon used moral meaning morale. Chandler, *The Military Maxims of Napoleon*, 57–58.
42. D'Este, *Patton: A Genius for War*, 237.
43. Codman, *Drive*, 272.

44. Patton diary, March 25, 1944, box 3, GSP LOC.
45. Sun Tzu as underlined by Patton in "Transcription of the Text of Sun Tzu on the Art of War, The Oldest Military Treaties in the World, Translated from the Chinese by Lionel Giles, MA," 1910, box 54, GSP LOC.
46. Patton diary, August 3, 1944, box 3, GSP LOC.
47. Blumenson, *The Patton Papers, Volume I*, 540.
48. Ibid., 555.
49. Jomini, *The Art of War*, 285.
50. U.S. Army, *Cavalry Drill Regulations 1916* (Washington, D.C.: U.S. Army, 1917), 158.
51. Blumenson, *The Patton Papers, Volume I*, 456.
52. Wilson, *Treat 'Em Rough!* 29.
53. D'Este, *Patton: A Genius for War*, 215.
54. Wilson, *Treat 'Em Rough*, 45.
55. Russell F. Weigley, *History of the United States Army* (Bloomington: Indiana University Press, 1984), 392.
56. Blumenson, *The Patton Papers, Volume I*, 539.
57. Patton in "Speaking Notes," June 2, 1918, box 2, GSP LOC.
58. Patton added, "The British supports follow in short columns, the French in skirmish line. I am uncertain which is the best formation. . . . Before the wilderness campaign General Grant told the President that in his opinion the Union Army had never been fought to its limit. Please pardon my presumption in suggesting that the same is true of the Tanks." Blumenson, *The Patton Papers, Volume I*, 531.
59. Ibid., 587.
60. Wilson, *Treat 'Em Rough!* 113.
61. George S. Patton Jr., "Report of Personal Experiences in the Tank Corps," 16 December 1918, in Patton, *Military Essays and Articles, 1885–1945*, 282.
62. Trevor N. Dupuy and R. Ernest Dupuy, *The Harper Encyclopedia of Military History* (New York: HarperCollins, 1993), 1075.
63. Bruce, *A Fraternity of Arms*, 270.
64. Blumenson, *The Patton Papers, Volume I*, 612. See also undated page 2 of statement by First Lieutenant Paul S. Edwards, Signal Corps, in folder 16, box 47, GSP LOC.
65. Blumenson, *The Patton Papers, Volume I*, 613.
66. See David Jablonsky, "Why Is Strategy Difficult?" in *The U.S. Army War College Guide to National Security Issues, Volume I: Theory of War and Strategy*, 4th ed., ed. J. Boone Bartholomees Jr. (Carlisle, Pa.: U.S. Army War College, July 2010), 8.
67. Ibid. Strategy moved to "the level of war at which campaigns and major operations are planned, conducted and sustained to accomplish strategic objectives."
68. Blumenson, *The Patton Papers, Volume I*, 867.

69. Jomini, *The Art of War*, 62.
70. Sun Tzu, *The Art of War*, ed. James Clavell (New York: Delacorte Press, 1983), 29.
71. Nye, *The Patton Mind*, 50.
72. Blumenson, *The Patton Papers, Volume I*, 635.
73. Winfield Scott, *Infantry Tactics* (New York: Harper and Brothers, 1835), introduction.
74. See the discussion of attrition strategy and the misunderstanding of Clausewitz in Weigley, *History of the United States Army*, 209–11.
75. Clausewitz, *On War*, 207.
76. "Despite his subtleties, the most evident thrust of Clausewitz was to support the kind of strategy of mass and concentration in furtherance of the goal of destroying the enemy army that U.S. Grant had relied on in 1864–1865 and both sides had fallen back on in 1914–1918." Weigley, *The American Way of War*, 211.
77. Weigley, *History of the United States Army*, 211.
78. Weigley, *The American Way of War*, 220.
79. Lucian Truscott Jr., *The Twilight of the Cavalry* (Lawrence: University Press of Kansas, 1989), 139.
80. Cited by Odom, *After the Trenches*, 39.
81. See D. K. R. Crosswell, *The Chief of Staff: The Military Career of General Walter Bedell Smith* (Westport, Conn.: Greenwood Press, 1991), 54.
82. Johnson, *Fast Tanks and Heavy Bombers*, 224.
83. Ibid.
84. Truscott, *The Twilight of the Cavalry*, 140.
85. Henry G. Gole, *The Road to Rainbow: Army Planning for Global War, 1934–1940* (Washington, D.C.: AUSA Institute of Land Warfare/Naval Institute Press, 2004), 125.
86. Crosswell, *The Chief of Staff*, 54–55.
87. Ibid., 253.
88. D'Este, *Patton: A Genius for War*, 332–33.
89. Blumenson, *The Patton Papers, Volume I*, 778.
90. D'Este, *Patton: A Genius for War*, 331.
91. Blumenson, *The Patton Papers, Volume I*, 801.
92. Ibid., 801–2.
93. Nye, *The Patton Mind*, 74.
94. Ardant du Picq, *Battle Studies*, in *Roots of Strategy, Volume 2*, ed. T. R. Phillips (Harrisburg, Pa.: Stackpole Books, 1940), 98, 208.
95. Nye, *The Patton Mind*, 75.
96. du Picq, *Battle Studies*, 224.
97. Ibid., 227.
98. Blumenson, *The Patton Papers, Volume I*, 820.

99. Ibid., 802.
100. Patton in "Advance Guard Demonstration, 27th Inf.," November 19, 1926, box 53, GSP LOC.
101. Ibid.
102. Blumenson, *The Patton Papers, Volume I*, 843.
103. D'Este, *Patton: A Genius for War*, 345–46.
104. Odom, *After the Trenches*, 129.
105. U.S. Army Field Manual 100–15, *Manual for Commanders of Large Units (Provisional), Volume I (Operations)* (Washington, D.C.: Government Printing Office, 1930), 7–8.
106. Ibid., 8.
107. Odom, *After the Trenches*, 125.
108. Blumenson, *The Patton Papers, Volume I*, 831.
109. George S. Patton Jr., "Mechanized Forces," *Cavalry Journal* (September-October 1933), in *Military Essays and Articles, 1885–1945*, 126.
110. Ibid., 123.
111. Ibid., 126.
112. H. E. Ely, "Battlefield Psychology," March 28, 1933, box 57, GSP LOC.
113. Ibid.
114. Ibid.
115. Ibid.
116. Ibid., 123. Patton cited von Seeckt's discussion of the lack of strategy in World War I. See also Thomas Mahnken, *Uncovering Ways of War: U.S. Intelligence and Foreign Military Innovation, 1918–1941* (Ithaca, N.Y.: Cornell University Press, 2002), 104.
117. See Farago, *Patton: Ordeal and Triumph*, 122.
118. See Christopher Duffy and Paul Harris, introduction to Heinz Guderian, *Achtung-Panzer!* (London: Arms and Armour, 1993), 15.
119. Ibid., 204.
120. Blumenson, *The Patton Papers, Volume I*, 834.
121. Farago, *Patton: Ordeal and Triumph*, 119.
122. D'Este, *Patton: A Genius for War*, 366–67.
123. Blumenson, *The Patton Papers, Volume I*, 929.
124. Ibid., 930.
125. Hirshson, *General Patton: A Soldier's Life*, 221.
126. D'Este, *Patton: A Genius for War*, 376.
127. George S. Patton Jr., letter to C. P. Stars, Commander 5th Cavalry Regiment, 22 July 1939, box 25, GSP LOC.
128. General Édouard Réquin cited by Mahnken, *Uncovering Ways of War*, 110–11.
129. Patton, "Address to officers and men of the Second Armored Division," Fort Benning, Georgia, May 17, 1941, box 45, GSP LOC.
130. Corum, *Roots of the Blitzkrieg*, 204.

131. Robert M. Citino, *Quest for Decisive Victory: From Stalemate to Blitzkrieg in Europe, 1899–1940* (Lawrence: University Press of Kansas, 2002), 276.
132. Grant T. Hammond, *The Mind of War: John Boyd and American Security* (Washington, D.C.: Smithsonian Institution Press, 2001), 139–42.
133. "Memorandum for the Chief Control Officer," 16 May 1940, box 53, GSP LOC.
134. Blumenson, *The Patton Papers, Volume I*, 952.
135. Blumenson, *The Patton Papers, Volume II*, 32.
136. Hirshson, *General Patton: A Soldier's Life*, 236.
137. Norris H. Perkins and Michael E. Rogers, *Roll Again Second Armored: Prelude to Fame, 1940–1943* (Surbiton, U.K.: Kristal, 1988), 25.
138. "Orientation on Maneuver," May 1941, 1, folder 12, box 25, GSP LOC.
139. Ibid., 4.
140. Patton, letter to Colonel William C. Crews, 7 March 1941, box 26, GSP LOC.
141. "Orientation on Maneuver," May 1941, 5.
142. Ibid., 6.
143. Patton described how, in Poland, the Germans had executed a double envelopment just as Hannibal's Carthaginians had done against the ill-disciplined Varro and his Romans at Cannae in 216 BCE. Patton told his men, "There is an old Latin saw to the effect that, 'To have a Cannae, you must have a Varro.'" Blumenson, *The Patton Papers, Volume II*, 11.
144. Farago, *Patton: Ordeal and Triumph*, 149.
145. Lande, *I Was with Patton*, 12.
146. Farago, *Patton: Ordeal and Triumph*, 152.
147. Ibid., 151.
148. Perkins and Rogers, *Roll Again Second Armored*, 11.
149. Ibid., 57.
150. Ibid., 66.
151. Farago, *Patton: Ordeal and Triumph*, 164.
152. U.S. Army Field Manual 100–5, *Operations* (Washington, D.C.: Government Printing Office, 22 May 1941), 23.
153. Patton, letter to Floyd GHQ, 1 August 1941, box 26, GSP LOC.
154. Hirshson, *General Patton: A Soldier's Life*, 241.
155. Ibid., 162.
156. See D'Este, *Patton: A Genius for War*, 396–97.
157. Crosswell, *The Chief of Staff*, 117.
158. Stephen Ambrose, *The Supreme Commander: The War Years of Dwight D. Eisenhower* (Jackson: University Press of Mississippi, 1999), 137.
159. Rick Atkinson, *An Army at Dawn: The War in North Africa, 1942–1943* (New York: Henry Holt, 2002), 376.
160. Hirshson, *General Patton: A Soldier's Life*, 311.
161. Atkinson, *An Army at Dawn*, 261.

162. D'Este, *Patton: A Genius for War*, 462.
163. Eisenhower, *Crusade in Europe*, 175.
164. Patton, letter to General James G. Harbord, 15 June 1943, box 27, GSP LOC.
165. Charles Whiting, *First Blood: Battle of Kasserine Pass, 1943* (New York: Steiner and Day, 1984), 240.
166. Patton, letter to Lieutenant General James B. Harbord, 26 April 1943, box 27, GSP LOC. Middle initial B. is *recte* G.
167. See Farago, *Patton: Ordeal and Triumph*, 241.
168. Headquarters II Corps, "Report on Operations Conducted by II United States Army Tunis 15 March–10 April 1943," 10 April 1943, 1, box 45, GSP LOC.
169. Blumenson, *The Patton Papers, Volume II*, 195.
170. See Codman, *Drive*, 106.
171. Montgomery, *The Memoirs of Field Marshal Montgomery*, 164.
172. Carlo D'Este, *Bitter Victory: The Battle for Sicily, 1943* (New York: HarperPerennial, 1988), 110.
173. Andrew J. Birtle, *Sicily: U.S. Army Campaigns of World War II* (Washington, D.C.: U.S. Army Center of Military History, 1993), 7.
174. Ibid.
175. Alexander added, "Both I and my staff felt that this division of tasks might possibly, on this understandable ground, cause some feeling of resentment." Farago, *Patton: Ordeal and Triumph*, 279.
176. Hirshson, *General Patton: A Soldier's Life*, 361.
177. All quotations in paragraph from Patton in Headquarters I Armored Corps, Reinforced, Letter of Instruction, 5 June 1943, folder 23, box 24, GSP LOC. See also Blumenson, *The Patton Papers, Volume II*, 262.
178. Ibid.
179. S. W. C. Pack, *Operation "HUSKY"* (New York: Hippocrene Books, 1977), 151.
180. Blumenson, *The Patton Papers, Volume II*, 290.
181. Patton, letter to Major General Kenyon Joyce, 26 September 1943, box 27, GSP LOC.
182. Clausewitz, *On War*, 99.
183. Yeide, *Fighting Patton*, 208.
184. Eisenhower, *Crusade in Europe*, 175.
185. Yeide, *Fighting Patton*, 214.
186. Gerald Astor, *Terrible Terry Allen, Combat General of World War II—The Life of an American Soldier* (New York: Ballantine Books, 2003), 210–11.
187. Birtle, *Sicily: U.S. Army Campaigns of World War II*, 21.
188. Bradley and Blair, *A General's Life*, 196.
189. Patton, letter to Walter Dillingham, 4 March 1944, box 28, GSP LOC.
190. German letter cited by Bradley, *A Soldier's Story*, 141.

191. Message 243-D Alexander to Patton, 17 August 1943, box 46, GSP LOC.
192. "The Commander-in-Chief's personal representative in the combat area," cited in "Lessons from Sicily," 20 November 1943, 4, box 46, GSP LOC.
193. Hanson, *The Soul of Battle*, 289.
194. Leo Barron, *Patton at the Battle of the Bulge: How the General's Tanks Turned the Tide at Bastogne* (New York: NAL Caliber, 2014), 54.
195. Ike said the change was to allow Patton to plan for Sicily, but Montgomery planned for the invasion while remaining in command. See Eisenhower, *Crusade in Europe*, 154.
196. See Bradley and Blair, *A General's Life*, 159.
197. Ibid., 390.
198. Royle, *Patton: Old Blood and Guts*, 106.
199. Irzyk, *Gasoline to Patton*, 162.
200. Crosswell, *The Chief of Staff*, 258.
201. Irzyk, *Gasoline to Patton*, 122.
202. Farago, *Patton: Ordeal and Triumph*, 641.
203. Steven J. Zaloga, *Lorraine 1944: Patton vs. Manteuffel* (Oxford: Osprey Publishing, 2000), 9.
204. Third U.S. Army, *After Action Report, Third United States Army, 1 August 1944–9 May 1945, Volume I* (Regensburg, Germany: Third Army Headquarters, 15 May 1945), 63.
205. Christopher R. Gabel, *Lorraine Campaign: An Overview, September–December 1944* (Fort Leavenworth, Kans.: U.S. Army Command and General Staff College, February 1985), 10.
206. "The XIX TAC conducted a larger proportion of close-air support missions out of their total combat missions than any other TAC in Europe." Zaloga, *Lorraine 1944*, 29.
207. Gabel, *Lorraine Campaign*, 11.
208. See Third U.S. Army, *After Action Report, Volume I*, 64.
209. Bradley and Blair, *A General's Life*, 336.
210. Robert S. Allen, *Lucky Forward! The History of Patton's Third U.S. Army* (New York: Vanguard Press, 1947), 134.
211. Patton diary, October 22, 1944, box 3, GSP LOC.
212. Rickard, *Patton at Bay*, 148.
213. Bradley and Blair, *A General's Life*, 343.
214. Eisenhower, *Crusade in Europe*, 338.
215. Montgomery, *The Memoirs of Field Marshal Montgomery*, 268–69.
216. Ambrose, *The Supreme Commander*, 549.
217. Bradley and Blair, *A General's Life*, 349.
218. Blumenson, *The Patton Papers, Volume II*, 595.
219. D'Este, *Patton: A Genius for War*, 678.
220. Farago, *Patton: Ordeal and Triumph*, 704.

221. Bradley and Blair, *A General's Life*, 358.
222. Farago, *Patton: Ordeal and Triumph*, 705.
223. Patton diary, December 20, 1944, box 3, GSP LOC.
224. Ibid.
225. See Crosswell, *The Chief of Staff*, 289.
226. Patton in "Conference Between Gen. Patton and Third Army Correspondents, Luxembourg, Luxembourg, Jan. 1, 1945," box 53, GSP, LOC.
227. Danny S. Parker, *Battle of the Bulge: Hitler's Ardennes Offensive, 1944–1945* (Conshohocken, Pa.: Combined Books, 1991), 209.
228. Rickard, *Advance and Destroy*, 107.
229. Harkins, *When the Third Cracked Europe*, 48.
230. Ibid., 50.
231. Ibid., 42.
232. D'Este, *Patton: A Genius for War*, 704.
233. Codman, *Drive*, 258.
234. Ibid., 222–23.
235. Blumenson, *The Patton Papers, Volume II*, 649.
236. Patton diary, March 9, 1945, box 3, GSP LOC.
237. Tedder cited in Patton diary, March 13, 1945, box 3, GSP LOC.
238. D'Este, *Patton: A Genius for War*, 711.
239. Third U.S. Army, *After Action Report, Volume I*, 304.
240. Farago, *Patton: Ordeal and Triumph*, 758.
241. Allen, *Lucky Forward!* 251.
242. Ibid., 254.
243. Barbara E. Boland, "American Blitzkrieg," *Military History Magazine*, 29 June 2002.
244. Allen, *Lucky Forward!* 254.
245. Ibid., 260.
246. Patton diary, March 22, 1945, box 3, GSP LOC.
247. Norman Gelb, *Ike and Monty: Generals at War* (London: Quill, 1995), 405.
248. Patton diary, March 23, 1945, box 3, GSP LOC. Note Patton and/or his typist misspelled "mangificient" in the original.

Chapter 3. Combined Arms
Epigraph: D'Este, *Patton: A Genius for War*, 811.
1. Farago, *Patton: Ordeal and Triumph*, 130.
2. Weigley, *History of the United States Army*, 334.
3. Patton, "Cavalry Work of the Punitive Expedition," *Cavalry Journal* (1917), in *Military Essays and Articles, 1885–1945*, 19.
4. Letter, Leonard Wood to Patton, 3 March 1916, box 25, GSP LOC.
5. Hofmann and Starry, *Camp Colt to Desert Storm*, 93.
6. Ibid., 94–95.

7. J. F. C. Fuller, *Tanks in the Great War* (London: Battery Press, 1920), 277.
8. Ibid.
9. Ibid., 277–78.
10. Headquarters commandant Robert Bacon, letter of endorsement, 3 October 1917, box 25, GSP LOC.
11. Fuller, *Tanks in the Great War*, 58–59.
12. Patrick Wright, *Tank* (New York: Viking Press, 2002), 68.
13. Gerard Chailand, ed., *The Art of War in World History* (Los Angeles: University of California Press, 1994), 922–23.
14. John Keegan, *The First World War* (London: Vintage, 2000), 369.
15. Ibid., 370.
16. Ibid.
17. Wilson, *Treat 'Em Rough!* 4.
18. See G. S. Patton Jr., "Light Tanks," 12 December 1917, in *Military Essays and Articles, 1885–1945*, 85–114. See also Blumenson, *The Patton Papers, Volume I*, 451.
19. Patton, "Light Tanks."
20. Blumenson, *The Patton Papers, Volume I*, 454.
21. Patton, "Light Tanks."
22. Blumenson, *The Patton Papers, Volume I*, 476.
23. Ibid.
24. Brigadier General F. C. Marshall, 165th Field Artillery Brigade, Camp Travis, Texas, letter to Patton, 17 March 1918, box 25, GSP LOC.
25. Wilson, *Treat 'Em Rough!* 36.
26. Blumenson, *The Patton Papers, Volume I*, 520.
27. Patton, "Status of Development on Tank Radio—May 1, 1918," box 54, GSP LOC.
28. Johnson, *Fast Tanks and Heavy Bombers*, 36.
29. D'Este, *Patton: A Genius for War*, 224.
30. Blumenson, *The Patton Papers, Volume I*, 554.
31. Ibid.
32. Ibid., 581.
33. D'Este wrote the attack "sowed the seeds of what was to become Patton's trademark employment of armor in World War II—the deep penetration. . . . He believed his tanks could have slashed into the German rear if only McClure's force had been larger." D'Este, *Patton: A Genius for War*, 245.
34. Yeide, *Fighting Patton*, 29.
35. Patton thought Craig seemed willing to depart from "most preconceived notions as to the proper use of tanks." See Blumenson, *The Patton Papers, Volume I*, 604.
36. Ibid.
37. Colonels E. E. Mitchell and G. S. Patton, "Notes on Tanks," 24 January 1919, box 54, GSP LOC.

38. Ibid.
39. Ibid., 642.
40. Patton also said, "Tanks exist to help infantry. They cannot help a mile in front any more than a mile behind." Ibid., 648.
41. George S. Patton Jr., "Tanks in Future Wars," *Cavalry Journal* (May 1920), in *Military Essays and Articles, 1885–1945*, 345.
42. Blumenson, *The Patton Papers, Volume I*, 654.
43. Ibid., 660.
44. "In between these lines, he said, was where we must make our first essay in exploitation." Ibid., 661.
45. Ibid., 660.
46. Jonathan M. House, *Toward Combined Arms Warfare: A Survey of 20th-Century Tactics, Doctrine, and Organization* (Fort Leavenworth, Kans.: U.S. Army Command and General Staff College, 1984), 61.
47. Fuller, *Tanks in the Great War*, 311.
48. Ibid., 313. Fuller envisioned "land ports" with underground defenses, fleets of aircraft attacking civilian population centers, and fleets of tanks battling each other.
49. Robert H. Larson, *The British Army and the Theory of Armored Warfare, 1918–1940* (Newark: University of Delaware Press, 1984), 93.
50. Fuller, *Tanks in the Great War*, 309–10.
51. Farago, *Patton: Ordeal and Triumph*, 97.
52. Hirshson, *General Patton: A Soldier's Life*, 151.
53. Blumenson, *The Patton Papers, Volume I*, 728.
54. Patton diary, May 9, 1945, box 3, GSP LOC.
55. Blumenson, *The Patton Papers, Volume I*, 729.
56. Hirshson, *General Patton: A Soldier's Life*, 151.
57. D'Este, *Patton: A Genius for War*, 296.
58. Patton, "Tanks in Future Wars."
59. Ibid., 345.
60. Finlayson, *An Uncertain Trumpet*, 63.
61. Johnson, *Fast Tanks and Heavy Bombers*, 26.
62. Ibid., 72.
63. Weigley, *History of the United States Army*, 599.
64. Finlayson, *An Uncertain Trumpet*, 31.
65. Odom, *After the Trenches*, 51.
66. For these book citations see Nye, *The Patton Mind*, 49–60.
67. George S. Patton Jr., "Comments on 'Cavalry Tanks'," *Cavalry Journal* (July 1921), in *Military Essays and Articles, 1885–1945*, 343.
68. George S. Patton Jr., "What the War Did for Cavalry," *Cavalry Journal* (April 1922), in *Military Essays and Articles, 1885–1945*, 343.
69. Blumenson, *The Patton Papers, Volume II*, 96–97.

70. George S. Patton Jr., "Armored Cars with Cavalry," *Cavalry Journal* (January 1924), in *Military Essays and Articles, 1885–1945*, 11–15. Also Blumenson, *The Patton Papers, Volume I*, 780.
71. Blumenson, *The Patton Papers, Volume I*, 781.
72. *Field Service Regulations 1923*, 11. See also Hofmann and Starry, *Camp Colt to Desert Storm*, 92–93.
73. Brigadier General Samuel D. Rockenbach, Office of the Commandant, HQ Tank School, letter to Patton, 5 February 1924, box 25, GSP LOC.
74. Patton called for heavy twenty-ton tanks to create a breakthrough and for speedy six- to ten-ton light tanks to exploit it. See Robert M. Citino, *Armored Forces: History and Sourcebook* (Westport, Conn.: Greenwood Press, 1994), 52.
75. Citino, *Quest for Decisive Victory*, 194.
76. See Mahnken, *Uncovering Ways of War*, 95.
77. Ibid., 96.
78. Johnson, *Fast Tanks and Heavy Bombers*, 73.
79. Bradley and Blair, *A General's Life*, 56.
80. Johnson, *Fast Tanks and Heavy Bombers*, 125.
81. John B. Wilson, *Maneuver and Firepower: The Evolution of Divisions and Separate Brigades* (Washington, D.C.: U.S. Army Center of Military History, 1998), 112.
82. Douglas Waller, *A Question of Loyalty: Gen. Billy Mitchell and the Court-Martial That Gripped the Nation* (New York: HarperCollins, 2004), 20.
83. The Mark C became the model adopted by the Japanese during World War II. Chris Ellis and Peter Chamberlain, *Fighting Vehicles* (London: Hamlyn, 1972), 83.
84. Patton found its recommendations too passive and wrote, "This is a poor paper." D'Este, *Patton: A Genius for War*, 341.
85. Blumenson, *The Patton Papers, Volume I*, 814.
86. Hofmann and Starry, *Camp Colt to Desert Storm*, 107.
87. Johnson, *Fast Tanks and Heavy Bombers*, 97.
88. Timothy K. Nenninger, "Organizational Milestones," in Hofmann and Starry, *Camp Colt to Desert Storm*, 40.
89. Patton, notation on Chief of Cavalry Office, "Procurement of one Christie Chassis modified as an Armored Car," February 19, 1929, box 53, GSP LOC.
90. Patton in "Special characteristics of track and wheel-type vehicles (Christie)," point 5, notebook, box 53, GSP LOC.
91. Patton, letter to Major E. C. McGuire, Cavalry School, May 20, 1929, box 53, GSP LOC.
92. See George A. Higgins, "The Operational Tenets of Generals Heinz Guderian and George S. Patton, Jr.," (master's thesis, School of Advanced Military Studies, U.S. Army Command and General Staff College, 1985).
93. General Fox Connor, HQ I Corps, letter to Patton, 3 February 1931, box 25, GSP LOC.

94. Colonel John S. Wood, note to Patton, 1932, box 25, GSP LOC.
95. Showalter, *Patton and Rommel*, 119.
96. George S. Patton Jr. and C. C. Benson, "Mechanization and Cavalry," *Cavalry Journal* (1930), in *Military Essays and Articles, 1885–1945*, 118.
97. Ibid.
98. George S. Patton Jr., "The Effect of Weapons on War," *Cavalry Journal* (November 1930), in *Military Essays and Articles, 1885–1945*, 42.
99. Patton, "Success in War."
100. Patton letter to Winston W. Ehrgett, 15 October 1930, box 25, GSP LOC.
101. See, for example, Hofmann and Starry, *Camp Colt to Desert Storm*, 112.
102. Johnson, *Fast Tanks and Heavy Bombers*, 135.
103. Hirshson, *General Patton: A Soldier's Life*, 195.
104. See George S. Patton Jr., "The Probable Characteristics of the Next War and the Organization, Tactics, and Equipment Necessary to Meet Them," dissertation, Army War College, February 29, 1932, in *Military Essays and Articles, 1885–1945*, 170.
105. Hofmann and Starry, *Camp Colt to Desert Storm*, 128.
106. Mahnken, *Uncovering Ways of War*, 103–4.
107. Ibid., 103. The punch in each of these powerful units was contained in its combination of a tank brigade, a motorized infantry brigade, and a motorized artillery regiment. Each of these was augmented with a reconnaissance battalion, an antitank battalion, an engineer company, and signal, service and supply units. Rigorous field tests dictated modifications to this organization.
108. Ibid., 105.
109. Johnson, *Fast Tanks and Heavy Bombers*, 120.
110. Hofmann and Starry, *Camp Colt to Desert Storm*, 122.
111. Ibid., 125.
112. Ibid.
113. The Military Intelligence Division published 170 *Tentative Lessons Bulletins* on Poland in the next two years. This one was by Lieutenant Colonel Sumner Waite, cited by Mahnken, *Uncovering Ways of War*, 108.
114. Robert M. Kennedy, *The German Campaign in Poland (1939)* (Washington, D.C.: Government Printing Office, 1988), 92.
115. See Farago, *Patton: Ordeal and Triumph*, 136.
116. John Mosier, *The Blitzkrieg Myth: How Hitler and the Allies Misread the Strategic Realities of World War II* (New York: HarperCollins, 2003), 72.
117. Mahnken, *Uncovering Ways of War*, 107.
118. Kennedy, *The German Campaign in Poland*, 131.
119. Mosier, *The Blitzkrieg Myth*, 74.
120. The Polish *Podolska* and *Wielkopolska* cavalry brigades were especially successful against the German 24th and 30th Infantry Divisions west of Warsaw. "And indeed the Germans themselves used cavalry units throughout the war,

beginning with September 1939, when a cavalry brigade was deployed out of East Prussia." Ibid., 74.
121. Kennedy, *The German Campaign in Poland*, 130.
122. Hofmann and Starry, "Army Doctrine and the Christie Tank," in *Camp Colt to Desert Storm*, 127.
123. "The manual failed to recognize that advances in ground and air mobility had fundamentally changed doctrine by creating new arms, redefining the combined arms team, and significantly altering the tempo and range of battlefield maneuver." Odom, *After the Trenches*, 134.
124. In Odom's words, "The maneuver plan was the *infantry* plan of maneuver, artillery's first task was to protect *infantry* units, and suppression of enemy artillery was indispensable for the success of the *infantry* attack. The manual even referred to division aircraft as *infantry* airplanes. . . . Indeed, synchronizing infantry fires and maneuver with artillery fire support continued to define combined arms operations." Ibid., 136.
125. Ibid., 142.
126. See Peter McCarthy and Mike Syron, *Panzerkrieg: The Rise and Fall of Hitler's Tank Divisions* (New York: Carroll and Graf, 2002), 71.
127. Of the 2,600 German tanks, 525 were light Mark Is that only carried machine guns, and 955 were Mark IIs armed with small 20-mm main guns. Their only quality tanks were 350 Mark IIIs with 37-mm guns and 280 Mark IVs and 228 Czech T-38s, both with low-velocity 75-mm guns. The French, on the other hand, had 300 Char B-1s that carried both a 47-mm gun in the turret and a 75-mm gun in the main body under 55-mm–thick armor. They also had 250 superb Somua tanks carrying 47-mm guns under 55mm of armor. While these tanks far outclassed the German vehicles, most of the French armor consisted of more than four thousand light tanks, many of World War I vintage, but even these matched up fairly well against light German vehicles when used in the defense. The British had 450 tanks in France, including nearly 225 modern Cruisers and Matildas with 40-mm guns and 75mm of armor plating. See ibid., 71–100.
128. "The French Army had neglected higher formation staff training for tank officers such as was needed for handling several divisions at once. This was in keeping with their belief that tanks should function either as infantry support or in the traditional cavalry roles." Ibid.,72.
129. Eugenia Kiesling, *Arming Against Hitler: France and the Limits of Military Planning* (Lawrence: University Press of Kansas, 1996), 157.
130. Mahnken, *Uncovering Ways of War*, 110–11.
131. This comparison of Patton and Guderian in doctrine comes from Higgins, "The Operational Tenets of Heinz Guderian and George S. Patton, Jr.," 182–87.
132. Nenninger, "Organizational Milestones," in Hofmann and Starry, *Camp Colt to Desert Storm*, 59.

133. Kent Roberts Greenfield, Robert R. Palmer, and Bell I. Wiley, *United States Army in World War 2: The Army Ground Forces—The Organization of Ground Combat Troops* (Washington, D.C.: U.S. Army Center of Military History, 1947), 325.
134. Headquarters 2nd Armored Division, General Orders No. 4, August 19, 1940, box 48, GSP LOC.
135. Johnson, *Fast Tanks and Heavy Bombers*, 222.
136. This meant about 287 light tanks and 120 medium tanks. See Christopher R. Gabel, "World War II Operations in Europe," in Hofmann and Starry, *Camp Colt to Desert Storm*, 146.
137. "As initially organized these divisions consisted of five principle elements: (1) command, (2) reconnaissance, (3) striking, (4) support, and (5) service." James A. Sawicki, *Tank Battalions of the U.S. Army* (Dumfries, Va.: Wyvern Publications, 1983), 16.
138. As Mahnken noted, "Maneuvers indicated that the initial organization lacked sufficient infantry. As a result, in 1938–1939 the infantry element of the Panzer division grew to four battalions." Mahnken, *Uncovering Ways of War*, 112.
139. Christopher R. Gabel, *The U.S. Army GHQ Maneuvers of 1941* (Fort Leavenworth, Kans.: U.S. Army Center for Military Studies, 1991), 25.
140. Hirshson, *General Patton: A Soldier's Life*, 233.
141. A letter from Patton to the corps commander began, "If and when we get real tanks." Patton, letter to Brigadier General Scott, 13 March 1941, box 26, GSP LOC.
142. Patton, letter to James B. Talvin, 6 February 1941, box 26, GSP LOC.
143. Blumenson, *The Patton Papers, Volume II*, 20.
144. Ibid., 36.
145. Patton, letter to Lieutenant Colonel W. C. Crane, GHQ Army War College, 25 April 1941, box 26, GSP LOC.
146. Patton, letter to Major General Jay L. Benedict, 25 July 1941, box 26, GSP LOC.
147. Ibid.
148. U.S. Army Field Manual 100–5, *Operations* (1941), 5.
149. Johnson, *Fast Tanks and Heavy Bombers*, 147.
150. Ibid.
151. The doctrine noted that when "confronted by an organized defensive position . . . the limited firepower of Infantry must be adequately reinforced by the support of artillery, tanks, combat aviation, and other arms." U.S. Army Field Manual 100–5, *Operations* (1941), 5.
152. Ibid., 279.
153. Patton, "Address to the Officers and Men of the Second Armored Division," Fort Benning, Georgia, May 17, 1943, 4, box 45, GSP LOC.
154. Ibid.
155. Patton, untitled draft, June 1941, folder 13, box 45, GSP LOC.

156. "A Lecture to the Officers of the 2nd Armored Division in Preparation for the Louisiana Maneuvers," August 5, 1931, box 45, GSP LOC.
157. Gabel, *The U.S. Army GHQ Maneuvers of 1941*, 49.
158. Patton, letter to Floyd at GHQ, 1 August 1941, box 26, GSP LOC. See also Blumenson, *The Patton Papers, Volume II*, 38.
159. Hirshson, *General Patton: A Soldier's Life*, 243.
160. "Address to the Officers and Men of the Second Armored Division."
161. Blumenson, *The Patton Papers, Volume II*, 44.
162. Patton, letter to McNair, 27 May 1941, box 26, GSP LOC.
163. George S. Patton Jr., "Notes on Tactics and Technique of Desert Warfare," 1942, in *Military Essays and Articles, 1885–1945*, 199.
164. Ibid.
165. Patton, untitled speech, May 9, 1942, folder 15, box 45, GSP LOC.
166. D'Este, *Patton: A Genius for War*, 410.
167. Blumenson, *The Patton Papers, Volume II*, 68.
168. Vincent Jones, *Operation Torch: Anglo-American Invasion of North Africa* (New York: Ballantine Books, 1972), 32.
169. Hirshson, *General Patton: A Soldier's Life*, 282.
170. Norman Gelb noted that Truscott was fearful of fratricide and that "he therefore declined to call for as much naval firepower support as could have been provided." Gelb, *Ike and Monty*, 233.
171. Patton, letter to Brigadier General F. C. Parks, 23 November 1942, box 26, GSP LOC.
172. Wilson, *Maneuver and Firepower*, 198.
173. Orr Kelly, *Meeting the Fox: The Allied Invasion of Africa, from Operation Torch to Kasserine Pass to Victory in Tunisia* (Hoboken, N.J.: Wiley, 2002), 45.
174. Martin Blumenson, *Kasserine Pass* (Boston: Houghton Mifflin, 1966), 51.
175. Hirshson, *General Patton: A Soldier's Life*, 308.
176. Blumenson, *Kasserine Pass*, 192.
177. Astor, *Terrible Terry Allen*, 164.
178. Eisenhower's orders as noted in Headquarters II Corps, "Report on Operation Conducted by II Corps United States Army, Tunisia, 15 March–10 April 1943," 3, box 45, GSP LOC. See also Farago, *Patton: Ordeal and Triumph*, 244.
179. John D'Arcy-Dawson, *Tunisian Battle* (London: MacDonald, 1944), 178.
180. Patton, letter to Major General Charles Herron, 21 April 1943, box 27, GSP LOC.
181. Astor, *Terrible Terry Allen*, 168.
182. Patton, "Notes on Combat," May 1943, folder 17, box 48, GSP LOC.
183. Headquarters II Corps, "Report on Operation Conducted by II Corps United States Army 15 March–10 April 1943."
184. Ibid., 169.
185. Blumenson, *The Patton Papers, Volume II*, 206.

186. Daniel R. Mortensen, *A Pattern for Joint Operations: World War II Close Air Support, North Africa* (Washington, D.C.: U.S. Army Center of Military History, 1993), 51.
187. Ibid., 362.
188. Bradley and Blair, *A General's Life*, 178.
189. Wedemeyer, *Wedemeyer Reports!* 221.
190. Hirshson, *General Patton: A Soldier's Life*, 355.
191. Blumenson, *The Patton Papers, Volume II*, 267.
192. "Their mobility was preserved as much as possible in order to facilitate prompt committal either to bolster the landing operation or to exploit the success achieved during that phase." Birtle, *Sicily: U.S. Army Campaigns of World War II*, 6.
193. See Farago, *Patton: Ordeal and Triumph*, 300.
194. Blumenson, *The Patton Papers, Volume II*, 293–94.
195. He added, "British observers were constantly astonished how quickly Americans got artillery pieces into position to fire. The self-propelled mounts enabled the Americans to start firing in minutes when, in the same conditions, the British would require hours." See Blumenson, *The Patton Papers, Volume II*, 286.
196. Ibid., 295–96.
197. He added, "Such methods assure victory and reduce losses, but it takes fine leadership to insure execution. General Keyes provided perfect leadership and great drive. The praise should be his." Ibid., 296–97.
198. Translation of captured German document, 3 August 1945, box 46, GSP LOC.
199. Blumenson, *The Patton Papers, Volume II*, 304.
200. "As such it had plenty to do: defending Palermo from an Italian Navy raid, giving gunfire support to Patton as he advanced along the coast, providing amphibious craft for 'leap-frog' landings, and ferry duty for heavy artillery, supplies and vehicles to relieve congestion on the coastal road." Samuel Eliot Morison, *The Two-Ocean War: A Short History of the United States Navy in the Second World War* (New York: Ballantine Books, 1963), 220.
201. Blumenson, *The Patton Papers, Volume II*, 314.
202. Farago, *Patton: Ordeal and Triumph*, 337.
203. Allied Force Headquarters, Lessons from the Sicilian Campaign, 20 November 1943, 11, box 46, GSP LOC.
204. Ibid., 12.
205. Headquarters VIII Corps, Memorandum for General Patton, 5 April 1944, 11, box 46, GSP LOC.
206. David N. Spires, *Patton's Air Force: Forging a Legendary Air-Ground Team* (Washington, D.C.: Smithsonian Institution Press, 2002), 27.

207. Bradford J. Shwedo, *XIX TAC and Ultra: Patton's Force Enhancers in the 1944 Campaign in France* (Maxwell Air Force Base, Ala.: Air University Press, 2001), 9.
208. Ibid.
209. Ibid., 10.
210. Spires, *Patton's Air Force*, 45.
211. Ibid., 142–43.
212. "Conference Between General Patton, General Weyland and Third Army Correspondents, December 9, 1944, Nancy, France," box 53, GSP LOC.
213. Hirshson, *General Patton: A Soldier's Life*, 439.
214. Headquarters VIII Corps, Memorandum for General Patton, 5 April 1944, 11, box 46, GSP LOC.
215. Ibid.
216. "On 16 April, a training memorandum, 'Use of Tanks in Support of Infantry,' written by the Army Commander, was issued." Third U.S. Army, *After Action Report, Volume I*, 3.
217. Patton diary, May 8, 1944, box 3, GSP LOC.
218. Blumenson, *The Patton Papers, Volume II*, 436.
219. Headquarters U.S. Third Army, "Tactical Use of Separate Tank Battalions," 15 April 1944, 2, box 46. GSP LOC.
220. Patton, *War as I Knew It*, 410.
221. Third U.S. Army, *After Action Report, Volume I*, 6.
222. Blumenson, *The Patton Papers, Volume II*, 455.
223. For the 1928, 1940, and 1943 organizations, see Wilson, *Maneuver and Firepower*, 124, 151, 186.
224. See George S. Patton Jr., "Notes on Combat Armored Divisions," 1944, www.pattonhq.com/textfiles/divnotes.html.
225. See Will Lang, "Colonel Abe," *Life Magazine*, 23 April 1945.
226. Third U.S. Army, *After Action Report, Volume I*, 4.
227. Patton diary, May 9, 1944, box 3, GSP LOC.
228. XX Corps, *XX Corps, Its History and Service in World War II* (Osaka, Japan: XX Corps Association, 1946), 53.
229. Ibid., 50.
230. Bradley and Blair, *A General's Life*, 317.
231. Zaloga, *Lorraine 1944*, 37.
232. Kenneth A. Koyen, *The Fourth Armored Division: From the Beach to Bavaria* (Munich, Germany: Herden Druck, 1946), 57.
233. Hirshson, *General Patton: A Soldier's Life*, 578.
234. George F. Hofmann, *The Super Sixth: History of the 6th Armored Division in World War II and Its Post-war Association* (Louisville, Ky.: The 6th Armored Division Association, 1975), 226.

235. Dated November 21, among German articles captured on 5 December. Ibid., 256.
236. Chandler, *The Military Maxims of Napoleon*, 74.

Chapter 4. Command and Control
Epigraph: Atkinson, *An Army at Dawn*, 403.
1. *Field Service Regulations 1923*, 11.
2. Patton, "Cavalry Work of the Punitive Expedition," 20.
3. Ibid., 21.
4. Patton, "Light Tanks," 104. Also, Blumenson, *The Patton Papers, Volume I*, 455.
5. Blumenson, *The Patton Papers, Volume I*, 604.
6. Showalter, *Patton and Rommel*, 94.
7. George S. Patton Jr., "The Obligations of Being an Officer," October 1, 1919, in *Military Essays and Articles, 1885–1945*, 220.
8. Patton, "Report of Personal Experiences in the Tank Corps," 261.
9. D'Este, *Patton: A Genius for War*, 234.
10. Wilson, *Treat 'Em Rough!* 109.
11. Ibid., 43.
12. Ibid., 118.
13. See the impact of Scharnhorst and Moltke regarding subordinate initiative. Walter Goerlitz, *History of the German General Staff, 1657–1945* (New York: Praeger, 1956), 75.
14. Patton, *War as I Knew It*, 357.
15. Patton diary, January 20, 1943, box 2, GSP LOC.
16. Headquarters I Armored Corps, "Notes on Combat," 21 April 1943, box 46, GSP LOC.
17. Headquarters Third United States Army, "Letter of Instruction No. 3," 20 May 1944, box 46, GSP LOC.
18. *Field Service Regulations 1923*, 7.
19. Ibid., 11.
20. Barbara Tuchman, *Stillwell and the American Experience in China, 1911–1945* (New York: MacMillan, 1971), 91.
21. Ibid., 298.
22. Hirshson, *General Patton: A Soldier's Life*, 152.
23. D'Este, *Patton: A Genius for War*, 296.
24. Ibid., 332–33.
25. George S. Patton Jr., "The Secret of Victory," 1926, in *Military Essays and Articles, 1885–1945*, 305.
26. Johnson, *Fast Tanks and Heavy Bombers*, 9.
27. Mahnken, *Uncovering Ways of War*, 95–96.
28. "Seeckt's great contribution to modern military thought was that, at the head of a 'disarmed' military that was little more than a glorified police force, he

continued to think in terms of a 'war of movement' (*Bewegungskrieg*)." Citino, *Quest for Decisive Victory*, 195.
29. Blumenson, *The Patton Papers, Volume I*, 801–2.
30. Headquarters I Armored Corps, "Notes on Combat."
31. Atkinson, *An Army at Dawn*,136.
32. Clausewitz, *On War*, 117.
33. George S. Patton Jr., "Why Men Fight," 1927, in *Military Essays and Articles, 1885–1945*, 406.
34. Ibid. See also Blumenson, *The Patton Papers, Volume I*, 817.
35. Bradley and Blair, *A General's Life*, 66.
36. D'Este, *Patton: A Genius for War*, 467.
37. "The Leavenworth system, imposing conformity and standardization, shaped several generations of graduates into a homogeneous pattern." Of the 657 Army War College graduates between 1934 and 1940, 436 made general. Gole, *The Road to Rainbow*, 124.
38. See Odom, *After the Trenches*, 120.
39. See Kiesling, *Arming Against Hitler*, 140–41.
40. "A key tenet of methodical battle was centralized decision making to ensure perfectly sequenced commitment of units." Odom, *After the Trenches*, 122.
41. Corum, *Roots of the Blitzkrieg*, 49.
42. U.S. Army (War Department), *Infantry Drill Regulations (Provisional) 1919* (Washington, D.C.: Government Printing Office, 1919), 93.
43. U.S. Army Field Manual 100–15, 6.
44. Patton, "The Probable Characteristics of the Next War," 175.
45. Ibid., 176.
46. Patton, "Mechanized Forces,"176.
47. Nye, *The Patton Mind*, 85–86.
48. Clausewitz, *On War*, 117.
49. Patton, "Success in War," 336.
50. Blumenson, *The Patton Papers, Volume I*, 908.
51. Ibid.
52. Ibid., 752.
53. Ibid., 753.
54. Mahnken, *Uncovering Ways of War*, 108.
55. George S. Patton Jr., "Training Memoranda to his Regiment," *Cavalry Journal* (July-August 1940), in *Military Essays and Articles, 1885–1945*, 362.
56. Patton, "Memorandum for the Chief Control Officer," 16 May 1940, box 53, GSP LOC.
57. Gabel, *The U.S. Army GHQ Maneuvers of 1941*, 64.
58. Ibid.
59. Ibid., 54. See also Farago, *Patton: Ordeal and Triumph*, 160.
60. Hirshson, *General Patton: A Soldier's Life*, 241.

61. Ibid., 162.
62. Patton, letter to Crews.
63. U.S. Army Field Manual 100-5, *Operations* (1941), 23–24.
64. Ibid.
65. Gabel wrote, "The fundamental goal was to make the maneuvers as much like real war as possible in order to test and train under near battle conditions." Gabel, *The U.S. Army GHQ Maneuvers of 1941*, 46.
66. "The section of the Umpire Manual dealing with tank-antitank combat raised even deeper concerns about realism and fairness. . . . Although antitank proponents had some valid objections to the Umpire Manual, armor advocates had even better reason to complain." Ibid., 48.
67. See Christopher Gabel, "Seek, Strike, and Destroy: U.S. Army Tank Destroyer Doctrine in World War II," Leavenworth Papers, No. 12 (Fort Leavenworth, Kans.: Combat Studies Institute, 1985), 3–6, 10, 14.
68. Farago, *Patton: Ordeal and Triumph,*164.
69. Ibid.
70. Hirshson, *General Patton: A Soldier's Life*, 242.
71. D'Este, *Patton: A Genius for War*, 377.
72. Von Seeckt's "Observations of the Chief of the Army: Direction of the German Army Training in 1925," quoted by Patton, letter to Crews.
73. Hans von Seeckt, "Observations by the Chief of the Army Command, Colonel-General von Seeckt, on Inspection of Maneuvers in the years from 1920 to 1926," October 12, 1928, translation, box 54, GSP LOC.
74. Patton, "Address to Officers and Men of the Second Armored Division."
75. Blumenson, *The Patton Papers, Volume II*, 37.
76. Ibid.
77. Patton, "Draft Address," June 5, 1941, folder 13, box 45, GSP LOC.
78. Ibid. See also Blumenson, *The Patton Papers, Volume II*, 39–40.
79. Blumenson, *The Patton Papers, Volume II*, 61.
80. William B. Breuer, *Operation Torch: The Allied Gamble to Invade North Africa* (New York: St. Martin's Press, 1985), 34.
81. Blumenson, *The Patton Papers, Volume II*, 94–95.
82. Atkinson, *An Army at Dawn*, 145.
83. Blumenson, *The Patton Papers, Volume II*, 98.
84. Ibid., 648.
85. George S. Patton Jr., "War as She Is," 1919, in *Military Essays and Articles, 1885–1945*, 377–78.
86. See Gladwell, *Blink*, 44.
87. "After World War II, Omar Bradley and some of the original members of the II Corps staff perpetuated the myth that Patton was a mediocre commander, ill served by a poor staff that more often than not failed to do its job—a view,

colored by deep prejudices against Patton, that was neither balanced nor accurate." D'Este, *Patton: A Genius for War*, 420–21.
88. Ibid., 422. It is interesting that Ike never liked Gay, thought he "does not impress others sufficiently," and often urged Patton to replace him. See Patton diary, February 11, 1944, box 3, GSP LOC.
89. Blumenson, *The Patton Papers, Volume II*, 347.
90. Ibid., 262.
91. Patton, *War as I Knew It*, 349.
92. Blumenson, *The Patton Papers, Volume II*, 653.
93. Patton, *War as I Knew It*, 255.
94. Patton, undated draft "Letter of Instruction," 1, box 46, GSP LOC. See also Blumenson, *The Patton Papers, Volume II*, 261.
95. Hirshson, *General Patton: A Soldier's Life*, 120.
96. Patton, for example, told Ike the plans for Torch were too complicated. Patton diary, August 14, 1942, box 2, GSP LOC.
97. Patton, letter to Brigadier General Harold B. Fiske, September 30, 1927, box 53, GSP LOC.
98. Patton, *War as I Knew It*, 397.
99. Ibid., 399.
100. Ibid., 401.
101. Hirshson, *General Patton: A Soldier's Life*, 560.
102. Ibid.
103. Third U.S. Army, *After Action Report, Volume I*, 164.
104. Blumenson, *The Patton Papers, Volume II*, 637.
105. D'Este, *Patton: A Genius for War*, 708.
106. Bradley and Blair, *A General's Life*, 300.
107. O. L. Spaulding Jr., "Studies in Applied History," undated, scrapbook, box 53, GSP LOC.
108. Blumenson, *The Patton Papers, Volume II*, 272.
109. D'Este, *Patton: A Genius for War*, 499.
110. Lande, *I Was with Patton*, 292.
111. Patton diary, September 2, 1943, box 3, GSP LOC. See also Blumenson, *The Patton Papers, Volume II*, 345.
112. Bradley and Blair, *A General's Life*, 317.
113. Atkinson, *An Army at Dawn*, 138.
114. The Army history noted, "By 1700 on D-Day 39% of the troops had been landed, but only 16% of vehicles and 1.1% of supplies were ashore." Charles R. Anderson, *Algeria-French Morocco* (Washington, D.C.: U.S. Army Center of Military History, 1993), 18.
115. Hirshson, *General Patton: A Soldier's Life*, 335.
116. Eisenhower, *Crusade in Europe*, 148–49.
117. Blumenson, *Patton: The Man Behind the Legend*, 183.

118. Bradley, *A Soldier's Story*, 68.
119. Farago, *Patton: Ordeal and Triumph*, 266.
120. Ibid., 473.
121. Brenton G. Wallace, *Patton and His Third Army* (Mechanicsburg, Pa.: Stackpole Books, 1946), 16–17.
122. See Crosswell, *The Chief of Staff*, 196. Patton often refers to Bedell as "Beedle" in his writings.
123. Patton diary, October 27, 1943, box 3, GSP LOC. See also Blumenson, *The Patton Papers, Volume II*, 366.
124. Patton diary, October 27, 1943.
125. Patton diary, May 31, 1944, box 3, GSP LOC.
126. Ibid., 6.
127. Ibid., 40.
128. Rickard, *Patton at Bay*, 85.
129. 12th Army Group G-4 Section, "Report of Operations (Final After Action Report)," 31, box 1314, records group 407, National Archives and Records Administration II (hereafter RG 407, NARA II).
130. Ibid.
131. D'Este, *Patton: A Genius for War*, 651.
132. Third U.S. Army, *After Action Report, Volume I*, 100.
133. Rickard, *Patton at Bay*, 126.
134. Only 4,559,000 ration accessory convenience kits of tobacco were received out of the 8,030,000 requested in September. Third U.S. Army, *After Action Report, Volume I*, 99.
135. Gabel, *Lorraine Campaign*, 22.
136. Ibid.
137. Ibid., 23.
138. Rickard, *Patton at Bay*, 158.
139. Patton diary, April 7, 1944, box 3, GSP LOC.
140. Ibid.
141. Ibid. See also Hirshson, *General Patton: A Soldier's Life*, 457.
142. Allen, *Lucky Forward!* 145.
143. Third U.S. Army, *After Action Report, Volume I*, 144.
144. D'Este, *Patton: A Genius for War*, 665.
145. Gabel, *Lorraine Campaign*, 30.
146. Patton diary, November 29, 1944, box 3, GSP LOC.
147. Atkinson, *An Army at Dawn*, 115.
148. Ibid.
149. See Breuer, *Operation Torch*, 202.
150. Blumenson, *The Patton Papers, Volume II*, 282.
151. Astor, *Terrible Terry Allen*, 196.
152. Patton diary, July 11, 1943, box 3, GSP LOC.

153. Birtle, *Sicily: U.S. Army Campaigns of World War II*, 14.
154. Hirshson, *General Patton: A Soldier's Life*, 355.
155. D'Este, *Bitter Victory*, 173.
156. Blumenson, *The Patton Papers, Volume II*, 267.
157. Clay Blair, *Ridgway's Paratroopers: The American Airborne in World War II* (Annapolis, Md.: Naval Institute Press, 1985), 75.
158. Ibid.
159. Blumenson, *The Patton Papers, Volume II*, 281.
160. Hirshson, *General Patton: A Soldier's Life*, 362.
161. Captain S. W. C. Pack added, "Fire was not to be opened above 6,000 feet when night fighters were operating over the convoys. It all sounds so logical but it is questionable whether compliance was practicable in the heat of battle." S. W. C. Pack, *The Invasion of North Africa, 1942* (New York: Scribner, 1979), 69.
162. Harry C. Butcher, *My Three Years with Eisenhower: The Personal Diary of Captain Harry C. Butcher, USNR, Naval Aide to General Eisenhower, 1942 to 1945* (New York: Simon and Schuster, 1946), 360.
163. Patton diary, July 12, 1943, box 3, GSP LOC.
164. Bradley added, "That loss of faith would have a distinct bearing on my own future, so the meeting was a turning point in my life as well as Patton's." Bradley and Blair, *A General's Life*, 184.
165. Butcher, *My Three Years with Eisenhower*, 352–56.
166. D'Este, *Bitter Victory*, 319.
167. Bradley and Blair, *A General's Life*, 185 (note).
168. Butcher, *My Three Years with Eisenhower*, 357.
169. Patton diary, July 12, 1943.
170. Gelb, *Ike and Monty*, 403.
171. Bradley and Blair, *A General's Life*, 189.
172. Atkinson, *An Army at Dawn*, 332.
173. Ibid., 347.
174. Whiting, *First Blood*, 196.
175. Bradley and Blair, *A General's Life*, 167.
176. D'Este, *Bitter Victory*, 546.
177. Charles Anderson, *Tunisia* (Washington, D.C.: U.S. Army Center of Military History, 1993), 27.
178. Hirshson, *General Patton: A Soldier's Life*, 415.
179. Montgomery, *The Memoirs of Field Marshal Montgomery*, 254.
180. Ibid., 75–76.
181. See Bernard L. Montgomery, "Some Brief Notes for Senior Officers on the Conduct of Battle," December 1942, box 57, GSP LOC.
182. Essame, *Patton, as Military Commander*, 216–17. See also Koch, *G-2: Intelligence for Patton*, 80, on the monitoring of the German buildup for the Ardennes.

183. Patton diary, December 16, 1944, box 3, GSP LOC.
184. Patton diary, December 17, 1944, box 3, GSP LOC.
185. D'Este, *Patton: A Genius for War*, 678.
186. Crosswell, *The Chief of Staff*, 283.
187. Patton diary, December 18, 1944, box 3, GSP LOC.
188. See Parker, *Battle of the Bulge*, 137.
189. Patton diary, December 18, 1944. See also Blumenson, *The Patton Papers, Volume II*, 596.
190. Bradley and Blair, *A General's Life*, 358.
191. Blumenson, *The Patton Papers, Volume II*, 597.
192. Third U.S. Army, *After Action Report, Volume I*, 169.
193. Ibid. Note that at the time an infantry division consisted of about 2,012 vehicles and an armored division, 2,650 vehicles. Many more vehicles resided in the support units under Third Army and its corps. George Forty, *The Armies of George S. Patton* (London: Arms and Armour, 1996), 75.
194. Ibid.
195. Patton diary, December 19, 1944, box 3, GSP LOC. See also Blumenson, *The Patton Papers, Volume II*, 596.
196. Patton diary, December 19, 1944. This passage is presented slightly altered, prioritizing the axes, in Farago, *Patton: Ordeal and Triumph*, 706.
197. Blumenson, *The Patton Papers, Volume II*, 599.
198. Farago, *Patton: Ordeal and Triumph*, 707.
199. Barron, *Patton at the Battle of the Bulge*, 59.
200. Ibid.
201. Kay Summersby, *Eisenhower Was My Boss* (New York: Prentice Hall, 1948), 286.
202. Patton diary, December 19, 1944. See also Blumenson, *The Patton Papers, Volume II*, 596.
203. Patton diary, October 29, 1945, box 3, GSP LOC.
204. Blumenson, *The Patton Papers, Volume II*, 599.
205. Patton diary, December 19, 1944.
206. D'Este, *Patton: A Genius for War*, 680.
207. Farago, *Patton: Ordeal and Triumph*, 708.
208. Patton diary, December 19, 1944. D'Este wrote that Patton answered he would attack on "the morning of December 21." D'Este, *Patton: A Genius for War*, 680. See the discussion on the difference in dates in Rickard, *Advance and Destroy*, 106.
209. Codman, *Drive*, 232.
210. Barron, *Patton at the Battle of the Bulge*, 60.
211. Codman, *Drive*, 230.
212. In *A Soldier's Story*, Bradley reported that Patton promised on 19 December that he could attack in forty-eight hours, or on 21 December (Bradley, *A*

Soldier's Story, 472), and in his second autobiography, he wrote that Patton promised to attack on 22 December (Bradley and Blair, *A General's Life,* 359).
213. Bradley and Blair, *A General's Life,* 359.
214. D'Este, *Patton: A Genius for War,* 680.
215. Ibid.
216. Hanson, *The Soul of Battle,* 310.
217. Patton diary, December 19, 1944.
218. Bradley and Blair, *A General's Life,* 363.
219. Ibid., 363–64.
220. Patton diary, December 20, 1944, box 3, GSP LOC.
221. Ibid.
222. Bradley and Blair, *A General's Life,* 357–58.
223. Harkins, *When the Third Cracked Europe,* 42.
224. See Third U.S. Army, *After Action Report, Volume I,* 169.
225. Patton diary, December 20, 1944. See also Blumenson, *The Patton Papers, Volume II,* 603.
226. Patton, *War as I Knew It,* 227.
227. Third U.S. Army, *After Action Report, Volume I,* 169.
228. Barron, *Patton at the Battle of the Bulge,* 64.
229. Patton diary, December 21, 1944, box 3, GSP LOC.
230. Allen, *Lucky Forward!* 176.
231. Hirshson, *General Patton: A Soldier's Life,* 575.
232. D'Este, *Patton: A Genius for War,* 683.
233. Allen, *Lucky Forward!* 177.
234. Ibid., 176.
235. See Hirshson, *General Patton: A Soldier's Life,* 579.
236. Parker, *Battle of the Bulge,* 143.
237. See Barron, *Patton at the Battle of the Bulge,* 66.
238. Patton diary, December 25, 1944, box 3, GSP LOC.
239. Bradley, *A Soldier's Story,* 473.

Chapter 5. Intelligence
Epigraph: Allen, *Lucky Forward!* 60.
1. Patton, "Address to the Officers and Men of the Second Armored Division."
2. Hammond, *The Mind of War,* 15.
3. U.S. Army Field Manual 2.0, *Intelligence* (Washington, D.C.: Headquarters Department of the Army, 17 May 2004), 8.
4. For an in-depth consideration of the nature of intelligence, see Jennifer E. Sims and Burton Gerber, eds., *Transforming U.S. Intelligence* (Washington, D.C.: Georgetown University Press, 2005), 15–18.
5. *Field Service Regulations 1923,* 25.
6. Robert B. Glass and Philip B. Davidson, *Intelligence Is for Commanders* (Harrisburg, Pa.: Military Service Publishing, 1948), x.

7. On Patton and dyslexia, see Blumenson, *Patton: The Man Behind the Legend*, 33–34.
8. Hirshson, *General Patton: A Soldier's Life*, 43.
9. Blumenson, *The Patton Papers, Volume I*, 778.
10. D'Este, *Patton: A Genius for War*, 349.
11. Patton, "Cavalry Work of the Punitive Expedition," 20.
12. Larson, *The British Army and the Theory of Armored Warfare*, 59–60.
13. Patton, "Report of Personal Experiences in the Tank Corps," 280.
14. D'Este, *Patton: A Genius for War*, 234.
15. Ibid., 234–35.
16. Blumenson, *The Patton Papers, Volume I*, 863.
17. Ibid., 909.
18. George S. Patton Jr., "Thoughts on Armored Warfare," undated, box 53, GSP LOC.
19. Patton, "War as She Is," 383.
20. Ibid.
21. Ibid.
22. *Field Service Regulations 1923*, 25.
23. Koch, *G-2: Intelligence for Patton*, 147.
24. Patton diary, February 26, 1945, box 3, GSP LOC. See also Blumenson, *The Patton Papers, Volume II*, 648.
25. U.S. Army Field Manual 100–5, *Operations* (1941), 23–24.
26. David Irving, *The War Between the Generals: Inside the Allied High Command* (London: Congdon and Lattes, 1981), 389.
27. "Montgomery was unimpressed by the danger, and planning did not change." See Russell F. Weigley, *Eisenhower's Lieutenants: The Campaign of France and Germany, 1944–1945* (Bloomington: Indiana University Press, 1990), 296.
28. Allen, *Lucky Forward!* 236.
29. Patton, "The Effect of Weapons on War," 39.
30. Patton, "Success in War," 333.
31. Bradley, *A Soldier's Story*, 33.
32. Farago, *Patton: Ordeal and Triumph*, 115.
33. Blumenson, *The Patton Papers, Volume I*, 913–14.
34. Hirshson, *General Patton: A Soldier's Life*, 195.
35. Ibid., 236.
36. Ibid., 240.
37. Patton, "Address to the Officers and Men of the Second Armored Division."
38. Ibid.
39. Patton, speech, May 9, 1942, folder 15, box 46, GSP LOC.
40. Patton, "Address to the Officers and Men of the Second Armored Division."
41. See Hirshson, *General Patton: A Soldier's Life*, 241.
42. Farago, *Patton: Ordeal and Triumph*, 162.

43. Ibid., 161.
44. Bradley and Blair, *A General's Life*, 99.
45. Patton, *War as I Knew It*, 358.
46. Ibid., 414.
47. Patton, letter to Floyd GHQ, 1 August 1941, box 26, GSP LOC.
48. Patton, letter to Colonel James C. Crockett, 25 July 1942, box 26, GSP LOC.
49. George S. Patton Jr., "Orientation on Maneuvers," May 1941, box 45, GSP LOC.
50. Hirshson, *General Patton: A Soldier's Life*, 127.
51. D'Este, *Patton: A Genius for War*, 464.
52. Ibid., 463.
53. Ibid., 477.
54. Breuer, *Operation Torch*, 254.
55. Atkinson, *An Army at Dawn*, 166.
56. Blumenson, *The Patton Papers, Volume II*, 133.
57. Patton diary, December 12, 1942, box 2, GSP LOC.
58. Atkinson, *An Army at Dawn*, 237.
59. Patton diary, December 8, 1942, box 2, GSP LOC.
60. Blumenson, *The Patton Papers, Volume II*, 139.
61. Blumenson, *Kasserine Pass*, 279.
62. Bradley, *A Soldier's Story*, 33.
63. Headquarters I Armored Corps, Reinforced, notes on combat, 21 April 1943, box 45, GSP LOC.
64. Ibid.
65. Ibid.
66. Ibid.
67. Headquarters I Armored Corps, Reinforced, Letter of Instruction, 5 June 1943, box 45, GSP LOC.
68. Ibid.
69. Pack, *Operation "HUSKY,"* 33. See also the discussion of plans in Montgomery, *The Memoirs of Field Marshal Montgomery*, 156.
70. "General Patton's Speech of June 21, 1943, delivered at General Conference (141) held at AFQ," 2, box 45, GSP LOC.
71. See Nye, *The Patton Mind*, 89.
72. G. F. R. Henderson, *Stonewall Jackson and the American Civil War* (New York: Da Capo Press, 1988), 196.
73. Ibid., 332–33.
74. "Transcription of the Text of Sun Tzu on the Art of War."
75. "Conference Between General Patton and Third Army Correspondents, 6th of November, Nancy, 1944," box 53, GSP LOC.
76. Patton diary, February 5, 1945, box 3, GSP LOC. See also Blumenson, *The Patton Papers, Volume II*, 635.

77. Charles B. MacDonald, *The Last Offensive* (Washington, D.C.: U.S. Army Center of Military History, 1993), 18.
78. United States Military Academy, Department of Military Art and Engineering, *Operations in Sicily and Italy* (West Point, N.Y.: United States Military Academy, 1950), 10.
79. Bradley and Blair, *A General's Life*, 182.
80. See Astor, *Terrible Terry Allen*, 199.
81. Ibid., 202.
82. Ibid.
83. It seemed like a minor event in the heat of battle, but Bradley felt forced to "borrow" units from the 2nd Armored Division to fill the gap between the 1st and 45th Divisions. See Hirshson, *General Patton: A Soldier's Life*, 368.
84. Bradley and Blair, *A General's Life*, 183.
85. 9th Division comments in Allied Force Headquarters, Lessons from the Sicilian Campaign, 20 November 1943, box 46, GSP LOC.
86. Ibid.
87. Ibid.
88. Pack, *Operation "HUSKY,"* 141.
89. Harold Alexander, *The Alexander Memoirs, 1940–1945* (New York: McGraw-Hill Book, 1962), 108.
90. United States Military Academy, *Operations in Sicily and Italy*, 13.
91. Patton diary, July 13, 1945, box 3, GSP LOC. See also Blumenson, *The Patton Papers, Volume II*, 285.
92. Bradley and Blair, *A General's Life*, 189.
93. Ambrose, *The Supreme Commander*, 221.
94. Blumenson, *The Patton Papers, Volume II*, 285.
95. "General Patton's Speech of June 21, 1943."
96. Patton diary, July 14, 1943, box 3, GSP LOC.
97. Pack, *Operation "HUSKY,"* 148.
98. D'Este, *Bitter Victory*, 401.
99. Ibid., 529–36.
100. Ibid., 529.
101. Ibid., 546.
102. Gelb, *Ike and Monty*, 404.
103. David Eisenhower, *Eisenhower at War 1943–1945* (New York: Vintage, 1987), 717.
104. Headquarters Third United States Army, Letter of Instruction No. 2, 3 April 1944, box 46, GSP LOC.
105. Ibid.
106. Ibid.
107. Headquarters Third United States Army, Letter of Instruction No. 3.

108. J. F. C. Fuller, *A Military History of the Western World, Volume III: From the American Civil War to the End of World War II* (New York: Funk and Wagnalls, 1956), 134.
109. Headquarters Third United States Army, G-2 Air Section, 10 May 1944, box 46, GSP LOC.
110. See Koch, *G-2: Intelligence for Patton*, 14.
111. Third U.S. Army, *After Action Report, Volume I*, 8.
112. For details on the assembly of the photographic center, see Koch, *G-2: Intelligence for Patton*, 59.
113. Ibid., 140.
114. Allen, *Lucky Forward!* 47–48.
115. Koch, *G-2: Intelligence for Patton*, 61.
116. Wallace, *Patton and His Third Army*, 205.
117. Third U.S. Army, *After Action Report, Volume I*, 3.
118. Ibid., 5.
119. Hammond, *The Mind of War*, 166.
120. Forty, *The Armies of George S. Patton*, 124.
121. Third U.S. Army, *After Action Report, Volume I*, 4.
122. In the creation of Public Affairs, Third Army followed First Army's example. Ibid., 6.
123. For Patton's history with Ultra, see Shwedo, *XIX TAC and Ultra*, 14–15.
124. Ibid., 55.
125. Ibid.
126. Interviews between General Patton, Schramm, Dunckern, and Meyer, folder 18, box 52, GSP LOC.
127. Nye, *The Patton Mind*, 82.
128. Baldwin, *Tiger Jack*, 75–76.
129. Blumenson, *The Patton Papers, Volume I*, 870.
130. Blumenson, *The Patton Papers, Volume II*, 271.
131. Patton, "War as She Is," 374–75.
132. Maurice, "Strategikon (Strategy)," trans. Col. O. L. Spaulding (undated), box 58, GSP LOC.
133. To understand how Clausewitz encouraged just such a process of synthetic experience, see Jon Tetsuro Sumida, *Decoding Clausewitz: A New Approach to On War* (Lawrence: University Press of Kansas, 2008), especially appendix one, "A Pictorial Representation of Critical Analysis."
134. Sun Tzu, *The Art of War*, 18.
135. Chandler, *The Military Maxims of Napoleon*, 55.
136. Clausewitz, *On War*, 136.
137. Patton, *War as I Knew It*, 400.
138. Third U.S. Army, *After Action Report, Volume I*, 230.
139. Allen, *Lucky Forward!* 206.

140. Patton, *War as I Knew It*, 238.
141. Blumenson, *The Patton Papers, Volume II*, 636.
142. Farago, *Patton: Ordeal and Triumph*, 758.
143. Rickard, *Patton at Bay*, 190.
144. XX Corps, *XX Corps, Its History and Service in World War II*, 149.
145. Ibid., 148.
146. Hofmann, *The Super Sixth*, 178.
147. Farago, *Patton: Ordeal and Triumph*, 665.
148. Third U.S. Army, *After Action Report, Volume I*, 126.
149. Patton diary, January 11, 1945, box 3, GSP LOC.
150. Ibid.
151. Wallace, *Patton and His Third Army*, 205.
152. Allen, *Lucky Forward!* 60.
153. Irving, *The War Between the Generals*, 369.
154. Hirshson, *General Patton: A Soldier's Life*, 595.
155. Blumenson, *The Patton Papers, Volume II*, 622.
156. Hofmann, *The Super Sixth*, 148.
157. "The XIX TAC conducted a larger proportion of close-air support missions out of their total combat missions than any other TAC in Europe." Zaloga, *Lorraine 1944*, 29.
158. Rickard, *Patton at Bay*, 78.
159. XX Corps, *XX Corps, Its History and Service in World War II*, 117.
160. Rickard, *Patton at Bay*, 101.
161. Farago, *Patton: Ordeal and Triumph*, 579.
162. Koch, *G-2: Intelligence for Patton*, 80.
163. Allen, *Lucky Forward!* 162.
164. Patton diary, November 25, 1944, box 3, GSP LOC.
165. Eisenhower, *Crusade in Europe*, 338.
166. Third U.S. Army, *After Action Report, Volume I*, 154.
167. Allen, *Lucky Forward!* 147.
168. Koch, *G-2: Intelligence for Patton*, 83.
169. Allen, *Lucky Forward!* 148.
170. Ibid.
171. Koch, *G-2: Intelligence for Patton*, 84.
172. Parker, *Battle of the Bulge*, 94.
173. Crosswell, *The Chief of Staff*, 281.
174. Bradley and Blair, *A General's Life*, 354.
175. Crosswell, *The Chief of Staff*, 281.
176. D'Este, *Patton: A Genius for War*, 676.
177. Allen, *Lucky Forward!* 161.
178. Bradley and Blair, *A General's Life*, 351.
179. Ralph Bennett, *ULTRA in the West: The Normandy Campaign of 1944–1945* (New York: Charles Scribner's Sons, 1979), 192.

180. See Parker, *Battle of the Bulge*, 39.
181. Third U.S. Army, *After Action Report, Volume I*, 160.
182. Farago, *Patton: Ordeal and Triumph*, 697.
183. Essame, *Patton, as Military Commander*, 216–17.
184. Bradley and Blair, *A General's Life*, 351.
185. See Hirshson, *General Patton: A Soldier's Life*, 569.
186. Bradley and Blair, *A General's Life*, 351.
187. Third U.S. Army, *After Action Report, Volume I*, 161.
188. Bradley and Blair, *A General's Life*, 353.
189. Allen, *Lucky Forward!* 163–64.
190. Bradley and Blair, *A General's Life*, 349.
191. Farago, *Patton: Ordeal and Triumph*, 695.
192. Ibid., 698.
193. Parker, *Battle of the Bulge*, 45.
194. Bradley, *A Soldier's Story*, 464.
195. Eisenhower, *Crusade in Europe*, 341.
196. Parker, *Battle of the Bulge*, 45.
197. Allen, *Lucky Forward!* 165.
198. Bradley and Blair, *A General's Life*, 354.
199. Farago, *Patton: Ordeal and Triumph*, 697.
200. Bradley and Blair, *A General's Life*, 356.
201. Bradley, *A Soldier's Story*, 450.
202. Farago, *Patton: Ordeal and Triumph*, 694.
203. Bradley and Blair, *A General's Life*, 356.
204. Farago, *Patton: Ordeal and Triumph*, 694.
205. Koch, *G-2: Intelligence for Patton*, 158.
206. Ibid.

Chapter 6. Breakout: Conceptualization

Epigraph: Irzyk, *Gasoline to Patton*, 77.
1. Patton diary, September 6, 1943, box 3, GSP LOC.
2. Patton diary, September 29, 1943, box 2, GSP LOC.
3. Patton diary, September 7, 1943, box 3, GSP LOC.
4. Patton diary, October 27, 1943, box 3, GSP LOC.
5. Patton diary, September 6, 1943.
6. Patton diary, September 17, 1943, box 3, GSP LOC.
7. Patton diary, September 29, 1943.
8. Ibid.
9. Ibid.
10. Patton diary, October 27, 1943.
11. Patton diary, December 7, 1943, box 3, GSP LOC.
12. Patton diary, September 7, 1943.

13. Patton diary, November 21, 1943, box 3, GSP LOC.
14. Patton diary, December 8, 1943, box 3, GSP LOC.
15. Patton diary, September 7, 1943.
16. Ibid.
17. Patton diary, January 1, 1944, box 3, GSP LOC.
18. Patton diary, January 3, 1944, box 3, GSP LOC.
19. Patton diary, January 18, 1944, box 3, GSP LOC.
20. Blumenson, *The Patton Papers, Volume II*, 398.
21. Marshall to General John Edwin Hull. See Farago, *Patton: Ordeal and Triumph*, 131. He added, "And don't feel too bad about this. Patton himself understands this. This is what makes it so easy to deal with the man."
22. Bradley and Blair, *A General's Life*, 218.
23. Bradley, *A Soldier's Story*, 229.
24. Blumenson, *The Patton Papers, Volume II*, 407.
25. Patton diary, January 26, 1944, box 3, GSP LOC.
26. Bradley and Blair, *A General's Life*, 219.
27. Farago, *Patton: Ordeal and Triumph*, 505.
28. Royle, *Patton: Old Blood and Guts*, 128–29.
29. Patton diary, January 27, 1944, box 3, GSP LOC.
30. Ibid.
31. Farago, *Patton: Ordeal and Triumph*, 381–82. See also Patton diary, January 27, 1944.
32. Patton diary, March 14, 1944, box 3, GSP LOC.
33. Ibid.
34. Patton diary, January 27, 1944.
35. Patton diary, February 18, 1944, box 3, GSP LOC.
36. Koch, *G-2: Intelligence for Patton*, 54.
37. Hirshson, *General Patton: A Soldier's Life*, 439.
38. "After World War II, Omar Bradley and some of the original members of the II Corps staff [who remained with Bradley] perpetuated the myth that Patton was a mediocre commander, ill served by a poor staff that more often than not failed to do its job—a view, colored by deep prejudices against Patton, that was neither balanced nor accurate." D'Este, *Patton: A Genius for War*, 420–21.
39. Shortly after, Ike made Patton replace Gay as his chief of staff as payback for his sitting on the orders to cancel the drive on Palermo. Gaffey replaced Gay.
40. Patton diary, February 10, 1944, box 3, GSP LOC.
41. Forty, *The Armies of George S. Patton*, 117.
42. Patton diary, February 11, 1944.
43. Hirshson, *General Patton: A Soldier's Life*, 437.
44. Patton, letter to Walter Dillingham, 4 March 1944, box 28, GSP LOC.

45. Patton, undated "Letter of Instruction," box 46, GSP LOC, and Patton, "Letter of Instruction No. 2," 3 April 1942, box 46, GSP LOC. See also Patton, *War as I Knew It*, appendix D, 397.
46. Patton, *War as I Knew It*, 399.
47. Ibid., 400.
48. Ibid., 401.
49. Third U.S. Army, *After Action Report, Volume I*, 1.
50. Patton diary, March 14, 1944.
51. Ibid.
52. Ibid.
53. Koch, *G-2: Intelligence for Patton*, 52–53.
54. Harkins, *When the Third Cracked Europe*, 50.
55. See comments penciled by Patton on the Michelin map of France, oversized box, RG 407, NARA II.
56. Shwedo, *XIX TAC and Ultra*, 72.
57. Bradley and Blair, *A General's Life*, 100.
58. See the various definitions offered by academics in James Gleick, *Chaos: Making a New Science* (New York: Penguin Books, 1987), 306.
59. Alan Beyerchen, "Clausewitz, Nonlinearity, and the Unpredictability of War," *International Security* 17, no. 3 (Winter 1992–1993): 59–90.
60. Third U.S. Army, *After Action Report, Volume I*, 6.
61. Ibid., 2.
62. Patton diary, March 28, 1944, box 3, GSP LOC.
63. Ibid.
64. Ibid.
65. See Carlo D'Este, *Decision in Normandy* (New York: Konecky and Konecky, 2000), 75–77.
66. Bradley and Blair, *A General's Life*, 235.
67. Patton diary, April 7, 1944.
68. Bradley, *A Soldier's Story*, 260.
69. Ibid., 244.
70. Montgomery, *The Memoirs of Field Marshal Montgomery*, 191.
71. D'Este, *Decision in Normandy*, 81.
72. Patton diary, April 13, 1944, box 3, GSP LOC.
73. "On 16 April, a training memorandum, 'Use of Tanks in Support of Infantry,' written by the Army Commander, was issued." Third U.S. Army, *After Action Report Volume I*, 3.
74. Blumenson, *The Patton Papers, Volume II*, 436.
75. Patton, *War as I Knew It*, 405.
76. Ibid., 410.
77. Ibid., 118.
78. Patton diary, April 13, 1944.

79. Patton diary, April 18, 1944, box 3, GSP LOC.
80. Third U.S. Army, *After Action Report, Volume I*, 6.
81. Hirshson, *General Patton: A Soldier's Life*, 459.
82. Patton diary, April 25, 1944, box 3, GSP LOC.
83. Patton diary, April 26, 1944, box 3, GSP LOC. See also Blumenson, *The Patton Papers, Volume II*, 441.
84. Patton diary, April 26, 1944.
85. Yeide, *Fighting Patton*, 217.
86. Ibid., 218, and Farago, *Patton: Ordeal and Triumph*, 407.
87. F. W. Winterbotham, *The Ultra Secret: The Inside Story of Operation Ultra, Bletchley Park and Enigma* (New York: Dell, 1976), 186.
88. Bradley and Blair, *A General's Life*, 222.
89. Ambrose, *The Supreme Commander*, 343.
90. Bradley and Blair, *A General's Life*, 222.
91. Ibid., 223.
92. Patton diary, April 27, 1944, box 3, GSP LOC.
93. Ibid.
94. Patton received this report from Hughes. Patton diary, April 30, 1944, box 3, GSP LOC.
95. D'Este, *Patton: A Genius for War*, 590.
96. Patton diary, May 1, 1944, box 3, GSP LOC.
97. Blumenson, *The Patton Papers, Volume II*, 450.
98. D'Este, *Patton: A Genius for War*, 589.
99. Bradley and Blair, *A General's Life*, 223.
100. Patton diary, May 1, 1944.
101. Yeide, *Fighting Patton*, 219.
102. Ambrose, *The Supreme Commander*, 345.
103. Blumenson, *The Patton Papers, Volume II*, 452.
104. Patton, "Notes on Combat Armored Divisions," 192.
105. Blumenson, *The Patton Papers, Volume II*, 455.
106. Third U.S. Army, *After Action Report, Volume I*, 4.
107. Patton diary, May 9, 1944.
108. Ibid.
109. Baldwin, *Tiger Jack*, 159.
110. Spires, *Patton's Air Force*, 45.
111. Patton, *War as I Knew It*, 108.
112. Spires, *Patton's Air Force*, 48.
113. XX Corps, *XX Corps, Its History and Service in World War II*, 53.
114. Ibid., 50.
115. Patton diary, May 10, 1944, box 3, GSP LOC. See also Blumenson, *The Patton Papers, Volume II*, 455.

116. Headquarters, 4th Armored Division, "Revision, Infantry-Tank Demonstration," 13 May 1944, box 54, GSP LOC.
117. Third U.S. Army, *After Action Report, Volume I*, 8.
118. Patton, *War as I Knew It*, 400.
119. Patton diary, May 1, 1944.
120. Patton diary, June 1, 1944, box 3, GSP LOC.
121. Montgomery cited by Blumenson, *The Patton Papers, Volume II*, 461.
122. Bradley and Blair, *A General's Life*, 243.
123. Ibid.
124. Patton diary, June 1, 1944.
125. Patton diary, June 2, 1944, box 3, GSP LOC.
126. Bradley and Blair, *A General's Life*, 251.
127. Ibid., 257.
128. Ibid., 254.
129. Montgomery, *The Memoirs of Field Marshal Montgomery*, 228.
130. Martin Blumenson, *Breakout and Pursuit* (Fort Leavenworth, Kans.: U.S. Army Center of Military History, 1961), 104.
131. Patton diary, June 6, 1944, box 3, GSP LOC.
132. Blumenson, *The Patton Papers, Volume II*, 465.
133. David Garth, *St-Lo* (Fort Leavenworth, Kans.: U.S. Army Center of Military History, 1994), 5.
134. D'Este, *Decision in Normandy*, 341.
135. Leo Daugherty, *The Battle of the Hedgerows* (St. Paul, Minn.: MBI Publishing, 2001), 42.
136. D'Este, *Decision in Normandy*, 341.
137. He added that the "watershed roads would always be firm enough to carry military transports no matter how much it rained." Farago, *Patton: Ordeal and Triumph*, 71.
138. Blumenson, *Breakout and Pursuit*, 105.
139. Eisenhower, *Crusade in Europe*, 260.
140. Blumenson, *Breakout and Pursuit*, 105.
141. Bradley and Blair, *A General's Life*, 263.
142. Bradley, *A Soldier's Story*, 308.
143. Blumenson, *Breakout and Pursuit*, 109.
144. Eisenhower, *Crusade in Europe*, 263.
145. Crosswell, *The Chief of Staff*, 247.
146. Bradley, *A Soldier's Story*, 318.
147. Bradley and Blair, *A General's Life*, 265.
148. Butcher, *My Three Years with Eisenhower*, 594–95.
149. Bradley, *A Soldier's Story*, 317.
150. Bradley and Blair, *A General's Life*, 264–65.
151. D'Este, *Decision in Normandy*, 345.

152. Ibid., 346.
153. Ibid., 345.
154. Bradley and Blair, *A General's Life*, 266–67.
155. Ibid., 267.
156. Ibid.
157. Ambrose, *The Supreme Commander*, 428.
158. Bradley, *A Soldier's Story*, 300.
159. Ambrose, *The Supreme Commander*, 432.
160. Blumenson, *Breakout and Pursuit*, 109.
161. Bradley and Blair, *A General's Life*, 264.
162. D'Este, *Patton: A Genius for War*, 610.
163. Farago, *Patton: Ordeal and Triumph*, 415.
164. Patton diary, July 2, 1944, box 3, GSP LOC. See also Blumenson, *The Patton Papers, Volume II*, 471.
165. Patton diary, July 2, 1944.
166. Farago, *Patton: Ordeal and Triumph*, 431–32. See also Blumenson, *The Patton Papers, Volume II*, 471.
167. Patton diary, July 2, 1944.
168. Ibid.; Blumenson, *The Patton Papers, Volume II*, 471.
169. The author is grateful to Jonathan W. Jordan, author of *Brothers, Rivals, Victors: Eisenhower, Patton, Bradley, and the Partnership that Drove the Allied Conquest in Europe* (New York: New American Library, 2011), for pointing out this issue. See also Patton diary, July 2, 1944.
170. Codman, *Drive*, 91. See also Blumenson, *The Patton Papers, Volume I*, xi–xiv.
171. Patton diary, July 3, 1944, box 3, GSP LOC.
172. Patton diary, February 11, 1944.
173. Bradley and Blair, *A General's Life*, 270.
174. Crosswell, *The Chief of Staff*, 248.
175. Blumenson, *The Patton Papers, Volume II*, 472.
176. Patton diary, July 4, 1944, box 3, GSP LOC.
177. Blumenson, *The Patton Papers, Volume II*, 478.
178. Patton diary, July 6, 1944, box 3, GSP LOC.
179. Farago, *Patton: Ordeal and Triumph*, 424.
180. Bradley and Blair, *A General's Life*, 270.
181. Daugherty, *The Battle of the Hedgerows*, 152.
182. Patton diary, July 7, 1944, box 3, GSP LOC.
183. Blumenson, *Breakout and Pursuit*, 117.
184. Bradley and Blair, *A General's Life*, 272.
185. D'Este, *Decision in Normandy*, 333.
186. Bradley and Blair, *A General's Life*, 272.
187. Montgomery, *The Memoirs of Field Marshal Montgomery*, 229.
188. Bradley and Blair, *A General's Life*, 277.

189. See D'Este, *Decision in Normandy*, 348.
190. Ibid., 349.
191. Ibid., 341.
192. Headquarters First U.S. Army, "Outline Plan Operation 'COBRA'," 13 July 1944, box 1532, RG 407, NARA II.
193. First U.S. Army, *First U.S. Army Report of Operations, 20 October 1943–1 August 1944* (Paris: First U.S. Army, 1944), 97.
194. Headquarters First U.S. Army, "Outline Plan Operation 'COBRA'."
195. Bradley, *A Soldier's Story*, 338.
196. Ibid., 329–30.
197. Headquarters First U.S. Army, "Outline Plan Operation 'COBRA'."
198. Bradley, *A Soldier's Story,* 329. In his memoirs Bradley also said, "Meanwhile the armor would dash towards Avranches and turn the corner into Brittany." In the Cobra plan, this was to happen much later.
199. Headquarters First U.S. Army, "Outline Plan Operation 'COBRA'," 2.
200. First U.S. Army, *First U.S. Army Report of Operations*, 97.
201. Headquarters First U.S. Army, "Outline Plan Operation 'COBRA'."
202. J. Lawton Collins, *Lightning Joe: An Autobiography* (Baton Rouge: Louisiana State University Press, 1979), 235.
203. Collins argued that stopping east of Coutances would allow Bradley to either encircle the Germans facing VIII Corps or go south to Avranches if conditions allowed. See Martin Blumenson, *The Battle of the Generals: The Untold Story of the Falaise Pocket—The Campaign that Should Have Won World War II* (New York: William Morrow, 1993), 131.
204. Patton diary, July 23, 1944, box 3, GSP LOC.
205. Patton diary, July 14, 1944, box 3, GSP LOC.
206. Farago, *Patton: Ordeal and Triumph*, 442.
207. Blumenson, *Breakout and Pursuit*, 104.
208. Patton diary, July 14, 1944.
209. Patton diary, July 23, 1944.
210. Patton diary, July 13, 1944, box 3, GSP LOC.
211. Patton diary, July 4, 1944. See also Blumenson, *The Patton Papers, Volume II*, 480.
212. See for example Bradley, *A Soldier's Story*, 328–40.
213. See, for example, Yeide, *Fighting Patton*, 231; Rickard, *Advance and Destroy*, 13; or Charles Whiting, *Bradley* (New York: Ballantine Books, 1971), 32–33.
214. D'Este, *Decision in Normandy*, 351.
215. Ibid., 350.
216. Daugherty, *The Battle of the Hedgerows,* 168.
217. Garth, *St-Lo*, 92.
218. Patton diary, July 16, 1944, box 3, GSP LOC.
219. First U.S. Army, *First U.S. Army Report of Operations*, 89.

220. Butcher, *My Three Years with Eisenhower*, 626.
221. Montgomery, *The Memoirs of Field Marshal Montgomery*, 231.
222. Patton diary, July 22, 1944, box 3, GSP LOC.
223. Bradley, *A Soldier's Story*, 348.
224. Ibid., 349.
225. Ibid., 353.
226. Bradley and Blair, *A General's Life*, 277.
227. Patton diary, July 23, 1944.
228. Ibid.
229. Ibid.
230. Blumenson, *The Patton Papers, Volume II*, 486.
231. Bradley and Blair, *A General's Life*, 279.
232. Irving, *The War Between the Generals*, 211–12.
233. Jimmy Doolittle and Carroll V. Glines, *I Could Never Be So Lucky Again* (Atglen, Pa.: Schiffer Publishing Ltd., 1991).
234. Ibid.
235. Farago, *Patton: Ordeal and Triumph*, 430.
236. Ibid.
237. Blumenson, *The Patton Papers, Volume II*, 488.
238. D'Este, *Decision in Normandy*, 410.
239. Hofmann, *The Super Sixth*, 56.
240. Koyen, *The Fourth Armored Division*, 14.
241. Doolittle and Glines, *I Could Never Be So Lucky Again*.
242. "Radio communications between bombers and ground forces, clearly visible targets, and agreed upon approach routes." See Johnson, *Fast Tanks and Heavy Bombers*, 217.
243. Bradley, *A Soldier's Story*, 349.
244. Bradley and Blair, *A General's Life*, 280.
245. Blumenson, *Breakout and Pursuit*, 96.
246. Ambrose, *The Supreme Commander*, 463.
247. Bradley, *A Soldier's Story*, 347.
248. Ambrose, *The Supreme Commander*, 464.
249. See Bradley and Blair, *A General's Life*, 281.
250. D'Este, *Decision in Normandy*, 404.
251. Ambrose, *The Supreme Commander*, 465.
252. Patton diary, July 27, 1944, box 3, GSP LOC.
253. Blumenson, *Breakout and Pursuit*, 310.
254. He hoped to be in Rennes within two weeks, but that would be nearly impossible. D'Este, *Decision in Normandy*, 405.
255. Blumenson, *Breakout and Pursuit*, 259.
256. See Hofmann, *The Super Sixth*, 56.
257. See Koyen, *The Fourth Armored Division*, 15.

258. Blumenson, *Breakout and Pursuit*, 310.
259. Hirshson, *General Patton: A Soldier's Life*, 500.
260. Wood also claimed, "Patton did not come along until after I had taken Rennes"—a patently untrue statement. Ibid., 501.
261. Blumenson, *Breakout and Pursuit*, 310.
262. Frank James Price, *Troy H. Middleton: A Biography* (Baton Rouge: Louisiana State University, 1974), 184.
263. Ibid., 186.
264. Showalter, however, argued, "Cobra, in fact, combined fire power and exploitation in a way familiar to American inter-war thinking." Showalter, *Patton and Rommel*, 365.
265. Bradley, *A Soldier's Story*, 355.

Chapter 7. Breakout: Execution

Epigraph: Hanson, *The Soul of Battle*, 299.
1. Blumenson, *Breakout and Pursuit*, 310.
2. Ibid., 311.
3. Patton diary, July 28, 1944, box 3, GSP LOC.
4. Farago, *Patton: Ordeal and Triumph*, 433.
5. Bradley, *A Soldier's Story*, 358.
6. McNair, now dead from the fratricidal Cobra bombardment, had been selected as the only one with the proper prestige to replace Patton as the FUSAG commander, and although McNair's death remained a secret, it was deemed imprudent to reveal Patton's presence in Normandy. As Stephen Ambrose noted, "The FORTITUDE deception plan added to the enemy's problems, for throughout June and two-thirds of July the German high command assumed that a second landing would be made north of the Seine and therefore held the Fifteenth Army in the Pas de Calais area." Ambrose, *The Supreme Commander*, 460.
7. Patton wrote, "While Third Army did not become operational until 1200 on the first of August, General Bradley appointed me to command it by word of mouth on the twenty-eigth of July and explained the plans for the initial use of two corps, the VIII (Middleton) on the right and the XV (Haislip) on the left." Patton, *War as I Knew It*, 96.
8. Patton diary, July 28, 1944.
9. Farago, *Patton: Ordeal and Triumph*, 454.
10. Blumenson, *Breakout and Pursuit*, 313.
11. Patton diary, July 28, 1944.
12. Hofmann, *The Super Sixth*, 56.
13. Koyen, *The Fourth Armored Division*, 16.
14. Farago, *Patton: Ordeal and Triumph*, 441.
15. Koyen, *The Fourth Armored Division*, 16.

16. Baldwin, *Tiger Jack*, 28.
17. Blumenson, *The Patton Papers, Volume II*, 491.
18. Patton diary, July 29, 1944, box 3, GSP LOC.
19. Patton, *War as I Knew It*, 97.
20. Blumenson, *The Patton Papers, Volume II*, 491.
21. Patton diary, July 28, 1944.
22. First U.S. Army, *First U.S. Army Report of Operations*, 106.
23. D'Este, *Decision in Normandy*, 405.
24. Bradley and Blair, *A General's Life*, 281.
25. Patton diary, July 28, 1944. See also Blumenson, *The Patton Papers, Volume II*, 491.
26. Shwedo, *XIX TAC and Ultra*, 10.
27. Ibid., 28.
28. Blumenson, *Breakout and Pursuit*, 323.
29. Ibid.
30. Patton diary, July 30, 1944, box 3, GSP LOC.
31. Ibid.
32. Koyen, *The Fourth Armored Division*, 25.
33. Farago, *Patton: Ordeal and Triumph*, 432.
34. Blumenson, *The Patton Papers, Volume II*, 493.
35. Butcher, *My Three Years with Eisenhower*, 627.
36. Harkins, *When the Third Cracked Europe*, 48.
37. Patton diary, August 1, 1944, box 3, GSP LOC. See also Blumenson, *The Patton Papers, Volume II*, 496.
38. Hofmann noted that "no further advance was contemplated." Hofmann, *The Super Sixth*, 66.
39. Patton diary, July 31, 1944, box 3, GSP LOC.
40. Ibid.
41. Ibid.
42. Allen, *Lucky Forward!* 72.
43. Farago, *Patton: Ordeal and Triumph*, 447.
44. Allen, *Lucky Forward!* 73–74.
45. Patton diary, August 1, 1944.
46. Bradley and Blair, *A General's Life*, 283–84.
47. Allen, *Lucky Forward!* 68.
48. See Shwedo, *XIX TAC and Ultra*, 37.
49. See Blumenson, *The Patton Papers, Volume II*, 493.
50. See Hofmann, *The Super Sixth*, 65.
51. Bradley, *A Soldier's Story*, 362.
52. Patton diary, August 1, 1944. See also Blumenson, *The Patton Papers, Volume II*, 495.

53. Patton diary, August 1, 1944. See also Blumenson, *The Patton Papers, Volume II*, 496.
54. Patton diary, August 1, 1944.
55. "Then another German position fell to the Air Corps and the Armored Force." Koyen, *The Fourth Armored Division*, 30.
56. Ibid., 31.
57. Shwedo, *XIX TAC and Ultra*, 8.
58. Montgomery, *The Memoirs of Field Marshal Montgomery*, 233.
59. Ibid., 234.
60. Shwedo, *XIX TAC and Ultra*, 37.
61. Koyen, *The Fourth Armored Division*, 29.
62. Ibid., 30.
63. Baldwin, *Tiger Jack*, 44.
64. Ambrose, *The Supreme Commander*, 469.
65. Eisenhower, *Crusade in Europe*, 309.
66. Bradley and Blair, *A General's Life*, 289.
67. Ibid., 290.
68. Ibid.
69. Ibid.
70. Hofmann, *The Super Sixth*, 72.
71. Bradley, *A Soldier's Story*, 360.
72. Farago, *Patton: Ordeal and Triumph*, 472.
73. Butcher, *My Three Years with Eisenhower*, 630.
74. Ibid., 635.
75. "Transcript of Conference between Lt. Gen. G. S. Patton, Jr., and Third Army Correspondents, 2100, 7 September 1944," box 53, GSP LOC.
76. Bradley and Blair, *A General's Life*, 285–86.
77. Headquarters Twelfth Army Group, "Annex No. 1—Operation Mao to Accompany Letter of Instruction No. 1 (undated)," box 1314, RG 407, NARA II.
78. Martin Blumenson, *The Duel for France, 1944: The Men and Battles that Changed the Fate of Europe* (New York: Da Capo Press, 2000), 160.
79. D'Este, *Patton: A Genius for War*, 630.
80. The operations officer was Brigadier General A. Franklin Kibler. Hofmann, *The Super Sixth*, 73.
81. Bradley, *A Soldier's Story*, 361–62.
82. Patton diary, August 2, 1944, box 3, GSP LOC.
83. Hofmann, *The Super Sixth*, 71.
84. Ibid., 75.
85. Farago, *Patton: Ordeal and Triumph*, 476.
86. Ibid., 480.
87. D'Este, *Patton: A Genius for War*, 627.

88. Bradley, *A Soldier's Story*, 358.
89. Koch, *G-2: Intelligence for Patton*, 31.
90. Blumenson, *The Patton Papers, Volume II*, 499.
91. Blumenson, *The Duel for France*, 205.
92. Farago, *Patton: Ordeal and Triumph*, 167.
93. Ambrose, *The Supreme Commander*, 469–70.
94. Blumenson, *The Battle of the Generals*, 160.
95. Farago, *Patton: Ordeal and Triumph*, 475.
96. Yeide, *Fighting Patton*, 254.
97. Patton, letter to Major General Kenyon A. Joyce, 6 August 1944, box 28, GSP LOC.
98. Farago, *Patton: Ordeal and Triumph*, 477.
99. Price, *Troy H. Middleton*, 188.
100. Patton diary, August 4, 1944. See also Blumenson, *The Patton Papers, Volume II*, 495.
101. Baldwin, *Tiger Jack*, 44.
102. Ibid.
103. Blumenson, *The Patton Papers, Volume II*, 499.
104. Three days earlier Patton had identified Angers as his objective. Farago, *Patton: Ordeal and Triumph*, 480.
105. XX Corps, *XX Corps, Its History and Service in World War II*, 70.
106. Patton diary, August 5, 1944, box 3, GSP LOC. See also Blumenson, *The Patton Papers, Volume II*, 495.
107. Shwedo, *XIX TAC and Ultra*, 48.
108. Koch, *G-2: Intelligence for Patton*, 31.
109. D'Este noted, "Although Patton was privy to the Ultra secret, until early August 1944 he had no idea that there existed a small, secret, special intelligence section attached to Third Army HQ which processed information passed from Bletchley Park." D'Este, *Patton: A Genius for War*, 653.
110. Patton diary, August 5, 1944. See also Blumenson, *The Patton Papers, Volume II*, 49.
111. See XX Corps, *XX Corps, Its History and Service in World War II*, 70–73. See also Patton diary, August 7, 1944, box 3, GSP LOC.
112. Interestingly Ike added, "Moreover, by this time the weather had taken a very definite turn for the better and we had in our possession an Air Transport Service that could deliver, if called upon, up to 2,000 tons of supplies per day in fields designated by any of our forces that might be temporarily cut off." Eisenhower, *Crusade in Europe*, 310.
113. Bradley, *A Soldier's Story*, 365.
114. Patton diary, August 7, 1944.
115. Bradley, *A Soldier's Story*, 368.
116. Bradley had not expected XV Corps to drive as far to the east as Le Mans. Bradley and Blair, *A General's Life*, 294.

117. Bradley, *A Soldier's Story*, 369.
118. Blumenson, *The Battle of the Generals*, 214.
119. Eisenhower, *Crusade in Europe*, 310–11.
120. Patton diary, August 7, 1944. See also Blumenson, *The Patton Papers, Volume II*, 503.
121. Shwedo, *XIX TAC and Ultra*, 58.
122. Yeide, *Fighting Patton*, 261.
123. Bradley and Blair, *A General's Life*, 294.
124. Patton diary, August 8, 1944.
125. See Blumenson, *The Patton Papers, Volume II*, 504.
126. Bradley, *A Soldier's Story*, 371.
127. Bradley and Blair, *A General's Life*, 298.
128. Blumenson, *The Battle of the Generals*, 207.
129. Bradley, *A Soldier's Story*, 373.
130. Ibid., 374.
131. Patton diary, August 13, 1944, box 3, GSP LOC.
132. Blumenson, *The Patton Papers, Volume II*, 504.
133. Hirshson, *General Patton: A Soldier's Life*, 513.
134. Bradley, *A Soldier's Story*, 369.
135. 12th Army Group G-4 Section, "Report of Operations (Final After Action Report)," 29.
136. Ibid.
137. Hofmann, *The Super Sixth*, 105.
138. Koyen, *The Fourth Armored Division*, 36.
139. Baldwin, *Tiger Jack*, 147.
140. Ibid., 146.
141. Ibid., 41.
142. Blumenson, *The Battle of the Generals*, 202–3.
143. D'Este, *Decision in Normandy*, 427.
144. Bradley, *A Soldier's Story*, 372.
145. Ibid., 429.
146. Bradley and Blair, *A General's Life*, 298.
147. Bradley, *A Soldier's Story*, 373.
148. Ibid., 371.
149. Patton diary, August 13, 1944.
150. Blumenson, *The Battle of the Generals*, 207.
151. Hirshson, *General Patton: A Soldier's Life*, 516.
152. He wrote, "For any head-on juncture becomes a dangerous and uncontrollable maneuver unless each of the advancing forces is halted by a pre-arranged plan on the terrain objective." Bradley, *A Soldier's Story*, 374.
153. Eisenhower, *Crusade in Europe*, 314.
154. Bradley, *A Soldier's Story*, 373.
155. Hirshson, *General Patton: A Soldier's Life*, 515.

156. Butcher, *My Three Years with Eisenhower*, 647.
157. See Ambrose, *The Supreme Commander*, 477–78.
158. Bradley and Blair, *A General's Life*, 299.
159. Bradley, *A Soldier's Story*, 373.
160. Blumenson, *The Battle of the Generals*, 210.
161. Blumenson, *The Patton Papers, Volume II*, 508.
162. Robert Howe Fletcher, letter to Patton, 12 August 1944, box 28, GSP LOC.
163. Patton diary, August 13, 1944.
164. Ibid.
165. Bradley, *A Soldier's Story*, 378.
166. Bradley and Blair, *A General's Life*, 302.
167. Patton diary, August 14, 1944, box 3, GSP LOC. See also Blumenson, *The Patton Papers, Volume II*, 510.
168. Ibid.
169. Bradley, *A Soldier's Story*, 375.
170. Ibid., 352.
171. Eisenhower, *Crusade in Europe*, 293.
172. Butcher, *My Three Years with Eisenhower*, 642.
173. Montgomery, *The Memoirs of Field Marshal Montgomery*, 239.
174. See XX Corps, *XX Corps, Its History and Service in World War II*, 79.
175. Blumenson, *The Duel for France, 1944*, 276.
176. Bradley and Blair, *A General's Life*, 303–4.
177. D'Este, *Patton: A Genius for War*, 643.
178. Patton diary, August 15, 1944, box 3, GSP LOC. See also Blumenson, *The Battle of the Generals*, 223.
179. Blumenson, *The Patton Papers, Volume II*, 521.
180. Bradley authorized him to advance halfway, to Trun, before changing his mind. Patton diary, August 16, 1944, box 3, GSP LOC. See also Blumenson, *The Patton Papers, Volume II*, 509.
181. Blumenson, *The Battle of the Generals*, 225.
182. Bradley had Hodges send Gerow to lead the advance to Trun near Chambois but told Patton that Gerow would not arrive for several days. See Blumenson, *The Duel for France, 1944*, 278, and *The Battle of the Generals*, 232.
183. Blumenson, *The Battle of the Generals*, 235.
184. Koyen, *The Fourth Armored Division*, 37.
185. Bradley and Blair, *A General's Life*, 304.
186. Blumenson, *The Patton Papers, Volume II*, 518.
187. Blumenson, *The Battle of the Generals*, 238.
188. See Farago, *Patton: Ordeal and Triumph*, 477.
189. Gelb, *Ike and Monty: Generals at War*, 343.
190. Ambrose, *The Supreme Commander*, 497.
191. Brooke, *War Diaries, 1939–1945*, 585.

192. Patton diary, August 19, 1944, box 3, GSP LOC. See also Blumenson, *The Battle of the Generals*, 223.
193. Blumenson, *The Battle of the Generals*, 245.
194. Patton diary, August 19, 1944.
195. XX Corps, *XX Corps, Its History and Service in World War II*, 102.
196. Ibid., 83.
197. Patton diary, August 19, 1944.
198. Harkins, *When the Third Cracked Europe*, 24.
199. Blumenson, *The Patton Papers, Volume II*, 522.
200. Patton diary, August 20, 1944, box 3, GSP LOC.
201. Harkins, *When the Third Cracked Europe*, 24.
202. Patton diary, August 21, 1944, box 3, GSP LOC.
203. Ibid.
204. Hirshson, *General Patton: A Soldier's Life*, 525.
205. XX Corps, *XX Corps, Its History and Service in World War II*, 82–84.
206. "Conference Between General Patton and Correspondents, Third Army, Luxemboug, March 17, 1945," box 53, GSP LOC.
207. Bradley and Blair, *A General's Life*, 314.
208. Patton diary, August 22, 1944, box 3, GSP LOC.
209. Montgomery, *The Memoirs of Field Marshal Montgomery*, 241.
210. Bradley and Blair, *A General's Life*, 314.
211. Gelb, *Ike and Monty: Generals at War*, 351.
212. Montgomery, *The Memoirs of Field Marshal Montgomery*, 241.
213. Irving, *The War Between the Generals*, 251.
214. Montgomery, *The Memoirs of Field Marshal Montgomery*, 242.
215. Ibid., 241.
216. Irzyk, *Gasoline to Patton*, 162.
217. Bradley and Blair, *A General's Life*, 315.
218. Ibid., 314.
219. Patton diary, August 23, 1944, box 3, GSP LOC.
220. Ibid. See also Blumenson, *The Patton Papers, Volume II*, 526.
221. Patton diary, August 23, 1944.
222. Ibid.
223. Ibid.
224. Baldwin, *Tiger Jack*, 155.
225. Patton diary, August 23, 1944.
226. Rickard, *Patton at Bay*, 57.
227. Hanson, *The Soul of Battle*, 307.
228. See Irzyk, *Gasoline to Patton*, 158.
229. Third U.S. Army, *After Action Report, Volume I*, 41.
230. Farago, *Patton: Ordeal and Triumph*, 567.
231. Third U.S. Army, *After Action Report, Volume I*, 40.

232. Irving, *The War Between the Generals*, 249.
233. Third U.S. Army, *After Action Report, Volume I*, 40.
234. Butcher, *My Three Years with Eisenhower*, 642.
235. Blumenson, *The Patton Papers, Volume II*, 528.
236. XX Corps, *XX Corps, Its History and Service in World War II*, 89.
237. Patton diary, August 25, 1944, box 3, GSP LOC.
238. Bradley and Blair, *A General's Life*, 316.
239. Gelb, *Ike and Monty*, 353.
240. Ambrose, *The Supreme Commander*, 508.
241. Patton diary, August 25, 1944. See also Blumenson, *The Patton Papers, Volume II*, 528.
242. Ibid.
243. XX Corps, *XX Corps, Its History and Service in World War II*, 88.
244. Hofmann, *The Super Sixth*, 114.
245. Third U.S. Army, *After Action Report, Volume I*, 43.
246. Koyen, *The Fourth Armored Division*, 38–39.
247. Patton diary, August 26, 1944, box 3, GSP LOC.
248. Patton diary, August 27, 1944, box 3, GSP LOC.
249. Patton diary, August 28, 1944, box 3, GSP LOC.
250. Farago, *Patton: Ordeal and Triumph*, 567.
251. Patton diary, August 29, 1944, box 3, GSP LOC.
252. 12th Army Group G-4 Section, "Report of Operations (Final After Action Report)," 27.
253. Ibid.
254. Ibid.
255. Third U.S. Army, *After Action Report, Volume I*, 46.
256. Patton diary, August 29, 1944.
257. Blumenson, *The Patton Papers, Volume II*, 529–30.
258. Ambrose, *The Supreme Commander*, 507.
259. Montgomery, *The Memoirs of Field Marshal Montgomery*, 242.
260. Bradley, *A Soldier's Story*, 405.
261. Rickard, *Patton at Bay*, 51.
262. 21st Army Group, *The Administrative History of the Operations of 21 Army Group on the Continent of Europe* (Germany: Allied Forces, 21st Army Group, November 1945), 45.
263. Ibid., 47.
264. Farago, *Patton: Ordeal and Triumph*, 583.
265. David P. Colley, *The Road to Victory* (New York: Warner Books, 2000), 57–58.
266. Ibid., 109.
267. D'Este, *Patton: A Genius for War*, 649.
268. Crosswell, *The Chief of Staff*, 269.
269. Ibid.

270. Martin van Creveld, *Supplying War* (Cambridge, U.K.: Cambridge University Press, 1977), 214. Note, however, John Lynn's objections: "When Creveld criticizes the logisticians who hampered Patton by stating that their calculations were in error, he obscures the point that these pusillanimous bureaucrats had an abundance of material in the first place precisely because earlier phases of planning had succeeded." John A. Lynn, *Feeding Mars: Logistics in Western Warfare from the Middle Ages to the Present* (Boulder, Colo.: Westview Press, 1993), 14. While true, Lynn's point does not seem to challenge the points made here.
271. Van Creveld, 213.
272. Ibid.
273. See Colley, *The Road to Victory*, 27.
274. Crosswell, *The Chief of Staff*, 257.
275. Baldwin, *Tiger Jack*, 154.
276. Third U.S. Army, *After Action Report, Volume I*, 47.
277. Baldwin, *Tiger Jack*, 69.
278. Ibid., 68.
279. XX Corps, *XX Corps, Its History and Service in World War II*, 93.
280. Patton diary, August 30, 1944, box 3, GSP LOC.
281. Ibid.
282. Blumenson, *The Patton Papers, Volume II*, 531.
283. Third U.S. Army, *After Action Report, Volume I*, 48.
284. Blumenson, *The Patton Papers, Volume II*, 531.
285. "Transcript of Conference between Lt. Gen. G. S. Patton, Jr., and Third Army Correspondents, 2100, 7 Sept 1944," 3.
286. Ibid.
287. Butcher, *My Three Years with Eisenhower*, 655.
288. Yeide, *Fighting Patton*, 276.
289. Ibid., 276–77.
290. Patton diary, September 2, 1944, box 3, GSP LOC.
291. Ibid.
292. See Rickard, *Patton at Bay*, 33–34.
293. Third U.S. Army, *After Action Report, Volume I*, 63.
294. See Irzyk, *Gasoline to Patton*, 213.
295. 12th Army Group G-4 Section, "Report of Operations (Final After Action Report)," 35.
296. Baldwin, *Tiger Jack*, 86.
297. "Transcript of Conference between Lt. Gen. G. S. Patton, Jr., and Third Army Correspondents, 2100, 7 Sept 1944," 2.
298. Patton diary, September 2, 1944.

Chapter 8. Death and Resurrection

Epigraph: Showalter, *Patton and Rommel*, 424.
1. Patton diary, May 8, 1945, box 3, GSP LOC.
2. Bradley, *A Soldier's Story*, 541.
3. Farago, *Patton: Ordeal and Triumph*, 791.
4. D'Este, *Patton: A Genius for War*, 733–34.
5. Patton diary, May 10, 1945, box 3, GSP LOC.
6. Memorandum of the Joint Chiefs of Staff No. 1067 (revised), 10 May 1945, box 52, GSP LOC.
7. D'Este, *Patton: A Genius for War*, 740.
8. Third Army Headquarters, "Notes for the Army Commanders," 28 September 1945, box 51, GSP LOC.
9. D'Este, *Patton: A Genius for War*, 738.
10. Blumenson, *The Patton Papers, Volume II*, 712.
11. Patton diary, May 14, 1945, box 3, GSP LOC.
12. Patton diary, May 18, 1945, box 3, GSP LOC.
13. Farago, *Patton: Ordeal and Triumph*, 808.
14. D'Este, *Patton: A Genius for War*, 736.
15. Ladislas Farago, *The Last Days of Patton* (New York: Berkley Books, 1986), 79.
16. Hirshson, *General Patton: A Soldier's Life*, 644.
17. D'Este, *Patton: A Genius for War*, 749.
18. Blumenson, *The Patton Papers, Volume II*, 723.
19. Patton at press conference, 22 September 1945, recorded in a Memorandum for Record, 27 September 1945, Headquarters Third United States Army, 1, GSP, LOC.
20. Blumenson, *The Patton Papers, Volume II*, 701.
21. Hirshson, *General Patton: A Soldier's Life*, 653.
22. Blumenson, *The Patton Papers, Volume II*, 735.
23. Undated article, "Shortage of Doctors," folder 7, box 51, GSP LOC.
24. Blumenson, *The Patton Papers, Volume II*, 727.
25. Hanson, *The Soul of Battle*, 273.
26. Blumenson noted, "They were willing enough to have their Army commander remind them of the glories of their service under him, but as for the future—well, they had come to a parting of the ways with Patton and all that he stood for." Blumenson, *The Patton Papers, Volume II*, 737.
27. Patton diary, May 16, 1945, box 3, GSP LOC.
28. D'Este, *Patton: A Genius for War*, 758.
29. Blumenson, *The Patton Papers, Volume II*, 725.
30. Showalter, *Patton and Rommel*, 413.
31. Patton diary, August 8, 1945, box 3, GSP LOC.
32. Ibid.
33. Blumenson, *The Patton Papers, Volume II*, 734.

34. Patton diary, August 8, 1945.
35. Patton diary, July 4, 1945, box 3, GSP LOC. See also Blumenson, *The Patton Papers, Volume II*, 724.
36. Bradley and Blair, *A General's Life*, 444.
37. Patton diary, August 18, 1945, box 3, GSP LOC.
38. Hirshson, *General Patton: A Soldier's Life*, 646.
39. Blumenson, *The Patton Papers, Volume II*, 742.
40. Farago, *Patton: Ordeal and Triumph*, 811.
41. Patton, Headquarters Third Army Memorandum, 27 September 1945, 1, box 51, GSP LOC.
42. Blumenson, *The Patton Papers, Volume II*, 744.
43. Wallace, *Patton and His Third Army*, 209.
44. Blumenson, *The Patton Papers, Volume II*, 748.
45. D'Este, *Patton: A Genius for War*, 739.
46. Patton diary, August 8, 1945.
47. Ibid.
48. Ibid.
49. See Hirshson, *General Patton: A Soldier's Life*, 659.
50. D'Este, *Patton: A Genius for War*, 761.
51. Hirshson, *General Patton: A Soldier's Life*, 656.
52. Ibid.
53. Patton diary, September 16, 1945, box 3, GSP LOC.
54. Blumenson, *The Patton Papers, Volume II*, 753.
55. Ibid., 758.
56. Farago, *Patton: Ordeal and Triumph*, 806.
57. D'Este, *Patton: A Genius for War*, 763.
58. In addition to these correspondents were Richard Kasischke of the Associated Press, Tryggue Strom of the Norwegian Broadcasting Co., Helgo Waale of Fremtiden, and Chester Wilmot of the British Broadcasting System. "War Correspondents at Headquarters Third Army Briefing 22 September," 22 September 1945, GSP LOC.
59. Farago, *Patton: Ordeal and Triumph*, 812.
60. D'Este, *Patton: A Genius for War*, 763.
61. Blumenson, *The Patton Papers, Volume II*, 763.
62. Hirshson, *General Patton: A Soldier's Life*, 657. See also Third Army Headquarters, "Memorandum: extract of the official diary of 22 September 1945," 27 September 1945, box 51, GSP LOC.
63. Patton diary, September 22, 1945, box 3, GSP LOC.
64. Blumenson, *The Patton Papers, Volume II*, 762.
65. Ibid., 763.
66. Hirshson, *General Patton: A Soldier's Life*, 663.
67. Blumenson, *The Patton Papers, Volume II*, 764.

68. D'Este, *Patton: A Genius for War*, 769.
69. Blumenson, *The Patton Papers, Volume II*, 767.
70. Ibid., 769.
71. Butcher, *My Three Years with Eisenhower*, 820.
72. See Farago, *Patton: Ordeal and Triumph*, 815.
73. Blumenson, *The Patton Papers, Volume II*, 770.
74. Ibid., 773.
75. Showalter, *Patton and Rommel*, 413.
76. U.S. Forces, European Theater Main, "Military Government United States Zone Law No. 8," box 51, GSP LOC.
77. Blumenson, *The Patton Papers, Volume II*, 776.
78. Hirshson, *General Patton: A Soldier's Life*, 665.
79. Blumenson, *The Patton Papers, Volume II*, 777.
80. Ibid., 778–79.
81. Patton diary, September 29, 1945, box 3, GSP LOC.
82. D'Este, *Patton: A Genius for War*, 771.
83. Patton diary, October 17, 1945, box 3, GSP LOC. Also see Third Army Headquarters, Memorandum (No Subject), 28 September 1945, box 51, GSP LOC.
84. See Hirshson, *General Patton: A Soldier's Life*, 669.
85. Patton diary, September 29, 1945.
86. Blumenson, *The Patton Papers, Volume II*, 783.
87. Patton diary, September 29, 1945.
88. Ibid., 786.
89. Ibid.
90. Hirshson, *General Patton: A Soldier's Life*, 668.
91. D'Este, *Patton: A Genius for War*, 772.
92. Patton diary, October 2, 1945, box 3, GSP LOC.
93. Blumenson, *The Patton Papers, Volume II*, 791.
94. Hirshson, *General Patton: A Soldier's Life*, 670.
95. Patton diary, October 1, 1945, box 3, GSP LOC.
96. Patton diary, October 7, 1945, box 3, GSP LOC. Also see Farago, *Patton: Ordeal and Triumph*, 819.
97. Blumenson, *The Patton Papers, Volume II*, 810.
98. Patton, "Notes on interview given Mr. McDermott, UP, by General Patton," 8 October 1945, box 51, GSP LOC.
99. Hirshson, *General Patton: A Soldier's Life*, 669.
100. Blumenson, *The Patton Papers, Volume II*, 786.
101. Ibid., 796.
102. D'Este, *Patton: A Genius for War*, 778.
103. Blumenson, *The Patton Papers, Volume II*, 800.
104. Patton diary, October 13, 1945, box 3, GSP LOC.

105. Patton cited by D'Este, *Patton: A Genius for War*, 780.
106. Blumenson, *The Patton Papers, Volume II*, 798.
107. Farago, *Patton: Ordeal and Triumph*, 820.
108. Ibid., 823.
109. D'Este, *Patton: A Genius for War*, 782.
110. Blumenson, *The Patton Papers, Volume II*, 812.
111. Patton diary, December 3, 1945, box 3, GSP LOC.
112. Ibid., 813.
113. Farago, *Patton: Ordeal and Triumph*, 828.
114. Hirshson, *General Patton: A Soldier's Life*, 678.
115. Ibid.
116. Blumenson, *The Patton Papers, Volume II*, 833.
117. Farago, *Patton: Ordeal and Triumph*, 831.
118. Bradley and Blair, *A General's Life*, 464.
119. Merle Miller, *Ike the Soldier: As They Knew Him* (New York: G. P. Putnam's Sons, 1987), 349.
120. Bradley and Blair, *A General's Life*, 467.
121. Crosswell, *The Chief of Staff*, 330–32.
122. Bradley and Blair, *A General's Life*, 464.
123. See Lewis Sorley, *Thunderbolt: General Creighton Abrams and the Army of His Times* (New York: Simon and Schuster, 1992), 105.
124. Trevor N. Dupuy, Curt Johnson, and David L. Bongard, *The Harper Encyclopedia of Military Biography* (New York: Booksales, 2000), 7.
125. Sorley, *Thunderbolt*, 107.
126. Ernest Dupuy noted that the "opinion of many professional officers" of the Doolittle Board was that "the standards of the 'old' Army were so high that the 'new' Army had not come up to them, instead of recommending such indoctrination as would bring the 'new' to the higher standard, recommended lowering the standard to meet the situation." Ernest R. Dupuy, *The Compact History of the U.S. Army* (New York: Hawthorne, 1973), 273.
127. Ibid.
128. See Weigley, *History of the United States Army*, 490–95.
129. See Thomas D. Boettcher, *First Call: The Making of the Modern U.S. Military, 1945–1953* (Boston: Little, Brown, 1992), 6.
130. See White House Office of Management and Budget, *Historical Tables, Budget of the U.S. Government, FY 2005* (Washington, D.C.: Government Printing Office, 2004), 45–52.
131. The Army and Air Force fell from 8.2 million men on the day of the Japanese surrender to about 1.5 million twelve months later. Bradley and Blair, *A General's Life*, 464.
132. Pogue, *George C. Marshall, Interviews and Reminiscences*, 253.
133. Sorley, *Thunderbolt*, 104.

134. Bradley and Blair, *A General's Life*, 487.
135. Weigley, *History of the United States Army*, 503.
136. Robert A. Doughty, *Leavenworth Papers: The Evolution of the U.S. Army Tactical Doctrine, 1946–76* (Fort Leavenworth, Kans.: Combat Studies Institute, 1979), 2.
137. Ibid., 5.
138. House, *Toward Combined Arms Warfare*, 147.
139. Doughty, *Leavenworth Papers*, 5.
140. Phillip L. Bolté, "Post–World War II and Korea," in Hofmann and Starry, *Camp Colt to Desert Storm*, 218.
141. Doughty, *Leavenworth Papers*, 2.
142. Bradley and Blair, *A General's Life*, 489.
143. Boettcher, *First Call*, 122.
144. Bradley and Blair, *A General's Life*, 475.
145. Ibid., 518.
146. Ibid., 500.
147. Ibid., 478.
148. D'Este, *Patton: A Genius for War*, 737.
149. William Manchester, *American Caesar: Douglas MacArthur, 1880–1964* (New York: Little, Brown, 1978), 683.
150. Doughty, *Leavenworth Papers*, 9.
151. Manchester, *American Caesar*, 683.
152. Dupuy and Dupuy, *The Harper Encyclopedia of Military History*, 1357.
153. Ibid., 1361.
154. See United States Military Academy, *Bugle Notes* 71 (West Point, N.Y.: United States Military Academy, 1979), 265.
155. Doughty, *Leavenworth Papers*, 7.
156. Bradley and Blair, *A General's Life*, 523.
157. Ambrose, *The Supreme Commander*, 105.
158. Weigley, *History of the United States Army*, 522.
159. Ridgway to Van Fleet, in *Major Problems in American Military History*, ed. John Whiteclay Chambers II and G. Kurt Piehler (New York: Houghton Mifflin, 1999), 390.
160. See Doughty, *Leavenworth Papers*, 10.
161. Manchester, *American Caesar*, 667.
162. House, *Toward Combined Arms Warfare*, 153.
163. Doughty, *Leavenworth Papers*, 11–12.
164. Hirshson, *General Patton: A Soldier's Life*, 693–94.
165. House, *Toward Combined Arms Warfare*, 153.
166. Maxwell Taylor, *The Uncertain Trumpet* (New York: Harper and Brothers, 1959), 15.
167. Bolté in Hofmann and Starry, *Camp Colt to Desert Storm*, 256.

168. Doughty, *Leavenworth Papers*, 12.
169. Hirshson, *General Patton: A Soldier's Life*, 685.
170. Taylor, *The Uncertain Trumpet*, 18.
171. Edgar F. Raines Jr. and David R. Campbell, *The Army and the Joint Chiefs of Staff* (Washington, D.C.: U.S. Army Center of Military History, 1985), 85.
172. House, *Toward Combined Arms Warfare*, 154.
173. Weigley, *History of the United States Army*, 522.
174. S. D. Badsey, "The American Experience of Armour, 1919–1953," in Harris and Toase, *Armoured Warfare*, 144.
175. House, *Toward Combined Arms Warfare*, 154–58.
176. Doughty, *Leavenworth Papers*, 17–18.
177. Edward F. Witsell, *Russian Combat Methods in World War II*, pamphlet no. 20–230, Department of the Army, November 1950.
178. Bradley and Blair, *A General's Life*, 511.
179. Taylor, *The Uncertain Trumpet*, 23.
180. Dupuy, *The Compact History of the U.S. Army*, 292.
181. Doughty, *Leavenworth Papers*, 19.
182. House, *Toward Combined Arms Warfare*, 158.
183. Doughty, *Leavenworth Papers*, 22.
184. Ibid., 23.
185. Ibid., 25.
186. Weigley, *The American Way of War*, 458.
187. H. R. McMaster, *Dereliction of Duty: Johnson, McNamara, the Joint Chiefs of Staff, and the Lies that Led to Vietnam* (New York: HarperPerennial, 1997), 22.
188. Doughty, *Leavenworth Papers*, 29.
189. Harry Summers Jr., *On Strategy: A Critical Analysis of the Vietnam War* (Novato, Calif.: Presidio Press, 1983), 115–16.
190. Donn A. Starry, *Armored Combat in Vietnam* (New York: Arno Press, 1980), 6.
191. Patton, *War as I Knew It*, 413.
192. Weigley, *History of the United States Army*, 545.
193. Doughty, *Leavenworth Papers*, 36.
194. Lewis Sorley, "Adaptation and Impact: Mounted Combat in Vietnam," in Hofmann and Starry, *Camp Colt to Desert Storm*, 342.
195. See James Kitfield, *Prodigal Soldiers: How the Generation of Officers Born of Vietnam Revolutionized the American Style of War* (New York: Simon and Schuster, 1995), 45.
196. McMaster, *Dereliction of Duty*, 45.
197. See, for example, McMaster on Wheeler's deceptions, *Dereliction of Duty*, 220–22, 303, 321, 331.
198. Summers, *On Strategy: A Critical Analysis of the Vietnam War*, 163.
199. See Doughty, *Leavenworth Papers*, 37.
200. D'Este, *Patton: A Genius for War*, 306.

201. Blumenson, *The Patton Papers, Volume II*, 624.
202. Ibid., 293–94, 8.
203. Colin Powell, *My American Journey* (New York: Random House, 1995), 132.
204. Doughty, *Leavenworth Papers*, 40.
205. Patton, *War as I Knew It*, 403.
206. Sorley, *Thunderbolt*, 233.
207. Summers, *On Strategy: A Critical Analysis of the Vietnam War*, 133.
208. Walt Ulmer and Mike Malone, "Study on Military Professionalism," U.S. Army War College, 30 June 1970, 108.
209. Kitfield, *Prodigal Soldiers*, 108.
210. Royle, *Patton: Old Blood and Guts*, 199.
211. D'Este, *Patton: A Genius for War*, 2.
212. Royle, *Patton: Old Blood and Guts*, 200.
213. Hirshson, *General Patton: A Soldier's Life*, 699.
214. Sorley, *Thunderbolt*, 335.
215. See Kitfield, *Prodigal Soldiers*, 146–48.
216. Doughty, *Leavenworth Papers*, 40.
217. Paul H. Herbert, *Deciding What Has to Be Done: General William E. DePuy and the 1976 Edition of FM-100-5 Operations* (Fort Leavenworth, Kans.: U.S. Army Command and General Staff College, 1988), 6.
218. U.S. Army Field Manual 100–5, *Operations of the Army Forces in the Field* (Washington, D.C.: Department of the Army, September 1968), 1-6.
219. Ibid., 5-1.
220. Patton walked with the division and called it "bad, the discipline poor, the men filthy, and the officers apathetic." Blumenson, *The Patton Papers, Volume II*, 497.
221. Ibid., 616, 619.
222. Herbert, *Deciding What Has to Be Done*, 15–16.
223. Ibid., 16.
224. George E. Knapp, "Antiarmor Operations on the Golan Heights, October 1973," in *Combined Arms in Battle Since 1939*, ed. Roger J. Spiller (Fort Leavenworth, Kans.: U.S. Army Command and General Staff College, 1992), 27.
225. Heidi Toffler and Alvin Toffler, *War and Antiwar: Making Sense of Today's Global Chaos* (London: Warner Books, 1993), 58.
226. Sorley, *Thunderbolt*, 299.
227. See F. H. Toase, "The Israeli Experience of Armoured Warfare," in Harris and Toase, *Armoured Warfare*, 163–64.
228. House, *Toward Combined Arms Warfare*, 173.
229. Citino, *Armored Forces: History and Sourcebook*, 116.
230. Herbert, *Deciding What Has to Be Done*, 30.
231. Kitfield, *Prodigal Soldiers*, 152.

232. William E. DePuy, "Keynote Address at the TRADOC Leadership Conference," 22 May 1974, Fort Benning, Georgia, in *Selected Papers of General William E. DePuy*, ed. Richard M. Swain (Fort Leavenworth, Kans.: U.S. Army Command and General Staff College, 1973), 115.
233. Toffler and Toffler, *War and Antiwar*, 58.
234. Patton, *War as I Knew It*, 405.
235. See Herbert, *Deciding What Has to Be Done*, 30–32.
236. Orr Kelly, *King of the Killing Zone* (New York: W. W. Norton, 1989), 13.
237. DePuy, "Implications of the Middle East War," in *Selected Papers of General William E. DePuy*, 86.
238. Kelly, *King of the Killing Zone*, 129.
239. DePuy, "Implications of the Middle East War," 87.
240. Patton, *War as I Knew It*, 413.
241. DePuy, "Infantry Fighting Positions," in *Selected Papers of General William E. DePuy*, 172.
242. Herbert, *Deciding What Has to Be Done*, 35.
243. Paul F. Gorman, *The Secret of Future Victories* (Fort Leavenworth, Kans.: Combat Studies Institute, 1992), III-16.
244. Herbert, *Deciding What Has to Be Done*, 41.
245. Blumenson, *The Patton Papers, Volume II*, 44.
246. Herbert, *Deciding What Has to Be Done*, 41.
247. Toffler and Toffler, *War and Antiwar*, 59.
248. Herbert, *Deciding What Has to Be Done*, 81.
249. Harry Summers Jr., *On Strategy II: A Critical Analysis of the Gulf War* (New York: Dell Publishing, 1992), 124.
250. Christopher Gabel, "Doctrine: Active Defense," in Spiller, *Combined Arms in Battle Since 1939*, 94.
251. Herbert, *Deciding What Has to Be Done*, 97.
252. Doughty, *Leavenworth Papers*, 43.
253. Kenneth Allard, *Command, Control, and the Common Defense* (Washington, D.C.: National Defense University Press, 1996), 178.
254. Toffler and Toffler, *War and Antiwar*, 66.
255. Kitfield, *Prodigal Soldiers*, 305.
256. Kelly, *King of the Killing Zone*, 240.
257. Paddy Griffith, *Forward into Battle: Fighting Tactics from Waterloo to the Near Future* (Novato, Calif.: Presidio Press, 1992), 166.
258. Allen, *Lucky Forward!* 72.
259. Blumenson, *The Patton Papers, Volume II*, 555.
260. Allard, *Command, Control, and the Common Defense*, 179.
261. DePuy, "Towards a Balanced Doctrine," in *Selected Papers of General William E. DePuy*, 315.
262. Kitfield, *Prodigal Soldiers*, 309.
263. Blumenson, *The Patton Papers, Volume II*, 43.

264. Patton, *War as I Knew It*, 357.
265. Summers, *On Strategy II: A Critical Analysis of the Gulf War*, 148.
266. U.S. Army Field Manual 100–5, *Operations* (Washington, D.C.: Department of the Army, 1986), 98.
267. Axelrod, *Patton: A Biography*, viii.
268. DePuy, "Towards a Balanced Doctrine," 316.
269. U.S. Army Field Manual 100–5, *Operations* (1986), 17.
270. Patton, *War as I Knew It*, 357.
271. Patton, undated draft address, June 1941, 2, box 45, GSP LOC. See also Blumenson, *The Patton Papers, Volume II*, 39–40.
272. U.S. Army Field Manual 100–5, *Operations* (1986), 17.
273. George J. Church, "How Much Is Too Much?" *Time*, 12 February 1990, 15–16.
274. Dean Fischer et al., "Sayings of Stormin' Norman," *Time*, 11 March 1991, 27.
275. Toffler and Toffler, *War and Antiwar*, 85.
276. Powell, *My American Journey*, 164.
277. Norman Schwarzkopf, *It Doesn't Take a Hero: The Autobiography of General H. Norman Schwarzkopf* (New York: Linda Grey Bantam Books, 1996), 200.
278. Rick Atkinson, *Crusade: The Untold Story of the Persian Gulf War* (Boston: Houghton Mifflin, 1993), 22.
279. James Blackwell, *Thunder in the Desert* (New York: Bantam Books, 1991), xxiv.
280. Schwarzkopf, *It Doesn't Take a Hero*, 381.
281. Ibid., 383.
282. Atkinson, *Crusade*, 403.
283. Powell, *My American Journey*, 518.
284. Schwarzkopf, *It Doesn't Take a Hero*, 463.
285. Ibid., 381.
286. Summers, *On Strategy II: A Critical Analysis of the Gulf War*, 199.

Chapter 9. The Limits of Legacy

Epigraph: Patton to his staff after operations in North Africa. Puryear, *Nineteen Stars*, 247.

1. John Walcott, "Does America Need an Army?" *U.S. News and World Report*, 11 December 1989, 22.
2. For manpower numbers see Church "How Much Is Too Much?" *Time*, 12 February 1990, 16. See also Richard Sisk, "Army Adapts to Fewer Troops in Europe," Military.com, 13 September 2013, http://www.military.com/daily-news/2013/09/13/army-adapts-to-fewer-troops-in-europe.html. See also Defense Manpower Data Center, "Total Military Personnel and Dependent End Strength By Service, Regional Area, and Country," 30 June 2015.

3. Sanjeev Gupta et al., "The Elusive Peace Dividend," *Finance and Development* 39, no. 4 (December 2002).
4. U.S. Army Field Manual 100–5, *Operations* (Washington, D.C.: Headquarters Department of the Army, 1993), 6–8.
5. Evan Thomas and Martha Brant, "The Secret War," *Newsweek*, 21 April 2003, 29.
6. Richard J. Newman, "Not by the Playbook," *U.S. News and World Report*, 7 April 2003, 27.
7. Evan Thomas and Daniel Klaidman, "The War Room," *Newsweek*, 21 April 2003, 31.
8. Barry McCaffrey, "Gaining Victory in Iraq," *U.S. News and World Report*, 7 April 2003, 26.
9. J. T. MacCurdy, *The Structure of Morale* (London: Cambridge University Press, 1943), 12–26. See also the discussion on this topic by Malcolm Gladwell, *David and Goliath: Underdogs, Misfits, and the Art of Battling Giants* (New York: Little, Brown, 2013), 136.
10. David Talbot, "How Tech Failed in Iraq," *Technology Review: MIT's Magazine of Innovation* (November 2004), 41.
11. Evan Thomas, and John Barry, "A Plan Under Attack," *Newsweek*, 7 April 2003, 29.
12. Michael Elliott, "The Devastating Attack on U.N. Headquarters in Baghdad Opens Yet One More Front in the U.S. War Against Terrorism," *Time*, 1 September 2003, 35.
13. Mark Thompson, "Broken Down," *Time*, 16 April 2007, 30.
14. Ibid., 32.
15. Victor Davis Hanson, "What Would Patton Say About the Present War?" *Imprimis* 33, no 10. (October 2004).
16. Thomas F. Talley, "Is Reorganization of the Army under the Unit-of-Action and the Unit-of-Employment Concept Consistent with the Army's Identity?" (master's thesis, U.S. Army Command and General Staff College, Fort Leavenworth, Kansas, 2004), 1.
17. See U.S. Army Field Manual 3–24, *Counterinsurgency* (Washington, D.C.: Headquarters Department of the Army, 2006), 47–49.
18. See James A. Baker and Lee H. Hamilton, *The Iraq Study Group Report* (Washington, D.C.: United States Institute of Peace, 2006).
19. See Michael Duffy, "What a Surge Really Means," *Time*, 15 January 2007.
20. Joel Roberts, "Senator Reid on Iraq: 'This War is Lost,'" CBS News, http://www.cbsnews.com/news/senator-reid-on-iraq-this-war-is-lost/.
21. See Daniel L. Byman, "The Resurgence of al Qaeda in Iraq," Brookings Institution, http://www.brookings.edu/research/testimony/2013/12/12-resurgence-al-qaeda-iraq-byman.

22. Aryn Baker, and Loi Kolay, "The Longest War," *Time*, 20 April 2009, 27.
23. Johnson, *Fast Tanks and Heavy Bombers*, 129.
24. Hofmann, "Army Doctrine and the Christie Tank," in Hofmann and Starry, *Camp Colt to Desert Storm*, 118.
25. "Armor School Moves Operations to Fort Benning," *Armor* (July–September 2013).
26. Ibid.
27. Ben Patton, "What Would General Patton Do in Iraq and Afghanistan?" Huffington Post, 21 March 2012, www.huffingtonpost.com/ben-patton/general-patton-iraq-afghanistan_b_1371117.html?
28. Bill O'Reilly, Fox News, 29 September 2014, http://www.foxnews.com/on-air/americas-newsroom/2014/09/29/war-isis-should-us-take-page-pattons-playbook.
29. Arthur Herman and William Luti, "How America's Drones Can Defeat ISIS," *Defense One*, 15 March 2015, http://www.defenseone.com/ideas/2015/03/how-americas-drones-can-defeat-isis/107565/.
30. Mark Thompson, "Pentagon and Its Allies Begin the Budget Death Watch," *Time*, 18 March 2015.
31. See Jessica Stern, "The Protean Enemy," *Foreign Affairs* 82, issue 4 (July/August 2003).

SELECTED BIBLIOGRAPHY

Archival Sources
George S. Patton Jr. Papers, Library of Congress, Washington, D.C.
National Archives and Records Administration II, College Park, Md.

Primary Sources
21st Army Group. *The Administrative History of the Operations of 21 Army Group on the Continent of Europe*. Germany: Allied Forces Europe, 1945.
Alexander, Harold. *The Alexander Memoirs, 1940–1945*. New York: McGraw-Hill, 1962.
Allen, Robert S. *Lucky Forward! The History of Patton's Third U.S. Army*. New York: Vanguard Press, 1947.
Bradley, Omar N. *A Soldier's Story*. New York: Henry Holt, 1951.
——— and Clay Blair. *A General's Life*. New York: Simon and Schuster, 1983.
Brooke, Alan. *War Diaries, 1939–1945*. Berkeley: University of California Press, 2003.
Butcher, Harry C. *My Three Years with Eisenhower: The Personal Diary of Captain Harry C. Butcher, USNR, Naval Aide to General Eisenhower, 1942 to 1945*. New York: Simon and Schuster, 1946.
Clausewitz, Carl von. *On War* (1882). Edited and translated by Peter Paret and Michael Howard. New York: Alfred Knopf, 1993.
Codman, Charles R. *Drive*. Boston: Little, Brown, 1957.
Collins, J. Lawton. *Lightning Joe: An Autobiography*. Baton Rouge: Louisiana State University Press, 1979.
Eisenhower, Dwight D. *Crusade in Europe*. Garden City, N.Y.: Doubleday, 1948.
First U.S. Army. *First U.S. Army Report of Operations, 20 October 1943–1 August 1944*. Paris: First U.S. Army, 1944.
Irzyk, Albin F. *Gasoline to Patton: A Different War*. Oakland, Calif.: Elderberry Press, 2005.
Jomini, Baron Henri de. *The Art of War* (1862). Westport, Conn.: Greenwood Press, 1974.
Koch, Oscar W. with Robert G. Hayes. *G-2: Intelligence for Patton*. Philadelphia: Whitmore Publishing, 1971.
Lande, D. A. *I Was with Patton: First-Person Accounts of World War II in George S. Patton's Command*. St. Paul, Minn.: MBI Publishing, 2002.
Montgomery, Bernard Law. *The Memoirs of Field Marshal Montgomery*. New York: Collins, 1958.

———. *Normandy to the Baltic.* London: Hutchinson, 1958.
Patton, George S. Jr. *War as I Knew It.* Boston: Houghton Mifflin, 1947.
———. *Military Essays and Articles, 1885–1945.* Edited by Charles M. Province. San Diego, Calif.: The George S. Patton Jr. Historical Society, 2002.
- "Armored Cars with Cavalry." *Cavalry Journal,* January 1924.
- "Cavalry Work of the Punitive Expedition." *Cavalry Journal,* 1917.
- "Comments on 'Cavalry Tanks.'" *Cavalry Journal,* July 1921.
- "The Effect of Weapons on War." *Cavalry Journal,* November 1930.
- "Light Tanks." 12 December 1917.
- "Mechanization and Cavalry." *Cavalry Journal,* 1930.
- "Mechanized Forces." *Cavalry Journal,* September-October 1933.
- "Notes on Tactics and Technique of Desert Warfare." 1942.
- "The Obligations of Being an Officer." October 1, 1919.
- "The Probable Characteristics of the Next War and the Organization, Tactics, and Equipment Necessary to Meet Them." Dissertation, Army War College, 29 February 1932.
- "Report of Personal Experiences in the Tank Corps." 16 December 1918.
- "The Secret of Victory." 1926.
- "Success in War." *Cavalry Journal,* January 1931.
- "Tanks in Future Wars." *Cavalry Journal,* May 1920.
- "Training Memoranda to his Regiment." *Cavalry Journal,* July-August 1940.
- "War as She Is." 1919.
- "What the War Did for Cavalry." *Cavalry Journal,* April 1922.
- "Why Men Fight." 1927.

———. "Notes on Combat Armored Divisions." 1944. www.pattonhq.com/textfiles/divnotes.html.
Pogue, Forrest C. *George C. Marshall, Interviews and Reminiscences.* Lexington, Va.: George C. Marshall Research Foundation, 1991.
Powell, Colin. *My American Journey.* New York: Random House, 1995.
Rooney, Andy. *My War.* New York: Times Books, 1995.
Schwarzkopf, Norman. *It Doesn't Take a Hero: The Autobiography of General H. Norman Schwarzkopf.* New York: Linda Grey Bantam Books, 1996.
Scott, Winfield. *Infantry Tactics.* New York: Harper and Brothers, 1835.
Summersby, Kay. *Eisenhower Was My Boss.* New York: Prentice Hall, Inc., 1948.
Sun Tzu. *The Art of War.* Edited by James Clavell. New York: Delacorte Press, 1983.
Swain, Richard M., ed. *Selected Papers of General William E. Depuy.* Fort Leavenworth, Kans.: U.S. Army Command and General Staff College, 1973.
Third U.S. Army. *After Action Report, Third United States Army, 1 August 1944–9 May 1945.* Regensburg, Germany: Third Army Headquarters, 15 May 1945.

Truscott, Lucian Jr. *The Twilight of the Cavalry*. Lawrence: University Press of Kansas, 1989.
U.S. Army (War Department). *Cavalry Drill Regulations 1916*. Washington, D.C.: U.S. Army, 1917.
———. *Infantry Drill Regulations (Provisional) 1919*. Washington, D.C.: Government Printing Office, 1919.
———. *Field Service Regulations 1923*. Washington, D.C.: Government Printing Office, 1924.
———. Field Manual 100–15, *Manual for Commanders of Large Units (Provisional), Volume I (Operations)*. Washington, D.C.: Government Printing Office, 1930.
———. Field Manual 100–5, *Operations*. Washington, D.C.: Government Printing Office, 22 May 1941.
———. Field Manual 100–5, *Operations*. Washington, D.C.: Government Printing Office, 15 June 1944.
U.S. Department of the Army Field Manual 100–5, *Operations of the Army Forces in the Field*. Washington, D.C.: Department of the Army, September 1968.
———. Field Manual 100–5, *Operations*. Washington, D.C.: Department of the Army, 1986.
———. Field Manual 100–5, *Operations*. Washington, D.C.: Headquarters Department of the Army, 1993.
———. Field Manual 2.0, *Intelligence*. Washington, D.C.: Headquarters Department of the Army, 17 May 2004.
———. Field Manual 3–24, *Counterinsurgency*. Washington, D.C.: Headquarters Department of the Army, 2006.
U.S. Department of Defense Field Manual 3–0, *Operations*. Washington, D.C.: Department of Defense, 27 February 2008.
United States Military Academy. *Bugle Notes* 71. West Point, N.Y.: United States Military Academy, 1979.
Wedemeyer, Albert C. *Wedemeyer Reports!* New York: Henry Holt, 1958.
White House Office of Management and Budget. *Historical Tables, Budget of the U.S. Government, FY 2005*. Washington, D.C.: Government Printing Office, 2004.
XX Corps. *XX Corps, Its History and Service in World War II*. Osaka, Japan: XX Corps Association, 1946.

Secondary Sources

Allard, Kenneth. *Command, Control, and the Common Defense*. Washington, D.C.: National Defense University Press, 1996.
Ambrose, Stephen. *Ike: Abilene to Berlin: The Life of Dwight D. Eisenhower from His Childhood in Abilene, Kansas, Through His Command of the Allied Forces in Europe*. New York: HarperCollins, 1973.
———. *Eisenhower, Soldier and Statesman*. New York: Simon and Schuster, 1990.

———. *The Supreme Commander: The War Years of Dwight D. Eisenhower.* Jackson: University Press of Mississippi, 1999.
Anderson, Charles R. *Algeria-French Morocco.* Washington, D.C.: U.S. Army Center of Military History, 1993.
———. *Tunisia.* Washington, D.C.: U.S. Army Center of Military History, 1993.
"Armor School Moves Operations to Fort Benning." *Armor*, July–September 2013.
Astor, Gerald. *Terrible Terry Allen, Combat General of World War II—The Life of an American Soldier.* New York: Ballantine Books, 2003.
Atkinson, Rick. *An Army at Dawn: The War in North Africa, 1942–1943.* New York: Henry Holt, 2002.
———. *Crusade: The Untold Story of the Persian Gulf War.* Boston: Houghton Mifflin, 1993.
Ayer, Fred Jr. *Before the Colors Fade: A Portrait of a Soldier, George S. Patton Jr.* Boston: Houghton Mifflin, 1964.
Axelrod, Alan. *Patton: A Biography.* New York: Palgrave MacMillan, 2006.
Baker, Aryn and Loi Kolay. "The Longest War." *Time*, 20 April 2009.
Baker, James A. and Lee H. Hamilton. *The Iraq Study Group Report.* Washington, D.C.: United States Institute of Peace, 2006.
Baldwin, Hanson. *Tiger Jack.* Fort Collins, Colo.: Old Army Press, 1979.
Barron, Leo. *Patton at the Battle of the Bulge: How the General's Tanks Turned the Tide at Bastogne.* New York: NAL Caliber, 2014.
Bartholomees, J. Boone Jr., ed. *The U.S. Army War College Guide to National Security Issues, Volume I: Theory of War and Strategy*, 4th ed. Carlisle Barracks, Pa.: U.S. Army War College, July 2010.
Bennett, Ralph. *ULTRA in the West: The Normandy Campaign of 1944–1945.* New York: Charles Scribner's Sons, 1979.
Beyerchen, Alan. "Clausewitz, Nonlinearity, and the Unpredictability of War." *International Security* 17, no. 3, Winter 1992–1993.
Birtle, Andrew J. *Sicily: U.S. Army Campaigns of World War II.* Washington, D.C.: U.S. Army Center of Military History, 1993.
Blackwell, James. *Thunder in the Desert.* New York: Bantam Books, 1991.
Blumenson, Martin. *Breakout and Pursuit.* Fort Leavenworth, Kans.: U.S. Army Center of Military History, 1961.
———. *Kasserine Pass.* Boston: Houghton Mifflin, 1966.
———, ed. *The Patton Papers, Volume I: 1885–1940.* Boston: Houghton Mifflin, 1972.
———, ed. *The Patton Papers, Volume II: 1940–1945.* Boston: Houghton Mifflin, 1974.
———. *Patton: The Man Behind the Legend, 1885–1945.* New York: William Morrow, 1985.
———. *The Battle of the Generals: The Untold Story of the Falaise Pocket—The Campaign that Should Have Won World War II.* New York: William Morrow, 1993.

———. *The Duel for France, 1944: The Men and Battles that Changed the Fate of Europe.* New York: Da Capo Press, 2000.
Boettcher, Thomas D. *First Call: The Making of the Modern U.S. Military, 1945–1953.* Boston: Little, Brown, 1992.
Boland, Barbara E. "American Blitzkrieg." *Military History Magazine*, 29 June 2002.
Breuer, William B. *Operation Torch: The Allied Gamble to Invade North Africa.* New York: St. Martin's Press, 1985.
Brighton, Terry. *Patton, Montgomery, Rommel: Masters of War.* New York: Three Rivers Press, 2008.
Bruce, Robert B. *A Fraternity of Arms: America and France in the Great War.* Lawrence: University Press of Kansas, 2003.
Chailand, Gerard, ed. *The Art of War in World History.* Los Angeles: University of California Press, 1994.
Chambers, John Whiteclay II and G. Kurt Piehler, eds. *Major Problems in American Military History.* New York: Houghton Mifflin, 1999.
Chandler, David, ed. *The Military Maxims of Napoleon.* London: Greenhill Press, 1994.
Church, George J. "How Much Is Too Much?" *Time*, 12 February 1990.
Citino, Robert M. *Armored Forces: History and Sourcebook.* Westport, Conn.: Greenwood Press, 1994.
———. *Quest for Decisive Victory: From Stalemate to Blitzkrieg in Europe, 1899–1940.* Lawrence: University Press of Kansas, 2002.
Colley, David P. *The Road to Victory.* New York: Warner Books, 2000.
Coram, Robert. *Boyd: The Fighter Pilot Who Changed the Art of War.* New York: Little, Brown, 2002.
Corum, James S. *Roots of the Blitzkrieg: Hans Von Seeckt and German Military Reform.* Lawrence: University Press of Kansas, 1994.
Creveld, Martin van. *Supplying War: Logistics from Wallerstein to Patton.* Cambridge, U.K.: Cambridge University Press, 1977.
Crosswell, D. K. R. *The Chief of Staff: The Military Career of General Walter Bedell Smith.* Westport, Conn.: Greenwood Press, 1991.
D'Arcy-Dawson, John. *Tunisian Battle.* London: MacDonald, 1944.
D'Este, Carlo. *Patton: A Genius for War.* New York: HarperPerennial, 1996.
———. *Decision in Normandy.* New York: Konecky and Konecky, 2000.
———. *Bitter Victory: The Battle for Sicily, 1943.* New York: HarperPerennial, 1988.
Daugherty, Leo. *The Battle of the Hedgerows.* St. Paul, Minn.: MBI Publishing, 2001.
Doughty, Robert A. *Leavenworth Papers: The Evolution of the U.S. Army Tactical Doctrine, 1946–76.* Fort Leavenworth, Kans.: Combat Studies Institute, 1979.

Duffy, Michael. "What a Surge Really Means." *Time*, 5 January 2007.
Duggan, William. *Napoleon's Glance: The Secret of Strategy*. New York: Nation Books, 2003.
Dupuy, Ernest R. *The Compact History of the U.S. Army*. New York: Hawthorne, 1973.
Dupuy, Trevor N. and Ernest R. Dupuy. *The Harper Encyclopedia of Military History*. New York: HarperCollins, 1993.
Dupuy, Trevor N., Curt Johnson, and David L. Bongard. *The Harper Encyclopedia of Military Biography*. New York: Booksales, 2000.
Earle, Edward Mead, Gordon A. Craig, and Felix Gilbert, eds. *Makers of Modern Strategy: Military Thought from Machiavelli to Hitler*. Princeton, N.J.: Princeton University Press, 1943.
Eisenhower, David. *Eisenhower at War 1943–1945*. New York: Vintage, 1987.
Elliott, Michael. "The Devastating Attack on U.N. Headquarters in Baghdad Opens Yet One More Front in the U.S. War Against Terrorism." *Time*, 1 September 2003.
Essame, Hubert. *Patton, as Military Commander*. Conshohocken, Pa.: Combined Publishing, 1998. First published 1973 by B. T. Batsford.
Farago, Ladislas. *Patton: Ordeal and Triumph*. New York: Ivan Obolensky, 1963.
———. *The Last Days of Patton*. New York: Berkley Books, 1986.
Finlayson, Kenneth. *An Uncertain Trumpet: The Evolution of U.S. Army Infantry Doctrine, 1919–1941*. Westport, Conn.: Greenwood Press, 2001.
Fischer, Dean et al. "Sayings of Stormin' Norman." *Time*, 11 March 1991.
Forty, George. *The Armies of George S. Patton*. London: Arms and Armour, 1996.
Fuller, J. F. C. *Tanks in the Great War*. London: Battery Press, 1920.
Gabel, Christopher R. *Lorraine Campaign: An Overview, September–December 1944*. Fort Leavenworth, Kans.: U.S. Army Command and General Staff College, February 1985.
———. *The U.S. Army GHQ Maneuvers of 1941*. Fort Leavenworth, Kans.: U.S. Army Center for Military Studies, 1991.
Garth, David. *St-Lo*. Fort Leavenworth, Kans.: U.S. Army Center of Military History, 1994.
Gelb, Norman. *Ike and Monty: Generals at War*. London: Quill, 1995.
Gladwell, Malcolm. *Blink: The Power of Thinking Without Thinking*. New York: Little, Brown, 2005.
———. *David and Goliath: Underdogs, Misfits, and the Art of Battling Giants*. New York: Little, Brown, 2013.
Glass, Robert B. and Philip B. Davidson. *Intelligence Is for Commanders*. Harrisburg, Pa.: Military Service Publishing, 1948.
Gleick, James. *Chaos: Making a New Science*. New York: Penguin Books, 1987.
Goerlitz, Walter. *History of the German General Staff, 1657–1945*. New York: Praeger, 1956.

Gole, Henry G. *The Road to Rainbow: Army Planning for Global War, 1934–1940*. Washington, D.C.: AUSA Institute of Land Warfare/Naval Institute Press, 2004.

Gorman, Paul F. *The Secret of Future Victories*. Fort Leavenworth, Kans.: Combat Studies Institute, 1992.

Greenfield, Kent Roberts, Robert R. Palmer, and Bell I. Wiley. *United States Army in World War 2: The Army Ground Forces—The Organization of Ground Combat Troops*. Washington, D.C.: U.S. Army Center of Military History, 1947.

Griffith, Paddy. *Forward into Battle: Fighting Tactics from Waterloo to the Near Future*. Novato, Calif.: Presidio Press, 1992.

Guderian, Heinz. *Achtung-Panzer!* London: Arms and Armour, 1993.

Gupta, Sanjeev et al. "The Elusive Peace Dividend." *Finance and Development* 39, no. 4, December 2002.

Hammond, Grant T. *The Mind of War: John Boyd and American Security*. Washington, D.C.: Smithsonian Institution Press, 2001.

Hanson, Victor Davis. *The Soul of Battle: From Ancient Times to the Present Day, How Three Great Liberators Vanquished Tyranny*. New York: Anchor Books, 2001.

———. "What Would Patton Say About the Present War?" *Imprimis* 33, no. 10, October 2004.

Harkins, Paul D. *When the Third Cracked Europe: The Story of Patton's Incredible Army*. Harrisburg, Pa.: Stackpole Books, 1969.

Harris, J. P. and F. H. Toase, eds. *Armoured Warfare*. New York: St. Martin's Press, 1990.

Harrison, Gordon A. *The European Theater of Operations: Cross Channel Attack*. Washington, D.C.: U.S. Army Center of Military History, 1989.

Henderson, G. F. R. *Stonewall Jackson and the American Civil War*. New York: Da Capo Press, 1988.

Herbert, Paul H. *Deciding What Has to Be Done: General William E. DePuy and the 1976 Edition of FM 100–5 Operations*. Fort Leavenworth, Kans.: U.S. Army Command and General Staff College, 1988.

Herman, Arthur and William Luti. "How America's Drones Can Defeat ISIS." *Defense One*, 15 March 2015. http://www.defenseone.com/ideas/2015/03/how-americas-drones-can-defeat-isis/107565/.

Higgins, George A. "The Operational Tenets of Generals Heinz Guderian and George S. Patton, Jr." Master's thesis, School of Advanced Military Studies, U.S. Army Command and General Staff College, 1985.

Hirshson, Stanley P. *General Patton: A Soldier's Life*. New York: HarperCollins, 2002.

Hofmann, George F. *The Super Sixth: History of the 6th Armored Division in World War II and Its Post-war Association*. Louisville, Ky.: The 6th Armored Division Association, 1975.

——— and Donn Starry, ed. *Camp Colt to Desert Storm: The History of U.S. Armored Forces*. Lexington: University Press of Kentucky, 1999.

Hogg, Ian P. *The Biography of General George S. Patton*. New York: Gallery Books, 1982.

——— and John Weeks. *The Illustrated Encyclopedia of Military Vehicles*. London: New Burlington Books, 1980.

Hooker, Richard D. Jr., ed. *Maneuver Warfare: An Anthology*. Novato, Calif.: Presidio Press, 1993.

House, Jonathan M. *Toward Combined Arms Warfare: A Survey of 20th-Century Tactics, Doctrine, and Organization*. Fort Leavenworth, Kans.: U.S. Army Command and General Staff College, 1984.

Huntington, Samuel P. *The Soldier and the State: The Theory and Politics of Civil-Military Relations*. Cambridge, Mass.: Belknap Press, 1985.

Infantry Journal Incorporated. *Infantry in Battle*. Richmond, Va.: Garret and Massie, 1939.

Irving, David. *The War Between the Generals: Inside the Allied High Command*. New York: Congdon and Lattes, 1981.

Johnson, David E. *Fast Tanks and Heavy Bombers: Innovation in the U.S. Army, 1917–1945*. Ithaca, N.Y.: Cornell University Press, 1998.

Jones, Vincent. *Operation Torch: Anglo-American Invasion of North Africa*. New York: Ballantine Books, 1972.

Jordan, Jonathan W. *Brothers, Rivals, Victors: Eisenhower, Patton, Bradley, and the Partnership that Drove the Allied Conquest in Europe*. New York: New American Library, 2011.

Keegan, John. *The First World War*. London: Vintage, 2000.

Kelly, Orr. *King of the Killing Zone*. New York: W. W. Norton, 1989.

———. *Meeting the Fox: The Allied Invasion of Africa, from Operation Torch to Kasserine Pass to Victory in Tunisia*. Hoboken, N.J.: Wiley, 2002.

Kennedy, Robert M. *The German Campaign in Poland (1939)*. Washington, D.C.: Government Printing Office, 1988.

Kiesling, Eugenia. *Arming Against Hitler: France and the Limits of Military Planning*. Lawrence: University Press of Kansas, 1996.

Kitfield, James. *Prodigal Soldiers: How the Generation of Officers Born of Vietnam Revolutionized the American Style of War*. New York: Simon and Schuster, 1995.

Koyen, Kenneth A. *The Fourth Armored Division: From the Beach to Bavaria*. Munich, Germany: Herden Druck, 1946.

Lang, Will. "Colonel Abe." *Life Magazine*, 23 April 1945.

Lanning, Michael Lee. *The Military Top 100*. Secaucus, N.J.: Citadel Press, 1996.

Larson, Robert H. *The British Army and the Theory of Armored Warfare, 1918–1940*. Newark: University of Delaware Press, 1984.

Leonhard, Robert. *The Art of Maneuver Warfare: Maneuver–Warfare Theory and Air-Land Battle.* Novato, Calif.: Presidio Press, 1991.
Liddell Hart, B. H., ed. *The Rommel Papers.* New York: Harcourt, Brace, 1953.
Life magazine. Cover, 7 July 1941.
MacDonald, Charles B. *The Last Offensive.* Washington, D.C.: U.S. Army Center of Military History, 1993.
Mahnken, Thomas. *Uncovering Ways of War: U.S. Intelligence and Foreign Military Innovation, 1918–1941.* Ithaca, N.Y.: Cornell University Press, 2002.
Manchester, William. *American Caesar: Douglas MacArthur, 1880–1964.* New York: Little, Brown, 1978.
McCaffrey, Barry. "Gaining Victory in Iraq." *U.S. News and World Report,* 7 April 2003.
McCarthy, Peter and Mike Syron. *Panzerkrieg: The Rise and Fall of Hitler's Tank Divisions.* New York: Carroll and Graf, 2002.
McMaster, H. R. *Dereliction of Duty: Johnson, McNamara, the Joint Chiefs of Staff, and the Lies that Led to Vietnam.* New York: HarperPerennial, 1997.
Miller, Merle. *Ike the Soldier: As They Knew Him.* New York: G. P. Putnam's Sons, 1987.
Morison, Samuel Eliot. *The Two-Ocean War: A Short History of the United States Navy in the Second World War.* New York: Ballantine Books, 1963.
Mortensen, Daniel R. *A Pattern for Joint Operations: World War II Close Air Support, North Africa.* Washington, D.C.: U.S. Army Center of Military History, 1993.
Mosier, John. *The Blitzkrieg Myth: How Hitler and the Allies Misread the Strategic Realities of World War II.* New York: HarperCollins, 2003.
Newman, Richard J. "Not by the Playbook." *U.S. News and World Report,* 7 April 2003.
Nye, Roger H. *The Patton Mind: The Professional Development of an Extraordinary Leader.* New York: Avery Publishing Group, 1993.
Odom, William O. *After the Trenches: The Transformation of U.S. Army Doctrine, 1918–1939.* College Station: Texas A&M University Press, 1999.
Pack, S. W. C. *Operation "HUSKY."* New York: Hippocrene Books, 1977.
———. *The Invasion of North Africa, 1942.* New York: Scribner, 1979.
Parker, Danny S. *Battle of the Bulge: Hitler's Ardennes Offensive, 1944–1945.* Conshohocken, Pa.: Combined Books, 1991.
Patton, Ben. "What Would General Patton Do in Iraq and Afghanistan?" Huffington_Post, 21 March 2012. www.huffingtonpost.com/ben-patton/general-patton-iraq-afghanistan_b_1371117.html?
Perkins, Norris H. and Michael E. Rogers. *Roll Again Second Armored: Prelude to Fame 1940–1943.* Surbiton, U.K.: Kristal, 1988.
Phillips, T. R., ed. *Roots of Strategy.* Harrisburg, Pa.: Stackpole Books, 1940.

Piatt, Walter E. "What Is Operational Art?" Thesis, School of Advanced Military Studies, U.S. Army Command and General Staff College, 1999.

Price, James. *Troy H. Middleton: A Biography*. Baton Rouge: Louisiana State University, 1974.

Puryear, Edgar Jr. *Nineteen Stars: A Study in Military Character and Leadership*. New York: Ballantine Books, 1971.

Raines, Edgar F. Jr., and David R. Campbell. *The Army and the Joint Chiefs of Staff*. Washington, D.C.: U.S. Army Center of Military History, 1985.

Reardon, Mark J. *Victory at Mortain: Stopping Hitler's Panzer Counteroffensive*. Lawrence: University Press of Kansas, 2002.

Rickard, John Nelson. *Patton at Bay: The Lorraine Campaign, 1944*. Washington, D.C.: Brassey's, 2004.

———. *Advance and Destroy: Patton as Commander in the Bulge*. Lexington: University Press of Kentucky, 2011.

Roberts, Joel. "Senator Reid on Iraq: 'This War is Lost.'" CBS News. http://www.cbsnews.com/news/senator-reid-on-iraq-this-war-is-lost/.

Royle, Trevor. *Patton: Old Blood and Guts*. London: Weidenfeld and Nicolson, 2005.

Sawicki, James A. *Tank Battalions of the U.S. Army*. Dumfries, Va.: Wyvern Publications, 1983.

Showalter, Dennis. *Patton and Rommel: Men of War in the Twentieth Century*. New York: Berkley Caliber, 2005.

Shwedo, Bradford J. *XIX TAC and Ultra: Patton's Force Enhancers in the 1944 Campaign in France*. Maxwell Air Force Base, Ala.: Air University Press, 2001.

Sims, Jennifer E. and Burton Gerber, eds. *Transforming U.S. Intelligence*. Washington, D.C.: Georgetown University Press, 2005.

Simpkin, Richard. *Race to the Swift: Thoughts on Twenty-first Century Warfare*. London: Brassey's, 1985.

———. *Red Armour: An Examination of the Soviet Mobile Force Concept*. London: Brassey's Defence Publishers, 1984.

Sisk, Richard. "Army Adapts to Fewer Troops in Europe." Military.com, 13 September 2013.

Skelenka, Stephan D. "General George S. Patton: Operational Leadership Personified." Thesis, Naval War College, 4 February 2002.

Sorley, Lewis. *Thunderbolt: General Creighton Abrams and the Army of His Times*. New York: Simon and Schuster, 1992.

Spiller, Roger J., ed. *Combined Arms in Battle Since 1939*. Fort Leavenworth, Kans.: U.S. Army Command and General Staff College, 1992.

Spires, David N. *Patton's Air Force: Forging a Legendary Air-Ground Team*. Washington, D.C.: Smithsonian Institution Press, 2002.

Starry, Donn A. *Armored Combat in Vietnam*. New York: Arno Press, 1980.

Stern, Jessica. "The Protean Enemy." *Foreign Affairs* 82, no. 4, July/August 2003.

Sumida, Jon Tetsuro. *Decoding Clausewitz: A New Approach to* On War. Lawrence: University Press of Kansas, 2008.

Summers, Harry G. Jr. *On Strategy: A Critical Analysis of the Vietnam War.* Novato, Calif.: Presidio Press, 1983.

———. *On Strategy II: A Critical Analysis of the Gulf War.* New York: Dell Publishing, 1992.

Talbot, David. "How Tech Failed in Iraq." *Technology Review: MIT's Magazine of Innovation*, November 2004.

Talley, Thomas F. "Is Reorganization of the Army under the Unit-of-Action and the Unit-of-Employment Concept Consistent with the Army's Identity?" Master's thesis, U.S. Army Command and General Staff College, 2004.

Taylor, Maxwell. *The Uncertain Trumpet.* New York: Harper and Brothers, 1959.

Thomas, Evan and John Barry. "A Plan Under Attack." *Newsweek*, 7 April 2003.

——— and Martha Brant. "The Secret War." *Newsweek*, 21 April 2003.

——— and Daniel Klaidman. "The War Room." *Newsweek*, 21 April 2003.

Thompson, Mark. "Broken Down." *Time*, 16 April 2007.

———. "Pentagon and Its Allies Begin the Budget Death Watch." *Time*, 18 March 2015.

Toffler, Heidi and Alvin Toffler. *War and Antiwar: Making Sense of Today's Global Chaos.* London: Warner Books, 1993.

Tuchman, Barbara. *Stillwell and the American Experience in China, 1911–1945.* New York: MacMillan, 1971.

United States Military Academy. Department of Military Art and Engineering. *Operations in Sicily and Italy.* West Point, N.Y.: United States Military Academy, 1950.

———. Department of History. *Campaign Atlas to the Second World War: Europe and the Mediterranean.* West Point, N.Y.: United States Military Academy, 1980.

Walcott, John. "Does America Need an Army?" *U.S. News and World Report*, 11 December 1989.

Wallace, Brenton G. *Patton and His Third Army.* Mechanicsburg, Pa.: Stackpole Books, 1946.

Waller, Douglas. *A Question of Loyalty: Gen. Billy Mitchell and the Court-Martial that Gripped the Nation.* New York: HarperCollins, 2004.

Weigley, Russell F. *The American Way of War: A History of United States Military Strategy and Policy.* Bloomington: Indiana University Press, 1973.

———. *History of the United States Army.* Bloomington: Indiana University Press, 1984.

Whiting, Charles. *Bradley.* New York: Ballantine Books, 1971.

———. *First Blood: Battle of Kasserine Pass, 1943.* New York: Steiner and Day, 1984.

———. *Patton's Last Battle.* Havertown, Pa.: Casemate, 1987.

Wilson, Dale E. *Treat 'Em Rough! The Birth of American Armor, 1917–1920.* Novato, Calif.: Presidio Press, 1989.

Wilson, John B. *Maneuver and Firepower: The Evolution of Divisions and Separate Brigades.* Washington, D.C.: U.S. Army Center of Military History, 1998.

Winterbotham, F. W. *The Ultra Secret: The Inside Story of Operation Ultra, Bletchley Park and Enigma.* New York: Dell, 1976.

Witsell, Edward F. "Russian Combat Methods in World War II." Washington, D.C.: Department of the Army, pamphlet no. 20–230, November 1950.

Wright, Patrick. *Tank.* New York: Viking Press, 2002.

Yeide, Harry. *Fighting Patton: George S. Patton, Jr., Through the Eyes of His Enemies.* Minneapolis, Minn.: Zenith Press, 2011.

Zaloga, Steven J. *The Renault FT Light Tank.* London: Osprey Publishing, 1998.

———. *Lorraine 1944: Patton vs. Manteuffel.* Oxford: Osprey Publishing, 2000.

INDEX

Aachen operations, 4, 17, 18, 49, 136
Abrams, Creighton, 219, 245–46, 258, 260–62, 265–66, 269, 274, 275
Active Defense doctrine, 267–68
Afghanistan, 278, 281
air operations and power: air-ground coordination, 75, 78, 79–80, 82–83, 108–9, 167, 193–94, 270–71, 305n170; close-air support missions, 82–83, 145, 297n206, 320n157; Cobra operation, 187–88; curriculum about and doctrine for, 31; doctrine for air power, 189; Korean War air-ground coordination, 252; Normandy breakout plan and use of, 161, 204; Normandy operations training, 166–67, 193; tactical air support, 282–83
AirLand Battle, 18, 268–71, 277–78, 281–82
American Expeditionary Force, 4, 25–31, 55–56, 57–58
antitank guns and defenses, 76–77, 79, 96–98, 310n66
Argentan operations, 163, 170, 172, 201–3, 205–7, 208–10, 212
Armor Center/Armor School, 245, 264, 266–67, 281–82
Armored Division, 2nd: Bradley borrowing units from, 318n83; command of, 38, 73–74, 122; maneuvers/exercises, 39–40, 74–77, 96–98, 124–25, 127–28; mission of, 122; Palermo operations, 135; Sicily operations, 80–82, 306n192
Armored Division, 4th: Bulge operations, 113–21; casualties in, 11, 12; Cobra operation, 180–85, 186; demonstration of doctrine with, 86–87; Normandy operations, 48, 87, 190, 204–5; Normandy operations training, 158–59, 166–67, 173; spearhead role of, 11; Third Army assignment of, 11
armored divisions: casualties in, 11, 12; Cobra operation, 180–85; doctrine for, 37–38, 84–88, 166; function and mission of, 40, 74–77; organization of, 84–86; reconnaissance and attacks by, 127; role in combat, 37; vehicles in, 314n193
Army, U.S.: all-volunteer force, 260–61; Army Ground Forces, commanding general of, 234; budget and manpower cuts, 31, 63–64, 246–47, 248, 272, 277, 280, 341n131; fighters, state of interest in, 245–46; force strength at end of World War I, 64; mission and focus of, 277–78; officers-enlisted relations changes, 231, 245, 341n126; postwar changes and budget cuts, 63–64; postwar leadership of, 243–45; re-deployment after war, 230–31, 338n26; reorganization of forces, 31, 254, 255–56, 280. *See also* warfare and warfare doctrine
Army Information Service (AIS), 138–39, 140–42, 167–68, 198–99
Army War College, U.S., 16, 26, 47, 69, 93, 94, 123, 232, 234, 309n37
artillery: autonomous function of, 55; coordination with tanks, 57, 58, 59; doctrine on use of, 25, 84–88; EMF role of, 67; French doctrine on, 67–68; infantry-artillery–based attrition doctrine, 18, 246–47, 261; pace of barrages, 59; serenade drills, 84
asymmetric warfare, 279
atomic weapons, 232, 247–48, 249, 254
attrition warfare: defensive strategy, 256–59; direct attack method, 76–77; doctrine for, 3–4, 5, 22, 25, 34, 167, 232, 282–83, 290n13; Gulf War, 272–76; infantry-artillery–based attrition doctrine, 18, 246–47, 261; Normandy operations, 170, 173–80; rejection of by Patton, 20, 25, 26–27, 34–35; strategy for, 30, 49–50, 282–83, 293n76; success of, 28–29; Tunisia operations, 42
Auftragstaktik (mission tactics), 14, 91, 93, 98, 121

| 361

Index

Bastogne operations, 50–51, 87, 115, 120–21
"Battlefield Psychology" lecture, 35
battles and operations: avoidance of battles, 1–2, 3–4, 39, 86; command and control and success of, 6–7; execution as more important than plans, 6, 92–93, 101, 308–9n28; judgement of Allied commanders during, 144–45; methodical battle doctrine, 87, 93–95, 309n40; military theory and history knowledge and winning battles, 35, 139–40, 144, 319n133; operations and intelligence, interaction between, 132–36; pauses after attacks, 25, 28, 33, 48, 57, 89, 93–94, 96–97, 177, 272, 309n40; rapid decision cycles and intelligence, 122, 138; rigidity in following plans for, 136; small actions by individuals and units and things get done, 99–100; winning war by fighting, 31. *See also* plans for battles and operations
Berlin and Berlin Blockade, 5, 203, 227–28, 248–49
blitzkrieg, 8, 37, 39, 71, 72–73, 249, 278
boldness, 13, 27, 33, 95–96, 121, 226, 267
bombing operations: close-air support during, 82–83; fratricide concerns and incidents, 108–9, 180, 181, 206, 328n242, 329n6, 333n153; Normandy operations, 170, 175, 180, 181–82; North Africa operations, 78; saturation bombing, 170
boots and trench foot, 107
Bradley, Omar: awards and decorations for, 241; books and websites about, 11; bridge game and champagne with Eisenhower, 112–13, 151; command and control doctrine of, 93, 177; command experience of, 3, 47; command over Patton, reason for, 14, 47; command style of Patton, criticism of, 7, 102, 103, 161, 287n47, 322n38; criticism of Patton and staff by, 15, 134, 155–56, 287n33, 310–11n87; discrediting of Patton by, 9; encirclement of Germans, plan and operations for, 195, 201–3, 205–8, 333n153; fratricide incidents, passing blame for, 180; funeral of Patton, 243; headlines, Patton interest in, 196; irritation of Montgomery with, 171; irritation with Montgomery, 171, 174; logistics, criticism of Patton about, 103, 104–5; loss of faith of Eisenhower in Patton as turning point in career, 110, 313n164; memoirs and criticisms of other generals, 8, 103; operation failures of, 17, 18; opinion about Patton, 231; overstrength of personnel, objection to request for, 161–62; Patton, weary of troubles caused by, 165–66; Patton opinion about, 2, 163–64, 177, 179, 196–97, 253; personality of, 3; promotion of, 47, 208; rank in list of influential leaders, 8; rein on Patton by, 132, 192; relationship with Patton, 5; rigidity in following plans by, 136; sports played by, 41; staff of Patton, criticism of, 118, 121, 310–11n87; success of Patton because little or no opposition, 87; tactical operations responsibilities of, 21; tactician, Patton skills as, 18, 87; tank use and the self-reliance and aggressive spirit of infantry, 4; traditional philosophies and practices of, 3; war against Russia, Patton warning about, 229, 248–49; war doctrine of and planning by, 5
breakthroughs: Cobra operation, 170–71, 172, 175–85, 186–89, 327n198, 327n203, 328n254, 329n6, 329n260, 329n264; tank formations for, 35, 60, 61, 69, 72–73, 300n44, 301n74
Brittany operations, 18, 137, 156–57, 160, 168, 172, 173, 179, 180–81, 192–97, 198, 199–200, 201, 211, 219
Bulge, Battle of the: Ardennes counteroffensive, 48, 50, 102, 112–13, 146–51, 225; bridge game and champagne while Germans attack, 112–13, 151; casualties from, 51, 225; command, control, and staff procedures for, 100, 112–21; date for Patton attack, 116, 314n208, 314–15n212; drive into center of Bulge, Eisenhower orders for, 11; failure of Allied efforts, 17; German radio silence before attack, 151; intelligence use during, 146–51; logistics for, 119–20; Patton command and reversal of operations under, 17, 112–21, 314n196; Patton vision for operations, 5; success against German counteroffensive, 120–21; traffic flow and troop movements for, 114, 119–20, 314n193

Caen operations, 112, 136, 156, 159, 162–63, 168–70, 171, 173, 174, 263
Calais operations, 1, 156, 157, 165, 171–72, 187, 216, 225, 329n6
Cambria operations, 56, 57, 76
Camp Meade, 62, 74, 92
cavalry: armored cars use by, 64–65; armored force compared to, 73; autonomous function of, 55; charge of and psychological effect of shock, 23; cohesion in the line and success of saber charge, 27; combat mobility of, 69; coordination with tanks, 68; defense of, 33–34, 68; demand for, 55; doctrine for, 13, 25; EMF role of, 67; German horse cavalry attacks, 71, 302–3n120; horse cavalry replacement by machines, 71, 302–3n120; intelligence use by, 126; love of Patton for, 13; Patton return to after World War I, 31; Polish horse cavalry attacks, 71, 302–3n120; pursuit phase of battle, 6; rapidity and shock for success with, 27; tanks in traditional role of, 58; writings about, 29
Cavalry School, U.S., 31, 67, 123
chaos: concept of in war, 161; continuous movement to create shock and, 28–29, 32–33, 128–29, 269; opportunities from, taking advantage of, 115, 272; order to chaos and making circumstances fit battle plans, 6, 93; shock and creation of chaos, 133
Clausewitz, Carl von, 5, 30, 44, 93, 95, 140, 161, 172, 286n24, 293n74, 293n76, 319n133
combined arms force: advocacy for, 55; AEF operations, 55–56; aircraft attacks on, 66, 301n84; battle drill for, 77; benefits of, 55; Cobra operations, 180–85, 186–89, 329n6, 329n264; combat mobility of, 69; creation of combined arms tank divisions, 73–77, 304nn136–138; diminished interest in, 247, 254; doctrine for, 18, 56, 57–62, 64–69, 75–77, 82–88, 163, 267–68, 299n35, 303nn123–124; exercises for training, 65–67, 74–77, 78, 82, 86–87, 166–67; French use of tanks and combined arms force, 72–73, 303nn127–128; German panzer force, 69, 71, 72–73, 74, 302n107, 304n138; infantry role in, 74, 304nn137–138; Normandy breakout, 87–88, 163, 193–203; North Africa operations, 77–80, 305n170; probes of enemy lines with, 126–27; pursuit and exploitation in battle, 6; radios for, 58, 62; renewed interest in, 255–56; Sicily operations, 80–82, 306n192, 306n197, 306n200; success and use of Patton war doctrine, 16, 86–88, 282–83
command and control: Bradley methods, 93, 177; criticism of Patton methods, 6–9, 96–98, 102–7, 287–88nn47–48, 322n38; doctrine on, 89, 91–92, 93–95, 120–21, 166–67; Eisenhower methods, 111–12; flexible command and control, 18, 92–93, 121; French doctrine, 93–94; front, commanding from, 129; from helicopters, 257; ignoring higher command, 110; individual initiative, discouragement of, 6; inter-service coordination problems, 108–9, 313n161; logistical planning, 103–8, 311n114, 312n134; methodical battle doctrine, 93–95, 309n40; Montgomery methods, 112; new and old weapons and, 98–99; Patton command and staff procedures, 112–21, 166–67; plans to fit circumstances or creating circumstances to fit plans, 125–26, 148; rear, commanding from, 129; rigid adherence to orders, 206; SHAEF deficiencies, 112; subordinate initiative and, 1, 14, 73, 89–91, 95–100, 166–67, 189–90, 262, 272, 308n13; success in battle and, 6–7; success of Patton while under proper command and control, 13–14
Command and General Staff College/General Service School: class rankings at, 32, 123; class standing and career opportunities, 31; command of, 244; conformity and standardization taught at, 309n37; curriculum at, 31; doctrine taught at, pressure to conform to, 31–32; mission of, 31; Patton graduation from, 16, 31, 32, 123; rank attained by graduates of, 309n37; student suicides at, 31; studying under blue light at, 32
communications: Bulge operations and communication problems, 118; Eisenhower scolding Patton about, 133–34; end of classical strategy and speed of, 5, 286n26; inter-service coordination problems, 108–9, 313n161; Normandy,

problems in, 168, 181, 328n242; North Africa, problems in, 108; radios for combined arms operations, 58, 62; reports from Patton, Eisenhower anger at not receiving, 109–10; Sicily paratrooper incident and problems with, 108–9, 180; time-sensitive nature of intelligence and speed of, 128–29. *See also* Ultra intercepts

concentrated blow doctrine, 34

corporate management culture, 257, 262

counterinsurgency doctrine, 280–81, 282–83

coup d'oeil concept, 5, 13, 20, 88, 286–87n28

Desert Storm, Operation, 272–76

Desert Training Center, 77, 99, 128, 231, 270

discipline, 27–28, 42, 230–31, 245–46, 262, 341n126, 344n220

Doolittle, James "Jimmy," 91, 102, 180, 181, 231, 245, 341n126

echeloned attacks, 28, 34, 59, 60, 61, 69, 75, 268

Eifel operations, 51, 102, 132, 142, 146

Eisenhower, Dwight D. "Ike": advance into Germany, decision about, 224–25, 226; appreciation for Patton skills by, 8, 202, 227; attacks after promotion of and Patton rescue of, 118; beach visit while Patton was fighting, 110; books and websites about, 11; Bradley orders and anger at Patton countermanding order, 133–34; bridge game and champagne with Bradley, 112–13, 151; command and control methods, 111–12; command experience before World War II, 3, 231–32; command style of Patton, criticism of, 7, 288n48; defense policy of and nuclear war, 232; discrediting of Patton by, 9; education of, 16, 32; funeral of Patton, 243; irritation with Montgomery, 171, 173; Italy operations plans, 111–12; leadership skills of, 41; logistical planning by, 107–8; logistical support for Patton, withdrawal of, 1, 48–49, 214, 220, 221; loss of faith in Patton by, 109–10, 313n164; loyalty of Patton to, reporters questioning of, 237–38; memoirs and criticisms of other generals, 7–8; notes loaned to by Patton, 32; operational art practice by, 21, 22; opinion about Patton, 2, 17; Patton, weary of troubles caused by, 165; Patton as great leader but poor planner, 103; Patton as one-man fire brigade or pit bulldog for, 17, 231; Patton in France, telling press about, 210; Patton opinion about, 163–64, 177, 253; Patton promotion, promise to Marshall about, 13–14, 155; Patton speech and decision about recall, 165–66; personality of, 3; philosophy instilled at Command and General Staff College, 32; as political general, 155; presidential interests of, 228, 240, 241, 253; promotion of, 118, 155; rank in list of influential leaders, 8; rein on Patton by, 132; relationship with Patton, 5, 109–10, 238–39, 313n164; relief of Patton command, 47, 297n195; reports from Patton, anger at not receiving, 109–10; rigidity in following plans by, 136; rocket list of promising officers, 244; shortages, information about for, 154; Soviet administration over Berlin, caution about, 227–28; sports played by, 41; strategy knowledge of, 22; success of Patton, reasons for, 14; sweeping maneuver, plan for, 40; tapping of Patton phone by, 234; traditional philosophies and practices of, 3; war doctrine of and planning by, 5; wishing for Patton at Normandy, 171

enemy: anticipation of reactions of, 7; attacking enemy and belief about strength of attacker, 24; attacking weakness rather than strength, 38, 40, 43, 122, 212–13; continuous movement to catch enemy and boost morale, 25, 26, 33, 269; death, wounds, and inflicting fear on, 43, 274–75; decision through selective concentration in tactical battle doctrine, 22; destruction of through mass and concentration, 30, 293n76; destruction through maneuver, 35; exploitation of weaknesses of, 20, 30, 86, 97, 126, 192; fear and worry of, 24, 43–44; fire, maneuver, shock, enemy decisionmaking, and destruction of enemy morale, 3–4, 20, 23–24, 30–31, 35, 268, 278–79, 280–81; grab enemy by the nose and kick him in the pants, 37–38, 40, 64, 127, 213, 265; riding enemy to death with tanks, 58; shock and creation of chaos, 133; unbalancing enemy, doctrine for, 22, 23–24; where to beat, focus on, 5, 54, 128

Enigma machine, 138–39. *See also* Ultra intercepts

execution as more important than plans, 6, 92–93, 101, 308–9n28

exercises. *See* maneuvers/exercises

Experimental Mechanization Force, British, 66, 67

Experimental Mechanization Force, U.S., 66–67, 68–69, 74, 84–86, 304nn136–137

exploitation: emerging opportunities, exploitation of, 60, 122, 192, 272, 279; enemy weaknesses, exploitation of, 20, 30, 86, 97, 126, 192; phase of a campaign, 6; points of little or no opposition, exploitation of, 18, 87; rapidity and success of, 37; tank formations for, 35, 60, 61, 69, 72–73, 81, 300n44, 301n74, 306n197; Third Army for at Normandy, 177, 182, 185; war doctrine of Patton use of, 6

Falaise operations, 5, 52, 112, 136, 163, 182, 201, 203, 204, 205–7, 209–11

fear: death, wounds, and inflicting fear on enemy, 43, 274–75; enemy is more worried than you, 24, 43–44; enemy's fear of the unknown, armored division advantage in production of, 38; fear of death, fear of the unknown, and unit cohesion, 35; never take counsel of your fears, 24, 43–44, 205, 271

Fickett, Edward, 138, 140–42, 167–68, 198

Field Officers' Course, Cavalry School, 31, 123

Fifteenth Army, 239, 240, 244

fire/firepower: enemy fire, reducing effectiveness of, 163; fire, maneuver, shock, enemy decisionmaking, and destruction of enemy morale, 3–4, 20, 23–24, 30–31, 35, 268, 278–79, 280–81; infantry adaptation with fire superiority, 64; infantry frontal assault, firepower, and destruction of enemy, 31–32; maneuver and exposure to, 27; rapidity of attacks, 43–44; superior firepower and battle outcomes, 5; theories on role of, 1–2

First Army: Bulge operations, 50, 112–15, 119, 146–51; casualties in, 11, 12, 49; Cobra operation, 179, 187; Hürtgen Forest operations, 49; Mortain operations, 200–201; Normandy operations, 155–56, 158–60, 162, 171–72, 177, 179, 198, 199, 205; Public Affairs section, 319n122; Rhine operations, 136; Seine operations, 217

Fort Benning, 38, 66, 73–74, 127, 128, 281–82

Fort Bliss, 94–95

Fort Clark, 35–36

Fort Knox, 68, 245, 265, 281–82

Fort Leavenworth, 31, 92, 263–64, 309n37. *See also* Command and General Staff College/General Service School

Fort Myer, 36, 37–38

Fort Riley, 31, 123, 281

France: American light tank school in, 27–28, 56–57; appreciation for Patton skills during operations in, 8; artillery doctrine in, 67–68; Bradley command in, 14, 47; command and control doctrine in, 93–94; fall of and ineffective use of combined arms force, 72–73, 303nn127–128; logistical support for operations, 105–8; news broadcasts in, 138; offensive drive across to Germany, 1; Paris, liberation of, 209–10, 211, 217; Patton as best man for invasion of, 155, 322n21; photographic reconnaissance of, 137; tank operations of, inspection of, 26; tank school and doctrine in, 56–57, 61, 303n128; war doctrine for World War II, 37. *See also* Normandy/Operation Overlord

frontal assaults: battle outcomes and, 5; infantry frontal assault, firepower, and destruction of enemy, 31–32; Patton opinion about, 4, 30; rear or flank attacks better than, 32, 35, 36–37, 38, 43–44, 73, 97, 127, 264–65, 266; strategy and tactics for, 4–5

Gaffey, Hugh, 14, 81, 100, 107, 158, 202, 207, 209, 223–24, 245, 322n39

Gay, Hobart "Hap," 100, 107, 115, 119, 158, 160, 200, 225, 228, 235, 241, 242, 244–45, 311n88, 322n39

Germany: administration of eastern American Zone by Patton, 227–29, 230, 232–40; broad front march into, 213–14, 215, 222–23; casualties of, 49, 50; defeat of, 213–14; denazification program in, 228, 230, 232–40, 279; dread of Third Army by soldiers, 88; halt on border and regrouping of defenses, 223–26; intelligence from interviews with captured soldiers, 139; mechanized panzer force of, 69, 71, 72–73, 74, 302n107, 304n138; night sound signals of German soldiers, 134; offensive drive across France to, 1; operational art and study of army operations, 21; opinions about and expectations for Patton operations, 133, 164–65; rapidity of advance and mission tactics of, 95–96; rearming for war with Soviets, 229; rebuilding of as buffer to danger from Russia, 239; retreat of soldiers, 205–7, 213; surrender of, 227; tank doctrine in, 65; tank use and retreat of German soldiers, 28–29, 59–60; withdrawal from Sicily, 136

Golan Heights battle, 262–65

Grant, Ulysses S., 4, 24–25, 49, 293n76

Great Britain: decisive battles, doctrine for, 22; EMF exercises, 66, 67; German spies in, 156; tank operations of, inspection of, 26; tank school and doctrine in, 57, 62

Guderian, Heinz, 8, 35, 37, 72, 73

Gulf War, 272–76

Halfmoon doctrine, 247–49

Hammelburg raid, 13, 17, 263, 288n74

haste, 101, 271

Hawaii, 33, 66, 124, 126, 128–29, 241

Helfers, Melvin C., 138–39, 141, 200

hero status and getting killed in action, 229

Hürtgen Forest, 17, 18, 49

infantry: autonomous function of, 55; combat mobility of, 69; combined arms force role, 74, 83–88, 304nn137–138; coordination with tanks, 57, 58, 60–63, 71, 75–77, 83–88, 300n40; delay between commitment of waves of troops, 28; doctrine on use and role of, 25; EMF role of, 67; emphasis from infantry to use of mechanized forces, change in, 4–6; fire superiority and adaptation of, 64; frontal assault by, firepower, and destruction of enemy, 31–32; infantry-artillery–based attrition doctrine, 18, 246–47, 261; intelligence use by, 126; manual for infantry and tank cooperation and training, 59; mission and focus of tactical doctrine, 4, 65, 72, 179, 286n17, 303n124; primacy of, 63–64, 65, 72, 75, 247, 255–56, 303n124; support from tanks, 57, 59, 63, 75, 247, 304n151; tank ownership by, 64, 71; tank use and self-reliance and aggressive spirit of, 4, 66; theories on role of, 1–2; vehicles in divisions, 314n193

Infantry School, 4, 6–7, 66, 93, 267

insurgents and counterinsurgency, 280–81, 282–83

intelligence: briefs and tracking information from intelligence reports, 137; Cobra operation, 188–89; collection and use during operations, 125–26, 136–39, 140, 142–51, 282; concept and definition of, 122–23; confusing enemy intelligence picture, 142–43, 164–65; counterintelligence, 131–32; demand for fresh, 123; development of methods for gathering, 128; doctrine on, 125–26, 279; duties and responsibilities of intelligence staff officers, 125; enemy weak spots, identification of, 122; first-hand observation, value of, 124, 189; front line visit to gather, 124–25, 129–30; integrated systems and war doctrine of Patton, 18; intelligent maneuver, 125; interviews as source of, 139; layered system for, 122, 138–39, 140–42, 146, 167–68; maneuvers and refining use of, 127–28; misfits assigned to intelligence duties, 126; negative information as important as positive, 128; Normandy roads and terrain, report about, 169, 325n137; North Africa operations, 129–30; operations and intelligence, interaction between, 132–36; Patton service as intelligence officer, 33, 126; Patton's Household Cavalry, intelligence gathering by, 137–38; probes of enemy lines to gather, 126–28; rapid decision cycles and, 122, 138; sources of, 125, 136–39, 332n109; success of war doctrine of Patton and use of, 16; support for operations with, 1–2, 15; tactical intelligence, refinements in, 130–31; Third Army staff for, 137–38, 140–42; time-sensitive nature of, 128–29; training on, neglect of, 130; understanding and employment of by Patton, 122; World War I operations, 123, 124. *See also* Ultra intercepts

Iraq, Gulf War, and Iraq war, 272–76, 278–80, 281

Islamic State of Iraq and Syria (ISIS), 282–83

Italy, 4, 17, 111–12

Jackson, Thomas "Stonewall," 24, 95, 131–32

Kasserine Pass attack, 9, 17, 41, 43, 79, 111, 118, 129, 130

Knutsford: Patton and Third Army at, 158; speech at, 164–66, 227

Koch, Oscar: Ardennes intelligence, 146–51; German counterattacks, prediction of, 215–16; intelligence collection of during operations, 125; intelligence system role, 140–42, 144; on intuition of Patton, 152; map of Western Front, 137; Normandy breakout intelligence, 160–61, 167–68, 198, 200, 332n109; Normandy operations training, 158; photographic interpreters team, 137; staff role of, 100; Ultra intercepts briefings for Patton, 138–39; war doctrine of Patton, success of, 40

Korea and Korean War, 18, 249–53, 254

leadership: actor/performer to create enthusiasm and motivation, 2, 14–15, 39; commanding from the front not the rear, 129; Eisenhower skills, 41; front line visits by commanders, 124–25; inspiration to do things men think they are not capable of, 14–15; morale and, 35; motivational style and success of Patton, 2–3, 42, 285n12; opinions about Patton, 1–3, 6–9, 102–7, 285n12, 287–88nn47–48, 322n38; Patton as great leader but poor planner, 103; ranking of influential military leaders, 8; skills of Patton, 41; temper, gift of a bad, 2. *See also* command and control

logistics: command and control and logistical planning, 103–8, 312n134; D-day operations, 311n114; Normandy breakout and withdrawal of support for Patton, 1, 17–18, 48–49, 105–8, 154, 161–62, 203–4, 214, 216–17, 219–26, 312n134, 332n112, 337n270; Tunisia operations, 103–8

Lorraine campaign, 48–49, 145

Louisiana maneuvers, 37, 39–40, 76, 96–98, 127–28

Lucky Strike operation, 170–71

Luxembourg, 113, 115–19, 144, 147, 150, 151, 242–43

MacArthur, Douglas, 11, 249–51

Maddox, Halley, 50, 100, 113, 141, 151, 158, 160

maneuver: adoption of Patton doctrine for, 269–72; approach movement, 58; attack movement, 58; casualty reduction through use of, 27, 31, 258; continuous advance to catch enemy and boost morale, 25, 26; continuous advance to create chaos and shock, 28–29, 32–33, 129, 269; cutting off enemy from support, 40; decisive maneuver, 76–77, 258, 274–75; destruction of enemy through, 35; direction of advance and enemy perception of threat, 23, 29–30; early lessons on, 24; exposure to fire and, 27; fire, maneuver, shock, enemy decisionmaking, and destruction of enemy morale, 3–4, 20, 23–24, 30–31, 35, 268, 278–79, 280–81; intelligent maneuver, 125; Korean War use of, 250–53; morale and, 258; Normandy operations and use of, 27, 47, 190–92; strategic maneuver, 4, 5, 30–31, 39–40, 74, 112, 286n24; surprise element of time or direction of attack, effectiveness of, 38, 126, 133; sweeping maneuver, success of, 44, 159; sweeping maneuver plan, 39–40, 159; tanks role in, 34–35; theories on role of, 5, 286n26; Tunisia operations, 5, 42; war doctrine of Patton for, 1–2, 13; war never won by, 31

maneuvers/exercises: Carolina maneuvers, 128; cavalry exercise near Manassas, 36; combined arms exercises, 65–67, 74–77, 78, 82, 86–87, 166–67; command and control criticisms during, 95–100;

criticism of Patton tactics and victories during, 5–6, 37, 40, 96–98, 127–28; Fort Benning to Panama City march, 74; goals and purpose of, 98, 310n65; Hawaii maneuvers, 66, 124; Louisiana maneuvers, 39–40, 76, 96–98, 127–28; methodical battle doctrine inadequacies identified during, 94–95; Normandy operations training, 158–59, 166–67; observation of and war doctrine development, 33; reconnaissance use during, 38, 127–28; tank brigade exercises, 62; teaching war doctrine through, 39–40; Tennessee maneuvers, 39, 74, 76, 96–97, 127; Texas maneuvers, 36, 44; umpire manual for, 97, 310n66; umpiring of by Patton, 37, 95, 96; unity of effort and independent action during, 40

Market Garden operations, 17, 18, 49, 126, 136, 225, 316n27

Marshall, George C.: Army budget and manpower cuts, opinion about, 246; books and websites about, 11; Bradley criticism of Patton to, 134; command experience before World War II, 3, 231–32; logistics, criticism of Patton about, 104–5; North Africa invasion, decline of assignment for, 8; officers for future war, collection of, 36; opinion about Patton, 2; Patton as best man for invasion of France, 155, 322n21; Patton as best tank man, 13, 55; Patton promotion, Eisenhower promise about, 13–14, 155; Patton speech and decision about recall, 165–66; postwar assignment of, 244; rank in list of influential leaders, 8; replacement of, 234; student solutions to problems, sharing of with class, 93; tank use and self-reliance and aggressive spirit of infantry, 4

mechanized forces/mechanization: British use of, 66, 67; combat mobility of, 69; curriculum about and doctrine for, 31; development of and doctrine for, 281–82; emphasis from infantry to use of mechanized forces, change in, 4–6; future of, 69; German panzer force, 69, 71, 72–73, 74, 302n107, 304n138; maneuvers, criticism of Patton use of during, 6; offensive reserve force, 69; organization of, 84–86; potential for use of, 56, 69; probes of enemy lines and use of, 126–27; renewed interest in, 255–56; speed and tempo of, 37, 72, 303n123; strategy for use of, 4–6, 29, 69; support for operations with, 33–35; theories on role of, 1–2, 4

Metz: advance on, 203, 204, 211, 214–15; breakthrough south of, 142–43; casualties at, 49; defense of, strength of, 17, 48; direct assaults against, mistake of, 17; German defenses at, 211, 226; limitations placed on Patton in, 15; Normandy breakout and intelligence about area around, 160–61; plan for, 105, 106–7; success at, 18, 87; withdrawal from, 145

Meuse River operations, 18, 215–16, 223–24

Meuse-Argonne offensive, 29, 89–90

Military Academy, U.S., 16, 123

military information, 123, 125, 128

mobile operations and strategy, 4–6, 29, 64, 69, 207

Montgomery, Bernard "Monty": advancement after D-day, 210; attrition war following Normandy victory, opinion about, 49; books and websites about, 11; Bradley promotion to co-equal to, 208; command, control, and battle success doctrine, 7; command and control methods of, 112, 120–21; command of forces for Normandy operation, 158–59; criticism of Patton by, 110; D-day operations, 168–69; decision through selective concentration in tactical battle doctrine, 22; discrediting of Patton by, 9; Eisenhower strategy, criticism of, 213–14; encirclement of Germans, plan and operations for, 201–2, 205–7; end of war, concern about role in, 217; funeral of Patton, 243; German capabilities, message about, 150; irritation of Eisenhower and Bradley with, 171, 173, 174; Italy operations plans, 111–12; logistical support for, 49, 214, 216, 220, 221, 225; memoir of, 7–8, 112, 134; operation failures of, 17, 18; Patton opinion about, 163–64; personality of, 3; planning by and changes to plans, 112, 125–26, 316n27; rank in list of influential leaders, 8; skills of Patton compared to, 8–9; tactical operations responsibilities of, 21; toast to, 168; toast to war being

over, 168; traditional philosophies and practices of, 3
morale: bad temper, divine wrath, and driving men beyond physical abilities, 2; continuous movement to catch enemy and, 25, 26, 33, 269; fire, maneuver, shock, enemy decisionmaking, and destruction of enemy morale, 3–4, 20, 23–24, 30–31, 35, 268, 278–79, 280–81; importance of moral greater than physical in war, Napoleon dictum on, 24; Italian forces, breaking morale of, 44; leadership and, 35; maneuver and, 258; news broadcasts in French occupied areas and, 138; professionalism and, 259, 261; role of in combat, 24; shock and morale boost for soldiers, 133; subordinate initiative and, 95; tank use and, 26; in Vietnam, 258–59; war as killing business, speech about, 38–39, 295n143
Mortain operations, 170, 175, 193, 194, 200–202, 203, 206, 207, 332n109
Muller, Walter "Maud," 100, 105–6, 113, 158, 160, 161, 216
musicians of Mars, 99, 272

Napoleon I: combined arms force, importance of, 88; coup d'oeil concept, 5, 286–87n28; Patton interest in, 24, 291n29; Patton leadership style compared to, 3; plans for campaigns, 92, 100, 140; rapid march and the moral of an army, 26, 291n41; strategic maneuver concept, 30; training of staff by, 100–102; warfare strategy of, 4, 23, 30
New Look national defense policy, 253, 255
Normandy breakout: combined arms use, 87–88, 163, 193–203; command and control for, 100; credit to Patton for, 190–91, 196, 207; decision points and adjustments to operations, 47–48; decision points and intelligence for, 160–61; effectiveness and success of, 48, 213–26; effectiveness of Patton as commander and, 153; encirclement of Germans, plan and operations for, 5, 195, 201–3, 205–8, 209, 333n153; end of war in a few days, prediction of, 203, 216–17; execution of, 186–226; German counterattacks, prediction of, 215–16; German weakness and retreat, 203, 205–7, 210–11, 213; halt on German border, 223–26; headlines for Bradley for, 196; intelligence for, 160–61, 167–68, 192, 198–99, 200, 332n109; limitations placed on Patton for, 156, 173, 179–80, 186, 205–7, 209, 333n153, 334n180; logistical support for and withdrawal of support for Patton, 1, 17–18, 48–49, 105–8, 154, 161–62, 203–4, 214, 216–17, 219–26, 312n134, 332n112, 337n270; logistical support withdrawal and future loss of life, 225; maneuver use, 27, 47, 190–92; map of, 218; no plans for, 163, 171, 177; Patton in France, secrecy about, 187, 196, 210; Patton influence on and role in, 184–86; plan for, 159, 160–61, 171–74, 178, 180–85, 190–91; shocks to surprise enemy, 160–61, 190, 198, 202; speed of advance during, 193–203, 212–13; sweeping maneuver for, 159
Normandy/Operation Overlord: attrition battle in, 170, 173–80; bombing operations, 170, 175, 180, 181–82, 329n6; Bradley command of, 47, 153, 155–56; British command of operations, 210–11; casualties from, 169, 170, 179; Cobra operation, 170–71, 172, 175–85, 186–89, 327n198, 327n203, 328n254, 329n6, 329n260, 329n264; communications for, 168, 171, 181, 328n242; D-day operations, 168–70; D-day plans, 158–59; Eisenhower objective and plans for, 4–5, 47–48, 49–50; failure of Allied efforts, 17, 163, 173–74, 181–82, 183–84; German defenses, regrouping and reinforcement of, 18, 48–49; linear advances in, 47–48, 157, 161; logistics for D-Day, 103, 311n114; Lucky Strike operation, 170–71; narrow front for, 165–66, 168, 208–9; Patton plans and operations, 5, 154–56, 157–58; plans for, 47–48, 49, 156–61, 162–63, 165–66, 194–95, 201, 208–9; plans not going far enough, 5, 157; reverse Schlieffen plan to envelop Germans in, 5, 171–72, 208–9; secrecy of plans for, 132, 158–59; SHAEF plans for, 47–48, 49–50, 156–57; strategic maneuver during, 27, 47, 112; strategy for, 157, 208–9, 213–14; training for, 158–59, 166–67, 173

North Africa operations: appreciation for Patton skills for, 8; casualties during, 129; combined arms operations, 77–80, 305n170; communications problems during, 108; decline of assignment by Marshall, 8; experience in Hawaii and execution of operations in, 126; failure of Allied efforts, 17; front line operations tours, 129–30; intelligence for, 129–30; lessons learned in, 136; reputation of Patton after, 9; Torch operation, 40–42, 129–30, 311n96; training for, 77. *See also* Tunisia

offensive operations, 150–51, 256, 269, 271, 274–76
open warfare/war of movement, 4–6
operational art, 21–24, 73
Overlord, Operation. *See* Normandy/Operation Overlord

Palatinate operations, 51–53, 142
Parker, Frank, 34, 56, 57, 66–67, 69, 73, 98
Patton, 260
Patton, Beatrice, 7, 172, 242–43, 253
Patton, George S. (grandfather), 24
Patton, George S., Jr.: accident, death, and burial of, 242–43; actor role to create enthusiasm and motivation, 2, 14–15, 39; analytical and inquisitive mind of, 123; appearance and dress of, 2, 173, 246; aversion to suffering and cruelty, 26–27; awards and decorations for, 241–42; baldness and studying under blue light, 32; boldness of, 13; books, websites, and TV series about, 11; career of, uncertain future of, 35–36, 47, 100, 153, 154–55; career opportunities and usefulness at end of war, 231, 232, 234, 238–39; complaints about, 234–35; confidence in, 165–66; drive, energy, self confidence, and optimism of, 14–15, 115, 119; education and homeschooling of, 24, 123, 291n29; education and professional training of, 7, 15–17, 31, 123–24, 289n96; Eisenhower discussions of potential assignments for, 234, 238–39; emotion when visiting Walter Reed Army Hospital, 229–30; events in life of, significant, xi–xii; explanation of success of, 15–18; heroes of, 24; influence and significance of, opinions about, 8, 17; injury of during World War I, 29; intellect of, 7, 15–17, 123–24; intuition of, 7, 143–44, 151–52; legacy of, 18–19, 253; letters by, 15–16; loss of faith in, 109–10, 313n164; loyalty of soldiers to, 9; loyalty to Eisenhower, questions about, 237–38; luck of, 8, 13; memoir from diaries, publication of, 7; military theory and history interests and knowledge of, 35, 64, 139–40, 144, 319n133; movie about, 260; news reports about, 25; nicknames for, 2, 9, 42; one-man fire brigade or pit bulldog for Eisenhower, 17, 231; opinion about Bradley, 2, 163–64, 177, 179, 196–97, 253; opinion about Eisenhower, 163–64, 177, 253; opinions about, 1–3, 15, 18–19, 231; personality of, 1–3, 13–15; politics, encouragement to get involved in, 240–41; popularity of and public fascination with, 11, 13; press conference with reporters, 235–37, 339n58; promotion of, Eisenhower promise about, 13–14, 155; rank in list of influential leaders, 8; recall of, threat of, 179–80, 196–97; recall threat and caution to not say anything controversial, 164–66; relationship with Bradley, 5; relationship with Eisenhower, 5, 109–10, 238–39, 313n164; reputation of, 9, 227, 231, 243; resignation, consideration of, 233, 236–37, 241; retirement of and restrictions on behavior, 236–37; return to Germany, saying goodbye before, 230; risk-taking nature of, 13; saddle of grandfather, learning to ride in, 24; as scapegoat, 239–40; sidelining and limiting operations of by Eisenhower, 1; speeches by, 15, 38–39, 164–66, 227, 229, 230, 295n143; sports played by, 41; success of, defense of, 18–19; success of, theories about, 13–16; tapping of phone of, 234; team player, attitude about Patton as a, 41; toast by and wishing for another war, 285n11; toast to Montgomery, 168; wounding of, 60
Patton, Ruth Ellen, 26, 229
Patton Bowl amphitheater, 38
Patton's boys. *See* staff of Patton
Patton's Household Cavalry, 137–38, 141
plans for battles and operations: changing plans as opportunities develop, 100;

complex plans, complaint about, 101, 311n96; decision points and adjustments to operations, 47–48, 160–61; emphasis on instead of on fighting, 232; execution as more important than plans, 6, 92–93, 101, 308–9n28; importance of, 6–7, 95; intelligence collection of during operations and change to plans, 125–26, 140, 316n27; intelligence for development of, 140; intelligence to confirm, 125–26; Patton as great leader but poor planner, 103; plans to fit circumstances or creating circumstances to fit plans, 125–26, 148; rigidity in following, 112, 136; simplicity, speed, and flexibility of, 6–7, 13, 14, 54, 99–102, 121, 166–67

Poland, 71, 233, 302n113, 302–3n120

political generals, 155, 227, 257

political instrument, war as, 44

pursuit, 6

reconnaissance units and patrols: aerial reconnaissance, 5, 57, 127, 136–37, 141, 148, 167–68, 250, 286n26; enemy weak spots, identification of, 122; function and mission of, 130–31; inquisitiveness of, 128, 131; maneuvers, use of recon during, 38, 127–28; mountain warfare reconnaissance, 131; night sound signals of Germans, training on, 134; during operations, 125–26, 136–39; probes of enemy lines, 126–28; war doctrine of Patton and use of, 126–27, 166

reincarnation, 140

Reorganization Objectives Army Division (ROAD), 255–56

revolt of the admirals and colonels, 254, 255

Rhine campaign: attacks and maneuvers, 51–53; crossing Rhine and deep thrust into Germany, 215; crossing Rhine and withdrawal of logistical support, 18, 224–25; plans for, 50–51; rigidity in following plans for, 112, 136; secrecy of plans for, 132; seizing crossing on, 219; strategic bombing for, 102; strategic maneuver for, 5

Russia/Soviet Union: administration of Berlin by, 227–28; atomic bomb detonation by, 254; beating of by Army, opinion about, 229; brutality of, reports on, 233; complaints about Patton from, 234; containment of and Army budget, 246, 248–49; danger from, opinion about, 228–29, 248–49; defensive war against in Germany, capabilities for, 248–49; operational art and study of army operations, 21; rearming Germans for war with, 229; Russian Front, map of, 137

Saint-Mihiel battle, 28–29, 59–60, 124

Schwarzkopf, Norman "Stormin' Norman," 273–76

Seine River operations: encirclement of Germans, 5, 195, 202–3, 207–8, 209; German counterattack, 213; German defensive line, 198, 210; Normandy breakout, 211–13, 215, 216–17, 219, 220; strategic maneuver, Patton call for use of, 5; success of Patton, 18

serenade drills, 84

Seventh Army, 43, 44, 46–47, 51–52, 81–82, 131, 135, 137, 155, 296n175

shock: concept of, 23; continuous movement to create chaos and, 28–29, 32–33, 128–29, 269; early lessons on, 24; effects of shock action and series of shocks, 24, 28–29, 37, 39, 268, 272; fire, maneuver, shock, enemy decisionmaking, and destruction of enemy morale, 3–4, 20, 23–24, 30–31, 35, 268, 278–79, 280–81; Normandy operations, 48–49, 160–61, 190, 198, 202; Palatinate operations, 51–53; psychological dimension of, 23, 32–33; Sicily operations success and, 46–47; surprise element of time or direction of attack, effectiveness of, 32, 38, 126, 133, 142–43, 264–65; tank use and creation of shocks, 27, 33, 60, 69, 72–73; war doctrine of Patton, 16, 18, 20, 53–54, 167

shock troops (*Stosstrupp*), 30, 60, 69, 90–91

Sicily: aerial reconnaissance for operations, 137; Bradley orders and anger at Patton countermanding order, 133–34, 318n83; casualties from operations in, 132–33; combined arms operations, 80–82, 306n192, 306n197, 306n200; experience in Hawaii and execution of operations in, 126; failure of Allied efforts, 17; German withdrawal from, 136; Husky operation, 42–47, 108–9, 131; intelligence and changes in plans and operations, 132–36; jeeps and trucks for operations, 43; lessons learned in and training Third Army, 136; limitations placed on Patton in, 15; logistics for, 104–5; Messina operations, 5, 44, 46–47, 81–82, 105, 112, 134–35, 136, 306n200; morale of Italian forces, breaking of, 44; Palermo operations, 5, 42, 43, 44, 81, 105, 135, 306n200, 322n39; paratrooper incident and communications problems, 108–9, 180; plans for operations, 42–43, 111, 131–32; Ponto Olivo airfield, capture of, 133–34; reconnaissance operations in, 131; reputation of Patton after operations, 9; rigidity in following plans in, 112; secrecy of plans for, 131–32, 135; slapping incidents, 8, 47, 100, 153, 154, 227, 285n12; speed of operations in, 80–81, 306n195; strategic maneuver coordination in, 112; strategic maneuver, Patton call for use of on, 5; success of Patton in, 18, 46–47; sweeping maneuver, success of, 44, 159

Siegfried Line, 5, 102, 119, 223, 226

slap on back while looking for a place to thrust the knife, 241

speed: flexibility and speed of operations, 6–7, 13, 14, 18, 54, 73, 121, 166–67, 193–203, 212–13, 226; flexibility and speed of operations and subordinate initiative, 73, 95–100, 166–67, 262, 272, 275; haste compared to, 101, 271; open warfare concept and, 5; rapidity and shock for success with tanks and cavalry, 27, 33; Sicily operations success and, 46–47; tempo of modern warfare, 37, 72, 303n123

staff of Patton: casualty chart kept by, 137; characteristics of effective staff, 100; code word for communication with, 119; criticism of, 118, 121, 153, 310–11n87, 322n38; faith in by Patton, 102; intelligence staff, 137–38, 140–42; loyalty of, 100; names of key men, 100; Patton's Household Cavalry, 137–38; postwar assignments for, 244–45; postwar influence of, 9, 244–45; quality of, 100, 104–5, 121, 310–11nn87–88, 322n38; stealing of good staff, 153; training of in war doctrine, 100–102, 121

strategy: classical strategy, end of, 5, 286n26; classical strategy, inadequacy of for modern warfare, 29; concept and definitions of, 5, 20–21, 30; coup d'oeil concept and, 5, 13; Eisenhower knowledge of, 22; goal of, 34; mobile strategy, 4–6, 29, 69, 207; operational art and, 21–23; Patton knowledge of, 2; responsibility for, 21, 29, 34, 292n67; war doctrine of Patton, 18, 22–24, 29–31

student complex, 99

subordinate initiative, 1, 14, 73, 89–91, 95–100, 166–67, 189–90, 262, 272, 308n13

successive effort doctrine, 34

Sun Tzu, 27, 30, 69, 132, 140, 292n45

Supreme Headquarters Allied Expeditionary Force (SHAEF): command and control deficiencies of, 112; limitations placed on Patton support from, 18, 105–8; logistical planning and mismanagement by, 154, 203–4, 220–23, 337n270; Normandy plans of, 47–48, 49–50, 156–57

surprise element. *See* shock

synchronization, 57, 58, 78, 89, 271–72, 273–74, 303n124

synthetic experience, 140, 319n133

Tactical Air Command (TAC), XIX: Bulge operations, 114–15, 119; close-air support missions, 82–83, 145, 297n206, 320n157; command and control style of, 189–90; coordination with Third Army, 82–83, 101–2, 166–67, 270–71; demonstration of doctrine with, 86–87; Normandy operations, 48, 87, 189–90, 193–94, 213; photographic interpreters from, 137; training for Normandy operations, 158–59

tactics: concept and definition of, 5, 21; infantry as center of doctrine on, 4, 179, 286n17; operational art and, 21–23; Patton as tactical commander, 21, 22; Patton knowledge and skills, 2, 5, 8–9, 14, 18, 87; responsibilities for tactical operations, 21, 29; tank tactics, 61, 300n40; war doctrine of Patton, 30

Tank Corps, 26, 27–28, 31, 61, 63

tanks: advocacy for, 68–69; attacks by compared to armored division attacks, 127; benefits of use of, 60–61; boldness as key to victory with, 27; breakthroughs and exploitation with, 35, 60, 61, 69, 72–73, 81, 300n44, 301n74, 306n197; British tank school and doctrine, 57, 62; cavalry doctrine applied to armor warfare, 13; cavalry role assumed by, 58; conditions for successful use of, 56, 61; coordination with artillery, 57, 58, 59; coordination with cavalry, 68; coordination with infantry, 57, 58, 60–63, 71, 75–77, 83–88, 300n40; creation of combined arms tank divisions and doctrine for use of, 73–77, 304nn136–138; death of, article about, 265; deep penetrations with, 59–60, 299n33; design and capabilities of, 62–63, 64–65, 66, 68–69, 70, 265–66, 301n83; doctrine for use, 56, 57–63, 64–69, 75–77, 83–88, 89–90, 92, 265–66, 299n35, 300n48; EMF role of, 67; emphasis on use of, 2; expertise with and best tank man, 13, 55; French tank school and doctrine, 56–57, 61, 303n128; French use of tanks and combined arms force, 72–73, 303nn127–128; future for use of, 247; German doctrine on, 65; German panzer force, 69, 71, 72–73, 302n107; infantry ownership of, 64, 71; infantry support from, 57, 59, 63, 75, 247, 304n151; leading infantry with in coordinated rushes, 60; light tank school in France, 27–28, 56–57; limited role for, 59, 72, 76; maneuver role of, 34–35; manual for infantry and tank cooperation and training, 59; marking to identify tanks, platoons, and companies, 124; mission of, 71; morale and use of, 26; Patton command experience with during World War I, 3, 25–31; primacy of in future wars, 34, 62, 63, 75, 300n48; production of, 67; radios for, 58, 62; rapidity and shock for success with, 27, 33; repair tank, suggestion for, 90; riding enemy to death with, 58; self-reliance and aggressive spirit of infantry and use of, 4, 66; shock and surprise from use of, 27, 33, 60, 69, 72–73; subordinate initiative in use of, 89–90; tactics for use of, 28–29, 61, 300n40; writings and lectures on use of, 27, 57–58, 59, 60, 61, 63, 64–65, 68;

World War I operations role of, 26–29, 55–56, 57, 59–60, 76
teamwork and team-play culture, 41, 60–61, 75–76, 99, 167, 255, 257
Tennessee maneuvers, 39, 74, 76, 96–97, 127
Texas, 35–36, 44
Third Army: activation for Normandy, 179, 180, 187, 329n7; administration of eastern American Zone, 227–29; Brittany operations, 156–57, 160, 168, 172, 173, 180–81, 201; Bulge operations, 113–21, 146–51; casualties in, 11, 12, 49; command of, 9, 154–56, 165, 187, 329n7; coordination with XIX TAC, 82–83, 101–2, 166–67, 270–71; dread of Germans for, 88; efficiency of, 104–5; as exploitation force, 177, 182, 185; front line operations tours, 1; halting of and limitations placed on, 205–7, 209, 334n180; headquarters and War Room of, 137; intelligence staff and system for, 137–39, 140–42, 332n109; lessons learned in operations and training of, 136; logistical support for, 1, 48–49, 105–8, 161–62, 216–17, 219–26, 312n134, 337n270; Lorraine campaign, 145; loyalty of soldiers in to Patton, 9; maneuvers in Texas, 36, 44; manpower shortages in, 107–8; maps in headquarters of, 137; Normandy operations, 48, 87–88, 156–60, 162, 171–72, 179, 182–83, 190–200; offensive drive across France to Germany, 1; overstrength of personnel, request for, 161–62; Palatinate operations, 51–53, 142; photographic interpreters from, 137, 141; psychological warfare section, 138, 140–42; publicity/Public Affairs section, 138, 140–42, 319n122; replacement of Patton as head of, 239; training for Normandy operations, 158–59, 166–67. *See also* staff of Patton
Torch operation, 40–42, 129–30, 311n96
Training and Doctrine Command (TRADOC), 261–62, 265, 267–68, 274
trench foot and boots, 107
trench warfare, 4, 64
Tunisia: aerial reconnaissance for, 137; failure of Allied efforts, 17; limitations placed on Patton in, 15, 40–42; logistics for, 103–4; Patton command of

operations, 41–42; rigidity in following operations plans, 136; skills of generals in, 8, 41; strategic maneuver use in, 5, 42, 112

Ultra intercepts: Ardennes attack and overreliance on, 148; Enigma machine decrypts, 138; German spies, identification of through, 156; German withdrawal from Sicily, 136; intelligence from and daily briefings on, 138–39, 140–42; Normandy breakout and intelligence about German movement, 194, 200, 332n109

Vietnam and Vietnam War, 18, 256–59, 260–61, 267, 279–80
Virginia Military Institute, 16, 123

War as I Knew It (Patton), 7, 172
war as killing business, speech about, 38–39, 295n143
war doctrine of Patton: aversion to suffering and losses, 26–27; basis for, 24; battles, role of and avoidance of, 1–2, 3–4, 39, 86; boldness as key to victory, 13, 27, 33, 95, 121, 267; decision cycles and points, 122; enemy reactions, anticipation of, 7; exploitation of points of little or no opposition, 18, 87; fire, maneuver, shock, enemy decisionmaking, and destruction of enemy morale, 3–4, 20, 23–24, 30–31, 35, 268, 278–79, 280–81; front line operations tours, 1, 6, 128; frontal attacks, attitude toward, 4, 30; knowledge of Patton about strategy, tactics, and techniques, 2; legacy of, 18–19; limitations and restrictions placed on Patton and, 1, 15, 17–18; maxim for, 37–38; mobile strategy, 4–6, 29, 69, 207; opinions about, 1–2, 15, 167; simplicity, speed, and flexibility of plans, 6–7, 13, 14, 18, 54, 99–102, 121, 166–67, 193–203, 212–13; speed, simplicity, boldness, 95–96, 226; strategy and tactics of and comparison to traditional doctrine, 3–7, 13, 20, 86, 166–67, 231–32; strategy concept, 18, 22–24, 29–31; success of, 1, 54, 153; success of because little or no opposition, 87;

success of, criticism of, 2, 5–6, 287n33; success of, defense of, 18–19; success of, explanation for, 15–18, 167; success of, misunderstanding of, 282–83; success of, theories about, 13–16; tactics concept, 30; where to beat enemy, focus on, 5, 54, 128. *See also* subordinate initiative
warfare and warfare doctrine: asymmetric warfare, 279; basis for doctrine on, 24–25; change in doctrine after Vietnam, 261–72; change in doctrine after World War II, 227, 246–59; doctrine built on next war being like last war, 63, 94, 227; doctrine on and comparison to Patton techniques, 3–7, 13, 20, 86, 166–67, 231–32; Halfmoon doctrine, 247–49; infantry mission and focus of tactical doctrine, 4, 286n17; influence of Patton of future doctrine, 240, 245; logistics and success in, 104; open warfare/war of movement, 4–6; pace, range, and nature of, changes to, 72, 303n123. *See also* attrition warfare; battles and operations; frontal assaults; strategy; tactics
West Point, 16, 56, 123, 232
Western Front, map of, 137
Weyland, Otto "O. P.," 82–83, 86, 101–2, 114, 119, 158, 166–67, 189–90, 204, 240, 252, 270
World War I: Allied strategy during, 25–31; attrition strategy during, 30, 293n76; attrition warfare during, Patton opinion about, 26–27; casualties during, 29; combined arms operations during, 55–56; end of classical strategy after, 5, 286n26; injury of Patton during, 29; intelligence use during, 123, 124; Patton command experience during, 3, 25–31, 36; tank use during, 28–29, 55–56, 57, 59–60, 76
World War II: appreciation for Patton skills during, 8–9, 227; blame and credit for, 228; casualties from European operations, 9–11, 12, 49, 50, 51; casualty chart kept by Patton staff, 137; command experiences of generals before, 3, 231–32; German surrender, 227; memoirs of general published after, 7–8; strategy for, 227, 228

About the Author

James Kelly Morningstar is a twenty-year Army veteran who served in the Gulf War and in a wide range of assignments, including tours in Germany, Bosnia, Washington, D.C., and at the National Training Center. He is a West Point graduate and now teaches military history at the University of Maryland. This is his first book.

The Naval Institute Press is the book-publishing arm of the U.S. Naval Institute, a private, nonprofit, membership society for sea service professionals and others who share an interest in naval and maritime affairs. Established in 1873 at the U.S. Naval Academy in Annapolis, Maryland, where its offices remain today, the Naval Institute has members worldwide.

Members of the Naval Institute support the education programs of the society and receive the influential monthly magazine *Proceedings* or the colorful bimonthly magazine *Naval History* and discounts on fine nautical prints and on ship and aircraft photos. They also have access to the transcripts of the Institute's Oral History Program and get discounted admission to any of the Institute-sponsored seminars offered around the country.

The Naval Institute's book-publishing program, begun in 1898 with basic guides to naval practices, has broadened its scope to include books of more general interest. Now the Naval Institute Press publishes about seventy titles each year, ranging from how-to books on boating and navigation to battle histories, biographies, ship and aircraft guides, and novels. Institute members receive significant discounts on the Press' more than eight hundred books in print.

Full-time students are eligible for special half-price membership rates. Life memberships are also available.

For a free catalog describing Naval Institute Press books currently available, and for further information about joining the U.S. Naval Institute, please write to:

Member Services
U.S. Naval Institute
291 Wood Road
Annapolis, MD 21402-5034
Telephone: (800) 233-8764
Fax: (410) 571-1703
Web address: www.usni.org